THE HABIT OF AUTHORITY

by the same author

DOCTRINES OF IMPERIALISM

THE IMPERIAL IDEA AND ITS ENEMIES

WEST-INDIA POLICY UNDER THE RESTORATION

THE HABIT
OF
AUTHORITY

Paternalism in British History

BY

A. P. THORNTON

'Democracy forms no element
in the materials of English
character.'

RICHARD COBDEN

London
GEORGE ALLEN & UNWIN LTD
RUSKIN HOUSE ' MUSEUM STREET

13382

PRINTED IN GREAT BRITAIN
in 11 *on* 12 *point Bell type*
BY SIMSON SHAND LTD
LONDON, HERTFORD AND HARLOW

PREFACE

The 'story of English liberty' is a famous story, often re-told. This book comments not on that story but on its context.

Paternalism is an old strand in its pattern, democracy a new. In Great Britain 'government *for* the people' was ultimately to be challenged by the other two components of Abraham Lincoln's celebrated trinity. But innovation does not assert itself against tradition without straining the principles of liberalism, and without making those who held such principles, as much as those who did not, conscious of the strain. The American Revolution was one comment on the problem set; the emergence of a British Labour party was another; modern colonial nationalism is a third. English attitudes to all three movements, and others akin, are here examined—and where it has seemed to me that the views on democracy of Americans, Australians, Canadians, and Scotsmen are relevant to the argument, I have trenched on the history of their communities.

University of Toronto   A.P.T.
31 December 1964

CONTENTS

NOTE

All works referred to in the footnotes are published
in London, except where otherwise stated.

INTRODUCTION

England's history is the history of a certain tradition and practice of governance—a tradition of successful paternalism.

It has been successful because the various kinds of men who have governed the country have shown themselves able both to change with changing circumstance, and to calculate the amount of the change. They have also known how to exploit an accompanying tradition, followed by those they have ruled— that of deference to authority. They congratulated themselves on their percipience at the time: their historians have continued to admire them since. Accordingly, the impression that Englishmen possess a political genius not readily granted to or at any rate found among others has become widespread, and not solely among the English themselves. No 'set book', no required text, has been their guide to this reputation: they were American colonists of the eighteenth century, a fraternity more literate head for head than their English kin, who paid more attention to the constitutional commentaries of John Locke and William Blackstone than these ever received at home.

Adaptability was therefore better thought of than prescription or principle. In the nineteenth century the Duke of Wellington, as is well known, had the gift of turning left or right in politics as though this were a simple parade-ground drill. That the government of the Crown must be carried on was the main, indeed the only correct objective for politicians to strive for. This he fittingly and famously illustrated in an emergency in November 1834, when he thought it right to hold all the Cabinet portfolios himself—and because he thought it right, it proved perfectly possible for him to do so. The Tory party of which he was sometimes head and always symbol he looked on as a regiment of Guards, protecting Crown, constitution and people alike from disorder.[1] A relieving garrison might be composed of officers with whom those of the outgoing regiment might not choose to dine, and of men who had been trained in a different, and therefore inferior, tradition: but since its duties would be precisely the same, the task of 'handing over' to it was one that in all respects must be punctiliously carried out.

[1] A. S. Turberville, *The House of Lords in the Age of Reform* (1958), p. 414.

13

This was an attitude that held then and has kept since its peculiar attraction. During the 1820s the Royal Navy's Captain Basil Hall had distinguished, during his travels among American republicans, 'a want of loyalty' as one of their chief characteristics. He was hotly attacked for this, as for most of his other opinions. But whatever its merits, it is not a charge that can readily be laid against the English at home, where the sense of status within the community was ever more profound than a devotion to rugged individualism. For, even when engaged in acts of revolution—in the homeland in the seventeenth century, in America in the eighteenth—the English had the habit of proclaiming themselves Tories, true Conservatives, wanting only to return the ship of state to a course it should never have left. English Radicals have convinced themselves that it was renovation, not innovation, that they sought. They have wished to revert to ancient principles that had been, in one way or another, by someone or other, wrongfully usurped. As a consequence, times of revolution have proved also to be times for enthusiastic research by antiquarian lawyers: as early as 1381 English peasants in revolt were raising legalistic points concerning the nature of land-tenure and their own status, appealing indignantly (and paradoxically) to Domesday Book as their authority.[1] The English record has its Whig interpretations, which differ: but it is a history of Toryism that is interpreted.

For it was always the abuse of authority, not the authority itself, that was the immediate target of attack, even although other targets might present themselves as a campaign progressed. The insistence in the *corpus* of English law on precedent betrays, perhaps, a consciousness among lawyers that it were well that any distinction between right and justice should not be allowed to deflect and distract the respectful compliance of the laymen of England with the laws that bound their behaviour. As late as 1947 no proceeding against the Crown could be taken without the *fiat* of the Crown's own principal law officer, the attorney-general. The political authority of the monarchy upheld the legal authority of the king's bench; and the respect paid to the one encompassed the other—and the opinions that the men who sat on it handed down. Accordingly, the 'genius of

[1] One wonders what they thought was in it. The Book was not printed until 1783.

English liberty' has been nurtured under the protection of governments more in sympathy with individual right than with any view of 'social justice', or of the rights of men in general.

It is clear, too, that government in England has been supported, to a degree uncommon in the history of other countries. The reasons for this deserve examination. But, apart from two essays by Professor Herbert Butterfield—his *Whig Interpretation of History* (1931) and *The Englishman and his History* (1944)—together with the comic masterpiece by Messrs Sellar and Yeatman, *1066 and All That* (1930)—they have not been closely examined. Why, for example, has it been so generally agreed that, *pace* the last work mentioned, William the Conqueror although a Bad Man effected a Conquest which was a Good Thing? The Saxon English of his own day did not think so —but they have since paid for this heresy by being signally ignored by English historians as factors of significance in the subsequent story of 'the making of England'. Had they produced a hero who defied the invader successfully, an English counterpart of Wallace or the Cid, they might not have been relegated so brusquely to the realms of folklore. As for the American Loyalists of 1776–83, who opposed the Conquest of the English Atlantic provinces by their own fellow-subjects, they have been served even worse. This may have occurred because the very existence of a majority of Saxons who dissented from William I, as of the minority of Americans who approved of George III,[1] draws attention to fissures in the English tradition of deference —for assuredly, the emergence of the United States of America and of the Republic of Ireland (to name no other examples) are evidence of marked failure in the record of English governance.

A considerable revenge has in consequence been taken by the English on the Americans and on the Irish. Ireland, the other island, still receives cavalier treatment in textbooks of British history. Not until the era following the twentieth century's second world war was serious attention paid in Britain to the development and culture of the United States—the British Association for American studies, a body founded by young dons

---

[1] Edward Channing however stated in his *History of the United States of America* (New York, 1905–25), III, 215, that more colonials fought for the British than against them.

THE HABIT OF AUTHORITY

to foster study of these matters in schools and universities, dates only from 1955. R. G. Collingwood, when he remarked that all history is the history of thought, might well have added that most history is the history of what the thinker thinks important.

Why he thinks it important depends very much on the history of his own ideas. Since this is so, a personal word is necessary. I here survey the record of modern England, from the standpoint of 'government *for* the people', because of my continuing interest in the history of the British Empire, and in the attitudes of mind that derived and still derive from its existence. There would never have been an Empire at all had there not been, in the English character, a habit of authority—and this habit would not have survived without its obverse, a habit of respect for its exercise. I could not avoid noticing, when working on *The Imperial Idea and Its Enemies* (1959) (itself written between the lines of the narrative histories of expansion), that I was leaving a gap between my own lines which I ought to try, at another time, to fill. To study the exportation and imposition of power overseas, without analysing English ideas on the role of paternalism at home, was plainly to deal with half only of an entire story.

For paternalism was as deeply entrenched on the Left as on the Right. The convinced imperialist of Alfred Milner's school, and the dedicated Fabian socialist of Sidney Webb's, can be found at the turn of the twentieth century irritably rounding upon one another with the accusation that there had somehow occurred yet another dishing of Whigs, and a theft of paternalist clothes. Both groups set themselves up as improving landlords. They were impatient of tenants, domestic or external, who stuck to their own myopic opinions. Efficiency and utility were written on the banners of both movements. The Fabians, like the imperialists, were determined to improve the stock and quality of the British race, and by so doing improve also the standard of intelligence among the rulers of the race, the men in power—who should, of course, be Fabians. Power was justifiable at all only so long and so far as it was equated with service. The majority of the British people, landless and moneyless, deserved as good, as meticulous an 'imperial governance' as did the inhabitants of Africa and India. So it was that both these argumentative groups developed a philosophy of action—one that involved, for the benefit of the governed, the widening and strengthening of the zones of a paternalist authority. No wonder, then, that they spoke each other's language and promoted each other's policies, while often angrily denying that they were doing anything of the kind.

The socialists were to win their battle, the imperialists to go down to defeat. This happened because the former finally obtained the consent of the governed, and the latter did not. Just why these things happened, and what their consequences entailed, are matters worth looking into.

Aristocracy, as Sir John Seeley once told his Cambridge students, 'rather tinges institutions than creates institutions peculiar to itself'. His successor Professor Butterfield has strengthened this metaphor, pointing out how, 'when the aristocracy was sent to the laundry, the dye ran out into the rest of the washing'.[1] The theme here, therefore, is the continuity of paternalism and its attitudes in the face of the rising principle of democracy. It seeks to show how this continuity affected, as it still does, class and convention, polity and politics; and how power, when transferred from the aristocracy to the ranks below, took its assumptions with it.

[1] J. Seeley, *An Introduction to Political Science* (1896), p. 255; H. Butterfield, *The Englishman and His History* (Cambridge, 1944), p. 126.

CHAPTER I

THE COLONIZATION
OF ENGLAND

England begins her modern history as a colony.

For two-and-a-half centuries she was governed by, and certainly for, a Norman-French élite. Once this élite had marshalled the ranks of society, it went on to regulate for its subordinates the codes and conventions by which they were henceforth to live. When at length the alien speech of this aristocracy had been absorbed into a common language, when Normans had become anglicized and Englishmen normanized in unascertainable proportions, these arrangements were not disturbed. Both the political power and the social polity which the aristocracy had organized remained intact. If and when they had an enemy, it was the monarchy, not the people. Indeed the aristocrats were free to spend most of the fifteenth century quarrelling with one another, a large part of the sixteenth century recruiting their numbers and expanding their influence, and much of the seventeenth century asserting themselves against the monarchy once more, without any fear that their order as a whole was likely to be displaced by an outraged populace. During this long time the bonds of what is familiar to the twentieth century as 'colonialism' became so powerful as to avoid any such pejorative definition altogether. The ranks of society, originally granted to it from above, became literally taken for granted, and were therefore undiscussed.

One period stands out as an exception to this—and, as an exception, it proves the rule. In the revolution of the mid-seventeenth century, when the gentry broke their own ranks and

18

disputed both the style and the nature of authority in England, at once everything that had been taken for granted fell into dispute. The organization of society as a whole was very closely discussed. 'Levellers' preached unknown doctrines of social justice, the 'Norman yoke' was so defined and vilified, the rights of freeborn Anglo-Saxons were simultaneously invented and invoked, and the commonalty which formed the ranks of the New Model Army learned not only the military but also the social authority of the sword—the sword, which had always been an exclusive symbol of gentle status. The axe that killed the king cut also the ties that bound together the various orders of men below the throne. It seemed possible for the society to recast itself, to seek another future, another horizon. But not enough men either saw this chance, or wished to take it, or could agree which path was the best one to follow. The horizon, if it was ever more than a mirage, was not reached; and, once the monarchy and all its attendant appurtenances of aristocracy had been restored, this period of social and political experiment was embalmed in men's minds, and in the history books, as the interregnum—in other words, as a break in the natural order of things, an aberration, an exception. It is still thought of as such.

For a colony can be reckoned a success when the ideas and attitudes of the rulers are readily, even eagerly, accepted by their subordinates. A Guianese writer of the 1880s reported a dispute between two Negroes, one from British and one from French Guiana. The first clinched the argument: 'You forget that *we* beat *you* at Waterloo.'[1] In Great Britain too, a like process of assimilation can be traced. Edmund Burke's most passionate appeals were always more to custom than to law; while John Stuart Mill remarked, in his *Representative Government* (1861), how unhesitating was the readiness of Englishmen to let themselves be governed by the higher classes. Every other observer agreed with him. The idea of 'station' appeared to have become rooted in English minds. Because this was so, the very many Englishmen who succeeded, some of them spectacularly, in raising themselves above their station, always knew well enough what they were about, and how much they were spending in the

[1] N. Darnell Davis, *Mr Froude's Negrophobia* (Demerara [British Guiana], 1888), p. 4.

effort. Yet their superiors, or 'betters'—these two terms being significantly identical—made the path of ascendancy for an ambitious and potentially valuable man as easy as possible, for they did not doubt their own ability, as officers of the best regiment, to knock the promising recruit into the correct shape. The Tudor monarchy promoted many such recruits; Stuart kings, in need of money, conscripted the wealthy into their nobility. But once enrolled, and so long as his powers of assimilation were equivalent to his talents, every such newcomer became thoroughly acceptable; and English genealogy, as a result, was seldom to look beyond the grandfather—or, if it did so, to worry about what it found there. In this way the authoritative group, from one age to another, put down roots of an extraordinary durability.

A great deal is commonly heard of the importance of class, of the distinctions of class, and of the fissures these distinctions have caused to open before the feet of an aspiring Englishman, pursuing happiness. In fact these are fissures that do not go very deep. They may make him stumble, but they will not cripple him. 'Class' is a concept invented amid the fluid conditions of nineteenth-century industrialism, the impact of which dislocated society and forced both those who abetted and those who opposed its processes to review all the existing attitudes. It is also a concept that more often confuses than guides. For example, it is surely true that the career carved out for himself by William Whewell, Master of Trinity 1841–66, who was the son of a Lancashire master-carpenter and had gone up to Cambridge with a scholarship from Heversham grammar school, would have been far harder to achieve in the last quarter of the nineteenth century than in the first.[1] Previous centuries had laid the main emphasis on a man's status and position—his rank, or (as the Tudor age called it) his 'degree' in society. It is only in times when the *parvenu* seems to be ubiquitous that stress is laid on the correct equipment he must have about him. The early seventeenth century therefore produced a great deal of literature on heraldry and etiquette for persons lately arrived at, or forcibly promoted to, gentility. (Oliver Cromwell himself refused a

[1] J. P. C. Roach, 'Universities and the National Intelligentsia', *Victorian Studies*, December 1959, p. 145.

knighthood from Charles I in 1629, and was fined £10 accordingly.) The mid-nineteenth century, building on foundations already laid, instituted the public school for the private processing of the sons of the successful, and for their instruction in the creed, code and accent of the gentry. In the twentieth century, and particularly since 1940, large numbers of Englishmen have swarmed through the class barriers that their fathers so diligently manned, only to get lost on the other side of them; for they have not found any route there that safely guides them, at least in the same large numbers, to positions of any significance. It is agreed that this sets a problem; and it is one for which nobody, at the present time of writing, has yet hazarded a solution.

Emancipation from class, like emancipation from anything, is never a final act, as many Englishmen are reminded if they revisit the scenes of their youth. But the Englishman who refuses to admit that any emancipation was necessary sets himself an even harder task. The idea that a man has a station has so long dominated men's minds that, if anyone publicly doubts the validity of this arrangement, he declares himself a rebel to society and has to suffer the penalties of so exposed a position. Vulnerability reduces his effectiveness, for a man who spends his time complaining it is a world he never made will not achieve that knowledge of the world which could help him remake it. Clive Bell in his *Civilisation* has noted of the artist in England how he must first break free from his environment before he can begin to make his positive statement. The great majority in England who will never be artists have to consume their own smoke, and the history of radicalism in English politics is one, on the whole, of inches painfully gained.

This innate regard for conservatism—the tendency in the English which, as Sir Ivor Jennings has recently observed, brings them to institutionalize everything, even radicalism—is defensive at base. The concept of 'law and order' was elevated from a necessity to a principle by the governors of England, and they exported it as such to colonies populated by their subordinates; so that, in time, a colonial governor was judged by his ability to keep matters quiet in the area of his responsibility. In 1829 the 'Colonial Reformer' Gibbon Wakefield remarked

how the best society at Sydney, New South Wales—where he
never set foot, but where circumstances, as he sensed even from
his rooms in Newgate jail, could hardly be otherwise than he
described—was convinced that the hallmark of respectability was
an invitation to dine at Government House.[1] A century later
this hallmark was still being sought. Methods of seeking it have
remained much the same, and have met the same obstacles. A
contemporary of Wakefield, the wife of the English Attorney-
General of Upper Canada, declared that she found in Toronto all
the evils and none of the advantages of the old and artificial
social system which prevailed at home in England, because of
the constant straining after a social standard which was, after
all, 'not quite within the reach of the ambitious provincial'.[2]

Normans of the mid-eleventh century cannot of course be
directly accused of frustrating ambitious provincials, or of
restricting the conventions of colonial towns. Yet the Normans'
habit of authority, developed in their original colonization of
England, governed the reactions of a long posterity. They were
the stage-managers of the historical pageant of the English-
speaking peoples, and the stage they set outlasted them.

The philosopher David Hume, who published the first volume
of his *History of England* in 1754, remarked of the Normans'
conquest that it would be 'difficult to find in all history a revolution more destructive, or attended with a more complete
subjection of the ancient inhabitants'. His book impressed
Augustin Thierry, and convinced him that English institutions
contained more aristocracy than liberty, despite the Whig
chorales on the latter theme. 'The idea struck me, that dates
from a conquest'[3]—and seventy years after Hume's account the
French scholar produced his own *History of the Conquest of
England by the Normans* (1825). This history resuscitated the
Saxons, sought to rebut the modern English notion that 'their

---

[1] E. G. Wakefield, *A Letter from Sydney* (Everyman edn., 1929), pp. 24 ff.

[2] Mrs Jameson however missed the point. (See J. L. Morison, *British Supremacy
and Canadian Self-Government*, Glasgow 1919, p. 27). As the New Zealander
Pember Reeves puts it, to the European visitor 'a colonial city is a third-rate town,
but to the pioneer who started there in a tent, it is victory'; *The Empire and the
Century*, ed. C. S. Goldman (1905), p. 466.

[3] G. P. Gooch, *History and Historians in the Nineteenth Century* (1920),
pp. 170-1.

ancestors were all utterly defeated and crushed in a single day',[1]
and rounded out the picture of Gurth and Wamba which had
recently delighted while somewhat mystifying the many readers
of Sir Walter Scott's *Ivanhoe* (1819). Thierry wanted to show
how the race of the invaders, although it put down deep roots,
had remained a privileged class. This he did, to be at once
attacked for his French presumption by Sir Francis Palgrave and
a series of scholars since, who were content to see in 'the making
of the English nation' only a process very much to the credit
both of all who took part in it and of their posterity.[2] 'Social
history' was not in vogue, for this was critical history, which
looked beyond the habits and attitudes of the aristocracy and
gentry. What was wanted was 'political history': a narrative,
written in acceptance, of the events which expressed in action
these habits and attitudes. The Norman invasion was, in its way,
an act of God: and if one belonged to that providential school of
historians which was also devoted to the idea of progress, it was
necessary to accept the visitation gracefully. If one was a
professional radical, however, it was equally necessary to do
nothing of the sort. Radicals believe in progress, but it is something that will come with the future, it has not occurred in the
past. They are naturally the enemies of that type of history which
argues that it has.

Among them was Tom Paine. In his *Rights of Man* (1791)—
a work designed to restore to the English people some sense of
the fitness of things—Paine states flatly that conquest and
tyranny, together with lawyers and tithes, had transplanted
themselves with Duke William from Normandy into England.
He adds,

And the country is yet disfigured with the marks.

To Paine, the chief disfigurement was the continued existence in
England of a monarchy and an aristocracy, both of which claimed
the powers they wielded by an appeal to hereditary rights.

[1] Thierry, *loc. cit.* (trans. W. Hazlitt, 1826), xxiii–iv.
[2] As did Sir William Temple, who writes in his *Introduction to the History of
England* (1695) of 'the happy circumstances of this famous conquest'. But Sir
Winston Churchill, Marlborough's father, and a Tory to Temple's Whig, had
already written in 1685 on 'the calamity of foreign servitude'.

These rights were, in Paine's opinion, so many fiddlesticks. William, 'the son of a prostitute and the plunderer of the English nation', had, in company with an armed banditti, parcelled out the country—bribing some parts of it by what their lawyers called charters, so that the other parts of it might be the better subjected to their will. And what had been the result of this? Why, the establishment of 'a vassalage class of manners' among the English, and their deprivation of any real role in the constitution of the country. Their deprivation, indeed, of a constitution at all; for the boast that the English constitution was unwritten because there was no need to write it did not strike Paine as that glorious safeguard of popular liberties which it was so often made out to be by those who held all political power securely in their own hands. The view, dear to English lawyers, that no rights obtained in England save those actionable at law, was the nefarious upshot of such an assumption. How great the contrast with the new American republic, where the successful revolutionaries, acting on earlier advice from Paine himself, had just taken good care to draw up for themselves a written instrument of government!

Paine reiterated that the government of England had arisen out of a conquest, and not out of society as a whole. Thus no 'social contract', whatever John Locke might have said a hundred years ago to gratify his patrons, the Whig oligarchs who had just emancipated themselves from the interference of King James II, had ever been made; and, as a direct result,

> though it has been much modified from the opportunity of circumstances since the time of William the Conqueror, the country has never yet regenerated itself, and is therefore without a constitution.

And where his contemporary Edmund Burke might rhapsodize that even a wrong, when mantled with the concealing folds of custom and tradition, became a right—or at any rate became all right, right enough, in time—Paine scoffs that what at first was plunder assumed the softer name of revenue. Indeed the same kind of thing went on that had only just been put a stop to (and of course for reasons far otherwise than those the oligarchs were likely to own to) in the commandeered province of Bengal. To be sure, the baronage of England had its monument at Runnymede, but no such honour had been done at Smithfield to mark the fall of Wat Tyler. But, he warned, the people of England had long memories, and did not share Burke's belief that passage of time agreeably romanticized the past by planing down its edges —for although 'not a courtier in England' would talk of the curfew-bell, 'not a village in England has forgotten it'. And what else were the hated Game Laws, debarring forever these same villagers of man's inalienable right to go out and shoot his own dinner, but another legacy from these same free-booting and predatory Normans, whose aristocratic successors were equally as determined to maintain their privileges? It was Paine's conviction that the people of England had never been fairly or candidly dealt with; and his writings, proscribed in 1792 but passing under cover from hand to hand throughout the country, illustrate the effort on his part to lead them to a light by whose aid they might be enabled to deal fairly and candidly by themselves.

Tom Paine's voice when raised is the kind that shatters glass. But, if we take a stand where he saw himself standing, as spokesman for the unrepresented people of England, the eagle glance he bends on Duke William and his friends has indeed a power of illumination. If the Normans are assessed as colonists and settlers, creators of an authoritarian 'New Order', their record for efficiency at the business certainly stands high: among their successors, perhaps only Cortez and his companions in sixteenth-century Mexico, or Pizarro and his brigands in Peru, can equal them.

The Normans were not the first depredators of England, only the most tenacious. They overlaid themselves on a society that had had time to integrate and to lose its previous colonial status, one indeed that had had the sophistication to develop something equivalent to a 'plural society' with the Danes in the eastern half of the country.[1] But the Normans, noted even in their own day as both a litigious and an imitative race, saw themselves as something more than predators. This role they were content to play in contemporary Sicily, where they fanned out from bridge-

[1] R. W. Lennard, *Rural England 1086–1135* (Oxford, 1959), p. 3.

heads in Messina (1061) and in Palermo (1072), in the process rescuing Christians there from their status of slavery to Muslims, and ultimately becoming the ruling group over a variety of races. In England, in contrast, they found a nation already in existence, and it was neither safe nor politic to seek to base their rule on force alone, although force had to be used. They therefore sought to justify their presence by an appeal to the authority and tradition of England's own laws and customs. Duke William, in his claim to the English throne, indeed laid on customary law a weight it could scarcely bear. Anxious not to be saddled with the reputation of a freebooter, of the same type as any one of his Northmen forebears, he decked out his claim with assumption and precedent. In his view, in the circumstances of 1066 in England, the lawful heir was driven against his will to win his rights by force from outside. Successful in his quest, he insisted always that he held his authority by English right according to English law, and, following his example, every Norman baron who took over an English manor claimed the same. In this way the Normans embedded themselves into the English system, and assimilated themselves into the English society so thoroughly that in time both their race and their tongue vanished entirely from sight.

But although they were to lose their racial identity, they never lost either the position or the habit of authority in the society as a whole. Moreover, the conversion of England to a new colonial status was extremely quick. By 1086 Worcester was alone among English sees in having an English bishop. This expropriation of the English ruling class may not have been Duke William's original intention, but the series of provincial revolts that broke out between 1068 and 1071, and the fact that, in Palgrave's words, 'the battleaxe of the Dane was always glittering before him',[1] determined him to be ruthless, and to employ none but Normans in positions of place and trust.[2] The monk of St Evroul, Orderic Vitalis, who completed his account of these transactions in 1127, tells us of two singular personages:

[1] Sir F. Palgrave, *Normandy and England*; in *Works*, III (Cambridge, 1921), 216.
[2] Cf. D. C. Douglas, 'The Companions of the Conqueror', *History* xxxviii (1943), that 'the possession of English lands by a Norman in 1086 offers no proof whatsoever that he or even one of his ancestors [*sic*] fought in a battle 20 years before'.

one, Guilbert Fitzrichard, who said he had accompanied his lord to England because such was his duty, but that stolen goods had no attraction for him and that he would return to Normandy to enjoy his own heritage there; another, a monk Guimond, who did not well see how he could be the religious leader of men whose manners and language he had no knowledge of, and whose kindred had been slain or enslaved. These were nonconformists indeed. Despite them, barons and churchmen, priests of fortune as well as soldiers of fortune, took over the temporal and spiritual control of the country, 'scale by scale on the dragon's back'. Castle and cathedral loomed from eminences throughout the land, with walls of a similar thickness; and the early Norman bishops went to the altar through rows of lances.

Colonized England, like colonized America six centuries later, had its frontier areas, Alsatias for the lawless and the refugee. These were 'the Marches', for the pacification of which a great lord would issue letters of marque to lesser men. The solitary Wulfstan of Worcester was the only churchman who dared make a pastoral visitation into Cheshire in Duke William's day; Norman bishops made visits of another kind. William of Malmesbury, writing 70 years afterwards, tells how Bishop Eudes [Odo] ravaged the Northern Marches, 'cutting the nerves' of Northumbria, a province once so fair, Christian, and flourishing. Behind the stockades of the Marches, the independence of whose commanders was to set a standing problem to the central authority until Tudor times, less than two hundred barons, and between five and six thousand knights, became the landowners of England.

Feudalism is a seventeenth-century expression and an intangible one at best. Land, however, is fact not fiction: a system of governance using it for a foundation must necessarily be solidly constructed. The system of land tenure established by the Normans linked the lord with the vassal. The lord rendered service to the king, the vassal to the lord, in return for the land held; and these ties were very rigorously defined in 'the law of the land', a capacious phrase. The cardinal 'feudal' doctrine, therefore, was this of knight-service. All land was held of the king. All other occupiers were tenants either of the king or of some lord holding of the king; the tie between the lord and his tenants was hereditary; and the extent of each man's holding determined the extent of his civil and political rights. The English had developed a complicated but workable system of social and political relationships; the Normans took from this what would fit into their larger scheme. The Domesday inquisition of 1083 gave Duke William information about his new country that he had to have, and as a result of it he took over direct control of lands that Edward the Confessor and Harold Godwinson, the last Saxon kings, had possessed, together with the lordship of all cities. Domesday has remained a quarry for many types of social investigator; it is certainly a record of English expropriation. Duke William owned close on fifteen hundred manors himself, and was generous in establishing the Church on the most solid of foundations; he took care, however, to scatter in diverse places the possessions of his followers, lest powerful satrapies, and the ambitions that normally go with them, emerged. Thus, to Henry de Ferrers was allocated 114 manors in Derbyshire and 96 in thirteen other counties; to Robert de Mortain went a grant of 193 manors in twenty different shires. To his own sons, whom doubtless he suspected of having inherited their father's taste for usurpation, Duke William gave nothing at all.

These were acts of settlement indeed. In them lies the revolution David Hume spoke of, the 'parcelling-out' that so upset Tom Paine. Behind them is the fact Thierry emphasized, that the tales of 'the outlaw' Robin Hood were for long 'the only national history that a man of the people in England transmitted to his sons, having himself received it from his ancestors';[1] and it is a comment on this, that 'Ned Ludd', mythical captain of the machine-breakers after 1811, should have been reputed to have his headquarters, too, in Sherwood Forest. The disappearance of the English freeholder, his absorption into villein-status, the imposition of the axiom *nulle terre sans seigneur*, were events whose implications time was never entirely to erase. The colonization of land elsewhere in the world was subconsciously to use the Norman model: for in just such a manner, regiment by regiment, were the officers of Cromwell's expeditionary army rewarded in Jamaica after their successful conquest of that

[1] *Norman Conquest*, II, 226.

Spanish island in 1655. In England the towns themselves served as island-colonies of the Normans. The old towns were brought directly within the sphere of Norman influence, while the new were founded by the Normans on the lands of the royal demesne or of the Church. Lay lord or spiritual, his political authority over his tenants was supreme. All townsfolk were manorial tenants, the sheriff was the local representative of the royal power, and the burgesses owed agricultural service before they were allowed to commute this to a quit-rent. Sometimes, in towns that did not expand, this was not done: the inhabitants of Manchester were still, in the mid-eighteenth century, taking their 'suit to the mill'—corn and malt to the lord's mill and bread to the lord's oven.

Nineteenth-century writers, living in an age when conquests, and their consequent displacement of persons, seemed to be as much part of a dim past as dinosaurs, so often hailed all this as a thoroughly beneficial process that it still takes some effort of imagination to calculate the issues that were here involved, and to assess the damage wrought by this wind of change. Thomas Carlyle reflected the Norman contempt for the Saxons, and indeed for the Scots as well—the former were drunkards and the latter verminous. In an acid passage of his *Frederick the Great* the pre-conquest Saxons 'lumber about in pot-bellied equanimity'.[1] Sir Walter Scott made an English hero of Richard Coeur-de-Lion, one of whose customary oaths was, do you take me for an Englishman? Macaulay bestowed the Whig accolade on Duke William, who was, whatever else he was, a success. Edward Freeman, writing at a time when kinder if more fanciful views about the destinies of the 'Anglo-Saxon race' were spreading abroad, played a more flattering light upon the original Anglo-Saxons themselves. He talked of patriots and the national party, and found in King Harold, who had previously been written down as a ruffian, a supporter of parliamentary government. Freeman resented the views of such as Paine, a radical, and Thierry, a Frenchman, and declared how utterly unjust it was to cast Duke William as a mere successful adventurer or brigand— as one who, in company with his gang of Normans (itself a misnomer, as they came from 'all Gaul'), set on foot a career in

[1] I, 415.

England of general spoliation. There was no one moment, Freeman argued, of general confiscation or general plunder; and proceeded to document the many diverse moments when these things took place.[1] Still later writers have wondered how the Normans managed to effect their conquest at all, and have decided that they must have done it with a considerable degree of help from the native English, as Clive did it with his sepoys in Bengal. The conquest itself has been reduced in scale to a 'triangular contest between a Norman duke, a Norwegian king and a West Saxon earl'.[2]

The Normans themselves appear to have prospectively agreed with Carlyle. In Papal circles in particular did they go to great pains to issue attractive propaganda about their 'enterprise of England'. They stressed that their aim there was to act as importers of European civilization, and especially so in the realm of the spirit. This note was struck from the outset. Duke William's first Archbishop of Canterbury, Lanfranc—who was from Lombardy—went out of his way to denigrate his Saxon predecessors, particularly the canonized Alphege: and this lead was followed by his own natural son Paul, whom he inserted as Abbot of St Albans, and who went to the length of actually disinterring the bones of *his* predecessors. A later generation of the ruling class had more sense in this respect. In 1138 Archbishop Toustain of York, marshalling forces to repel an invading army of Scots, refugee Saxons, and renegade Normans, invoked the help of the Saxon saints Cuthbert and Wilfrid and raised their banners to stir the emotions of his Saxon levies, successfully as it turned out: and this battle was gratefully remembered as the Battle of the Standard. Similarly, it was a Norman, Geoffrey of Monmouth, who first collated the tales of Arthur and the Round Table, thus successfully Normanizing that hero for ever; while Henry II ensured that much respect was paid to the supposed tomb of Arthur when it was unearthed at Glastonbury in 1189.

These were evidences of adaptability, creditable both to the compassion and the confidence of the alien rulers. Yet the Welsh chiefs, pleading to Henry II for the security of the church of

[1] E. Freeman, *The Norman Conquest*, III (2nd edn., 1876), 13.
[2] D. C. Douglas, *The Norman Conquest and English Historians* (University of Glasgow, 1946), p. 25.

St David, made an eloquent case for themselves, and must have
echoed many an English thought. 'These bishops,' they said,

> come from another land, detest us, us and our country; they
> are our mortal enemies; how can they take an interest in the
> welfare of our souls? They have been placed among us, as in
> ambush. . . . Whenever an expedition is making ready in
> England against us, suddenly the primate of Canterbury
> places an interdict upon the territory they propose to invade;
> and our bishops, who are his creatures, hurl anathema upon
> the whole people in a body, and, by name, upon the chiefs who
> arm to fight at their head. Thus all among us who perish in
> the defence of our country die excommunicate.[1]

Some things are perhaps too painful to recall with accuracy.
Dr Graeme Ritchie has commented how until recently English
historians regularly described a twelfth-century Archbishop of
York as Roger of Bishopsbridge, which seems to suggest that
Roger was of English birth and that Bishopsbridge is in York-
shire, 'whereas it is Pont l'Evêque'.[2] The Archbishop Toustain
referred to above is usually found under the name of Thurstan,
to which he is unlikely ever to have answered. Similarly,
Scotland's first Stewart was a Breton, and it was the Scottish
King David I (1124–53) who, by giving to a certain Robert de
Brus the *potestas* of some two hundred thousand acres in Annan-
dale, brought that family out of Yorkshire into the history of
Scotland—in neither of which places, so Tom Paine would have
argued, had it any 'right' to be.

Unlike her southern neighbour, Scotland was not colonized.
On that 'non-event' much has since depended: indeed, those
scandalized by the amount of bloodshed in the angry pageant
that normally passes for medieval Scottish history have argued
that the country was left uncivilized as a result.[3] The lowland
country was 'planted' by Normans in much the same way as,
later that century, they made plantations in Ireland; but this was

[1] Thierry, *Norman Conquest*, II, 118.
[2] R. L. Graeme Ritchie, *The Normans in Scotland* (Edinburgh, 1954), p. xxiii.
[3] Cf. the historian W. E. H. Lecky's point of view: it was a calamity that,
while England was conquered by a single battle, it took the Normans 400 years to
subdue Ireland.

done under the aegis of native Scottish kings, who were never to suffer the fate of Sicilian satraps, or Welsh and Irish chiefs. In Duke William's own time Malcolm Canmore's Scotland became a place of refuge for the English and Danes of Northumbria, as well as for disgruntled Normans who reckoned that they had not received their due from their master. It was fortunate for Scotland that, once William had 'harried' the North of England, there was no settled and ordered community hard against her southern borders, a community that could well have acted as a springboard towards further colonization—the role that Cheshire was to play for North Wales and Shrewsbury for mid-Wales, as later would Pembrokeshire for Leinster and, to go further afield in time and place, Devon for 'the Newfoundlands' and Ulster for the American coastal settlements. The Scottish border and the northern English marches long remained a no-man's-land wherein only now and then, and for specific purposes, would the forces of authority show their faces. It was the Cistercian order, whose first house in England was founded in 1128, that was to act as the agent of cultural imperialism south of the Tweed and north of the Trent.

The Conqueror's son married Malcolm Canmore's daughter, and thereafter high life at the Scottish Court, in the Church and in the baronial society of the lowlands became thoroughly Normanized. David I, ablest of the heirs to this tradition, 'shared the profound respect of twentieth-century historians'[1] for the feudal system of administration perfected by Henry I of England. Between 1124 and 1130, David set out to establish much the same system of governance in Scotland, issuing Charters in the approved style, and leaving as legacy a string of royal burghs that are still extant—Edinburgh, Aberdeen, Stirling and Berwick among them. (Rutherglen, now a southeast proliferation of the City of Glasgow, was David's burgh: Glasgow itself was an ecclesiastical property.)

Thus royal castles, royal burghs with royal sheriffs, and an abundance of abbots all reflected in Scotland the fashionable trend of the power to the south; and, as in the south, they set up small Norman colonies in themselves, with a spreading influence. In one direction the influence spread farther than it did in

[1] Ritchie, op. cit., p. 184.

England itself, for Grahams, Sinclairs and Ramsays in Scotland have long survived Mowbrays, Veres and Bohuns in England.[1] Scottish commoners were not prevented, as were their Saxon neighbours, from adopting the surnames of the gentry, for what would have been considered pretentious in the conquered was not reckoned so by fellow-countrymen, albeit of a higher class. In Scotland the earl or baron bestowed a fief on each son, and each in turn on his, 'till the blood of the highest noble in the land was flowing in that of the working peasant, at no remote interval'. By these processes it became 'rare to find a Lindsay, a Hay, a Drummond, in the lower orders, who has not some tradition at least of descent from the houses of Crawford, Errol, or Perth'.[2] Other Scottish surnames, such as Bailie, Fletcher, Lorimer, Porter and Falconer, remain to reflect the Normanized system of local husbandry and administration.

What the working peasant thought of this transformation in his social system has not been recorded, but certainly he did not suffer the same degree of displacement and denigration as the Saxon English. Villein-status was not implanted in Scotland. The laird was not in fact, what he appears in name, a lord of the Norman-English pattern, and Scotland, unabashed by a conquest and unblessed by forest laws, had no need to produce—or later to pretend to have produced—either an Arthur or a Robin Hood. She lacks both a Domesday Book and a peasants' revolt, and, as will be discussed later, lacks also that sense of 'station' and acquiescence that was to be for so long a legacy in the southern kingdom. The differences between England and Scotland have never been so much national as social; when, in the 1860s, the Radical John Bright was campaigning for a Reform Bill, he was much struck by the intellectual difference between his Scottish and his English audiences, and remarked that it was the Scots and not the Irish who deserved home rule.[3] The Irish of Bright's day wanted this because they had been deprived of it, originally by Normans. The Scots, whose political history had always been their own responsibility, had no such axe to grind, and, never

[1] But perhaps they survive elsewhere. It was a tradition in the family of Daniel Boone, the Kentucky trailblazer (1734–1820) that the eldest son should be called Squire. The Boones had emigrated in the 1660s from the English west country.
[2] Lord Lindsay, *The Lives of the Lindsays*, I (1849), 117–19.
[3] G. M. Trevelyan, *Life of John Bright* (1913), p. 84.

having in their daily round encountered many gentlemen, they had developed no feelings towards them either of deference or dislike.

That all Duke William's companions were gentlemen became first a polite fiction and then an accepted axiom among their posterity. Armies are composed of officers and men, and Thierry was to speak darkly about the drovers and weavers of Normandy and Brittany becoming great magnates in England. In contrast, a historian of Scotland sees the Normans as heroes, uniting 'the courage and fierceness of the Old Sea-King to the polished suavity of the Frank'.[1] This has certainly been the more durable image: there has been a consistent habit among Englishmen, perhaps partly due to their national unease in the presence of the French language, to consider such a name as Hugo de Ranville as more high-sounding and *ipso facto* high-born than, say, that of Alfred of Lee. One of the Norman villains[2] in *Ivanhoe* bears the name of Front-de-Boeuf—which is not, when examined, notably patrician. The Scottish Lord Lindsay in his account of some members of his own house, *The Lives of the Lindsays* (1849), speaks of the first Lindsay, or Limesay, as a gentleman of Duke William's train; but his own further evidence above shows that the sire in question was a *protégé* of Lanfranc's son Paul, the Abbot of St Albans, who, whatever else he was, was no gentleman and unlikely to take for his boon companions there those who were such. The Danish scholar who in 1830 described the Saxons as persons to whom no gentleman would wish to be introduced was possibly nearer the truth than he could have supposed[3]—perhaps very few gentlemen actually *were* introduced. Palgrave refers to 'that rascal rout', and there can be no doubt that the Normans themselves distinguished between those of rank and 'temporary gentlemen', however high-flown the names of these latter, or broad their purloined estates, had since become. Passage of time however helped to wash away these original distinctions, and 'Creole' Normans, becoming at once more patriotically 'English' and more loyal to the idea of caste, doubtless instructed their grandsons that their own grand-

---

[1] Hill Burton, *Life of Simon Lord Lovat* (1847), p. 3.
[2] This word began in lowly station and has in modern times sunk farther still.
[3] Douglas, *Conquest and English Historians*, p. 31.

sires, whatever their background, had known the Conqueror well.

It may be that Normans who stayed in Normandy developed as hearty a contempt for their brethren in England as the Anglo-Normans were later to display towards those of their own number who had gone to settle in Ireland, and who succumbed to the spell of the harps and mists of that island, losing much of their original racial arrogance in the process. Similarly, the Normans of Munster and Leinster accused their kin in Connaught of going regrettably native. But, when Normans in England called themselves English, they were describing their own geographical location rather than identifying themselves in any way with the subject-race. A sense of distinctiveness, if not of isolation, early descended upon the Anglo-Normans. Archbishop Lanfranc often spoke, although it may have been without a driving conviction, of 'we English' and 'our island'. Yet he had more right to do so than most, for at least the Church over which he presided was the one area of authority and influence from which even the earliest of the Norman governors, professedly the carriers of the torch of Christian European civilization, could not exclude their English subjects. Indeed the Church of this period played a role not unlike that fulfilled by 'government service' in twentieth-century colonies in Africa; it set down a ladder into the lowest reaches of society, up which the natives might climb. In the long-run the controversial doctrine of 'benefit of clergy'—a privilege whereby everyone in orders 'had his first crime free'[1]—proved more acceptable to the people at large than ever it did to the Norman and Angevin kings themselves. Accordingly Archbishop Thomas Becket, the devoted adversary of Henry II who was murdered in his cathedral in 1170, became the first popular English hero, less perhaps because he was a 'holy blissful martyr for to seek' than that he represented, at long last, a point of view different in kind (whatever its other merits) from that of the foreign oligarchy as a whole.

Moreover, the native English had a value as soldiers, and by exploiting this were able to find some release from their depressed status. As early as 1073 Duke William recruited many among them for his invasion and reduction of the province of

[1] G. R. Elton, *England under the Tudors* (1955), pp. 14–15.

Maine, where they burned and plundered with a savage ferocity that may have indicated a suppressed desire to behave similarly against their own Norman overlords, whose soldiers had recently wreaked so much devastation in the English north. In 1087 Duke William's son Rufus either trusted his subjects less or disliked them more; having mustered some 20,000 of the old English fyrd, or national levy, he absconded with their expense-money of ten shillings per head and used this to employ foreign mercenaries in their place. But they were certainly Englishmen who, forty years after Hastings, helped Duke William's youngest son on the field of Tinchebrai to annex his ancestral duchy to the English Crown. Robert d'Eu had Englishmen in his train when he conquered Pembrokeshire early in the twelfth century; and subsequently Fitzstephen had English settlers from Pembroke in his expedition to Leinster in May 1169. Irish adventures always had an attraction for the native English, for in Ireland at least they were not, as in England, confined to the lowest degree: to the Irish themselves that was allocated. In the Anglo-Norman 'pale' in Ireland Henry II granted to merchants of Bristol the same liberties of trading as they enjoyed in their own town—a forerunner of those 'extraterritorial rights' in foreign lands which nineteenth-century imperialists were to prize so highly. The Normans did not, because they could not, make feudatories of the native Irish. A local magnate could only treat them as allies or enemies, and preferred to do the latter. It was possibly fitting that it should have been the only English pope in history, Adrian IV, who gave his blessing to Henry II's plans for the reduction of Ireland.

It was an enterprise that proved to be protracted. The need to enact the Statute of Kilkenny in 1367, which enjoined the use of the English language, forbade the use of Irish names, and prohibited both political neutrality and racial intermarriage, indicates that the Normans had not made the desired impact on the manners of their subordinates. Indeed, if one follows the line of thought of the Irish Nationalist leader John Redmond, the actual processes of colonization were to come to an end only in 1903, with the passage of the Land Purchase Act: 'the reconquest of the soil of Ireland by the people'.[1]

[1] Denis Gwynn, *Life of John Redmond* (1932), p. 105.

But if in Ireland there were at best only unwilling feudatories, in England there was a sufficient minority at least—for one cannot know what the majority thought, or even be certain what they did—who were prepared to make use of what opportunities were presented them. The army and the Church had early established themselves as the two institutions that provided employment, irrespective of the place or degree of birth of entrants. Of these two, it was the Church, since it was a supra-national organization, that offered most. Its officers, unlike those of the army, had no need to be gentlemen: they were required only to be intelligent, adaptable, and loyal to their superiors, by whose favour alone they could expect promotion. But both institutions played a great part in giving the native English a stake of a kind in their own country, and, as a consequence, signally assisted the process of welding together the colonizers and the colonized in one 'race'. Lord Lindsay's eulogy of this process—one that is badly documented, as the clergy composed the only group among the conquered that produced its own historians—is typical of many. 'I need not expatiate,' says he,

> on the blessings which have accrued to England through the Conquest—the regeneration of the Saxon race through amalgamation with the Norman, and the birth from that union of a still higher offspring, the Saxo-Norman English-man, inheriting the principle of independence from one parent, and that of Order or Reverence from the other, with all they imply, of antagonism and progression, as represented in the Constitution of Great Britain.[1]

(The historian of the British Army, Sir John Fortescue, does not expatiate but puts this case more bluntly: 'England now passed,' he observes, 'to her great good fortune, under the sway of a race that could teach her to obey.')[2] Englishmen were using Norman Christian names, though not surnames, by the reign of Henry II, although Saxon and Danish names remained prevalent in the north and east of the country until the time of John and Henry III. John, the first ruler to appoint a genuinely English Archbishop

[1] Lindsay, *Lindsays*, I, 14.
[2] Fortescue, *History of the British Army*, I (1899), 7.

of Canterbury in the person of Stephen Langton, was also the first to style himself 'King of England' instead of 'King of the English';[1] but that was not so much an act of grace towards his native subjects as the assertion by Jehan Sans Terre of his ultimate attainment of a territory he could call his own. It was not an action that brought him much credit with the Celtic annalists of Ireland, who, with an Irish disregard of these fine distinctions, continued to refer to him as they had done in the past, as the son of the King of the Saxons.

Even if, in England, a new 'race' was coming into being, its leadership stayed firmly in hands it was accustomed to. It was the Creole Norman baronage, after 1205 severed from their connections with and property in Normandy itself, which raised the loudest objection to the horde of Angevin, Poitevin, Savoyard and Brabanter 'aliens' which both John and his son Henry III saw fit to import to fill positions of importance in the administration of England. The barons' sense of self-importance increased as they saw themselves inevitably committed to a purely English future. They needed to make that future secure. In the name of a general equity and justice they imposed on these two monarchs charters which enumerated their own privileges, and called them 'rights', applicable in theory to all dwellers in the realm. In just such a fashion, but with less success, did the boyars of eighteenth-century Russia impose a charter on Tsarina Anne (1731), who tore it up amid the applause of her people, who preferred the traditional autocracy of a paternal monarch to the 'liberties' of a self-seeking oligarchy. Yet a Russian prince, admittedly a tyrant, might appeal to the Russian people to support his tyranny, for it could be said, and it was said, that he was their 'little father'.[2] No 'king of the English' could expect to be so regarded. He could not appeal with any chance of success to people whose language he did not speak and whose 'liberties' it was to his own interest and to that of his nobility to keep on the curb.[3] The people would never

---

[1] 'Rex Anglorum'—ruler *over* the English. Usage changed: when Napoleon I became Emperor of the French, and Louis Philippe became King of the French, they indicated their wish to identify themselves *with* the people.

[2] And cf. Edward Thornton, *History of India*, IV (1843), 377: '[Under Joseph II] the Hungarian peasantry stood up to a man for the liberty of the lash.'

[3] John's Charter was not printed until 1759.

rally with enthusiasm to a king as alien to them as their own immediate lords: thus both the Yorkists and the Tudors were later to stand on a base of *dynastic* popularity that their royal predecessors, however personally engaging, had never enjoyed.

In England, the game of politics was for aristocrats only. It was baronial, not popular, intransigence that made it impossible for Edward II, succeeding his powerful father Edward I in 1307, to make another inventory of his kingdom on the Domesday model, as he wished to. On the strength of the monarchy, on the aptitude of the incumbent for his job, the health of the state—that is to say, the efficiency of its institutions—was henceforth to depend; and whether at any one time the monarchy or the baronage was the stronger was not a problem that the English people themselves were set to solve. They were patients, not agents; whoever held the ring, it was their role to remain within it, and for their own security they must have hoped that their own particular lord, did he set out on a career of opposition to the royal authority, would prove a shrewd hand at the game.

But they cannot have been collectively restive, or more would have been heard of them. Rules designed to curb 'overmighty subjects' certainly improved the security of subjects who had no might at all: the popular view was that strong kings like Henry II and Edward I were the best kings, for the practical advantages of king's peace and king's bench were obvious to the remotest peasant in the dimmest shire. Still, no record of popular affection for either of these kings has come down to us. The old Norman law of 'presentment of Englishry'—under which a corpse was presumed to be that of a Norman (so that a fine might be levied on the hundred) unless it could be proved to be English—was on the statute-book as late as 1341. Five years later, however, the Plantagenet Edward III was able to count on a degree of genuine national feeling among the 'commons', else he would not have troubled to publish at large in London and other towns, in order to arouse general indignation, the details of a French plan for yet another conquest of England—to be mounted, like its predecessor, from Normandy.

The statesmanship of these authoritarian kings has been much admired. Certainly their successful marshalling of the various ranks of men, so that each man within his own degree had an ascertainable position, with rights belonging to it, gives them a better claim to fame than any of their egocentric expeditions into France. Liberty cannot exist except within a framework of settled law. Settled law requires an accepted authority to establish and support it. To obtain this acceptance was necessarily a protracted and difficult task for the rulers, and until it had been got there could be no liberties beyond those they thought safe to allow. They sought their own security; but, since this was also a goal sought by their subordinates, they were able to make a common system of justice the safeguard of internal social peace. This system demanded the backing both of an effective judicial organization and of an unquestioned political supremacy. It required also the establishment and recruitment of a school of 'interpreters', to deal with whatever technical questions of canon or feudal law might arise; and, throughout the English record, there was never to be a shortage of churchmen or lawyers to act as 'lions under the throne'. To systematize law and order, to organize both a national security and a widespread sense of it, was the prime principle of the Anglo-Norman kings and of their Angevin and Plantagenet successors. It was this principle that the Tudors—now no longer believed to have invented a 'New Monarchy', as none was needed if the old one was properly put to work—later took over, refurbished, and applied afresh. Men who promoted able administration were genuinely serving the interests of the majority of the subjects of the Crown, and were recognized by these subjects as doing so.

Exceptional times proved this recognition the rule. Forty years after 'presentment of Englishry' had disappeared from the statute-book some Englishmen at least were prepared to present themselves as critics of the order of things that had been established among them. This they did during the 'hurling time' of Wat Tyler—the peasants' revolt of 1381. Outrages were indeed committed on persons and property, but on nothing like the scale of those that the French *jacquerie* had already indulged in. But the criticism of the established institutions cut very deep. John Ball looked forward to the abolition of serfdom and spoke of the lure of freehold tenure, the same lure that was one day to people the North American continent, so that there came a time when William Cobbett would find American farmers treating 'as a sort of romance' his harrowing tales of English tithe.[1] Ball also dwelt with feeling, as did Tom Paine four centuries after him, on the ingrained iniquities of lawyers, the men who held in their keeping in their mysterious Inns of Court the parchments written in Latin and French that contained the title-deeds of the lands of England. Jack Straw stated that Wat Tyler himself, had he lived to lead the revolt to success, would have left no clergy at all in the land, save the mendicant orders. Straw can be believed. The Church of the day was reckoned a hard landlord, and a town on its demesne was likely to enjoy far fewer municipal liberties than another under the royal protection. It was the clash between clergy privilege and burgher frustration that animated the long history of 'town and gown' quarrels in the two English universities. In 1381 the town of St Albans was still a manor on the lands of the richest of English abbeys (and was to remain so until the Reformation); and while some of the townsmen aired their grievances in true English style by casting back to a dubious charter of liberty granted them by long-gone Offa King of Mercia, wilder spirits nailed up a rabbit on a gallows to indicate the fate of the game laws. In London spirits still wilder beheaded the chancellor-archbishop, and held the city itself at their mercy.

The aristocracy however, led by their young King Richard II, rallied to meet these tests. The Earl of Salisbury, during the council-of-war held in the Tower how best to cope with the mob invasion of London by Tyler's men, put it squarely. 'If we begin,' he said,

> what we cannot carry through, we should never be able to repair matters. It will be all over with us and our heirs, and England will be a desert.[2]

But they did carry it through, it was not all over with them, and their heirs were to pay closer heed to the opinions of the commonalty. Seventy years later Jack Cade's tone was milder

---

[1] Quoted by Allan Nevins, *America Through British Eyes* (New York, 1948), p. 40.

[2] So says Sir John Froissart, *Chronicles*, trans. Berners, III (1901), 234.

than Tyler's. Cade had grievances indeed to express, but he distinctly stated that he was not blaming lords, gentlemen, lawyers, bishops or priests for the condition of affairs of which he complained. So generous an exculpation had a long future before it, but it made Tyler rather than Cade the hero of the early Victorian Chartists, social reformers all. Yet the French historian Taine, visiting the Chartists' England, came to the conclusion that the labourers and the middle classes really *wanted* to have the aristocracy in charge of the nation's business.[1] The middle-class Radical leader Richard Cobden, whose radical-ism never trenched on matters of social reform, had already underlined Taine's point. 'That which the French really prize,' he observed, 'and the English trouble themselves little about, is the absence of privileged inequality in their social system.'[2]

This privileged inequality was a necessary corollary to the aristocratic governance of England. Indeed, its presence was essential to the very idea of aristocracy. The aristocrat must not only think himself to be such, but must have other people around him who agree with him. In mediaeval England townsmen and merchants certainly agreed with him. The English town and its municipal life developed 'under the guidance or at any rate with the authority of the kings, barons and bishops'.[3] The towns with their guilds, companies, fees, markets, fairs, had their privileges and liberties, but these were held 'as of grace', and not as a right. What can be granted can always be recalled—or at least the attempt may lawfully be made, as was to be made plain to the corporation of the City of London so late as the reigns of Charles II and James II. The mercantile class was associated rather than allied with the rulers: the single government of England that was willing to allocate considerable political power to merchants was Cromwell's Protectorate. Otherwise they remained in a position of comfortable subordination, capable of forming a political 'interest' but never a government, and, if successful in their commercial enterprises, graduating via either money or marriage or both into the ranks of the gentry.

[1] Hippolyte Taine, *Notes on England*, ed. E. Hyams (1957), pp. 155 ff.
[2] R. Cobden, *Speeches* ed. J. Bright and J. E. Thorold Rogers (1870) II, 333.
[3] F. M. Powicke, *Mediaeval England* (1945), p. 24.

Thus the governance of an English town was not designed to supply a seed-bed for democracy: mayors and corporations themselves saw to that. Nor was the English parliament. Not until Tudor times was parliament a regular part of the government of the country, and not until Charles II was restored to his throne in 1660 was it made a *permanent* part of the government of the country. Tudor monarchs had very clear ideas as to its station: it was there to be informed, to raise supplies, and to register approval of the royal policies. The mediaeval parliamentary writ of election sent to all the sheriffs declared that the persons who were to be elected to the House of Commons from the burghs must be 'two of the more discreet burgesses, capable of work'.[1] It was well understood that the work they must be capable of was the work of carrying through whatever legislation might be initiated by the king and his great councillors. The less discreet burgesses, were there such, were not supposed to appear at Westminster. When in 1603 James I enfranchised the universities of Oxford and Cambridge, he made use of the same formula: the divines there were to return as their parliamentary burgesses two of their 'more discreet and sufficient men'. They did so, by methods peculiar to themselves: for Oxford refused to allow a candidate for parliamentary election to approach within ten miles of its jurisdiction, while Cambridge, although admitting the candidate, did not permit him to speak.

As for the other representatives of the commons, the knights of the shire, they were both likely to be and reckoned on as being even more amenable than townsmen. It was Richard II's habit to instruct the sheriffs to nominate the knights of the shire. His Lancastrian successors Henry IV and Henry VI did the same, which occasioned one of Jack Cade's thoughtful complaints against the world as he found it in 1450—the freedom of election for knights of the shire

had been taken from the people by the great men who send letters to their tenants to choose such men as they [the people] approve not.[2]

[1] C. H. Haskins, *Growth of English Representative Government* (New York, 1948), p. 6.
[2] E. and A. Porritt, *The Unreformed House of Commons*, I (1903), 21.

The Tudors managed the county elections in the same way, and Henry VIII, determined to 'reform' the Church with the connivance of his people, and accordingly with a very crowded parliamentary programme to put through, would not have increased the number of seats in parliament from 296 to 334 (which included the 'shiring' of Wales) had he not been confident of being able to complete, under Thomas Cromwell's expert management, what he had set out to do.[1] In particular the royal duchy of Cornwall served as a valuable channel through which reliable men could be returned to parliament—or, if we accept one hostile opinion, provided a means whereby the back benches could be filled with greedy courtiers and expectant lawyers. It was in Cornwall, which from the time of Edward VI to that of William IV enjoyed the franchises allotted to no less than twenty-one boroughs, that the most diligent of all royal political managers, George III, served his apprenticeship at the game.

The rulers had no misgivings as to the propriety of these practices, nor could it have been explained to them why they might have had some. In 1586 Elizabeth I instructed the sheriffs to let the principal persons in the cities and boroughs understand 'that we think they will do very well to nominate in their free elections those whom they elected before'—in other words, they ought to return the compliant characters who had sat in her last parliament. Elected members who seemed disinclined to compliance she brought sharply up short: liberty of speech, she admonished the Commons in 1593, did not imply a permission to members 'to speak there of all causes as him listeth'.[2] In a reign of 45 years, she summoned Parliament ten times only, and no session lasted longer than two months. Her Stuart successor James I followed this line of conduct, telling the Commons not to meddle in matters of state, and tearing up the Protestation they presented to him as a result (1621). James cautioned the electors to avoid the choice of any persons either noted for their superstitious blindness or for their turbulent humours. They

[1] At the time of the Reformation the Church held one-third of the lands of England—but it had, it seems, lost the respect and loyalty of its tenantry. Was this because its members were as low-born as the tenants themselves?

[2] Porritt, *op. cit.*, p. 377.

were also to take especial care not to be misled by such as were
unripe and immature, or by all 'curious and wrangling lawyers'.
When, despite this counsel, the population at Westminster of
curious and wrangling lawyers continued to increase, his son
Charles I devised the neat expedient of having the most
vociferous among them appointed sheriffs, thus removing them
from the parliamentary scene. Charles maintained close liaison
with the justices of the peace in the shires, but the boroughs
eluded him, as these under malign influences of lawyers and
merchants had begun to fall more and more into the hands of
Whig dissenters. Charles' successor Cromwell was no Whig;
and, unable to come to terms with those who—known candidly
as 'malignants'—wished to perpetuate dissent and disaffection
for their own sakes, first reformed the borough franchise and
then dispensed with parliament altogether.

The problem remained to confront the restored Charles II in
1660, and it was resolved by withdrawing public recognition
from nonconformity of all kinds. The Corporation Act of 1661
confined all municipal office to royalist Anglicans. The Test Act
of 1673 made it impossible for anyone other than a royalist
Anglican to hold any office of state or command in the army or
navy. These measures, by assuming that all dissenters in
religion were *ipso facto* radically Whig in politics, certainly
helped to bring that undesired state of affairs about. The later
Stuarts were indeed more active than their forebears in the
control of—or, as it was now coming to be classified, interference
with—the lower House. Charles II's long parliament of 1661–
79, although it fell out with him in the end, was notoriously
'Cavalier and pensionary', for it was he who invented that
system of 'influence' which unplaced Whigs were later to accuse
George III of perfecting. In the last four years of his reign, when
he was enjoying a comfortable pension from King Louis XIV,
Charles followed the example of both his father and Cromwell
and dispensed with the advice of his lieges. Unhampered
accordingly, he set out to attack, with the use of medieval *quo
warranto* procedure, two such formidably entrenched centres of
disaffection as the Corporation of London and the chartered
Colony of Massachusetts—with signal success. But his brother
James II had to have recourse to parliament, because, like

Henry VIII and Mary I before him, he intended to put through a religious revolution. He was the first king to make, in the autumn of 1687, an avowed 'election tour'; for he would have needed a parliament very well packed indeed if he was ever to carry out the sweeping plans he had made for refashioning the institutions of England both at home and in the colonies in America. The tour gave him a personal, but not a political success. He showed royal displeasure accordingly: the borough of Kingston-upon-Hull, which had refused to elect the royal nominee, had 1,200 soldiers quartered on it as a punishment.

The word 'radical' was not then coined, but it is plain that the exclusion of professed dissenters, wranglers and troublemakers of all kinds from the lower house of parliament, was a consistent aim of the executive from the outset. In 1664, in the island colony of Barbados, the king's governor Lord Willoughby gave voice to an opinion held by many generations of the highly-placed. In a contentious Speaker of the Assembly there Willoughby claimed to have rediscovered 'John Cade himself, a great Magna-Carta-man and Petition-of-Right-Maker', who had taught the planter-legislators 'to dance to the Long Parliament's pipe'.[1] Him he promptly deported. It was an action that Simon de Montfort, cast by the Victorians as the hero of the earliest movement towards representative government, would have applauded; for that formidable baron had taken good care to ensure that the knights and burgesses he caused to be summoned in 1265 to a national assembly at Lewes were persons who could be relied upon to abet him in his political plans, which were both immediate and complex. De Montfort and others of his kind certainly recalled what some of the Victorian seekers after constitutional pedigree sometimes forgot, that representation in the English parliament was not originally grounded on any right whatever, but on feudal obligation. Parliament was the king's high court, and feudal law required that his tenants should do suit and service at the lord's court for the lands they held of him, if and when they were summoned. The king could not exact more than the recognized feudal dues without consent, and it was clearly more convenient that consent

[1] A. P. Thornton, *West-India Policy under the Restoration* (Oxford, 1956), p. 65.

should be given by representation of communities than by each individual separately.

This being the background of the representative 'system', one could not expect to find, and indeed one does not, the emergence of any belief that there could exist such a thing as a 'loyal opposition'. This, at once the oddest and most sophisticated of modern English political inventions, would have seemed a meaningless fantasy to de Montfort, or for that matter to Edward I or Henry VIII. George III, on the throne between 1760 and 1820, was never able to grasp the notion; and even Victoria had continual trouble with it and could absorb it at all only by identifying it, more or less adequately, with the machinations of Mr Gladstone. The general view of those who were involved or interested in affairs of state—always a minority—sympathized with this official attitude. Only in an emergency could a matter of 'politics' be expected to gear the majority to concerted action. The doings of James II provided one such emergency, but such cases of crisis were rare. Normally it was proper, and because it was proper it was expected, that a gentleman should support the king's government. If one was not a 'King's Friend' (a definition invented by George III), what was the alternative—to cast oneself as a King's Enemy? This was a dismaying role, with malignant overtones, for in English history the most famous of all the king's enemies were the seventeenth-century 'Independents' who killed King Charles I. The men who did that never found themselves an honoured niche in popular estimation, and whatever their motives and ideals, they were hardly classifiable as 'discreet and sufficient'. How right and reasonable, therefore, to insist always on these qualifications in legislators: they would form perhaps a dull assembly, but a 'sound' one.

Thus Toryism was an ingrained English point of view before it was ever a political party, and even when it had fashioned its own party its attitudes overlapped the limitations that political allegiance imposed.

Security was its aim, moderation its method. Its strength lay in the lands of the shires of England, and was reflected in the institutions of England, themselves reared on the philosophical and practical foundations of property-right. By the eighteenth century one such institution, one both powerful and successful, was the Whig party: and the men who governed its affairs were Tories. The distinguished historian William Lecky, himself a Tory, has described the Whig governments of Sir Robert Walpole and the Duke of Newcastle as

> in the true sense of the word, Conservative governments: that is to say, governments of which the supreme object and pre-occupation was not the realization of any unattained political ideal, or the redressing of any political grievances, but merely the maintenance of existing institutions against all assailants.[1]

Assailants have not been lacking; but Conservative governments have remained the rule in England.

The recruitment and increase of the English gentry since Tudor times had entailed a like expansion of the sphere of their conventions and ideals, the imposition of their own brand of cultural imperialism. This was to govern the attitudes even of those—or, it is possible to argue—particularly of those who struck out against its tide. The peasants who in 1643, under cover of the disturbed conditions of the civil war, attacked the estates of the Earl of Suffolk, saw clearly how matters stood: 'if they took not advantage of the time, they shall never have the opportunity again'.[2] They were right. Charles I and Oliver Cromwell, who were otherwise not much of a mind, were alike paternalists. They agreed on their interpretation of the phrase 'the liberties of the people', which they heard bandied about on all sides. There was an inherent menace in it. The King spoke his mind on his scaffold. He told the people assembled to watch him die that their liberty and freedom consisted in their *having* government: 'It is not their having a share in government; that is nothing pertaining to them.' Five months later, the Long Parliament, inheritor of the authority of all three estates, passed an Act establishing the English Republic (May 19, 1649), which decreed that henceforth all writs were to run in the name

---

[1] W. E. H. Lecky, *A History of England in the Eighteenth Century*, II (edn. of 1892), 94.
[2] *Lords' Journals* VI, 21.

of 'the Keepers of the Liberties of England'. Thus liberty, like everything else in the community, needed its warders—eternal, and necessarily powerful, vigilants. Cromwell, although no friend to this parliament, assented to this. Government must be for the good of the people, and not for what pleased them. Society must keep its ranks in close formation: 'A nobleman, a gentleman, a yeoman—that is a good interest of the land and a great one.' Together with his lieutenant and son-in-law Ireton, Cromwell objected to the notions current among his own soldiers, whose 'Independency' in religion had distorted their political ideas, on the matter of the Englishman's 'birthright':

> that by a man's being born here he should have a share in that power that shall dispose of all things here, I do not think it a sufficient ground.[1]

It was anyway not the business of a soldier to have ideas; although he should 'love what he knows', he was not asked or supposed to seek what was not to be had. For Cromwell was no Leveller, as he proved when he had a number of that persuasion shot.

This fundamental harmony of view as to the right basis of governance and authority explains the similarities in kind between the two opposing groups. The civil war began in men's minds, as a problem in liberty and authority. It was therefore a matter for the educated, one not supposed to concern the common people, whose 'liberties' were presumably to be guarded whatever happened, and whoever won. The war was neither expected nor desired to turn into a 'class struggle': Cromwell's embarrassment when elements of the common people began to assert their own surprising view of the state of their liberties was accordingly profound. Mixed motives were also common to both sides. In the eyes of countrymen, the justice of the peace was the most visible symbol of the royal authority. It would be interesting to compute how many justices took up arms against the King; and also to conjecture the reaction of those to whom they were accustomed to dispense the royal justice. There were

[1] G. P. Gooch, *English Democratic Ideas in the 17th Century* (Torchbook edn., New York, 1959), p. 138.

some peers who thought that the forces of the parliament would prove stronger than those of the King, and chose the winning side: Pembroke and Salisbury, says Clarendon of two such, 'had rather the King and his posterity should be destroyed than that Wilton should be taken from the one and Hatfield from the other'.[1] There were some also from the lower orders, merchants and the like, who had got themselves gentlemen's estates, but not the esteem and reputation of a gentleman, and who hoped that their support of the parliamentary cause would bring them this. Among the lords, the King drew his main support from the families that had been ennobled by his father James I and himself. The members of the families which had been elevated to the peerage before 1603, James' accession, were about evenly divided between the royalists and the parliamentarians. The Sidney family set an example. Leicester began on Charles's side, and then became neutral; his brother-in-law Northumberland was on the side of parliament; his son-in-law Spencer was with the King; and his sons, Viscount Lisle and Algernon Sidney, were with parliament.[2] Charles in his straits was obliged to add thirty-eight more members to the peerage, an increase of 20 per cent—but this alone could not win him the day.

Men had forgotten how to be moderate. But they did not forget that their ultimate aim was security. Both sides fought for this. Social revolution was therefore kept at bay so long as this parity of view obtained. Levellers themselves objected to the name with which they were saddled, protesting that all the 'levelling' they wanted was a better distribution of justice. They stood for manhood suffrage,[3] annual parliaments, and complete religious liberty (except for Papists and prelatists). But what else would these things bring, but social revolution? And what was justice, but the opinions of those who judge? Their leader 'Freeborn' John Lilburne told the lords to their faces that they were encroachers and usurpers, while the politicians in the ranks of the army sought a redistribution of parliamentary seats as

[1] Clarendon, *History of the Rebellion*, ed. W. D. Macrae (Oxford, 1888) III, 495.

[2] Paul Hardacre, *The Royalists during the Puritan Revolution* (The Hague, 1956), pp. 10 ff.

[3] But cf. H. N. Brailsford, *The Levellers and the English Revolution* (1961), pp. 693-4.

well as, or in the name of, this same 'justice', arguing that the franchise should be extended to all who were not servants or beggars. Cromwell and Ireton, less interested in the achievement of justice than in the successful imposition of law, opposed this too, and in the Instrument of Government established in 1654 no one was granted the franchise who did not possess property valued at £200 a year.

Government was certainly to be remodelled—but it was not to be destroyed, far from it. The execution of the King had been followed within the week (February 7, 1649) by the abolition of the House of Lords, the logical step: but the concentration of political power in different (and, as it was argued, more righteous) hands made little difference in kind to the *ethos* of governance itself. It was to be made more efficient, more far-reaching than before, for the greater good of the people subordinated to it. The inclusion of Scotland in this new polity illustrates this determination. Some looked on it as a great condescension by the parliament of England 'to permit a people they have conquered to have a part in the legislative power',[1] but as it turned out it was no great part; for when twenty-one members were elected from Scotland to Westminster under this new dispensation in 1654, they were mostly officers in the English army of occupation or officials of the English executive in Scotland. English authority extended into other Scottish spheres. The Council of State directed commissioners to visit and reform, *inter alia*, the universities, colleges, and schools of learning in Scotland, so that they might

> alter and abolish such [statutes] . . . as you shall judge not agreeable to the good of this Island, or inconsistent with the government of this Commonwealth[2]

—clearly an outlook that does not have in it much care for the 'liberties' of the people, or for ideas of democracy.

There were extremists ready to propound such ideas, and one group of them displayed a curious sense of history. The 'Diggers', a communist sect that began to dig the soil of St George's

[1] Edmund Ludlow, ed. C. H. Firth, *Memoirs*, I (Oxford, 1894), 298.
[2] C. S. Terry, ed., *The Cromwellian Union* (Edinburgh, 1902), p. xviii, lvii.

Hill in Surrey, there to plant parsnips, carrots and beans, and even to threaten the security of the 'park pales' of the great, held opinions genuinely revolutionary. Their leader Gerrard Winstanley told the authorities that Christ was the head leveller and that riches were impossible to obtain by honest means—an opinion no Christian nation has ever found itself able to accept. One of the Digger tracts of 1647 was entitled *St Edward's Ghost*, a flattering reference to the Confessor, the last of the Saxon kings. King Charles, in contrast, was constantly referred to as the last of the Norman kings. By their victory over the King, the direct successor of William the Conqueror, the 'enslaved people of England' had recovered themselves, at long, long last, from the effects of the Conquest. Yet it was clear, to Diggers at least, that the people did not as yet enjoy the benefit of this victory. Nor could they, so long as the use of the common land was withheld 'from the younger brothers' by the lords of manors, men who still 'sat in the Norman chair' and upheld that tyranny as if the kingly power were yet in force. 'Your aim,' Winstanley accused,

> was not to throw down tyranny, but the tyrant.

The regicide government had not made good its compact with the people of England. It had promised 'that if we would adventure person and purse to recover England from under that Norman oppression you would make us a free people'. But no one was free, whose society was still encumbered with lawyers and clergy and tithes, those firm adjuncts of Norman power (another argument Tom Paine was to put to use). It was not for nothing, the Diggers declared,

> that the kings would have all their laws written in French and Latin, and not in English—partly in honour to the Norman race, and partly to keep the common people ignorant of their creation-freedoms, lest they should rise to freedom themselves.

As for rule by parliament, herein there could be no improvement, no hope for a true revolution. For who was it had the franchise? Freeholders and landlords: and who were they, but 'the Norman common soldiers, spread abroad in the land'? Whom did such elect to sit in the parliament, 'but some very rich man, who is the successor of the Norman colonels and high officers'? This last of course was unlikely to be true, as the possession of wealth had promoted many a man whose forebears would never have been allowed even to speak to a Norman lord; but even if they had some of the details of their indictment wrong, the Diggers kept a firm hold of their sense of social injustice. In one of their songs they went to the heart of the matter as they saw it:

But the gentry must come down, And the poor shall wear the Crown—Stand up now, Diggers all.[1]

But, just as in Wat Tyler's 'hurling time', the Norman yoke was not removed and the gentry did not come down. There was no one to take their place—nor, as it turned out and became clear even to presbyterians in not too long a run, was there anyone who could succeed King Charles I save King Charles II. The gentry indeed expanded, as it had done in Tudor times when fattened with the rent-rolls of monastic lands. By 1660, lands in south-eastern England which had been forfeited by fifty royalists had been distributed among 257 people.[2] These 257, and others like them, became Tories at once. Ireton's stubborn rebuttal to unlanded 'democrats' and their point of view was to win the support of many future generations of proprietors. In sum it involved the argument deduced from 'a stake in the country', of which Tories in Disraeli's day were still making much. Rulers and voters alike, said Ireton, should be those persons 'in whom all land lies, and those incorporations in whom all trading lies'— all those who had a 'permanent fixed interest in the country'. It was up to democrats to use what wit and talent they owned to get for themselves such a 'fixed interest'. No one had closed the door on them; but no one saw any need to dispense with the door, either. Status was something a man had to win: it was not something other men owed him.

[1] On the Diggers see G. H. Sabine, *The Works of Gerrard Winstanley* (Cornell U.P., 1941), p. 259 ff.; Gooch, *English Democratic Ideas*, p. 187; C. H. Firth, ed., *The Clarke Papers* (Camden Society, 1894), IV, 215 ff.

[2] Joan Thirsk, 'The Restoration Land Settlement', *Journal of Modern History*, xxvi (1952), p. 315.

But republicanism itself could never win itself a status. It was its own impermanence, the loose stones of theory on which and of which it was built, that undermined it and brought it down at the last. It was the political counterpart of religious sectarianism. It was founded on conviction, not on reason. It denied fellowship, since it was open to every republican to think himself a better republican than his fellow. Something so fissiparous could find no secure home for the idea of sovereignty, and therefore, no basis for its authority. Lacking these things, it could make no appeal to loyalty, and its ablest servants were men who thought more of their own careers than of their country. The deluge that, doubtless, would come after them was something they had no way of making any concern of theirs: Cromwell himself was miserable because he could not. Thus republicanism opened no window on any clear horizon. Its chief disadvantage, in men's eyes, was its unpredictability, its inevitable tendency to resort to desperate remedies. Having no security, it was *capable de tout*. With no precedents to follow, its practices were stumbling, and only the direct use of military force could get for it the kind of obedience that, since no one gave this who was not compelled to, was bound to dissipate at the first favourable opportunity. The like dilemma faced republicans who were democrats, and republicans who were nothing of the sort. The democrats correctly saw that the removal of the prop of monarchy had weakened the entire social structure, and put in question every English institution. The ranks of society, the orders and degrees, need no longer be marshalled in feudal array. The land itself could be put to different use, and an age of non-enclosure, of a peasant proprietary, might dawn. The republican government however denied forcibly that this was the corollary of their own actions, and slowly built for itself an enmity among those who had supported it as vindictive as any that burned in a royalist bosom. But, in whatever direction, left or right, these arguments swayed, the upshot was that republicanism demanded a constant attention from everyone to 'politics' of all kinds. It seemed to need constant analysis and inspection. Armed with idealism, it interfered in every sphere of life in this world and the next. The English nation was not composed of Diggers, of argumentative extremists, of fanatics and improvers. On a nation the great majority of which desired only to be left to mind their own business, the doctrines of republicanism laid too heavy an intellectual load—as in future other radical policies were also to do.

The royalists may indeed have been 'wrong but romantic'; and if they were romantic, it was because they had the traditional ways of life on their side. In an age when innovation ruled, a new glamour attached itself to these ways. Indeed many royalist gentlemen cared little for the cause of the bishops; but they had, and followed, an obvious loyalty to the person of the King who had made that cause his own. Once the King had been made away with, no other 'Single Person', despite all Cromwell's constitutional ingenuities, could expect to command a similar fidelity. The Diggers had the right of it: the 'kingly power' was in force—in force, but not in authority. Thus, having destroyed two of the greatest English institutions, the monarchy in 1649 and the parliament in 1653, Cromwell as Protector had to spend his time trying to restore both of them on some new basis of permanence. But the means he used to do this was the Army— an institution that did not have then, and was never to obtain, the customary loyalty of the English people. The Army indeed dressed its authority in parliamentary clothes, but its officers did this less because they thought it best, in A. F. Pollard's famous phrase, 'to fix a legal wig upon the point of the soldier's sword', less to ease their conscience, than to establish precedents that a less agitated generation could faithfully follow. They saw to it that the electors to their Barebones Parliament were proper Puritans, devout members of congregations, men neither likely nor expected to be 'discreet and sufficient', but certainly men who feared God and were of approved fidelity and honesty, the characteristics that the zealous Army men insisted upon.

These 'Saints' constituted a body of devoted improvers. Their ideas were commonsensible enough but their methods seldom were, and they were suspected, even when innocent, of having diverse axes to grind. Among other things they hoped to be able to rewrite the laws of England—those mysteries of black-letter, Norman-French, bad Latin—in an intelligible and compassable form, and this alone well illustrates the impracticable patterns their idealism took. Naturally their radicalism brought down on their heads the wrath of lawyers, soldiers and clergy, and finally that of Cromwell himself. The subsequent parliament, that which assembled under the Instrument of Government, was indeed a soberer and more practically-minded body, but again it lacked the vital and enduring spark—it could not be conservative as no one was agreed on what ought to be conserved. Cromwell's constant soul-searchings, public and private, concerning what was and what was not a 'fundamental' in government clearly indicate how far common agreement on this fundamental matter was lacking. His insistence that a written constitution was necessary, one that should contain for ever those fundamentals, reflects his wish to put down enduring republican roots in English soil: they were descendants of his disciples in New England, not in Old, who were at last to see his point. But as he could not establish his fundamentals, he ended by governing alone, as 'thorough' as Charles' agent Strafford had been, and as dangerous to men's peace of mind and hopes for the future. When he died in 1658 he was hated by royalists and republicans —by Presbyterians, Independents, Levellers and Saints alike.

Of these groups only the first, as has been noted, had a history, had that 'permanent fixed interest' in the country whose desirability Ireton had emphasized. Thus the restoration of the Stuart monarchy, and with it the restoration to their respective places in society of grandee, squire, parson and lawyer, was accompanied by the disappearance for ever of Saints from politics, of religious nonconformity from polite society for the same length of time, and of Levellers for another hundred years. The speed with which this happened struck contemporaries of the process, and has continued to puzzle posterity. What became thereafter of the members of Cromwell's army—that formidable engine which was at once the mainstay of the Protectorate and the admiration of the powers of Europe—history has not recorded.

Accordingly, the arrangements made at the Restoration put the old governing class back in the saddle. Parliament retained its victories of 1641, and it was in fact 'the-King-in-Parliament' which was henceforth the legislative authority in the country. But the Game Laws were restored, enclosures were continued and 'park pales' were no longer menaced by Diggers and their like. That this might be made the more improbable, the lords-lieutenants in the counties were given a firmer control of the local militia. In the long run, most of the royalists, as a result of private acts in their favour, orders from the House of Lords, private settlements, or litigation, recovered the lands that had been lost during the interregnum. The gentry's newer recruits were not however disturbed. Those who had after 1649 bought lands from the Crown or the Church or from 'delinquents'—the current term for active royalists—had worried greatly lest a restored king would dispossess them again. This anxiety was mended, however, when Charles II before his return issued a proclamation prohibiting the forcible repossession of lands by royalists or anyone else, pending a decision by Parliament or a lawful eviction of the tenants.[1]

These 'new men', like the lower ranks of Cromwell's army, were also successfully absorbed into the restored English society. They settled on their lands, spiritually supported by the presence of Anglican clergy, who were back in their pulpits by Christmas Day 1660; and they naturally tended to agree with Charles II's aphorism, that dissent was no religion for a gentleman. Henceforth a social frontier divided every English village, with 'Church' as the watchtower of the aspiring classes and 'chapel' as that of those who either would or could not aspire. While the village of Bray enjoyed the paternalism of its squire as well as of its vicar, the Church fell under the dominating ethos of the gentry. Its higher ranks indeed often became indistinguishable from the nobility of whose 'order' it formed part, so that it might be said that an eighteenth-century bishop regarded his benefice 'as an estate to which was attached the performance of certain ecclesiastical duties'. Secular Toryism could well afford to base itself on the doctrine of 'Church and State', knowing with accuracy which was the more important partner. This was to explain its desertion in 1688 of James II, who was the real revolutionary of that time in that he wanted to give to the Church—but not to the Anglican Church—the superior role.

Nor was it to be expected that the parliamentary reforms of the Protectorate, with their disturbing overtones of social justice, would be permitted to survive the republican regime.

[1] Hardacre, *Royalists during Revolution*, p. 157.

Cromwell's Instrument of Government had reduced the representation of the boroughs from 430 to 139 seats, but it had increased the county representation from 100 to 261 seats—a step which clearly indicated where, if loyalty to his kind of authoritative principle was anywhere to be found, Cromwell hoped to find it. The East Anglian counties, with their radical tradition, had been singularly favoured in this redistribution: to Lincoln, Norfolk and Suffolk were allotted ten county members apiece instead of two, while Essex was awarded thirteen. Cornwall was stripped of its boroughs, its twenty-one being reduced to four. Elsewhere several other boroughs, which the eighteenth century was to know as 'rotten', were disfranchised: these included Gatton, Grampound and Old Sarum. (The very existence of the latter, to become the most notorious of all, had been thought scandalous even by James I.)[1] The total number of English and Welsh representatives in the House of Commons was reduced from 530 to 400. But all these changes, including the parliamentary union with Scotland, were reversed on the brusque principle that anything effected by regicides was bound to be wicked; and political radicalism, tarred with this brush, went under cover while 'the unreformed House of Commons' remained, virtually untampered with, until 1832.

For the English Revolution of 1641–60 had sown more ideas than anyone ever wanted to reap. The English Revolution of 1688–9, which was to leave the aristocracy that had been restored in 1660 free to operate as an oligarchy, was far less significant intellectually. But in these latter events, far more so than in the turbulence of the mid-century, Milton's 'even temper of the English mind' was better reflected.

[1] Porritt, *Unreformed Commons*, p. 307.

CHAPTER II

THE ESTATES OF THE REALM

Innovation was now to cease: there had been something too much of it.

A generation that had been hammered by it was succeeded by others whose hope was to live mentally undisturbed and socially comfortable. They were fortunate, in that the economic expansion of the country allowed them both room and time to do so. James II was the last of the innovators, and Jacobites were considered, until the apparition in England of 'jacobins' (men who sympathized with the principles of the French Revolution of 1789) as the last of the possible disturbers of the domestic peace. *Quo warranto*, by what warrant?, is a formidable lever for prising open the locks of society, as John Ball and Jeremy Bentham, social critics in their different eras, diagnosed: for once men start to ask and examine, they may see as little point in having monarchs and magnates as in having monks. To avoid stirring up trouble, so that such questions would stay not only unasked but unformulated, therefore became the common aim of politicians. Since action, the use of an initiative, could be construed as provocative, it was best to take no action at all. One of Edmund Burke's *obiter dicta*, clearly designed to reduce mental strife to a minimum, adorns the age. 'A spirit of innovation,' he decrees, 'is generally the result of a selfish temper and confined views.'[1]

It was because he always wanted the sleeping dogs to lie, and had such skill in getting them to do so, that Sir Robert Walpole proved so durable a pillar of his society. Toleration became the accepted practice in politics, in an age whose seniors could re-

[1] Quoted in Lord Hugh Cecil, *Conservatism* (1912), p. 16.

member the axe falling on the necks of William Russell and Algernon Sidney. This did not happen because Walpole and his contemporaries were better and more humane men than their fathers. They were less worried. Since they were not confronted with any opposing, dangerous principle, they could afford to tolerate what did not alarm. They were Whigs from whose Whiggism all revolutionary tendencies had been purged. They had no wish to use their political supremacy to set about repealing such Tory legislation as the Test and Corporation Acts, to mount any far-reaching programme for reform, or indeed to legislate at all. Heirs of glorious days in 1688—when the landed oligarchs had finished the work, begun in 1641, of curbing the prerogatives of the Crown—they looked back to that event as to a final settlement. And they looked no farther back, for the success of the English Revolution never redeemed the earlier English Rebellion from discredit. In consequence, an entire generation of high-principled and adventurous men was buried in an oblivion which the publication of histories of their era by Clarendon (1702) and Burnet (1724) only briefly dispelled. Cromwell was left stamped with the mark of the regicide, an extremist beyond both the political and the social pales; while the first Earl of Shaftesbury, with greater claims to Whig canonization, was thankfully replaced in the hagiography by William of Orange, who had still better claims than he. Utopia, guarded and patrolled by self-appointed 'Keepers of the Liberties of England', was for the future to remain an untravelled country, of which the conjectural maps were declared lost. For these, Paine and many a later English radical, English misfit, and Irish refugee, substituted a chart of the American republic, dreaming 'the American dream' long before it became an American myth: a dream of the Utopia that was to be found on the Susquehanna, across the wide Missouri, at the end of the Oregon trail, by the Great Salt Lake, or even in Philadelphia, in the morning.

But Englishmen who were content to accept the style of their life in England accepted also the polity that governed it. They agreed with Burke, that 1688 was 'a parent of settlement, not a nursery of future revolutions.' Even Tom Paine added a wry assent, with his own twist to it. The Bill of Rights was a bargain between the Crown and the magnates, a new Magna Carta, and as little altruistic as the old:

> you shall have so much, and I will have the rest; and with respect to the nation, it said, for your share you *shall have the right of petitioning*.

The men of property had constructed a constitution for their own security; and, by a further and honestly-named Act of Settlement (1701) they entailed the Crown itself upon a restricted class of persons on whom they felt they could continue to rely—Protestants, who would uphold both the Church of England and the gentry who were its communicants. Their next task was to breed a general respect for this settlement, to establish its authority, so that as many as possible would come to agree without hypocrisy that it was, indeed, a glorious business. Time and circumstance helped the Whigs do this, and in a century studded by international rivalries and wars they easily appealed to the patriotism of the people. They spread their paternalist mantle alike over the welfare of merchants and Dissenters, and thus reinforced their authority with the support of classes whose ingrained toryism and respectability of character the official Tories, with their emotional attitude to Church and State, had never seen fit to recognize. It was a notable achievement. Eighteenth-century England, ruled by men whose conscience and property were at ease, developed as a free community, free sometimes to a point of rumbustious licence. The licence, however, was permissive. The community lived in an enclosed estate, whose 'improving' landlords were always better able to cope with the rowdy politicking of Grub Street and Gin Lane than with the intellectual radicalism promoted by that minority of tenants who wanted to know what, if anything, lay beyond the enclosing walls. As Burke reiterates, custom has a deeper influence on men than law itself. When custom had become traditional, when the British Constitution itself was acceptable in the form of a collection of precedents and conventions, it had as strong a bond as law. Blaise Pascal had given some guidance on this: lawgivers, he advised, should cause law

> to be regarded as authentic, eternal, and to conceal the beginning of it—if we do not wish it to come soon to an end.

Accordingly, the Whig purpose was always to propagate the idea that no other ideas existed than their own, that their own ideas marched with the interest of the community as a whole, and therefore that no new adventures were necessary.

It was a practice with a consistent history. The earliest Whigs, whose principles had been genuinely revolutionary, had worked towards the same end. In his republican handbook, *Oceana* (1656), James Harrington had insisted that gentlemen made the best republicans, and that those who owned the land of a country had the right to make its laws.[1] The laws would then become as hereditary, and as customary, as the ownership of the land itself. Once made, therefore, along these proper principles, they would need no further overhaul, and might indeed, as the 'Saints' had already suggested, be compassable in 'a big pocket-book'. In 1688 the Earl of Shaftesbury, more than half a republican and the leader of the 'country party' against the Court, who had been lucky to keep his head on his shoulders when Russell and Sidney lost theirs five years before, warned that it was not safe to make over the estates of the people in trust to those who had none of their own. This was one Whig idea that opponents could applaud, and it was made statutory by a Tory ministry in 1710. They passed an Act which required that, to sit in parliament at all, a knight of the shire must possess a landed income to the value of at least £600 *per annum*, and a burgess one of at least £300. There were always ways around these qualifications—but they were ways without menace, ways that only a wealthy man with an already established personal and political influence could take. To open a career to talent, or to discover that this was what one had actually done, was often either the pleasure or the dismay of the great patron. The elder Pitt, once he had been translated as Chatham to the House of Lords, gloomily dismissed the entire House of Commons as 'a parcel of younger brothers', natural dependents. His own son William, together with Burke, Fox, and Sheridan, were landless and moneyless men who were made to qualify for their

[1] H. F. Russell Smith, ed. (Cambridge 1914). In New England special provisions were made in the 'Body of Liberties' to prevent the infliction of corporal punishment on 'gentlemen'. Harrington's ideas were also adhered to in Ireland, by Roundhead and Royalist alike. Between 1641 and 1687 2 1/3 m. acres were transferred from Catholic to Protestant hands; *ibid.*, p. 26.

seats by being supplied with rent-charges to the statutory amount by a patron: Lord Verney for example served Burke in this manner from 1761 to 1774, and it was Lord Temple who in 1768 gave John Wilkes land in Middlesex to qualify him as a freeholder. In 1793 Charles Grey, leader of the movement for parliamentary reform, calculated that out of 558 members of the Commons, 307 were returned by patrons. Passage of time made no great difference to the figures. In 1827 John Wilson Croker, editor of the *Quarterly Review*, did the sum again, and reckoned that in a House augmented by 100 Irish members 276 were still patronized in this way.

Landowners were thus able to make not only the laws but to provide a majority of the legislators.[1] (In Ireland, the case could be seen at its expected extreme. 216 out of 300 members were elected by boroughs and manors, and of that 216, 176 were elected by individual patrons.)[2] The man of genuinely independent means in such a situation stood out. In the English parliament of 1780–84, when the younger Pitt held Appleby for a patron (Sir James Lowther) while Charles Grey represented a county (Yorkshire), it was Grey who had the higher prestige; and Pitt took care to remedy the situation, for from the election of 1784 to his death in 1806 he represented the University of Cambridge as its burgess. The property qualifications for a parliamentary candidate were indeed to survive Grey's Reform Act and the fall of the unreformed parliament in 1832. In 1838 personal property was substituted for landed property, but the valuations remained the same, and another twenty years passed before a Conservative ministry finally repealed the Act of 1710.

It has been estimated that three-quarters of all members of parliament, in the century between 1734 and 1832, drew their main income from landed rents. It is not therefore surprising that we do not find during this period any evidence of a struggle of parties, which a modern politician would recognize as deserving the name. There was no formed phalanx in opposition, with a much better legislative programme in its collective

---

[1] Note also the Nullum Tempus Act, 9 Geo. III, c. 16, which 'made 60 years of quiet possession of Crown lands a bar to any action for recovery on the part of the Crown'.

[2] Lecky, *History of Ireland in the Eighteenth Century*, I (edn. of 1892), 195.

pocket, ready to produce it the moment the opinion of the electorate veered in its favour. Not only was there no opposition and no programme, but there was no electorate to speak of, and whether there was a public opinion or not was a matter for argument. Nor did anyone in politics want these things to exist. The notion, later strongly propagated by doctrinaire Liberals and Socialists, that one party (their own) follows a line of principle while the other merely either strives for or clings to office, would have meant little to eighteenth-century politicians. Everybody strove for, or clung to, office: it was the natural thing to do. It was not a matter of morals; indeed, Lord Shelburne had to endure his reputation as a 'jesuit' in Berkeley Square because he had the habit of claiming higher aims in public life than anyone was prepared to allow either him or it. All the political contests were part of the same game. The game was played by men interested in the same thing—the exercise of political influence —and their only difference lay in their opposite opinions who was better fitted for this prize.

In his *Idea of a Patriot King* (1738) Bolingbroke observed that a people might be

> united in submission to the prince, and to the establishment, and yet be divided about general principles, or particular measures of both.

But Bolingbroke's ideas, those of an ex-Jacobite Tory, were thought strange. After all, there could be no division about general principles, for what was there to disagree about? As for measures, although the elder Pitt 'the great Commoner' might cry for a policy of 'measures, not men', he was both eccentric and unpredictable, a phenomenon that gave cause for alarm. Indeed his own failure throughout his political career to gather about his measures a body of men or an 'interest' upon which he could rely, only served to prove to politicians more satisfactorily equipped that there was something seriously amiss with his theory in the first place. Kinship counted for a great deal here, for the consanguinity of many a Whig political 'connexion' gave it at once flexibility and force.

Time made few inroads into Whig complacence. In the twi-

light of 'the Grand Whiggery' in 1883, Lord Cowper, confiding
to a magazine his 'Desultory Reflections of a Whig',[1] remarked
that Whig principles, as he understood them, were based upon
a study of the history of England. It was, indeed, 'non-historical'
for a member of the governing class not to be a Whig—or, if he
could not claim Whiggism by right of birth and membership in
'the great-grandmotherhood',[2] not to admit his adherence to
Whig principle. He did not mean to imply (Lord Cowper pursued his theme) that every wise measure in English political
history had been carried through by Whigs. No—but he
thought nevertheless that it might fairly be maintained that
when such measures were carried through by Tory leaders,
those leaders for the moment—and of course for that moment
only—assumed the character of their opponents, 'and found
their own followers more or less reluctant.' Here was a view of
history destined to leave a profound impression on the history-
books. When shortly afterwards (1899) the Whig Sir George
Otto Trevelyan produced his *History of the American Revolution*,
he devised a character-part for King George III so 'true to life',
as Whigs saw life, that it was only by the solid industry of a
later Tory historian who was not English at all that it was
finally discarded. Sir Lewis Namier's reading of the king's role
in politics was not new, for Sir John Seeley[3] had propounded it at
Cambridge in 1886, but Tory interpretations of history have
never enjoyed a providential right to immediate acceptance.

Lord Cowper had in mind both the measures and the men of
his on time. But in the Whig heyday of the previous century
attention to measures was seldom called for, and Tories found
little to compromise their consciences over once they were re-
assured that the Whigs—unlike their own lost leader, James II
—would respect the established Church. Indeed the Whigs retained the established Church, but it could hardly be said that
they respected it; and this was an omission of grace that always
troubled the more thoughtful Tories. It was perhaps not true, as
a Russell of pure Whig pedigree was later to assert, that Whigs

[1] In *The Nineteenth Century*, May 1883, p. 731.
[2] The phrase is G. W. E. Russell's, who adds that it is as difficult to become a
Whig as to become a Jew: 'A Protest against Whiggery', *Nineteenth Century*,
June 1883, p. 923.
[3] See his *Introduction to Political Science*, p. 283.

regarded the Church of England as a subdivision of the Home Department maintained for the promotion of morals, with parliament as her absolute master;[1] but certainly the general laxity of the Whig outlook could never harmonize with the Tory view that the Act of Establishment was merely an act of recognition by the State of the role of the Church in society, in much the same way as a charter of incorporation recognized and respected the existing liberties of an extant township. Pragmatism and practicality, a thoroughly secular view of life, with a suitable appreciation of its good things—these were the marks of the Whig, and whether or not one wished to be of their number depended primarily on individual temperament.

Certainly Whigs were highly professional in their attitude towards 'politics', a sphere of activity they may well be said to have invented. Lord Cowper's own direct ancestor, the Lord Chancellor to King George I, may be included among the inventors, for it was he who handed a paper to that King which stated that, since the House of Hanover derived its title purely from the Revolution, it must rest for support on those who sincerely approved the Revolution. Tories had not approved it, they had merely been caught up in a Whig tide, and many of them still had their ideas totally dishevelled. If, then, one wished to be a professional politician, it was necessary to become a Whig—which meant, for all intents and most purposes, finding a patron among the grandees.

That the country in fact needed the services of any such *genus* as the professional politician the country gentry took leave to doubt. The toryism of this group, since it did not include any political ideas at all, needed no capital letter to grace it. Such men saw the point of having a man like Walpole to preside over a condition of growing economic prosperity; of having a man like the elder Pitt (even if no man, anywhere, was ever quite like the elder Pitt) to guide England to victory in the Seven Years' War (1756–63); of having a man like his son to repair the internal damage wrought by the protracted combination of George III, Lord North, and the rebellion in the American colonies (1770–83); and of having a series of unremarkable men successfully keeping at bay the forces of the

[1] Russell, 'Protest', *ibid.*

French Revolution and its heir, the Emperor Napoleon I. These were all affairs of moment, which required the attention of trustworthy persons. But the backstairs intrigues of Ins and Outs, between one Whig 'gang' and another, at one time upbraiding the King for his choice of vizier, at another time fawning on him for the boon of his vizierdom—these were affairs of no moment at all. The Tory gentry were to like much better the attitude of a latter-day Stanley, strayed into the wrong century; for the fourteenth Earl of Derby, although three times Prime Minister to Queen Victoria, continued to look on political office as an unwelcome interruption of his other careers in Lancashire and on the Turf. The Tory criticism of place-seeking, so rife in Whig administrations, was particularly bitter, although such criticism perhaps came ill from a fraternity in society that had no need to seek a place at all. Whig activities were reckoned to have given England the reputation in Europe, long before Napoleon expressed his view of it, of being a nation of shopkeepers. Both the Bank of England and the new East India Company, created by the Whig administration under William III, were distrusted by the Tory gentry as enclaves of political and financial power—a point of view that the disastrous 'South Sea' speculations of 1720, and the perpetuation of Whig power in Bengal adumbrated in Charles James Fox's India Bill of 1783, served to impress on two different generations of Tories.

During his long tenure of office Walpole had made it one of his chief tasks to try to reconcile these two great 'interests'; and from a natural inclination he leaned more to the side of the squires than to that of the merchants. He was therefore more interested in whittling down that bane of the gentry, the landtax—four shillings in the pound in 1692, but down to one shilling by 1732—than in paying off the interest on the National Debt, which the gentry regarded as yet another Whig job for robbing their own posterity. His successors were less adept at removing this long-standing grievance, or less well placed to do so. The flamboyant presence at Westminster of many a East-India or West-India 'nabob' served to focus the underlying hostility to money as the key to political influence: Burke noted how 'the East Indians almost to a man, who cannot bear to find that their present importance does not bear a proportion to their

THE HABIT OF AUTHORITY

wealth' supported the theories of the French Revolution.[1] Chatham in 1770 suggested that the constitution would enjoy an infusion of health if one member per county were added to the representation, as a balance to the 'mercenary boroughs'. His son William Pitt as Prime Minister created fifty-six peers, but took care that only one of them was a banker; if we can believe Disraeli's *Sybil*, they were all 'second-rate squires and fat graziers.' By the 1780s, almost a quarter of the national revenue was derived from the land-tax—and this although the receipts from the customs and excise were double under North and Pitt what they had been under Walpole. The protests of the gentry concerning this course of events find expression in the polemics of William Cobbett, a paternalist radical who disliked democracy, having seen it working to his own detriment in the United States, and whose radicalism consisted in seeking to restore the good old days when democracy had not been thought of. He fulminated, in 1804, how his own generation had witnessed

> the almost entire extinction of the ancient country gentry, whose estates are swallowed up by loan-jobbers, contractors, and nabobs.[2]

It is always difficult to give any effective political expression to a grievance of such a kind, which is not so much a positive hurt as a nagging sense of discontent. Very often the gentry did not trouble to try, confining their opinions on the world as they found it to the hunting-field, to their diaries, to the club, or to the justices' bench in quarter sessions. Oratory and rhetoric had doubtless their value at Westminster, but even Whig grandees knew better than to make some passionate appeal to the sacred principles of English liberty when they were surrounded by their guests at their own dinner-tables in their own country seats. The most assiduous of Whig borough-mongers was reluctant to do his mongering among merchants, and as a consequence the richer radicals, men who although perforce allied with the Whigs despised them as time-servers, and who were

[1] *Thoughts on French Affairs*, December 1791.
[2] G. D. H. and M. Cole, *The Political Opinions of William Cobbett* (1944), p. 61.

68

determined to construct a parliamentary platform of their own, had first to make use of the system they were determined to abuse: such men as David Ricardo, Joseph Hume, and Samuel Romilly all bought their seats outright. In the same fashion, a Whig lord-lieutenant of a county was just as unlikely as a Tory to appoint a tradesman to the local magistracy.

The passage of time, the multiplication of legislation, the rise of the middle-classes into political ascendancy, and the perfecting of a disciplined party-system in English politics did not alter these attitudes. It was still necessary to follow silken guide-ropes through society. In his *Decline of Aristocracy*, Arthur Ponsonby, a member of the inner circle who had deliberately gone outside it, commented on the degree of social pressure that was invariably put on the Liberal peers of that day (1908):

> If they advocate reductions in the Navy, attack the policy of Imperialism, favour land reform, or support the claims of workers against employers, they simply cannot expect to be called upon in the same friendly way by their neighbours.

And even if a peer was stout-hearted enough to ignore this ostracism, his lady might well not be—for was there not 'something almost pathetic today in the stampede at a Liberal social gathering to catch a glimpse of the diamond tiara of the very rare Liberal countess?' It was indeed not for foolish reasons that the Victorians had decreed that politics—which by definition meant Whig (or Liberal, or Radical) politics, the politics of men who wanted to *do* something—should be debarred, along with religion, women, food, and money, from polite conversation.

Nor had Whig enthusiasm for the cause of political liberty ever inclined them to welcome a political contest for its own sake. Palms were better enjoyed without the dust; and between 1760 and 1800 the rulers had an ample experience of this, as in the seven general elections less than a tenth of the county seats, which returned 122 members to the Commons, were contested at all. The canvassing of votes, where it had to be done, was not particularly arduous in a system wherein, of 513 members for

England and Wales, 254 sat for constituencies that contained only 11,500 votes in all. The boroughs, which returned 432 M.P.'s, were notoriously more likely to produce radical surprises of one kind or another, and the zest with which the borough elections were manipulated bears witness to the confidence of the great men in their own political skills as well as to the importance they set on any extension of their own personal influence. The boroughs had many and various kinds of franchise, but only twenty of them had more than 1,000 voters and all of them were manipulable: even a 'scot-and-lot' borough like the city of Westminster itself, where every one of the 11,000 householders had a vote, could not fail to be blandished by the presence of a Whig duchess on its hustings, and the voters usually had the grace to repay favours granted by returning one Whig and one Tory.

In other types of borough more forthright methods could be used. Borough-mongers would buy up the freeholds and burgage-tenures in a small borough, with a view to reducing the number of electors to a manageable number. The result was the creation of 'nomination boroughs', and a hopeful politician would often pay his patron £1,000 a year for the seat as long as he held it. Lord Lonsdale (the same Sir James Lowther who had patronized Pitt) would send a colony of Cumberland miners to his borough of Haslemere in Surrey, to meet the residential qualification required of voters there: in the House of Commons itself, his nine members for nomination boroughs were known as Lowther's Ninepins. In his old age Lord (John) Russell looked back to the system as he remembered it, and told a story how one noble lord, being asked who should be returned for one of his boroughs, named a waiter at White's club; but as he did not know the man's Christian name, the election was declared void and a fresh election was held, when, the name having been ascertained, the waiter was duly elected.[1] The story may not be true; but it is not impossible that it could be true.

A constituency, after all, was something that came into being only when an artificial boundary had been drawn around a piece of land. The view of property-right that governed the holding of land was logically applied to the disposal of the con-

---

[1] Earl Russell, *Selections from Speeches and Despatches*, I (1870), 24.

stituency accordingly, and of the parliamentary seats attached
to it. The more land held, the greater the owner's influence in
the constituency. The system known as 'fagot holdings' illustrates this. A wealthy landowner would cut his acres into strips
more or less exactly equal in value to the qualifications required
of a voter. He then assigned them out, making their new holders
legal and indubitable freemen for the time of the election. When
the election was over, the land was re-conveyed back to him.
Sometimes, however, he did not insist on re-conveyance. Oldfield's *Representative History* quotes county Down as an example. 'It contains 30,000 freeholders, who elect the friends of
the Marquis of Downshire [Lord Castlereagh's father] without
a contest. To ensure this object, the Marquis's estate has been
divided, subdivided, and again divided, until it has become a
warren of freeholders.' The Reform Act of 1832 did not abolish
this type of byplay, it only required that property cited in
qualification of a franchise should have been held by the voter for
a year. Both Pitt's scheme for a reform of the parliamentary
representation in 1785, and Lord John Russell's of 1823, took
for granted this assessment of the franchise as property, for both
of them proposed to compensate the holders of nomination
boroughs for their loss in any redistribution of seats. The right
of a man to do what he liked with his own was one that had not
caught the attention of Tom Paine, but this was the concept that
both unified the 'unreformed' House of Commons and made its
practices generally acceptable. Seats in parliament were gambled
for, gambled away, advertised for sale in the gazettes, seques-
tered for debt, and bequeathed to the fortunate. Presentation to
a borough, like presentation to a living in the Church, was a
perquisite of landed property, and the 'right type' of character—
a quality hard to define, but instantly perceptible in its absence—
was expected to fill the place in both.

Thus the use of 'influence', in these and other ways, was a
feature of the British Constitution, accepted as such by those
who operated it: Erskine in 1797 spoke amicably of its 'mild and
seducing dominion.'[1] A patron had his duties as well as his
rights, and these were of a kind he cannot greatly have liked—
being overcharged by local tradesmen, over-subscribing to local

[1] *Parliamentary History*, xxxiii, 654.

charities, procuring favours for electors and for the cousinhood
of electors. Anthony Trollope's diligent Whig Duke of
Omnium, a mid-nineteenth century Prime Minister, filling
Gatherum Castle with people whom he would not have cared to
introduce to his friends, underlines this point. Addressing a
county meeting in Wiltshire in 1780, Charles Fox flattered his
audience when he assured them that, accustomed as he was to
the House of Commons, he had never before spoken to an un-
corrupt assembly. In neighbouring Devon a generation later,
Cobbett told the burghers of Honiton how wicked it was to take
bribes, only to have them laugh in his face. His candidacy was
defeated, and he was unconsoled when his opponent (Lord
Cochrane) assured him that his own electoral success had cost
ten guineas per voter. Both before and after the Reform Act, a
contested county election, when it did occur, was cripplingly expensive to the contenders, for the freeholders had all to be
brought to the county town, and there maintained and blandished
for days together. Contesting Northumberland unsuccessfully
in 1826 cost Lord Howick—or, more accurately, his father, Lord
Grey—some £14,000: a marked contrast to the tactics of the
Radical Brougham in Yorkshire in 1830, who made it a condition that his supporters should pay the bill.

There can be no doubt that the buying and selling of votes,
together with the pervasive atmosphere of flunkeyism that surrounded these transactions, sensibly or insensibly implanted a
contempt in the minds of many gentlemen for the very idea of
a free election and for the great principle of representation
itself, preventing them from ever paying respect or even attention to idealistic radicals who were always proclaiming the
natural goodness and incorruptibility of man. De Maistre's
celebrated comment on this never failed to strike an English
chord. In his time, he wrote, he had seen Frenchmen, Italians,
and Russians—he even knew, thanks to a reading of Montesquieu, that one might be a Persian—

> but as for *Man*, I declare I never met him in my life; if he
> exists, it is without my knowledge.

English gentlemen were used to dealing with men; they left it to others who had no stake in the country to conjure up the notion of mankind.

Influence, management, and manipulation were nevertheless three features of the Constitution that escaped any explanatory appraisal from William Blackstone—but then, Blackstone delivered his celebrated *Commentaries on the Laws of England* (1765-9) originally as a series of lectures to the young gentlemen of England, the country's future rulers, at the University of Oxford; had he been addressing the benchers of the Inns of Court he might well have omitted some of his rapter flights and interjected some examples of how things actually worked. The main political purpose of the Whigs after 1760, in so far as they were able to sink their personal rivalries in order to concert it, was to prevent the Crown from exercising its constitutional powers of patronage effectively. Chatham (although not an acceptable Whig) summarized their gloom as he surveyed 'the profligacy of the times, the corruption of the people, and the ambition of the Crown'. Nothing could be done about the times, but corruption and ambition were politically manageable, or at any rate negotiable. The various Whig 'connexions' wished to attack not 'influence' itself, but its use in the wrong hands—in hands, that is to say, other than their own. When North was in power Burke declared himself unable to see many on the side of the ministry save those who were attached to it 'by golden hooks', men who enquired 'nothing more concerning any question, but what are the commands of the day.' He spoke sadly also of the chains of influence, 'that tied us to an unfaithful shore'[1]—a view that goes far to explain the detestation of George III, the commander of the beach referred to, for Whigs of Burke's type. Dunning's motion, that the influence of the Crown had increased, was increasing, and ought to be diminished (April 6, 1780), was carried by eighteen, but the Tories, however much peppered by petitions from the county associations, would not support ambitious plans for a purification of parliament, to be brought about by establishing a better system of representation. If they suspected the Crown, they had an equal suspicion of the people, and an even deeper suspicion of Whigs who, waving their home-made banner of liberty, would

[1] *Parliamentary History*, xxi, 1.

assuredly use popular aspiration for their own ends.

North himself had noted in January 1770, at the time of the popular agitation that Wilkes should be allowed, after he had been expelled three times, to take his seat for Middlesex, how many of these petitioners were 'dupes to the crafty and the factious', who had signed papers that they had never read, and had determined questions that they did not know.[1] Ten years later, following hard upon the success of Dunning's motion, the viciously destructive riots instigated in London by Lord George Gordon underlined the dangers of any kind of extra-parliamentary pressure—petitions, meetings, associations, and the like. Accordingly the general election of the summer strengthened North's ministry, only three counties and fifty-nine boroughs being contested. Horace Walpole commented that now the Court might have what number it chose to buy.

To many Whigs, reform of parliament seemed one way to stop the creeping influence of the Crown, of which they were all so afraid. When they came into power in 1782, under Rockingham and then Shelburne, they debarred contractors from the Commons and revenue officers from the franchise, Pitt declaring that the House constituted both 'the parent and the offspring of corruption.' Pitt's early opinions however were never allowed to govern his later practices. George III, resolved never to undergo again his experiences of 1783, when he was the captive of ministers—Portland, Fox, and North—who would not even let him know whom they were appointing to *his* ministry, turned to Pitt to rebuild a system of influence that would not be contaminated with the record of American disaster. After the Lords at his direct instigation had thrown out Fox's India Bill in December 1783, both the King and Pitt had their chance. Expected by the Tory gentry both to rescue the King from the Whigs and to purify the parliament, Pitt triumphed in the general election of March 1784, so remarkably that no further planning to gain these objectives was necessary.[2] He took over the role that North had deserted, that of the King's principal friend; and, once he had seen his motion for parliamentary re-

---

[1] *Parliamentary History* xvi, 759.

[2] The election produced 174 'new faces' in the House of Commons; Asa Briggs, *The Age of Improvement* (1960), p. 84.

form defeated in 1785 by 248 votes to 174, did nothing more along that line. He was content to marry influence with efficiency in the best early manner of Walpole, and so managed to allay the fears of the previous decade.

Nevertheless, if Blackstone failed to see, or to note, that influence was a self-perpetuating feature of the constitution he so admired, it was not lost sight of by two such differing European observers as Frederick the Great of Prussia and Jean-Jacques Rousseau of Geneva. To Frederick, England was only *une espèce de Pologne*, where the magnates were for ever contending with one another in the manipulation of the elective system, and which was saved from Poland's own sad fate only by an accident of geography. To Rousseau, the vaunted pretensions of the English to political liberty were so much nonsense, as the affairs of the English people were kept firmly in the hands of their nobility, whose embarrassments at the time of a general election were never likely to be considerable. An English voice from an English colony had already dismissed these home-grown English pretensions anyway: for to Benjamin Franklin the so-called mixed monarchy of England, of which his contemporary the French *savant* Montesquieu had taken so rose-coloured a view, was 'nothing but an aristocratic republic',[1] rather poorly disguised.

In his *Thoughts on the Present Discontents* (1770) Burke insisted that the House of Commons had not been instituted to be 'a control *upon* the people . . . it was designed as a control *for* the people', a somewhat fine distinction whose point escaped his audience, both gentle and simple. He was to argue later, in 1784 when measures for parliamentary reform were before the House, that 'you have an equal representation because you have men equally interested in the prosperity of the whole'. Burke's reputation has always varied in direct proportion to the amount of radicalism present in the English polity at any one time, but it seems clear that he lacked commonsense. This explains in turn how it was that Burke's contemporaries in the House, men so much less gifted than he, would not bother to listen to him until, at the time of the French Revolution, he began to reflect and

[1] Quoted in E. Ruggiero, *History of European Liberalism* (Oxford, 1927), p. 12.

ultimately to mould their own fears for the security of their society.

His central attitude was, however, always clear. Men required, for their own sakes and in their own best interests, to be controlled. Here he certainly spoke for his Whig superiors, whose attitude to the purposes of government were consistent throughout. Even the maverick Duke of Richmond, who was the first to incubate aristocratic notions of parliamentary reform (1780), who wanted a broader base, a wider franchise for the constitution to rest upon, never lost sight of the fact that the people were to be *led*. Lord Grey was of the same opinion. His ministry of 1830, which was to carry reform through, had in it thirteen peers or sons of peers, one baronet, and only one untitled commoner. Looking for men of real capacity, Grey naturally looked for them in the only place he thought it possible to find them, among men of his own rank. These were the zealous aristocrats who abolished fifty-six nomination boroughs and took a member apiece from another thirty boroughs, thus leaving themselves 143 seats to redistribute. The shock of these proposals when they first put them forward was the greater in that very few members of this cabinet had previously supported any sweeping measure of parliamentary reform. Yet there was meaning and method in this: for, if a sweeping reform was necessary, it was equally necessary that they should be moderates rather than radicals who used the broom. In such matters reluctance was better than zeal.

It was Lord Grey in old age, not Charles Grey in his youth, who passed the Reform Act. Hopes he had had when young, forty years back, of discovering new horizons for the constitution, of strengthening the bonds of community within the English nation, had been blighted by the outbreak of the French Revolution. When in 1792 he had put forward his motion, it had been opposed by the Prime Minister, Pitt, on the formidable ground that it might prove to be 'the preliminary to the overthrow of the whole system of our present government.' Pitt of course did not suspect Grey or his 'New Whig' friends, Fox, or Sheridan, of being capable of treason. What he was afraid of was the marshalling behind their innocuous façade of the kind of people, the majority of them as yet invisible but no less a menace for that, who were prepared with French revolutionary encouragement to overthrow what Pitt himself described as the best constitution that was ever formed on the habitable globe. With these words Pitt ushered in forty years of a petrified toryism, to the applause of the shires and amid the sounds of splintering in the Whig party itself.

Fox maintained, with much justice, that the greatest innovation that could be introduced into the Constitution of England 'was to come to a vote that there shall be no innovation in it'[1]—for what was the English record, but a story of assertion and claim, above all of movement? But there were very many who held that if change was not necessary, it was necessary not to change. Those whom Burke designated as 'Old Whigs' found out that it had now become necessary to display that innate toryism of outlook they had always known they possessed. Flattered by the mirror Burke held up to them, they saw themselves as an aristocratic party, equally removed from 'servile Court compliances' (an old and officially Tory habit) on the one hand and from 'popular levity, presumption, and precipitation' on the other.[2] The 'New Whigs' were by implication prone to either group of errors. Why, they claimed to believe that some promise for mankind lay behind the doctrines of the Revolution—and what else was involved in these doctrines, but 'an absolute grant of every kingdom to the inferior orders', who were and who ever would be the many? Men holding such views necessarily gave up any hope of getting political power in that generation.

Burke no more than Pitt seriously supposed that Fox wished to overturn society and enthrone the lower orders. Since democracy was à la mode, fashionable gentlemen with a taste for political science would naturally patronize it. Burke however saw politics with an Irish intensity which his contemporaries never understood, and often thought absurd. Before publishing his *Reflections on the French Revolution*, he wrote to Philip Francis that he intended no controversy with the radical idealists—

1 Briggs, *op. cit.*, p. 110.
2 Lecky, *England*, VI, 452.

with Dr Price, or Lord Shelburne, or any other of their set.
I mean to set in full view the danger from their wicked
principles and their black hearts[1]

—a curious method of avoiding controversy. His *Reflections*
were written in 1790, before there had been any degeneration in
the moral fervours of the politicians in Paris, while Louis XVI
still reigned and Robespierre was unheard of; and it was the
arrival of the dooms Burke had prophesied that made him a
major figure of his time. He spent the best part of the decade in
a kind of mental thunderstorm, ending it with the plea that the
place of his burial should be kept secret, lest vindictive democrats dug up his bones for desecration. On the whole, whatever
the merit of these ringing arguments, his influence was bad.
His opinions on the horrors of social revolution, and on the
impropriety of any change at all, became the commonplaces of
dinner-tables, and both the *ethos* and the methods of the landowners of England hardened accordingly.

The commons of England had been unaccustomed to hear
from their overlords such accusations as were now being
brought, that they were a 'swinish multitude', capable of trampling with their hooves all that was fine and fair in the English
heritage. Here was a symbol for the new age that was entering
in.

Yet the malevolence Burke feared, Paine hoped, was in the
hearts of the English people was nowhere widespread. The
hearts of the Birmingham citizens who in July 1791 mobbed a
radical 'Bastille dinner' and looted the property of the advanced
thinker Joseph Priestley, were surely in their rightful place.
Their cry was for 'Church and King', although this hardly
affected the amount of scoundrellism displayed. But it was a
signal that the old symbols still commanded the old loyalties,
that things English had not been displaced by things French.
Throughout the upheavals in France, where warring idealists
set out once again on a search for those fundamentals of government that had eluded Cromwell, the people of England stayed
content to be governed by unpaid local authorities who, for the
reason that they possessed property and rank, were reckoned

[1] *Letters of Edmund Burke*; ed. H. Laski (Oxford, 1922), pp. 283–4.

justly authoritative. Political radicalism and the interplay of novel ideas made as little appeal to the majority as it had ever done or was ever to do. The governors, confusing rowdyism with ambition, would have done better to trust to the common-sense of the governed, and to dispense with the machinery of coercion that they so hastily assembled and so clumsily used. Decisions at quarter sessions continued to mean more to more people than did sessions of the House of Commons. This should have comforted Burke; for if the people were not thinking of 'politics' at all they could hardly be meditating political and social revolution in a French or 'jacobin' style. Indeed he had himself noted as much before, during the time of the rebellion in the American colonies, when he wrote to his chief Rockingham that any remarkable robbery on Hounslow Heath was able to stir up more general conversational excitement than all the disturbances in America.[1] In 1794 the Habeas Corpus Act was suspended and a rigid censorship of both speech and publication imposed, and this could hardly have been done without some great popular outcry had the multitude been so radically mutinous against the established order as its alarmists supposed.

Yet that they were right to be alarmed, if wrong about the dispositions and predilections of their countrymen, is indisputable. It was certainly true that jacobinism *was* subversive of the established order of things, of ideas and institutions alike. Allegedly jacobin principles on the lower decks of the Fleet at the Nore in 1797 provided one dreadful illustration of the pass to which things might come. It was Burke's most penetrating complaint of Fox and his followers, that they hailed the doctrine of the rights of man because of its innate generosity of spirit, but without stopping to consider what calamities the establishment of these self-appointed 'rights' might bring about.[2] The New Whigs asked only 'whether the proposition be true? —Whether it produces good or evil, is no part of their concern.' Yet it was never possible to separate the merits of any political question from the men who were concerned in it. Measures, after all, depended on the characters of the men who put them forward: the

[1] C. S. Emden, *The People and the Constitution* (Oxford, 2nd edn. 1956), p. 183.
[2] And it was Fox's most penetrating comment, that if Burke had taken the popular side he would assuredly have been hanged.

style of one reflected the other. And what kind of men had
taken upon themselves in Paris the right to prescribe for
humanity at large? Men unknown to the English political
world—

> the National Assembly has not 50 men in it (I believe I
> am outside of the number) who are possessed of an hundred
> pounds a year, in any description of property whatever.

It was a theme worth enlarging:

> . . . that the virtue, honour and public spirit of a nation
> should be only found in its attorneys, pettifoggers, stewards
> of manors, discarded officers of police, shopboys, clerks of
> counting-houses, and rustics from the plough, is a paradox,
> not of false ingenuity, but of envy and malignity. It is an
> error, not of the head, but of the heart.[1]

And was such a collection of persons likely to be able to remain
on a plane of high intellectual enquiry?—

> Successful pillage . . . speaks more forcibly to the interests
> and passions of the corrupt and unthinking part of mankind,
> than a thousand theories.[2]

The *cahiers* of grievance sent in from the French peasants to
those who claimed to represent them in the National Assembly
in 1789 had indeed referred in lawyerly preambles to rights of
man and the like, but they dwelt a lot more heavily on the
iniquities of tithe and taxes and game laws. These were all
familiar grievances among the English peasantry too—and
here lay the omen of future troubles. For men will naturally
work from the known to the unknown: what begins as a dispute
about taxation ends in a rebellion against sovereignty itself,
what sets out to constitute a club where like-minded and high-
minded men may meet and discuss reforms may well end as a
revolutionary junto—the very thing that had happened to the

[1] Burke to W. Weddell, January 31, 1792; Laski, *Letters*, pp. 339–40.
[2] *Ibid*. 364.

French jacobins themselves, whose original members had included such diverse characters as the future (1830–48) King Louis Philippe, Count Mirabeau, Lord Edward Fitzgerald, Talma the actor and David the painter.

Whatever else may be said of them, the jacobin chieftains Saint-Just and Robespierre were not lacking in idealism. Saint-Just for example spoke and wrote much on the essential harmony of society, a theme after Burke's own heart: but he argued that the society fashioned under the *ancien régime* had failed to produce this harmony, and that it would be attained only when all the elements of social existence had been put in their proper place. This raised a host of questions. For where was the proper place? Who was to be allocated to it? Who was to make the allocation? Robespierre planned to bring about a state of affairs wherein the government would genuinely be *of* the people, and not just *for* the people. All state and administrative offices should be elective; universal suffrage was a natural right. He agreed with Rousseau, that the representative system in Great Britain was a fraud, a plot perpetrated against the people. There, the alliance between the executive and the legislature was merely a cloak for the exercise of power by the oligarchy which controlled both. (That this was not an example of simple jacobinical wrongheadedness may be shown by reference to the views of contemporary Americans, who in drawing up their Constitution (1787–9) took great pains to separate the two branches of government, for that very reason, that neither would be able directly to influence the other.) Robespierre took it for granted that the English nation, composed chiefly of merchants, must be morally inferior to the agricultural French people—this notion, too, he had derived from Rousseau, and shared with Thomas Jefferson. He considered it an axiom, that the people were bound to be generous, reasonable, magnanimous, and moderate. If certain groups of men appeared who were none of these things, then by definition they were not people at all and deserved no consideration whatever. That general 'will', which Rousseau had diagnosed as the moving force of a political society, might indeed best be expressed through a minority, provided that the minority was composed of people who were indeed people. If even a National Assembly was found to contradict the general will, it must be dispensed with. And if a case arose where the people could not perceive what policies would obtain their own best interests, then those essential policies must be imposed on them by those of a keener insight. To the charge that this was just another kind of tyranny, Robespierre responded with genuine indignation. How was it possible for representatives of the people to tyrannize over the people—that is to say, over themselves? It was an absurdity. Yes, let the people claim its liberty, when it is oppressed—

> but when liberty is triumphant, and when tyranny has expired, that one should forget the general good in order to kill his country by preference of one's personal good, this is mean villainy, punishable hypocrisy![1]

The logic-chopping that must take place before an adequate foundation for totalitarian democracy can be built made as little appeal to English minds then as it has since. A subsequent generation of radicals was to raise a heated debate, whether the government of Great Britain had prosecuted war with France for twenty-two years for the sake of genuine 'British interests', or merely in order to scotch the snake of democracy. It was rather a pointless debate, as the government of the day was unable to regard these two aims as in any way alternative. It was to the interest of the country to fight and to go on fighting the French, for if French democratic principles were allowed the victory, then French tyranny at once arrived in their train and the polity of the English nation would be entirely destroyed. It could hardly be argued that such an outcome would be to the interest of any member whatsoever, however radical, of the English nation. The ruling class of the 1790s assessed 'democracy' in the same scales as the ruling class of the 1920s assessed 'Bolshevism'. The maintenance of the cause of law and order and 'legitimacy' in Europe was bound up with the maintenance of the authority of the English ruling class. King Louis XVI's execution in 1793 was a symbol, for no one could argue either that he was a tyrant or even that he was a political obstacle in the style of King Charles I. 'Not the despotism of a prince', said

[1] J. L. Talmon, *The Origins of Totalitarian Democracy* (1955), p. 113.

Burke, 'but the condition of a gentleman, was the grand object of attack.'[1] The Duke of Brunswick, and the embittered noble émigrés who gathered under his banner in Europe made no very agreeable allies for any kind of English Whig—but there they were, the only available representatives of the European aristocracy. Thereafter their various national armies were kept in coalitions, paid and equipped for the field by a lavish disbursal of 'Pitt's guineas', the mercantile wealth of England, £16 millions of which were thus disposed of between 1791 and 1805—and not to the 'Allied' armies only, as Napoleon's legions frequently marched in Nottingham's boots. The French themselves became aware of paradox here. It seemed odd to them that the same government in England, which supported Brunswick in the name of liberty, should later oppose Napoleon because he was hostile to freedom. Brunswick's original manifesto of July 25, 1792, which threatened the total destruction of Paris and its citizens, and spoke of crimes committed for which there was no remission, was far more bloodthirsty than anything Napoleon ever produced.

Pitt himself set out authoritatively the English point of view in January 1793. He found it impossible to make any distinction between the progress of French opinions and the success of their armies. French armies carried the democratic principle with them as one of their chief weapons. In November 1792 the National Convention had offered its assistance to all people wishing liberty: what was this but an open invitation to a general popular uprising? In explanation of this France's ambassador in London, Chauvelin, had been instructed that what was meant was that France would never demean herself by assisting rioters, but that she would certainly respond to the 'general will' of a people that desired to break its chains. To Pitt this appeared more a distinction than a difference. A subsequent French decree in December, whereby France announced that she would treat as an enemy a people which refused to accept liberté and égalité and continued to give its adherence to its prince and privileged castes, was aimed at the Dutch, whose frontiers were already guaranteed by Great Britain; while a French assertion that one of the rights of man was assuredly to enjoy free navigation on

[1] Laski, Letters, p. 340.

rivers, God's gifts to humanity at large, was aimed at the Scheldt, whose security was also a particular British interest. It was therefore perfectly plain that the Revolution in France was founded upon principles which were, as Pitt expressed it, inconsistent with every regular government, and which were hostile to hereditary monarchy, to nobility, to all the privileged orders, 'and to every sort of popular representation, *short of that which would give to every individual a voice in the election of representatives.*'[1] He agreed with Burke, that as much injustice and tyranny had been practised in a few months by a French democracy as by all the arbitrary monarchs in Europe—and no doubt agreed with him too, although he did not say so, that 'if we continued at peace with France there would not be ten years of stability in the government of this country.'[2]

It is worth a considerable emphasis that democracy, as it first appeared to educated English minds, was just another name for the exercise of ignorance and tyranny, blended together in an unpleasant mould of self-righteous hypocrisy. It was for long to retain its reputation. 'Democracy' was a word that was to conjure up for subsequent generations a jumble of memory and hearsay about Wilkes' squalid campaigns, the American rebellion, the Gordon riots, the 'Terror' in Paris of September 1792, the killing of King Louis XVI in January 1793, the slave rebellions in the English and French West Indies, Irish 'treachery', and naval mutinies at Spithead and the Nore. Of this latter event, Burke in his despair wrote that he would not be surprised to see the French navy convoyed by the British navy to an attack upon Great Britain (something that never crossed the minds of the men between decks). Democracy had set the world awry, and it was a debateable point in English ruling circles whether Napoleon's France was in fact more misguided and malevolent than Jefferson's republic across the Atlantic. In August 1814 a British army burned the public buildings in Washington—a treatment which, as John Quincy Adams indignantly exclaimed, no European nation would have dared mete out (or even have thought of meting out) to any capital in

[1] Writer's italics. January 4, 1793; quoted in *The Political Writings of Richard Cobden*, ed. F. W. Chesson, I (1903), p. 301.
[2] February 18, 1793, *ibid*. 319.

Europe.[1] It was the continuance of this dislike between patrician and plebeian that throughout the nineteenth century was to hamper all the efforts made on both sides to foster a better Anglo-American relationship.

The fallen angels, mused the governor of Nova Scotia in 1799, were originally, according to the poet Milton, happy, prosperous, and well-disposed in heaven. 'Yet Satan introduced corresponding societies, I believe, and dissensions soon followed.'[2] The vindictiveness in the relations between the orders of English society, which Cobbett noted as a new thing, was born of this feeling of fear and contempt. Francis Place thought that the words 'lower classes', as applied to workingmen and tradesmen, had lessened the respect paid to the aristocracy 'more, perhaps, than any other single thing whatever.' And what, after all, Cobbett inquired in 1815, were these 'jacobin principles' so dreaded by the aristocracy? Only 'that governments were made for the people, and not the people for governments.'[3] But none of the governors of England believed this, and they turned all their rancour on Radicals who propagated so carelessly so foolish a notion. 1817 repeated the repressive legislation of 1795, while William Lamb [the future Lord Melbourne, Prime Minister 1835–41] complained that all the petitions that were being showered down on the House of Commons were not in fact, as they professed, asking for reform —'but for revolution, since they prayed for annual parliaments and universal suffrage.'[4] A remark of that kind, better described as Bourbonism than as anti-jacobinism, was what brought the mild-mannered Jeremy Bentham to describe the House of Lords of the 1820s as more dangerous than a pack of wolves. It was a period when ranks were closed and the sense of community lost: the period of 'Peterloo' and the Six Acts, of Luddite machine-breakers and rick-burners under command of a non-existent Captain Swing. George Canning, whose historical reputation is that of a liberal Tory, was careful how far he took his liberalism, and opposed Russell on parliamentary reform. The flame of

[1] J. Q. Adams, *Writings*, ed. W. C. Ford, V (New York, 1917), 320.
[2] H. T. Manning, *British Colonial Government after the American Revolution* (New Haven, 1933), p. 191.
[3] Cole, *Cobbett*, p. 115.
[4] *Parliamentary Debates*, xxxv, 790.

liberty, he observed, must not have its purity impaired or its extinction hazarded out of a desire to render it more intense and radiant.[1]

Flames of liberty matched in radiance those from the hayricks of England, and could not therefore be expected to command the approval of the squirearchy. Grey himself declared in 1827 that, in any struggle between democracy and aristocracy, his part was taken, 'and with that order to which I belong I will stand or fall.'[2] Among his order were many who had patronized French democracy but could find no place for its fellow at home. Lord Lauderdale, who in his hot youth had been observed by Professor Dugald Stewart of Edinburgh University, calling himself 'Citizen Maitland' and standing on Paris street corners shouting for liberty,[3] became a hardened Tory, leading his Scottish brother peers in formed phalanx against the Reform Bills of 1831 and 1832. The Chartists' programme for constitutional reforms in the 1830s and '40s was based on the Duke of Richmond's programme of 1780, but they had to fight their battle unpatronized by any 'respectable' leadership from grandee, squire, or merchant. Democracy was not something that could be trafficked with without loss of reputation: Burke's *Reflections* had ensured this as the continuing majority view.

Thus, Richard Cobden's charge, made in 1853, that the aristocrats of England had deliberately gone to war in 1793 for for their own self-preservation was not one that would have seriously incommoded the aristocrats themselves. The thing was plain on the face of it. The Tory historian Archibald Alison remarks, without seeing a need for extenuation, that Pitt's government used the occasion of war with France to 'draw off the ardent spirits', to put obstacles in the path of 'democratic ambition' and 'the desire of power under the name of reform' which was growing 'among the middle ranks.'[4] A prominent member of Pitt's Cabinet, Earl Fitzwilliam, had asserted robustly and without contradiction from his colleagues that the

[1] Russell, *Speeches and Despatches*, I, 34.
[2] 2 H[ansard] 17, 1261.
[3] H. W. Meikle, *Scotland and the French Revolution* (Edinburgh, 1912), p. 49.
[4] Quoted in Cobden's pamphlet, *England in 1793 and 1853; Writings*, ed. Chesson, I, 273. Lecky, *History of England* VII, accuses this pamphlet of gross misrepresentation.

war was expressly undertaken to restore order in France and to effect the destruction of the abominable system that prevailed in that country. Events proved him right, and proved also that public opinion was with him. Those who stood out against it had short shrift. The Duke of Norfolk—a Howard who was also a Protestant was perhaps inevitably a New Whig—was dismissed from his lord-lieutenancy of the West Riding of Yorkshire for raising his glass in 1798 to toast 'Our Sovereign, the people'. A flash of post-prandial enthusiasm might however be permitted a nobleman who was a notorious eccentric; it could not be allowed to those whose enthusiasms were of another kind, and who came from a sphere of life where eccentricity could neither be afforded nor accepted.

The English reform societies were earnest and improving bodies, and perhaps because of these qualities their influence was never extensive. The Constitutional Information Society, founded in 1780 in the train of Richmond's efforts, and led by Major Cartwright and John Horne Tooke (of Eton and Cambridge) was the best-known. The London Corresponding Society, founded in 1792 by a master-shoemaker from Falkirk, Thomas Hardy, was more honest in its opinions than was permissible, and its addiction to the works of Tom Paine, already proscribed, was to prove its downfall. The 'corresponding' of its title was conducted with the National Convention in Paris and with kindred enthusiasts throughout the county; but the members were so far from conspiracy and guile that they published their views on all possible occasions, usually in language which could be construed by the authorities to mean anything they pleased. In November 1792, for example, after Dumouriez' victory at Jemappes, the society presented an address to the French Convention which declared a hope that in no long time the French might have an opportunity of sending a similar congratulatory address to a National Convention in England. Many members were dissenters; and it was always Pitt's opinion that if dissenters were admitted to civic rights they might use their power to overthrow the establishment of the Church of England. They might be expected, therefore, to conjoin with the parliamentary reformers, and to form 'clubs' after the French model—for what, if one referred to Burke once more, were enthusiasts for parliamentary reform but 'amateurs of the French Revolution'? Moreover, with a subscription that stood at a penny a week, their influence was expected to be widespread. Francis Place described its members as being 'of the lower and middling class of society *called the people.*' It was therefore not surprising, he added, that some of those gentlemen who had been so strenuous for reform in 1782 scarcely knew, or wanted to know, those who were associated for a reform in 1791.[1]

Certainly such a society could expect to have a greater influence at large than that of the aristocratic 'Friends of the People', composed of New Whigs who could afford a two-and-a-half guinea annual subscription. Dangerous radicalism was unlikely to be bought at such a price, as William Godwin himself ruefully remarked of the first edition of his extremely radical *Political Justice* (1793), which was published in a large quarto priced at four guineas. Thus the Corresponding Society, and Hardy himself, was the first target of the government. Pitt's attorney-General, Sir John Scott [the future Tory monolith, Lord Chancellor Eldon], made it a direct charge that Hardy had advocated representative government—

representative government, the direct contrary of the government which is established here![2]

Hardy had, moreover, worked upon the passions of men whom Providence had placed in the lower but useful and highly respectable situations in life, in order to irritate them against all whom its bounty had blessed by assigning to them situations of rank and property.[3] Hardy escaped the just wrath of his betters because the indictment was wrongly drawn; for Sir William Holdsworth has given his opinion that if Hardy had been tried for a seditious, and not a treasonable, conspiracy, it is unlikely that even all Erskine's forensic skill could have got him an acquittal.[4] But if Hardy escaped, the Society itself was not to be

[1] British Museum, Place MSS., 27814, 400.
[2] G. M. Trevelyan, *Lord Grey of the Reform Bill* (1920), pp. 39–40.
[3] State Trials, xxiv, 272.
[4] In his *History of English Law*, XIII (1952), 163.

allowed to do so—Place himself admits that its final disappearance in 1799 was popular among the shopkeepers and artisans.

The Friends of the People, whose very title illustrated the paternalist attitude, and which included among them Charles Grey, Sheridan, and other New Whig members of parliament, were looked on by the government less as seditious than as a bad influence on the people at large. Had Hardy been convicted, Pitt might well have moved against his ex-colleagues: Grey at least was convinced of this. But these Friends of the People did not ask, like the Corresponding Society, for universal suffrage and annual parliaments. Their approach was at once less intellectual and less radical. They asked only for freedom of elections—which ought to be held more often—and for 'a more equal representation.' They declared, in the language of every other English reformer that has ever been heard of (including Thomas Jefferson in colonial America, who owned to an admiration for the liberty-loving polity of the original Anglo-Saxons), that they wanted

not to change, but to restore: not to displace, but to reinstate the Constitution upon its true principles and original ground.

Whatever that original ground had been composed of, the Friends denied that they were appealing to 'the Rights of the People in their full extent', for this was the indefinite language of delusion, 'opening unbounded prospects of political adventure', the last thing any Whig, New or Old, would want. Yet there was some semantic inconsistency here, for while Grey insisted that his friendship for the people did not imply that he was also a friend to the doctrines of Tom Paine, he added that he was not to be deterred 'by a name' from acknowledging that the rights of man was the foundation of every government. This was to wander a little too far both from John Locke and Whig history, and in rebuttal of the vagary came a stout Tory answer from Charles Jenkinson. We ought not to begin first, he pointed out,

by considering who ought to be electors, and then who ought to be elected; but we ought to begin by considering who ought to be elected, and then constitute such persons electors as would be likely to produce the best elected.[1]

It was therefore ridiculous for the Friends of the People to put forward, as they did in their reform motion of 1797, the doctrine of household suffrage—with who knew what inflammatory consequences in the minds of householders?

The Friends of the People remained an aristocratic, London-club movement, with Brooks's as its principal headquarters. There were in England no local branches. But in Scotland there were many groups that borrowed the attractive name. In these however there was no touch of aristocracy. The Glasgow branch charged its members threepence a quarter, and had a membership to match. Glasgow and Paisley weavers (who had already staged an effective strike in 1787, before any French example had been put before them), briefless Edinburgh advocates such as Thomas Muir (an assiduous circulator of Tom Paine's proscribed works), were men who might very well mean what they said, and the fact that they were in Scotland put an edge on the government's determination to discipline them so severely that in future, whatever they continued to mean, at least they would not venture to say it. A British Convention on the Paris model was actually assembled at Edinburgh in the autumn of 1793: its full title was, 'the British Convention of the Delegates of the Friends of the People associated to obtain Universal Suffrage and Annual Parliaments.' The 'delegates' called themselves 'citizens', and it would be hard to say which of these new-fangled terms, the one democratic and the other republican, sounded the most menacing overtones. When its leaders were arrested, the Lord Advocate advised the jury that the whole object of the Convention was not, as was said, a reform, but a subversion of parliament:

a determined and systematic plan and resolution to subvert the limited monarchy and free constitution of Britain, and substitute in its place, by intimidation, force, and violence, a republic or democracy.

Its leaders were thereupon transported to New South Wales,

[1] May 1793; Briggs, *Age of Improvement*, p. 60.

despite orders sent from the Paris Convention to the French Admiralty to intercept the ship taking them there.

Universal suffrage was looked on as a genuinely revolutionary and therefore shocking ideal. At the trial of Thomas Palmer, another Scottish 'martyr', the jury were instructed that the subjects of Great Britain had never enjoyed universal suffrage, and were warned that, if ever they were to enjoy it, they would not long enjoy either liberty or a free constitution. It was a heartfelt view. At Thomas Muir's trial in August–September 1793, it was stated again, the more vehemently as the arch-Tory Lord Braxfield was on the bench. The jurymen at Muir's trial were all members of the Goldsmiths' Hall Association, which had not only struck Muir's name off its roll, but had even offered a reward for the discovery of any person circulating Paine's works—the very offence of which the prisoner was accused. Muir's impassioned address to this body, which lasted for three hours, was to become a favourite piece for declamation in New England school-houses, a result which would have pleased him mightily. At the time it pleased neither the jury nor Braxfield, who took the opportunity to state a view of governance that embarrassed even Cabinet members in London: 'A government in every country', he decreed:

> should be just like a corporation; and, in this country, it is made up of the landed interest, which alone has a right to be represented. As for the rabble, who have nothing but personal property, what hold has the nation on them? What security for the payment of their taxes? They may pack up all their property on their backs, and leave the country in the twinkling of an eye. But landed property cannot be removed,[1]

and thus the constitution founded upon it could not be improved upon. Muir was sentenced to fourteen years' transportation;. but he was more fortunate than the British Convention leaders. He escaped from Botany Bay in February 1796 on an American ship specially despatched there for the purpose, and went to France where he advised the Directory that the Scottish people were much readier for, and had more capacity to accomplish, a revolution than ever the English would be.

[1] Meikle, *Scotland and the Revolution*, p. 134; State Trials, xxiii, 545.

THE HABIT OF AUTHORITY

Although this was an opinion that singularly irritated the Irish dissident Wolfe Tone, who described Muir as a vain and obstinate blockhead, it was one that seemed to the English Cabinet to describe well enough the actual state of affairs. In Scotland, which had a population of a million at the turn of the century, there were under 4,000 voters, and 'less than 400 inhabitants who had any real influence on election returns'. With the exception of Edinburgh, all the towns were grouped into districts, and each district was allowed one member. The corporations of each of the towns in the district elected a single delegate; and the four or five delegates, thus elected, met together, and elected the member. For example, Glasgow, with a population of 80,000, elected one delegate, chosen by the self-elected corporation of thirty-two. In no county in Scotland did the number of voters exceed 240, and in one it was as low as nine; indeed, in Bute at the general election of July 1830, only one voter—the Sheriff—could be discovered, who elected himself. Thus the farmer, the manufacturer, and the artisan—all of whom were better educated than their English counterparts—had no voice in the election of representatives at all, and none of them could believe that the sixteen peers and forty-five members of the Commons at Westminster represented anything but the obligation made at the Treaty of Union in 1707. If indeed they represented something beyond this, it could only be the views of Henry Dundas.

Dundas, Pitt's trusted lieutenant, a product of Edinburgh High School and University, and known familiarly and not without affection in that city as King Harry the Ninth, was the real ruler of Scotland. Originally he had been given the keepership of the Scottish Signet by Lord Shelburne's administration in 1783, and to this office was explicitly attached 'the recommendation to all offices which should fall vacant in Scotland'.[1] The auditorship of the Scottish exchequer, which Dundas also held, was supplemented with a right of appointment to certain offices in the West Indian colonies. When his presidency of the Board of Control of the East India Company is also borne in mind, it is not surprising that he was looked on by the aspiring Scottish gentry as a man whose ear it was absolutely essential to

[1] H. Furber, *Henry Dundas* (Oxford, 1931), p. 193.

stand close to: the Indian Board of Control was still regarded by Sir Walter Scott in 1821 as 'the corn chest for Scotland, where we poor gentry must send our youngest sons, as we send our black cattle to the South.'[1] Moreover, after 1791 Dundas' own nephew and son-in-law Robert was the Lord Advocate, the head of the Scottish bar.

This, then, is the genial manipulator whose imposing monument in Edinburgh's George Street is fittingly set off by another (erected in 1844 by Chartists)[2] to the Scottish martyrs, even more imposing, on Calton Hill. Dundas knew all the '400 inhabitants' whom it was necessary to know, and did all his electoral work and a great deal of his political patronage through them. In September 1781 he had sent his instructions north that Edinburgh, even at that time showing signs of restiveness, must not be left in the political charge of some 'knot of themselves', but must be put under some respectable patron on whom the government could rely. In 1796 the mere sending of instructions was not enough—at a time when not Edinburgh only, but a large tract of the Scottish Lowlands, was less restive than actively seditious. (Lord Adam Gordon, the military commander-in-chief in Scotland, had already very sensibly assured him that the troubles in the highlands had a lot more to do with sheep than with politics.) Dundas complained to his friend Lord Hobart, the Governor of Madras, that he had actually been obliged to go up in person to Edinburgh, to prevent the return of any one member for Scotland hostile to government: 'the thing has never happened since the Union, and the temptation was strong to make the experiment.'[3] But the experiment was not made, even although it brought forth Scotland's liveliest election for a century; in Dunfermline, for example, one candidate kidnapped the provost and councillors and got his colliers to intimidate the townsmen with bludgeons. This resolute person was not, however, elected. Dundas' political machinery took this strain, and others, in its stride.

[1] *ibid.*, p. 33.
[2] T. B. Macaulay, then Edinburgh's M.P., carefully absented himself from the foundation-stone ceremony in August 1844; G. S. Veitch, *The Genesis of Parliamentary Reform* (1913), p. 298.
[3] Furber, *op. cit.*, p. 264.

To the London viewpoint that Dundas brought north with him, Scottish political consciousness must have appeared far more alert and awake than it actually was. Muir, Palmer and the others were given a far rougher passage from the law than Hardy and Horne Tooke experienced in England, simply because no one in England, or in alliance with the English government, had any means of judging whether the upsurge of democratic principle in Scotland was the first signs of some great explosion from the depths of society, or merely the scum on the surface of an otherwise stagnant pool. Certainly nobody in London could expect to turn to one of Scotland's representatives at Westminster, and get from him an informed and accurate estimate.[1] In English eyes Scotland was anyway something of a political risk: men still remembered 1745, and they did not doubt that there were other men in Scotland who remembered it even more vividly. This particular picture was exaggerated on both sides of the Border, and has continued to be so, until Charles Edward's band of some 11,000 has suffered the same inflation as 'the Companions of the Conqueror'. If all the Scottish families who, even by the time Walter Scott was in his middle age, were claiming to have had a representative 'out in the Forty-Five' had been telling the truth, the Prince must have had untold legions at his back.

But since this last Jacobite rising the English had been unwilling to allow to Scotland a militia after the English style, and only the French emergency brought them to reconsider this. Dundas wrote in 1792 that he had become convinced that it would very soon be necessary to aid the military forces in Scotland 'by arming, under proper authority, bodies of men of respect, and who can be trusted.'[2] His reluctance to do this was underlined by the Lord Provost of Glasgow, who was equally averse to giving arms to the lower classes. (A very similar problem was shortly to agitate the minds of the West Indian planters, who had to decide whether or not it was politic to arm their Negro slaves.) In the meantime Dundas revived the office

[1] This was to prove a continuing lack. Of the sixteen representative peers of Scotland in 1962, eleven had been educated at Eton, the other five at other English public-schools.

[2] Meikle, *op. cit.*, p. 95.

of Lord-Lieutenant (an official who had been imposed on Scotland just after the Jacobite rising) and gave him authority to raise volunteers to ensure internal tranquillity. But the continuation of French invasion-scares forced him to put through a Militia Act for Scotland in 1797, and he was grimly prepared to dub as 'jacobinism' the uproar in the Lothians and elsewhere that accompanied this measure. It was indeed a fortunate circumstance for Scotland that Dundas was not a nervous or particularly imaginative man, else she would have fared far worse.

Perhaps it might also be assumed that the Edinburgh Whigs who valued Dundas' friendship and had frequently put it to use were men of a somewhat similar stamp, easy-going and disinclined to panic because some idealistic young men got carried away with their up-to-date notions. To such men Burke's *Reflections* had seemed overwrought, and the book never had the impact in Scottish intellectual circles that it had among its English readers. The best retort to it came from the Scottish historian, James Mackintosh, whose *Vindiciae Gallicae* patiently dissected some of Burke's wilder accusations against the French, yet expressed a hope that the Revolution would invigorate the spirit of freedom in Scotland. If this spirit failed to find expression, it was not because of a lack of parliamentary representation, or because it fell a victim to the coercive Acts. It was due to the fact that the leaders of Scottish society disliked its enthusiasm. Scottish society, with centuries of strife and unrest for its history, had only recently become comparatively comfortable: democrats bid fair to make it thoroughly uncomfortable once more. Respectable members of the branches of the Friends of the People tended to dissociate themselves from some at least of the people—those who began to burn Dundas in effigy, to instigate disorders, and to flaunt red caps and trees of liberty in the more extreme French style. The odd poet, the occasional professor, might be allowed some licence: some of Robert Burns' 'Tree of Liberty' poems have not survived, 'for obvious reasons', as Dr Meikle doucely comments.[1] At the University, Professor Dugald Stewart, at whose philosophical feet both Lord Palmerston and Lord John Russell were soon to sit, was considered to

[1] Meikle, *op. cit.*, p. 121.

be what would nowadays in identical circumstances be called left-wing. This was not unjust. Stewart had been an early enthusiast for the Revolution, and had been in Paris in 1789. (On one occasion he gave a Scottish friend a snuffbox, as a birthday present for the friend's newborn son, inscribed 'Rights of Man' on the lid. The son, unable to refuse the gift at the time, took his revenge on Stewart later by growing up to become Archibald Alison, the Tory historian of the French Revolution.) Stewart remained a marked man, and Francis Jeffrey's father would not allow him to attend Stewart's lectures on philosophy as a result. In case of further harm, the Historiographer Royal for Scotland published at Dundas' request an edition of Aristotle's *Politics*, 'as peculiarly calculated to counteract the wild and dangerous principles afloat'. But it is one of the hazards of life, that one's offspring will when young be exposed to radical poets and professors, and it was not one that comfortable Edinburgh magnates considered worth paying too much attention to. For the atmosphere of the time there is no better barometer than the *Memorials* of the Whig judge, Henry Cockburn, an ironically tolerant book that looks back on this troubled time not with anger, but with a sympathetic and unsentimental understanding.

Such an outlook was justified by events: 'United Scotsmen' were always counted in a few hundreds where United Irishmen teemed in their thousands. But Scottish opinion, although it proved no exception to the anti-jacobin rule, was to swing with the radical tide towards a demand for parliamentary reform. The electoral alliances made by Dundas were too solid easily to give way, and they survived him. The solid conservatism of elders and presbyters, their continuing disapproval of such elements as Glasgow weavers and Sunday schools—which were reckoned at the outset as providing some kind of democratic 'fifth column', and abominated by such Tory grandees as the Duke of Atholl—continued indeed to reflect the even eighteenth-century temper. But change was due, and felt to be due, by thoughtful men who were catholic enough in their tastes to take the argumentation of the *Edinburgh Review* as a matter of course, and to enjoy the *Quarterly Review* for the commonsense of its opinions. After all, if Irish Catholics, a potentially

dangerous squadron if ever there was one, could be granted the
right to vote in large numbers in 1829—even although the
forty-shilling freehold had been scrapped in Ireland in favour of
a £10 county franchise—who had the right to deny it to loyal
and Protestant Scots? If Scotland's middle-classes did not produce a Daniel O'Connell it was because they did not want to,
and because they had confidence that the English Whigs would
play O'Connell's part for them. Edinburgh celebrated the 'July
Days' of Paris in 1830 with a large and ultra-respectable ban-
quet, and the city's petition for parliamentary reform that year
had 21,000 signatures, refreshingly authentic, upon it. Grey's
Reform Bill, presented March 1, 1831, envisaged granting to
Scotland another 80,000 voters; thereafter, even if all the Scottish peers voted against it in a body (as they did, in the predictable company of the English bishops), and the posterity of
Dundas's 'electors' were dubious at the way things were going,
the popular enthusiasm was too strong to withstand. Before
the Reform Act passed Scotland was represented by 40 Tories
and 5 Whigs, after it passed by 44 Whigs and 9 Tories. The
country was happy to remain loyal to their Whig benefactors
and to their Liberal successors, until 1885.

It was no paradox that it was through this medium that Scottish conservatism could most readily express itself. The Scots,
composing a mobile society that attached importance to 'respectability', certainly, but did not consider either birth or
landed property as necessary elements of it, were never able to
become Tory in the English sense, or to ally themselves without social discomfort to an officially Tory, or aristocratic Conservative, party. Yet Dundas had gauged the situation correctly: Scotsmen were of all men the least likely to revolt, so
long as there were opportunities in the wider world open to
their talents.

In England the estates of the realm in these adversities had
stood firm. Scotland, an estate of its own realm, did the same.
Thus in both countries self-styled Friends of the People were
relieved to find that the people were, after all, their friends.
Although Canning was to hail Pitt as the pilot that weathered
the storm, while the people continued to think him treacherous
as well as vindictive (so that Ireland celebrated his death in

THE HABIT OF AUTHORITY

1806 with a general gaol-delivery),[1] the main point was that the ship the pilot headed into the weather was itself a stout ship, with a disciplined crew. The lowland Scots, although they did not marshal themselves in ranks and degrees, believed as firmly as their English neighbours in the merits of law and order; and, even if more inclined to 'democracy', an argumentative race bred to the intellectually aristocratic concepts of Calvinism was unlikely to promote that kind of democracy which made a virtue of counting heads, many of which were empty. What was Rousseau's 'general will', after all, but one of those French fancies? If, moreover, the Scots since the Union of 1707 had made a poor showing in the English representative system, that may well have been for the self-satisfied reason the historian Alison suggested in 1834: that Scotsmen even before the Union had already

> effected a settlement, on the most secure and equitable basis, of all the great questions which it is the professed object of the Liberal Party to resolve.

Certainly since the Union, Scotland had been content to assimilate what she thought useful from the southern kingdom. This was a great deal: it included England's overseas empire, although it excluded her religious, legal, and educational systems. In consequence, in the French National Convention of 1793 the jacobin Count Kersaint had called Scotland a dependent colony of England. Moreover, in the industrial age that was arriving, both Scotland and Ireland, juridically non-existent, were to become more than ever economically dependent on England and on the mercantile commerce of the British Empire. Yet Kersaint was wrong. Scotland was not a colony of England, because the Scots—unlike the Irish—did not think of themselves as in any way subordinate. This lack of 'nationalist' resentment, the feeling indeed that it was they who had a position to exploit, they owed to their history.

These were attitudes which in the nature of things could neither be taught to nor caught by others. Because this was so, Scotsmen were very often regarded, then and later, with marked exasperation—as men with a fifth ace. For the other dependen-

[1] G. D. H. Cole and R. Postgate, *The Common People, 1746–1946* (1961), p. 180.

cies of England, the genuine colonies whose earliest history was the history of a handful of Englishmen, were able to fashion a 'nationalist' outlook only by piecing together a mosaic of attitudes derived from their English masters and managers. Having done this, they had then to try to find some kind of 'national' activity to fit their aspirations. Whatever the upshot in a particular case, this was always a formidable task. It was also exhausting, since it was continuous: no one generation could be absolutely sure that in its own day, at least and at last, the work had been finished. To find a particular and durable 'way of life', to establish an identity, is harder for nations than ever it is for men themselves.

Accordingly, on what grounds and with what assumptions colonies were founded, how colonists came to resent their dependence on a distant authority, and how they perpetuated the habits they had learned beneath it, are matters of importance.

It was in an American accent that the voice of democracy first arrested the attention of the ruling classes of England: it was the success of American rebellion that gave them their first defeat. How they reacted to the shock of this event, how long a shadow it threw, is part of this story as a whole.

CHAPTER III

ENGLISH AUTHORITY OVERSEAS

I

Men need justification for what they do. Where none is ready to hand, they go out and find some.

This is what was done by English colonists in America, whose leaders by the mid-eighteenth century were ready to claim a status in the world other than that which their history had so far allotted them. It was Adam Smith's diagnosis that the principal men in America 'had chosen to draw the sword in defence of their own importance'—and this is, surely, the real cause of the American Revolution.

In America Englishmen had conserved, and extended, the radical ideas of the previous century, venerating the puritan temper and the libertarian aims of such men as Pym and Hampden long after these had been discredited among the land-owning oligarchy at home. They believed that the puritan society in America had been founded on revelation and reason, and that nothing had since happened to depreciate the value and utility of both in coming to a proper judgment on men and affairs. In 1765 the opinion of John Adams of Massachusetts was that 'government was a plain, simple, intelligible thing'. An educated society could take commonsense for its guide and see a plain thing plainly, the more so since it was not hampered by an unquestioning adherence to those 'two systems of tyranny' which the Normans had brought with them into England and confederated together there the better to support their own supremacy. The systems Adams referred to were those of the feudal and the canon law—systems which, in contemporary

England, 'though greatly mutilated', were not yet destroyed, since much of their domineering spirit still remained.[1] Colonial leaders thus laid claim to independence of mind and outlook long before they were able to produce convincing arguments—which indeed were never easy to come by—that they had a 'right' to political and constitutional independence. They wanted to make the world they lived in match their criteria of commonsense, and they believed that they had a right to do this for the simple reason that they were in the right. They had their own grain, which the enforcement of English habits of authority would score and wound. (It was an accusation that was one day to be levelled in India against the British *Raj*.)

This claim to intellectual superiority shocked English opinion. Colonies were, by definition, dependencies. It followed that colonists were dependents. Dependents had no right to self-assertion. Nothing could be clearer. Colonies were anyway desirable at all only in so far as they contributed to the prosperity of their parent state. From this standpoint, the economic uselessness of the New England colonies in the imperial system of reciprocal trade gave England more right to quarrel with the colonists than *vice versa*: the New Englanders had always been notoriously 'stiff-necked', even although they had been granted more mercantile and military aid than they would ever give or think of giving in return. A colonist in America had the same status and duty as a parishioner in Sussex. He was a subject of the Crown, who could be allowed no greater pretensions than his homekeeping kin. Indeed he might fairly be allowed less, as he enjoyed more privileges than these kin, who had for over a century paid the bill for the defence of the American settler's home against both the French and the Indians. Moreover, every colony had some form of written constitution, which made it clear to the colonist where, in law, he stood. No such safeguard protected the Englishman at home, as John Wilkes' long and noisy campaign against the governmental abuse of general warrants had abundantly shown. A cry for 'the liberties of Englishmen' was unlikely to awaken the sympathies of those Englishmen who could hear in it only a cry for licence and the

[1] John Adams, 'Dissertation on the Feudal and Canon Law', April 1765, in *Life and Writings* (ed. C. F. Adams), III (New York, 1851), 447–64.

reduction of their own sphere of authority.

English Whigs who did publicly sympathize with these American fervours were careful not to carry their sympathies too far. Their Tory critics could however point out that they carried them farther than consistency allowed. Edmund Burke, who as agent in London for the colony of New York spent much of his time in the 1760s advising the Assembly there how best to obstruct the legislation of the English parliament, was never able to explain to anyone's satisfaction his very different reaction to the constitutional experiments instituted by Frenchmen in 1789 and 1790: Harold Laski once acutely commented how good a case might be made out for the thesis that what there is of liberalism in Burke derives rather from the impulse of compassion than from any typical sense of right.[1] Chatham might rhapsodize about the wonder of three million Americans animated by the glorious spirit of Whiggism, but another of his rhetorical flourishes announced his determination sooner to subscribe to the Catholic doctrine of transsubstantiation than to any doctrine of sovereignty by right for the colonies. His later declaration that, if colonists attempted to manufacture goods for themselves in defiance of the will of parliament, he would be the first to demand that the British army and navy should blast them out of their workshops, does not indicate any very profound revolutionary spirit, Whig, glorious, or other. It was thus left to the Society for the Bill of Rights to send a subscription to rebellious Boston, and to the Constitutional Society to raise subscriptions in 1775 for the victims of Lexington and Concord.[2]

But it was in part as a defence against the wounding reproach that by approving American restiveness they were fostering the dread 'democracy', that the Whigs were so studiedly moderate in their proposals for reform in England itself. They would not allow any innovations that promised seriously to interfere with the votes of the boroughs they controlled, and the majority of them eased their conscience by going not a step beyond their support for Burke's plan of 'economical reform' (1782), which although it cut down the distributable sinecures and pensions to £90,000 a year, left the genuine abuses untouched.

[1] In his introduction to Burke's *Letters* (Oxford 1932), p. xv.
[2] John Horne Tooke was given a year's sentence for raising such a subscription.

One Whig argument on America became a myth, mainly because of its ready acceptance by the Americans themselves—whose historians were naturally in the field with their justifications of the American Revolution long before any British historian was able to bring himself to recount, and at the same time to try to account for, the unpleasantness he knew as the American Rebellion. (Whig historians sidestepped the awkward implications of both 'Revolution' and 'Rebellion': to them, it was a 'War of Independence'.) This myth was that George III, having subjugated America, intended to extract a permanent revenue from the colonists (in the fashion of Barbados, which had since 1664 paid a fixed duty on the value of its exports), and to use the money to subvert the liberties of England. It was a charge Whigs might well have levelled against James II ninety years back, for of him it was true; but, since at that time they were too busy keeping their footing at home to care what was going on out of sight, they omitted to do so. Had George III devised such a plan, he would have conciliated the Americans, not coerced them. But he wished only to uphold the British Constitution, which as he saw it included the right of the king to choose men who would carry out faithfully the measures he approved of. That this was not at all a silly idea is illustrated by American rebels' own attitude to it: for, when they drew up a Constitution for the United States, they gave to their own President precisely those powers. Among English Whigs, however, the King was unable to find many such men.

For this, the majority of them did not forgive him—or his appointed agents either, for Whigs successfully attached the name of Tory, with the capital letter, both to Lord North and to his ultimate successor, the younger Pitt, two 'King's Friends' who went to their graves believing themselves as orthodox in their own kind of Whiggism as Walpole had been in his. Whigs who leagued in opposition never developed to any extent the idea of loyalty, making what capital they could out of the war, and out of the mistakes made by the 'little minds' directing it. Indeed they evinced the same kind of intellectual superiority to which they took such exception when they met with it in the attitudes of the American colonists. In doing so, they got out of touch with popular sentiment. The Tory gentry in parliament thought themselves better informed, and naturally disliked both the rebels in America and those in England who, by encouraging rebels, perpetuated rebellion. Tories were either amused or scandalized by Whig claims to altruism in the conduct of public affairs, domestic or imperial, and many felt that General Howe, the idle Whig commander of the English forces in America, was a better candidate for the title of Father of the regrettable American republic than his opponent General Washington. But in 1783, after they had combined to oppose Fox's attempt to put through an India Bill that would have served to make the revenues of Bengal a perpetual Whig perquisite, they voted with Shelburne's Whig ministry to bring the American war to an end. They did this because it had clearly become necessary, in the national interest, to do so. Thereafter, Tories adhered to their natural leader, the King. With him, they turned their backs on the cynical coalition of Fox with North, and in broad phalanx supported the younger Pitt, the King's own choice as his rescuer. George III himself never saw any reason to change his stoutly conservative views. He told Pitt in 1788, and Pitt agreed, that the American war had been the most justifiable any country had ever waged.[1]

The Whigs had used the fact of American Rebellion to exploit the domestic political situation to their own advantage. They never developed insight, however, into the factors that underlay the American Revolution (and even a century later the Whig historian Sir G. O. Trevelyan could not be got to see that there was any distinction between these two titles for what was, after all, an identical series of events). Insight could not be expected where interest and knowledge were lacking. Burke and Adam Smith both complained that 'underling tradesmen' had had too much say in the organization of England's imperial business, and they were right: but it was a say they had got by default. English merchants were better informed about American conditions than were the gentry and the grandees at Westminster and Whitehall. From the outset, therefore, the merchants opposed any parliamentary taxation of the colonies. Every colonial customer was a debtor: the planters of Virginia, for example, had always lived on credit, borrowing on the future

[1] E. A. Robson, *The American Revolution 1763–83* (1955), p. 29.

sales of tobacco crops still to be planted, and investing the money in lands as yet unproductive across the Alleghenies and in the Ohio Valley. It was therefore not only the present value of the colonial trade, but even more the assessment of the indebtedness involved, that brought English and Scottish merchants to concert together in 1766, 1768 and 1775 in order to obtain the repeal of Grenville's Stamp Act, of Townshend's Act and of North's Prohibitory Act. Yet merchants knew well enough that, although a show of solidarity might prevent the politicians from plunging too far into unrealism, they were still unlikely to be consulted when the ministry was resolved to take an initiative. They could only hope to mitigate the consequences.

It was for this reason that they deplored the intransigent and intemperate language with which the irritated American colonists reacted to the politicians' activities. In 1769 merchants in London pointed out to merchants in Philadelphia, that had a petition been presented from *them* on the principle of the inexpediency of the taxation measures, instead of from the Assembly of Pennsylvania denying the right of the British parliament to institute any such measures at all, the laws complained of 'would ere now have been repealed'. As late as 1774 the mercantile class was still urging for a peaceful settlement; the Lord Mayor of London offered hopefully to put up the sum of £20,000 as security for the £8,000 worth of the East India Company's tea which now lay at the bottom of Boston harbour— a sum he was sure, he said, the Bostonians would repay.[1] But the country gentry saw no reason to believe this, or to see anything amid the diversity of legal points the colonists were now making other than an intent on their part to live scot-free at others' expense. Since the peace of 1763 the landed classes of England had lived at a considerable financial disadvantage in comparison with the mercantile interest, which did not pay much in landtaxes and had reaped an agreeable commercial harvest amid the rampant profiteering of the Seven Years' War. If colonial contribution, on what was after all a very minor scale, could ease the burden of the land-tax, then the colonists—who were not, whatever bombast they went in for, a particular *genus* of man-

[1] D. M. Clark, *British Opinion and the American Revolution* (New Haven, 1930), p. 81.

kind—should make such a contribution. Certainly they had no excuse for not doing so in an era when the general commerce and prosperity of the American colonies was booming. The imposition of the Stamp Act would have cost the colonists a shilling per head per year: people who considered this an intolerable and unjust burden were plainly people whose other views deserved very little consideration indeed.

Colonial uproar was thought the more irritating in that, apart from its being based on inadequate ground, it deflected the attention of the politicians from matters far more significant. The imperialism invoked during the war by the elder Pitt had faded as Chatham faded to unimportance in the House of Lords. Britain after 1763 was a sated empire. Her European rivals indeed considered her both swollen and decadent, an unlovely pair of qualities. Some of the more reflective English statesmen saw the dangers inherent in this European assessment, and thought it highly likely that the French, so badly humiliated at the Peace of Paris, would take the first opportunity to seek their revenge. It was better, accordingly, for England to live remotely, and if possible obscurely, out of the international limelight. Thus the importance of the American rebellion (1776–83) lay less in vociferous argument about constitutional right than in the fact that both France and Spain, still in Bourbon 'Family Compact', exploited the British involvement with it as their great oppor- tunity to reverse the European balance of power in their own favour, an opportunity of a kind that was unlikely to recur. It was their intervention that saved George Washington and his accomplices from ending their careers ingloriously on an English scaffold, as traitors to their country. It made the entire quarrel a matter of international significance, and one of first-class importance to educated opinion in England itself. How to extricate the country from the hornets' nest into which a series of well-intentioned statesmen, considering only the state of the domestic economy, had plunged their hand, became the main objective of the gentry in the House of Commons.

These were men who had long distrusted active policies on principle. It was they who had opposed the expulsion of John Wilkes from the Commons—rightly, as Wilkes in parliament proved much less effective as a popular agitator than he had been outside its walls. It was they who since 1770 had rallied to the King and to his managerial Prime Minister Lord North—and who had yet supported Dunning's motion in 1780 that the influence of the Crown in parliament had become too powerful, and ought to be curbed. It was they, as already noted, who ultimately allowed the Whigs to carry the motion that the war should cease. They did all these things because they were constantly looking for a secure middle way. If they finally deserted their own Lord North because his policy of coercing the Americans had proved ineffective, that assuredly did not attest to any sympathy on their part for American Whiggism and its pretensions to nationalism and democracy.

By 1783 peace with France and Spain—and in consequence with the American rebels, satellites to these Powers—had become an essential 'British interest'. Thus the Americans' claim to independence received the stamp of recognition, if never the seal of approval, of the European powers at Versailles. It was a momentous step, recognized as such. From it this generation in England learned a lesson which it was to entail on its successors, so impressively that the effects of it took close on a century to wear off: that the greater the extent of territory possessed overseas, the greater the vulnerability of Great Britain in Europe. Britain's insular position allowed her to dispense with a standing army, while the strength of her navy made it easy for her to influence in her own favour the policy of any country that had a coastline. But, if Britain obtained a series of land frontiers here and there throughout the world, she at once discarded these natural advantages, and became a far easier prey to other imperial nations which did possess standing armies. The embarrassment of just this state of affairs in India vis-à-vis Russia, and in Canada vis-à-vis the United States, was to hamper the freedom of British foreign policy throughout the nineteenth century. If bargaining was to be done, British statesmen wanted to do it in negotiable currency. While the world's centre of gravity remained in Europe, as it did until 1917, British flags flying briefly over far places—war-time trophies such as Havana and Manila (1762), Buenos Aires (1808) and Java (1811)—could not affect this fundamental point. Castlereagh at Vienna in 1815, like Harley at Utrecht in 1713, was content to barter colonial possessions as counters, the better to play the diplomatic game in Europe.

This self-centred concentration on the European aspects of Empire explains how there arose the general opinion that, to quote once again Sir John Seeley's aphorism of 1881, Great Britain had got control of half the world in a fit of absence of mind. The century Seeley was looking back on as he spoke gave him some grounds for saying so—although the remark was always, and was always intended as, an exaggeration. Certainly after 1783 British statesmen were most reluctant, even while circumstances forced their hand (as they did, for example, in Southern Africa), to extend the area of their responsibilities. But if a corporate absence of mind may be claimed—yet, does such a thing exist as a corporate presence of mind?—individual inattention is hard to prove.

The individuals who since the days of the Normans in Ireland had extended the enterprises of England overseas had never suffered from a lack of concentration on their particular task. They knew very well what they were about, and why they were about it. The ultimate failure of the medieval English monarchy to control and colonize large areas of France convinced both the nation and its monarchs that a state-enterprise on so great a scale had laid too heavy a burden on a small country: Mary Tudor's grief at the final disappearance of her French patrimony, the loss of Calais in 1558, is symbolic less of what might-have-been than of what never should have been attempted. But over-seas activity had appealed to Englishmen long before the English state could afford to lay claim to a 'colonial policy' at all. This was not, as romantics have claimed, because Englishmen were naturally adventurous by birthright and had salt-water in their veins—surely a charge hard to bring home to the average Shropshire lad at any time—but because beyond the horizon lay greater opportunities, social and economic, than could ever be got in the narrow, closely-graded world at home. Many of the merchant-venturers of the sixteenth century were 'unlanded gentry', younger sons and youngest sons of younger brothers, and it was from them that emerged the kind of man who was content to spend a gainful life in Havana or Cadiz in the free days of the Emperor Charles V before the Reformation divided

ENGLISH AUTHORITY OVERSEAS

the world into hostile ideological camps, or who would travel to
the Levant or to the Azores or to Surat without taking, wanting
to take, or thinking of taking his national flag in his baggage.
Long, however was the imperial future that lay before all
such.

The unlanded gentry were, and are, a migratory race by com-
pulsion—men ready to get themselves careers in commerce, in
the Church, in the law, in foreign armies, or in 'the Newfoundlands'—wherever they had a chance to improve their patrimony.
As Tom Paine was morosely to observe, your aristocrat begins
his career of dominion in the nursery, by trampling on his younger brothers and sisters. It was a training that bred in these dis-
possessed a remarkable degree of initiative, and the best of
them learned how best to live by their wits. Their creation and
manipulation of joint-stock companies was one means by which
they progressed towards a new place in the world, so that they
might transmit an easier heritage to their sons. They appealed
for aid where they could get it. The Tudor monarchs, like other
grandees, invested in a likely venture and were accordingly
gratified by success, as Francis Drake's knighthood attests. The
Stuarts continued this tradition: both Charles II and James II
were prominent stockholders of the two African Companies
(1663, 1672), whose main business was transporting African
slaves to the American plantations.

But for a state-enterprise as such, Ireland, always half a
colonial and half a domestic problem, supplies the best of these
early examples. Henry VIII, trying to impose some kind of
'indirect rule' on the Irish, had much ill-fortune, mainly because
his principal agent in the matter was the unprincipled Earl of
Kildare. It was therefore in the reign of his daughter Mary
(1553–8) that the first English colony proper was established in
Leix and Offaly—where until 1921 the names of King's and
Queen's Counties (a reference to Philip II of Spain and Mary
herself) commemorated the deed. This settlement was made for
strategic reasons: to extend the zone of security of the old
Anglo-Norman pale. It was a strategy whose commonsense
continued to impress Mary's successors. In July 1587 her sister
Elizabeth I wrote to Sir Henry Sidney in Leinster, approving a
suggestion he had made

that some gentlemen of good houses within our realm here may be induced to come over [to Ireland] with their own tenants and friends . . . and so by continuance of time to establish those countries with English birth and government.[1]

Objections by the native Irish to this policy were expected, and discarded.

The policy hardened after an Irish rebellion in the south of the island. After 1583 the districts of Cork, Kerry and Limerick lay at the disposal of the English, and the Crown Title Act of 1585 cleared the way for an English colonization. Here we find the first appearance on the stage of Irish history of a fraternity well known, if never loved. These were 'the Undertakers', land-agents whose task it was to arrange the importation from England of gentlemen landlords, farmer-tenants, and labourers, all of whom were attracted by terms such as these: twopence per acre for land in Munster, no rent to be paid for the first five years of settlement, and only a half-rent payable for the subsequent three years. Circulars and prospectuses abounded. In the pro-vince of Munster Sir Walter Ralegh and Sir Richard Grenville disposed of 42,000 acres to 320 families from the English west country. Ventures of this kind were expensive; but even the hazards of Irish landlordism provided valuable experience, which helped turn the minds of enterprising promoters and undertakers towards schemes for further expansion, farther afield. Ralegh and his cousin Sir Humphrey Gilbert went on to issue very similar prospectuses to attract magnates, merchants and misfits to 'the Newfoundlands' of North America. Between 1582 and 1584 Gilbert disposed, on paper, of nearly nine million acres—none of which had ever been surveyed—of what even at that time he had the imagination to call 'New England'. In this case, it would have been a patient stockholder indeed who sat still and awaited his dividend. Twenty years later, Ulster was filled by another set of undertakers with needy Scotsmen, noted by Lecky as a class very little fitted to raise the low moral level of that province. Still, the Ulster 'plantation' raised the social level of the many Englishmen who, for £1,080 apiece, bought their

[1] D. B. Quinn, *Voyages of Sir Humphrey Gilbert* (Hakluyt Society, 1940), I, 119–20.

baronetcies—a rank created by James I in 1611, whose proceeds were supposed to pay for the work of colonization in Ulster.

Whoever promoted it, colonization was a gamble. Yet even in the short run, the lure of freehold tenure was to prove stronger than less tangible magnets like 'El Dorado' in Guiana or a north-west passage to the Pacific. Colonies of settlement were founded, fitted out, and maintained by young men who were determined to make their fortune out of them. It was hard work that made them hard men, and they systematized forced labour for white men and black men wherever it was possible to do so: genuine intractables, like the Caribs of the West Indies, were exterminated. There was never any question who was master.

As a microcosm of the process, the settlement of the Somers Islands [Bermuda] may stand: between 1609 and 1612, this tiny territory was partitioned as the property of eight 'tribes' of landowners. This pattern was copied on an ever-extending scale. Barbados, the Carolinas, Maryland and Pennsylvania all began life as 'proprietary' settlements, paternally governed by a magnate or by a group of wealthy associates. It was thought that men with so personal a stake in their own piece of country would spare no efforts to make their settlements a success. This belief fortune did not always favour: and colonial proprietors battered by economic misfortune were often glad enough to return their charter and their rights under it to the Crown. Even so, hopes of profit and prestige to be got from some colonial satrapy continued to attract. As late as 1763 the Earl of Egmont was petitioning the Crown for the proprietary of Prince Edward Island, together with the backlands of the Ohio valley which had just been relieved of their French sovereignty. In this second bid Egmont was not successful; but his disappointment was probably less than that of the landowning gentry of Virginia, who, having already granted out two million acres in the Ohio country, were speculating to the same tune in the Mississippi valley. Hemmed in by the establishment of two new British 'pales' in North America—for the Proclamation of 1763 debarred further territorial expansion to the west, and the Quebec Act of 1774 from the north-west and north—Virginian planters saw themselves faced with the virtual bankruptcy of their economic and social system, and were thus the readier to ally themselves, many of

111

them doubtless with set lips, with the wilder political radicals in their own midst.

Colonists who claimed the rights of freeborn Englishmen usually forgot that Englishmen were in fact born subjects of the Crown, and, if they were of the post-1689 generation and after, were also subject to the authority of the Crown as expressed through the English parliament. Since the English parliament had, between 1689 and 1763, seldom interested itself in the internal affairs of the colonies, their inhabitants had some excuse for their bad memories. The Crown itself was indeed known and respected. It was preferred as a landlord to any magnate, perhaps because, as Sir Lewis Namier has described it, it was distant, sublimated, and symbolically paternal. In the seventeenth century the Crown itself took a distinctively personal view of this relationship. Charles I gave Quebec back to France in 1632 to encourage them to pay his French wife's dowry; Charles II's wife brought Portugal's property of Bombay with her in 1662 as part of her dowry; Charles II sold Dunkirk to the French, to whom it had never belonged, and retained the Cromwellian conquest of Jamaica from the Spaniards, to whom it had always belonged; his brother James when Duke of York disposed of the lands of the Dutch province of New Amsterdam in America [New York, 1664] before the Dutch were even aware that the English intended to make war on them at all.

But those colonists whose dwelling-place, together with the status they had allocated to themselves within it, was not thus passed from hand to hand as diplomatic counters, had had time to develop settled opinions as to their own destiny. These opinions, independently arrived at during a period when their state of dependency was not underlined, held political and legal implications that were never fully understood even by those who held them: so that, in the long run, the founding of the United States of America was to come as a surprise to the majority of 'Americans' themselves. In the seventeenth century the in-grained radicalism of New England had more a religious than a political bent; but, as Cromwell had found out, the one attitude easily influenced the other. Indeed, that one form of protestant-ism was a stepping-stone to another was always clearer to the colonists' English overlords than to themselves; on this point, the younger Pitt in the 1790s held the same view as Charles I in the 1630s. To both, the political menace inherent in 'Dissent' was obvious. The Massachusetts Bay Company, because it was regarded by the government of Charles I as a useful safety-valve for dissent, was granted a very liberal charter accordingly (1629): it was better that wrangling puritans should pollute the air of New rather than that of Old England with their various and irreconcilable dogmas. Massachusetts naturally took advantage of the breakdown in English authority in the mid-century to carry dissent as far as it could well go. It elected its own governor, carried on its domestic business without reference to England, and once indeed (1654) went to war with French colonists in America without consulting the government at home. On its own authority, it shed the province of Connecticut and assimilated the provinces of New Hampshire and Maine, and in 1652 set up its own mint.

This frontier intransigence was at once widespread, contagious, and heritable: Boston and Salem were always sallyports for attitudes and ideas as well as for ships and cargoes. Royalist planters in Barbados were the first Englishmen overseas who took public exception to the legislation of the English parliament, on the ground that the Navigation Act of 1650, which curtailed the free trade on which the colony had thrived during the twenty-five years since its foundation, amounted to taxation without representation. It was a cry remembered and repeated by the planters of Jamaica—many of them 'Old Standers' of Cromwell's expeditionary army—when in 1678 they refused to vote a perpetual revenue to the Crown. But, from the time of the restoration of the monarchy in 1660, this colonial assertiveness was matched with the resolution of the Crown to set its American estates in order. Charles II was in particular personally determined to put an end to the state of affairs wherein his American possessions were governed, as he complained, by persons he did not know in a manner they would not confess to. Thus, freebooting and corrupt governance in the West-India plantations was curbed; New York was fashioned into a trim patrimony for the Duke of York and his friends; Virginia's tidewater gentry, encouraged to copy English Cavalier habits, put down a radical revolt with more than Cavalier severity;

magnates interested themselves in the settlement of Carolina; and, after some false starts, the manners and customs of the New England politicians and merchants were thoroughly investigated by the Crown, their 'independency' arraigned, and the over-liberal charter of Massachusetts recalled (1684).

The process of establishing the royal authority in the colonies, and the necessary respect for it in the colonists, was one that could never be finally accomplished, as England did not have the means of effectively policing and patrolling so vast an area; even in the nineteenth century, the idea of *pax Britannica* was to depend as much on the tacit consent of Europe as on British naval power. Yet, by the time James II fled his country, the twelve colonies in America were recognized as royal properties, and their inhabitants had acquiesced in their status as subjects of the Crown. The underlying assumptions were these: that only the authority of the Crown could ensure the good governance, and with it the essential military protection of His Majesty's subjects wherever under the sun they might live; and that only Crown-appointed officials could be relied upon to enforce the series of Navigation Acts whose purpose was to bind together, to their mutual benefit, the properties of England in one self-sufficing commercial emporium. These ideas were not reckoned on either side of the Atlantic as something far-fetched, or impossible to accept.

But the initiative of the Stuarts was not followed up. The opportunity of habituating colonists to the presence of an active imperial authority was lost. The accession of William III in 1689 ushered in a generation of European wars. These, although they indeed had their extra-European repercussions, necessarily withdrew the attention both of Westminster and Whitehall from the internal affairs of the English colonies. As it was, while the habit of authority was exercised by the various English politicians to whose notice came what problems of colonial administration there were, they did not realize (and so were taken aback when consequences arose from) the fact that a different climate of opinion was emerging in the colonies—one that was bound to lead the colonists to put their own self-interest before anything else. If there was no overt clash before 1763 between the one set of opinions and the other, that was because no occasion was given. Moreover, the colonists, physically dependent on British armed forces for their protection against the French, had no wish to raise nice constitutional objections to the exercise of British power in their midst. The presence of the French in Canada was, as Lecky noted, an essential condition of the British imperial power in America. The conquest of New France by the British removed the element of self-interest that had kept the colonists loyal to British codes of regulation for their conduct.

Members of the English parliament, although always vigilant against any unwarranted exercise of the royal prerogative, did not foresee an attack on their own prerogatives from such a quarter. They knew that colonies existed, mainly because of the ostentatious presence in their own lobbies of both an East-India and a West-India 'interest'. Some members had served in colonies, but always as part of the authoritative hierarchy, observers of but not participators in the local scene. It was this parliamentary disinterest that gave the Crown and its agents their chance to administer the colonies, uninspected. Colonial patronage provided a means whereby George III and his ministers were able to reward their faithful without running a gauntlet of criticism at Westminster. The Quebec Act of 1774, following hard upon North's Regulating Act for the East India Company's governance of Bengal, was the first parliamentary statute directly to constitute a colony and to organize its institutions; but even then, it more accurately summarized the opinions of the soldier-governor of the province, Sir Guy Carleton, than any informed view from front or back benches in the House of Commons.

Acts that 'regulated' provinces varied in severity in ratio to their distance from the seat of government. Distance bred lenience; for Quebec, conquered in 1763, was granted a benevolence of treatment that Scotland, conquered in 1746, had not enjoyed. The 'Heads of Regulations in Scotland' included the garrisoning of rebellious districts, the substitution of private jurisdictions by the establishment of a circuit of justices-in-eyre (this being contrary to the terms of the Treaty of Union of 1707), the transportation of common rebels, the regranting of 'Jacobite' lands, and the permission to tenants holding property to a value of £40 to purchase their lands from their landlords, 'so as to hold directly from the crown'.[1] *Habitants* in Quebec had no such 'new order' forcibly imposed upon them; and their Catholicism did not debar them, as it did their contemporaries in Ireland, from the exercise of civil rights.

Thus it was under the Crown's 'distant and sublimated paternalism', and not under any watchful eye of parliament, that the 'old representative system' in England's American colonies developed. By 1750 twenty-one out of thirty-one overseas possessions had representative Assemblies. Three colonies—Connecticut, Rhode Island and Maryland—did not have to submit to the Crown the Acts of their Assemblies for acceptance or rejection. In three corporate colonies, Massachusetts, Rhode Island, and Connecticut, the Governor's Council was selected without reference to Great Britain: in Massachusetts indeed the Council was elected by the Assembly, an assertion of the doctrine of 'responsible government' which continued to be rejected by British governments for the next century. Thomas Pownall, who had been Governor of Massachusetts, noted in his book *The Administration of the Colonies* (1765) *that*

> the people of the colonies say, that the inhabitants of the colonies are entitled to all the privileges of Englishmen; that they have a right to participate in the legislative power

—but, as the majority of Englishmen in England did not have that right nor were in possession of many privileges, this was not a statement that could count on approval from those who considered that obedience to the laws of the land was a man's first duty. On this point men so automatically at odds with each other's opinions as Chatham and the two judges Camden and Mansfield cordially agreed. The executive and legal authorities in England looked on the colonial Assemblies as ancillary to the colonial governor's executive council, and their approval of the principle of representation illustrated in them did not incline them also to favour the notion that these Assemblies had any 'right', got from some 'law of nature' which no English jurist

[1] L. H. Gipson, *The British Empire before the American Revolution*, I (New York, 1936), 185.

could find in the law-books, to invade the province of the executive.

It is worth emphasis that colonists themselves were never prepared to admit a right of representation too far. The attitudes of propertied Englishmen overseas reflected those of their own kind at home.

The eighty-four members of colonial Virginia's House of Burgesses were elected by men who owned 100 acres of uncultivated land, or 25 acres of cultivated land with a house upon it. Virginia, with its counties and parishes and tithes, its laws of primogeniture and entail, its Anglican clergy and its Scotch-Irish [Ulster] dissenters, provided a better model of Old England than ever the colonies of New England had done—even although the closeness of the resemblance was often over-emphasized by many of the colony's 'old families', whose pedigrees in fact could not have borne any very rigorous inspection. The social distinctions between tidewater and piedmont [foothill] country were firmly maintained, and indeed to this day the atmosphere and condition of the State of West Virginia markedly contrast with those of the State of Virginia itself. In the colony of South Carolina, the forty-five members of whose House of Assembly were elected by those freeholders fortunate enough to enjoy possession of 500 acres and twenty Negro slaves. In Massachusetts, the vote was not granted, as in England, to the 40s freeholder: the qualifying value was £3. As late as 1790 only one in ten of the male residents of the city of New York owned sufficient property to be qualified to vote for the Governor of their state. Maryland, which had been established in 1632 as a refuge for oppressed Catholics, had by the mid-eighteenth century instituted the severest anti-Catholic laws in North America, and contained the best Anglican livings. Between 1763 and 1783 over 20,000 convicts transported from British gaols entered the colony, where their masters often treated them more severely than they did their Negro slaves, since Negroes cost them money and convicts did not. This operation was, however, attended with far less of the humanitarian outcry in England than greeted the establishment of Botany Bay in New South Wales (1787) as a penal settlement. Colonies in America had long been looked on as receptacles for

English undesirables: it was the novelty in the idea of treating a new and perhaps immensely valuable continent in the same way that roused these generous emotions.

Georgia had been founded in 1732–3 along different lines. It was an early example of 'systematic colonization': a philanthropic venture for the rehabilitation of the poor and distressed. But men once rehabilitated became determined to enjoy the right of a colonist to have both rum and Negro labour, and by 1750 had both. In Jamaica, all freeholders (including Jews, a unique privilege) had the vote: enfranchised planters were required to maintain on their estates one white man or woman for every thirty Negro slaves, and one for every 150 head of livestock. This attempt to keep the white population of the island to a certain level was, however, doomed to failure. It was not likely that the offspring of these maintained whites remained 'white' for long; to this day pride is taken in the West Indies in the proveable existence of a Scottish grandmother, a *rara avis* as a Scottish grandfather is not.

Colonial leaders thus instinctively, without concerting together on the matter, thought it best to confine participation in the affairs of government to those who had some stake in the country. This habit of authority at least had survived Englishmen's Atlantic crossing. Assemblymen were supposed to be, and generally were, genuinely representative of the 'respectable' element of the community: it was this indeed that made them a force to be reckoned with. The members of the governor's executive council were men of the same stamp. In a governor's private instructions, issued by the Secretary of State on the King's behalf, would appear variants of this formula: the councillors he chose to advise him had to be

> men of good life, well-affected to our government, of good estates and abilities, and not necessitous people or much in debt.[1]

There was no insistence that such a man, once appointed, had to *be* there to give his valuable counsel: one councillor of New York was absent from his home for thirty years. This was only

[1] L. W. Labaree, *Royal Government in America* (New Haven, 1930), p. 136.

an extreme example of the accepted British practice which, for example, allowed Wellington while commanding on the field of Vimiero (1808) also to hold the post of Chief Secretary for Ireland.

Moreover, it seems to have been a theory that well-affected men of this kind would be liable to propagate more of the same. In Virginia, of ninety-one councillors appointed throughout the colonial period, nine surnames account for one-third of them. In 1766 John Wentworth, Governor of the colony of New Hampshire, had eight relatives on his council of twelve members. Even Connecticut, with popular election to the council, went on electing the same people and their kin. These were people who, since it was their task to accompany the governor through his daily agenda of public business, were of all colonists the closest to the administrative principles of British governance. As a consequence, they became identified with it and identified themselves with it: it has been estimated that between a half and two-thirds of those who had at one time or another sat on a governor's council became Loyalists to the Crown during the American Revolution. For this habit of mind, these and other Loyalists were to be meted out a spectacular vilification by those who, their social inferiors in status, quite correctly accused them of not being in love with the principles of democracy. They were, and who could doubt it?, 'inveterate enemies to their country, to reason, to justice and the common rights of mankind'. They were, as one broadsheet called them, 'infamous parricides', who were and would always remain irrevocably hostile

to virtue, America and the human race.

(These last three were long to be regarded as an interchangeable emotional currency—a valuation that was to arouse a corresponding distaste in those who, for the life of them, could never see any point in the equation.)

In contrast to his council, the colonial governor, although his life was a hard one, did not have it made the harder by having to strike ambivalent attitudes. He was there to rule the colony, as the king's representative; and if he could do that the better by making use of the people's representatives he would certainly do so. In fact, every governor discovered that he had to do so, since the burgesses in Assembly were the sole source of a money-supply by which the administration of the colonial government could be financed, for no landowner in England, forever complaining about the land-tax, would have given his support to a ministry that asked him to vote money for the costs of maintaining an independent colonial executive in every one of England's colonies of settlement. The cost of the general colonial administration, including the upkeep of the regiments overseas, was already formidably high. By mid-century American quit-rents were producing a sum of some £16,000 a year, as against a total colonial expenditure of some £420,000; it was, indeed, the vastness of this sum that brought George Grenville to try and allay the unease of the English gentry, by making colonists themselves foot a small portion of this bill. The problem that faced Grenville and others was greater in scale but the same in essence as that which faced every colonial governor: what ends to establish, and how to make them meet.

The governor's main task was to collect a sufficient number of influential people in the colony around him to help him carry through both the things he wanted to do, and the things he had been told to do in his instructions, always a lesser number. He had accordingly to blandish the Assembly to his way of proceeding without having any financial wherewithal to help him do it—a job that would have baffled both the Whigs' Duke of Newcastle and the Tories' Lord North. A governor who had hoped to find a rest-cure in a colony, or at least a refuge from further personal indebtedness, was likely to be a disappointed man. Professor Labaree has calculated that, of the 300-odd governors of colonies who ruled in America between 1624 and 1785, one in four either had a title or was due to inherit one; forty-five had been members of parliament and another nine were going to be; forty-eight were graduates from either Oxford or Cambridge (a surprisingly small number, and an interesting point in itself); over twenty were benchers of one of the Inns of Court; and fifteen were Fellows of the Royal Society. This group has very often been accused by American historians as possessing only second-rate abilities. The statement echoes the long-standing colonial resentment: that English statesmen thought that any party hack, half-pay unemployable, or impoverished nephew would be adequate in a colonial post, which, being a second-rate sort of place anyway, did not warrant the services of anyone better. This opinion contains something of the truth, but not all of it.

The views of such a group of men were certainly predictable. Radicalism of any kind would have no part in them; and the experience of ill-requited military service which large numbers of them had in their past may perhaps have atrophied both their wits and their consciences. But this is a charge easier to make than to prove.

For it would have been difficult, as already suggested, for Solon himself to have built up an effective paternalist system in colonies where the governor had no power of the purse—as was the case in every one save Virginia—and where officials holding important administrative posts were appointed not by him but by a royal patent, issued to some court favourite or to some client of some creditor, over his head. In the eyes of the colonists, naturally enough, a good governor was one whose financial embarrassment guaranteed his amenability to their wishes. These wishes were usually negative. They wanted him not to take some particular action, but to take none—to look the other way while something went on that he would, had he been able, have put a stop to. An irascible despatch from Lord Balcarres in Jamaica in 1799, after the issues of American rebellion had been solved and settled, illustrates the dilemma of the colonial executive in both the century that was ending and the one that was about to begin. How far, he demanded of the Duke of Portland, could a governor expect local support without control of 'the loaves and fishes'? After all,

> no person ever supposed that a vice-Royalty could be maintained without the patronage.[1]

Portland, then Home Secretary, was not the man to disagree, having never supposed so himself. The loss of the thirteen American colonies had caused a great rent to appear in the fine

[1] Manning, *British Colonial Government*, p. 111.

meshes of the system of colonial patronage, but fortunately something remained. Before Portland left office in 1801, he was able to provide for many of his nephews and grandsons by granting to them the reversions to some of the most valuable offices in the old West-India colonies, and to some of the same in the newly-conquered colonies as well. Office was a property; and, as Balcarres plainly believed, the greatest officer should be endowed with the largest amount of property. The self-evident good sense in this could not, to an eighteenth-century mind, be called in question. Nor was it a concept that was due to disappear with the eighteenth century. Lord Acton once commented how the 'spoils system' of the American republic, much traduced in British governing circles in his own day, was merely something the democrats had adapted from the oligarchs of George III.[1]

The predicament of colonial governors, however, remained unnoticed by English statesmen at large until after 1763. By then it was too late to rectify the situation. The Seven Years' War, called in America the French and Indian War, had greatly strengthened the pretensions of the colonial Assemblies to behave, and become, like so many miniature Houses of Commons. Their control of the purse-strings, and their interference with military operations, greatly hampered the imperial direction of the war throughout the entire American theatre for the first two years of its course. But when in 1758 the elder Pitt's ministry promised reimbursement of their expenditure, they rallied with a will to the common cause, granting lavish bounties to assist enlistment, and rejecting any temptations to parsimony since it was not their debt but Great Britain's that would bear the burden. Victory over the French, and success on the floors of their debating-chambers, inflated both the confidence and the oratory of the colonial politicians. Remembering their ebullient war-time generosities, they could not but think the subsequent efforts of the Grenville and Townshend ministries to use some colonial revenue to pay for a colonial establishment of 10,000 British troops as a disastrous break from that immediate precedent.

George III's ministers, with his cordial approval, had in fact

[1] In his review of Bryce's *American Commonwealth*; *English Historical Review*, iv, April 1889, p. 390.

returned to the task that the Stuarts had been compelled to lay aside. The American estate was indeed now to be controlled, and by a far better administrative equipment for doing so than any that the Stuarts had had at their disposal. The laws of trade and navigation, designed to regulate not only colonial but imperial commerce as a whole, were now to be extended. They were also to be enforced, since it was reckoned that, at a conservative estimate, some £700,000 worth of goods were smuggled into American ports in any one year. Regulations that had lapsed and were suddenly resuscitated caused more resentment than the issue of any new edicts would have done. The memory of close on three generations of evasion of the Commercial Acts helped to arouse an immediate indignation in the colonists, when it became clear to them that the British Government was in earnest about bringing this evasion to an end. In New England, whose history of illicit trading was nearly as hallowed as that of the provinces themselves, the indignation was naturally the keener. Townshend's imposition of further duties on colonial imports, following the repeal of Grenville's Stamp Act, further convinced the colonists that Britain was determined to cramp their rightful commercial prosperity and growth. His establishment of an American Board of Customs Commissioners caused Boston to lose to the city of New York the honour of being the chief port of illegal entry. British commissioners, customshouse officers and judges of the court of admiralty were now active in all the Atlantic towns; and the aggrieved merchants resolved to set out to convince the farmers of the interior, to whom these officials were unknown, how intolerable a tyranny was abroad in the land.

The colonists were unable for long, however, to make any very effective constitutional case out of this situation, which bore an unfortunate resemblance to that of someone who, engaged in stealing jam from the cupboard, suddenly has the door slammed on his hand. The Declaration of Independence of 1776, listing the various oppressions and 'usurpations' of George III, makes only one reference, and that not a clear one, to the Acts of Trade. It was the resentment caused by the British determination to raise a revenue from the colonies which underlay the argument about liberty. Raising revenue from colonies was admittedly a novelty; and innovation lends itself more easily than renovation to attack from a high ground of principle.

Broad doctrines of natural law, the rights of Englishmen, and the spirit of the British constitution—all three of them regarded in English political circles as notorious will-o'-the-wisps, the kind of thing 'that devil Wilkes' had used as stock-in-trade—were marshalled by the colonists to combat this innovation. In rebuttal, all British statesmen, including those Whigs who were the most critical of the ministerial handling of the American dispute, or hungriest for office, or both, rallied to support the concept of British sovereignty over British subjects. Burke later found himself explaining that in encouraging the Americans he had had no thought of subverting this concept. 'On a supposition that the Americans rebelled to enlarge their liberty,' he insisted in his *Appeal from the New to the Old Whigs* (1791), 'Mr Burke would have thought very differently of the American cause. He always firmly believed that they were purely on the defensive in that rebellion. He considered the Americans as standing at that time in the same relation to England as England did to King James II in 1688.' Less subtle Tories were content to assert that British sovereignty, exercised by the Crown-in-parliament, was best epitomized in the right to tax. This symbol of sovereignty was certainly thought of as far more important than the comparatively small sum of money that the various methods for colonial taxation were expected to raise. A peppercorn, in acknowledgment of the right (as Lord Clare exclaimed), was of more value than millions without it. His point had a history: in the time of the great proprietaries in colonial America, there had been many a peppercorn, many a rose, many an ear of wheat, paid to the Crown by the grandees in graceful acknowledgment of this same sovereign right.

As they took up their constitutional ground, colonists were driven in their irritation to make assertions that were plainly untrue. John Adams insisted in 1775 that the authority of the British parliament had never been admitted 'as of right' in the internal affairs of the colonies. Daniel Webster in 1826 declared that 'our ancestors' had never admitted themselves subject either to British ministers or to parliament. This became an American axiom; and the success of George Bancroft's *History of the United States* (1834–40) ensured its impact on American school textbooks for the next three generations, linked with a characterization of George III that would have scandalized even those of his English contemporaries who distrusted him most. A genuine sense of grievance was implanted in both English and American minds. The English concentrated, as was to remain their habit, on the legality of their authority in their patrimony overseas. The Americans concentrated, as later 'Dominions' within the British Empire were to do, on questions of status. Each side in consequence thought the other's case irrelevant at best: at worst, mendacious.

Much sprang from this. Had the colonists had a catalogue of deliberate oppression to record, had they been able to claim they were provoked beyond reason, they would also have been able to rally their forces unanimously against the British power, and the American 'Tory' or 'Loyalist' would never have emerged. But in the event they were unable to do this. Their war of independence had in it many aspects of a civil war. The British, in their turn, would have accepted defeat in 1783 with a better grace, and in time the posterity of that generation might well have come to admit both the fact of British oppression and the right of American colonists, as true-born Englishmen, to rebel against it. As a further consequence, the whole course of Anglo-American relations for a century to come would have been very greatly improved, and democracy would have got itself a better reputation sooner than it did. But the continuing misunderstanding in England of the colonists' case—the denial indeed that they had a case at all—laid a train of unpleasantness. There was bred into several generations of educated Englishmen a contempt for things and ideas American, and the accompanying belief that a plebeian race, not upheld by any aristocratic principle of fair dealing, was capable of resorting to any kind of moralizing argument if it happened to suit their immediate book. Images evoked, for example, by appeals to the 'Monroe Doctrine' or to 'manifest destiny' were always very different in England from those accepted in the United States.

Since neither side was prepared to give direct battle on the ground chosen by the opposing party, the struggle for colonial subjection—or alternatively, for American independence—had to be waged in a zone mined with dangerous and indeed undefinable assertions about 'rights'. Englishmen were seldom at ease in such territory, and had no map of it. They felt indeed that they were expert in diagnosing a perilous political situation —such as had been brought about by the revolutionary tendencies of James II in 1688—but they could see nothing of a similar kind in the tea-cup politics of the American colonies, where, since no 'contract' had ever been made with anyone, no one could reasonably complain that a contract had been broken by someone. For colonists to tell those who were, after all, their lawful rulers and protectors that they were misconstruing the British Constitution, could hardly seem anything other than impertinence.

Lawyers in America made much, for example, of the political writings of John Locke. In England Locke had long been used as a quarry by politicians with a taste for political science: Bolingbroke in particular, forcibly relegated from the political battlefront to the study, had enhanced Locke's reputation for wisdom, and French *savants* had reflected it back again to England. Locke had also served as an excellent philosophical apologist for the Whig Revolution of 1688, and his *Two Treatises on Civil Government*, although antedating that event, had contributed to its subsequent reputation for gloriousness. The Whig hierarchs had by no means forgotten that a large part of the philosopher's own career had been passed under the patronage of that indubitable if controversial Whig hero, the great first Earl of Shaftesbury himself; Shaftesbury's less radical political progeny now found out that books, even good books, on political science might be misapplied by people to whom they were not addressed and to whom they were not intended to refer. When Locke took as his central doctrine the sovereignty of the people, he meant the sovereignty of parliament. Misguided Americans ignored this point completely, and implied that he had been referring to something else—although to what, they were unable to verify from the actual texts of Locke himself, a most conservative thinker. They concentrated instead on Locke's view of natural law, natural right. But British pragmatism had never been at home with such abstract concepts. It was rare to hear them spoken of in the House of Commons, for although Charles Fox could quote Lucretius with the best of them, and the front benches enjoyed bandying apposite apophthegms from accepted classical authors, the number of squires who had actually read and digested Locke's *Treatises* must always have been few.

Nor, indeed, had appeals to any law of nature been much heard of in the American colonies prior to 1763. For there was one law of nature—or what seemed like such—that had long loomed over America, so that it appeared that only time would tell whether nature herself would or would not enforce it. It must often have occurred to thoughtful men that the natural destiny of North America might well lie in the hands not of the English race, but of the French, who controlled the two great re-entrants into the continent, the valley of the St Lawrence and the valley of the Mississippi. While a French domination was feasible, there lay a natural inhibition on colonial Englishmen from appeals to natural right; for, if the historical record was closely scanned, it might seem that the French in America had some natural rights of their own. But, when the French pressure was lifted, when the English race controlled both Quebec and the Ohio Valley, the atmosphere on the Atlantic seaboard was at once much freer, the superiority of the English race was held to have been vindicated, and colonial lawyers had room and time to take a broader view.

Thus, Locke's doctrine of the supremacy of the legislature— by which he meant, as indeed his English readers claimed he meant, the supremacy of the British parliament over the Crown —was used by the colonists to support their contention that the colonial legislatures were superior to the prerogative. His insistence that taxes could not be levied without the consent of the people—by which he meant that the king could not raise money without the consent of the people's representatives in parliament—was used by the colonists to support their argument that parliament had no right to tax them without their own consent. His belief that subjects had a right, indeed a duty, to rebel if their governors did not themselves obey the law—a justification for those Whig 'Exclusionists' who, distrusting Charles II's brother James (rightly, as it turned out), wished to debar him from the succession—was adapted by the Americans as sanction for their disobedience to a government they did not agree with. Locke himself had confessed that he made his intellectual discoveries 'by steadily intending his mind in a given direction', a direction doubtless given him by Shaftesbury. Americans however seemed determined to intend their minds in quite a different direction. To Englishmen, it could only appear that here was another case of the devil quoting scripture for his own ends. They did not hesitate to say so.

The ultimate success of the colonists' rebellion did not lower the temperature, or reduce the scale, of this mutual recrimination. The British were ready to admit a startling degree of military incompetence on their own part, but maintained that time and better generalship could have rectified the local failures in America, and that victory would have been theirs had it not been for the malicious intervention of the Bourbon Powers. On the other side, more Americans probably disliked Great Britain more intensively after 1783 than before 1776. It was the opinion of New York's Alexander Hamilton that in 1773 only about half of the colonists were 'Whig'—that is to say, anxious to rid themselves entirely of British control. At that time all the leaders of colonial opinion, including Hamilton himself, were thinking more of the righteous nature of their protest than of their ultimate purpose in making it. They knew the kind of thing they wanted to stop better than they knew what they wanted to start. In this war, as in others, 'war aims' made a late entry on the scene. War itself took charge of events, as it has a way of doing, and of opinions with them. During its course many colonists, and of course all of their leaders, crossed a personal Rubicon and could not, even had they wanted to, return to their abandoned allegiance. But the myth propagated by Bancroft and other American historians, that every colonist, convinced of the righteousness of his country's cause, stoutly fought the British redcoats—with stirring reference to a degree of corporate valour in the 'insurgent husbandmen' which General Washington himself was often hard put to it to perceive—took long to dissipate. Even now, if Americans have stopped believing this, it is more because they have stopped thinking about the matter at all than that they have investigated the claim and found it false.

A modern commentator has pointed out that Americans have, in fact, 'forgotten' the Loyalists, their 'Tory' ancestors who remained faithful to the allegiance they were born in. Yet this is an oblivion that has settled on a sizeable group of people, for in the American Revolution there were twenty-four *émigrés* per thousand of population, compared with a figure of five per thousand in the better-publicized French Revolution.[1] The American *émigrés*, 10,000 of whom were eventually to settle on British soil in Canada and Nova Scotia, were unable to return to remind their neighbours that other views were tenable besides their own, because after 1779 their lands and property in all the thirteen colonies were expropriated, and no restitution was ever made. Anyone who did not declare himself a rebel to King George was declared a traitor to 'America' (whatever that meant in 1779) by those who were rebels; and treated accordingly. The closest parallel to this displacement of persons lies in Cromwell's behaviour in Ireland. There, 6,000 landowners were deprived of their property, which the Crown did not restore after 1660, since it preferred to arrange the payment of an hereditary revenue from the newly-inserted owners as a *quid pro quo* for recognition of their future security of tenure.

American democracy was thus born amid popular intolerance, an embarrassment of situation of which, as Tocqueville was famously to observe sixty years later, it was unlikely ever entirely to free itself. Bancroft, to whom democracy was not a form of government at all but

a destiny of perfection, proceeding as uniformly and majestically as the laws of being and as certain as the decrees of eternity,

never mentioned the tarring and the feathering, the activities of Judge Charles Lynch, or the plight of the Virginia magnates, who, deeply committed against the King, had to stand back and watch their own Whig followers loot and despoil their Anglican churches in a fine presbyterian fury. But the treatment of the Loyalists, about which even the government of Louis XVI protested to its American allies, and for whose compensation and resettlement the British Government ultimately spent over

[1] R. R. Palmer, *The Age of Democratic Revolution* (Princeton, 1959), p. 189. Benjamin Franklin's only son was a Loyalist.

£3 million, remained in British minds as a symbol of democratic tyranny. When ten years later the revolutionaries in Paris similarly overstepped the bounds of acceptable behaviour, it became a fixed idea with the English governing classes that, whenever 'the people' were given their head, they at once lost it: and no English politician ever troubled to make those careful, indeed often laboured, distinctions between republicanism and democracy that American politicians were anxious to make clear from the outset. Both were reckoned as simple synonyms for popular licence. The fact that, during the presidency of Thomas Jefferson (1800–08), the government of the United States thought Napoleon a better champion of liberty than England, was only another, and not a particularly surprising, illustration of the ingrained wrongheadedness of professional democrats. Similarly, the American attack on Canada in 1812 was taken as a still further symbol of cupidity, resentment, and meanness of mind.

Yet if English politicians had paid a closer attention to the motives of American behaviour, they might have been better equipped to deal with the democratic radical movements that were soon to arise in England itself. They might at least have rid themselves of many of the fears that inhibited their own behaviour.

If American leaders laboured to distinguish their terms of reference in government, it was because they were anxious to prevent social revolution from accompanying and overtaking the political revolution that was involved in their rejection of the sovereignty of the Crown. Gouverneur Morris of New York, two years before the Declaration of Independence was issued, was confiding to Richard Penn of Pennsylvania his fears that 'the heads of the nobility' were growing dangerous to the gentry—'and how to keep them down is the question'.[1] For Morris and many like him it remained the question. If the vote was given to people who had no property, he was prophesying in 1787, they would sell it to the rich. (This was certainly true of his own New York State a hundred years later.) Too many appeals to liberty had been made: and as a result liberty, like everything else, must

[1] Dixon R. Fox, *The Decline of Aristocracy in the Politics of New York* (New York, 1918), p. 143.

now be 'checked and balanced'. The Declaration of Independence itself had been a 'campaign document', carefully contrived for an immediate political end. In it, equality was postulated only as a basis for the claim of liberty; it was a philosophy intended more for British than for local colonial, American consumption. The subsequent ricochet of its language to France, and the curious glosses the French put upon it, was not foreseen, and not liked: John Quincy Adams always indignantly denied that the American Revolution proceeded from the same principles as the French Revolution. This, he exclaimed, was 'a disgraceful imputation'.

Disgraceful or not, it was one whose implication could not be avoided. Leading Americans thought it one thing to propagate grievance, and lead revolt, but quite another to let political revolt degenerate into social revolution. Herein the assistance of George Washington, the prestige of whose presence was unassailable, proved of untold service to the conservative forces in America who sought, above all things, stability in govern- ment. These 'Federalists', who wanted to fashion a strong central executive for the Union, had in the upshot to be content with a system of governance wherein nothing much for either good or evil could be done at all unless there was some prepon- derant combination of 'interests' in the legislature. But at least stability was preserved. The people were indeed sovereign, but the Constitution was designed to head them off from playing the role of George III. As a somewhat sour Canadian historian expressed it in 1908 (five years before the American Charles Beard fluttered comfortable conservative dovecotes in his own country by publishing his *Economic Interpretation of the Constitution*):

The government so formed was not formed 'of the people', for a large number of the people were excluded from any share in it. It was not formed 'by the people' for they who formed it did not represent the people, having the suffrages of but a part of them. It was not formed 'for the people', for those who formed it took excessive care that the interests of the people should be subservient to those of the landed and moneyed classes.[1]

[1] A. H. Johnston, *Myths of the American Revolution* (Toronto, 1908), p. 156–7.

Thus, six signatures only are common to both the Declaration of Independence of 1776 and the Constitution of the United States of 1791. It was not until 1840, when all the delegates to the Federal Convention held in Philadelphia between 1787 and 1789 were dead, that the first records of the debates held there were published. The American Constitution was not an 'open covenant openly arrived at', for the reason that, at the time, there was no strong body of opinion that wanted it to be any such thing.

It was Washington's own conviction that mankind when left to themselves were unfit for their own government. From this it followed, that they were certainly unfit to *make* their own government. The views of the governed, Alexander Hamilton concurred, were often 'materially different' from those who govern. John Adams added a verdict which was to sway more public action in the United States than its devotional school of historians was ever ready to admit: 'Very few men who have no property have any judgment of their own.' Washington himself as president maintained semi-royalist pomp, and until Jefferson's regime the president's chair was called his throne. Jefferson's own outlook, although his intellectual habit of mind inclined him to look for simplicities where very often these were not present, was very much that of the paternalist. To him, the landed interest, rooted in the soil and imbued with its natural virtues, was a more moral institution than any likely to be fashioned by a knot of merchants and bankers led by Hamilton. Who was Hamilton, but 'the servile copyist of Mr Pitt', a man 'so bewitched by the British example as to be under the thorough conviction that corruption was essential to the government of a nation'? Who, Hamilton retorted, was Jefferson, but 'an atheist in religion and a fanatic in politics'?

This celebrated quarrel, between the country squire and the merchant, between agrarian Virginia and commercial New York, symbolized the growing antagonism of these two 'interests'. Yet in an English sense both Jefferson and Hamilton were Tories. The Toryism of Jefferson was similar to that of the English shires, the Toryism of Hamilton presaged the state of affairs that was to come, the industrialism that, while ever wishing to expand, distrusted anything 'radical' in politics—by

which it meant something active—that would threaten the
prosperity of the state as a whole. The heirs of the Federalists,
who had put such emphasis on the need for strong government,
turned out to be Republicans who thought that government best,
which did least. The heirs of Jefferson, the paternalist who
stressed the virtues of the yeoman, were to be 'Jacksonian
democrats', who, while they agreed indeed with Rousseau's concept of a general will, and with Jefferson himself that the great
body of the people could never deliberately intend to do wrong,
were enemies of just that type of aristocratic paternalism that
Jefferson represented. These paradoxes were to have their
English parallels: 'Tory democracy' in the late nineteenth
century could have found room for Jefferson, Radicals battling
against the 'money power' would have accommodated Jackson.
Both groups might have looked back to Jefferson's other views
with some nostalgia, but with no intention of seeking to translate
them to political practice. Jefferson objected both to workshops
and to cities, the mob in which added 'just so much to the support of pure government as sores do to the strength of the
human body'. This might be true, but it was never a truth
capable of political manipulation.

Yet Jefferson won his immediate day, for a landed aristocracy
governed the United States for a whole generation, its foreign
and commercial policy (in neither of which was it interested or
competent) stirring the depths of Federalist pessimism. 'We
are now in the Roland and Condorcet act of our comedy,' wrote
a saddened New Yorker in 1801; 'whether we go on to the
Danton and Robespierre acts depends on time and accident.'[1]
The non-appearance of an American Danton or Robespierre in
fact depended on more than time or accident. There was sufficient
common ground between the 'factions', whose very existence
the Federalist James Madison of Virginia so deplored, for the
Constitution to survive and to take root, so that, in future, both
parties were to vie with each other in its 'correct' interpretation.
The republican principle was the great bond, and this had a lot
less to do with democratic fervours than English critics of the
United States supposed. It was agreed on all sides, that the
proper successor to George III as sovereign was the people.

[1] Fox, *Decline of Aristocracy in New York*, pp. 5–6.

The only source of dispute lay in the varying assessments that were made, how best to give this popular sovereignty its full expression. American politicians have from that day to this run for office, not for principle. The principle can be taken for granted: the important question is, who is really the best representative of the people? (A very similar preoccupation had beset the Grenville, Bedford, Rockingham and other groups of English Whigs in the mid-eighteenth century. The same things were to be done, but some people were better equipped than others to do them.)

The main intellectual difficulty faced by this first generation of American statesmen was presented by the doctrine of equality, which no one seriously believed in.

As Jeremy Bentham points out, the equality of men lies chiefly in their cordial devotion to themselves. Egotism is the great common denominator of human attributes. Unfortunately, by its very definition, it is not one that is likely to lead men harmoniously to combine. Hamilton was strongly of Burke's opinion, that the passions of men would not conform to the dictates of reason and justice, without constraint. Only a government of laws could safeguard liberty, and such a government must have ample power to execute its laws. Stability and order in government were essential to public strength and to private security and happiness, the pursuit of which was already one of the professed aims of Americans. Since liberty was the great thing, equality must go by the board: for it is inequality, not equality, that is the natural outcome of a state of liberty. The people did not possess the discernment and stability necessary for systematic government. The voice of the people was not, or not necessarily, the voice of God. To the rich and well-born, therefore, should be given a distinct and permanent share in the government, for

it is admitted, that you cannot have a good Executive upon a democratic plan.

After all, if one looked through the rich and poor of the community, the learned and the ignorant, where did virtue predominate? The republic was, at base, a moral idea, and only moral and virtuous men were fitted to operate it. 'If we incline too much to democracy,' Hamilton warned in June 1787, 'we shall soon shoot into a monarchy.'

The outlook implicit here could not have failed to command the respect of Pitt and his Cabinet. The governors of England had never needed to establish a written constitution, as in each generation political power was entailed on the same sort of people who had previously held it. For the Americans to start their public life by instituting a fixed constitution, in the conviction that, since the same sort of people would always know best how to operate it, the same sort of people would always be elected to do so, could only seem to English oligarchs a surprisingly sensible idea. The ten amendments passed by Congress, however—particularly the first, which prohibited any establishment of religion, or any curtailment of free speech and assembly —struck a more dangerous, democratic note. Moreover, one of Jefferson's notions, that no law should run for longer than twenty years without revision, as change was inevitable, was as unlikely to appeal to American Federalists as to English Tories, who only enjoyed employing it against the Charter of the East India Company. Federalists agreed that the true principle of a republic was that the people should choose whom they pleased to govern them. Madison considered that a pure democracy was always liable to tyranny. By pure democracy, he meant a society consisting of a small number of citizens who assembled and administered the government in person. While doing this they were indeed very likely to sacrifice the weaker party or an obnoxious individual. Such a democracy continually exposed its own incapacity for regular deliberation and concerted measures, and was consequently apt to turn in relief to some ambitious magistrate who was prepared to rescue them from their own state of confusion, provided they agreed to retire from that sphere of executive governance altogether. It was otherwise with a republic—by which he meant a government in which a scheme of representation took place. This opened a different prospect, and promised 'the cure for which we are seeking'.

It was a worthy quest. It had been reserved to Americans, wrote Hamilton in the first of the *Federalist* papers, by their conduct and example, to decide the important question, whether societies of men are really capable or not of establishing good government from reflection and choice, or whether they are destined for ever to depend for their political constitutions on accident and force.

Here was the essence of that great 'American experiment,' the course of which was to be watched closely and critically by European governments, and sympathetically by European peoples, for the next 130 years. It was because Americans themselves considered that their way of life under their republican institutions was not just an alternative to European methods of governance, but something very much better than these, that accounted for that strain of moralism in American policy which so irritated foreign observers. For the old divine right of kings Americans appeared to have substituted the divine right of peoples, and the one opinion as much as the other disquieted all who, in a secular age, disliked any appeal from the world of politics to higher powers whose nature could not be accurately ascertained. The common gibe at Gladstone in the 1880s, that it was not his concealment of an ace in his sleeve that was so vexatious as his apparent assumption that Providence had put it there, was very often applicable to the actions and attitudes of American governments and people alike. But it was this optimism that carried Federalists and Jeffersonians through the early years of their mutual dislike to an eventual 'era of good feelings'. The conservative elements in the United States continued to attach importance to the old English idea of 'a stake in the country', and they devised a middle-class society whose attachment to social 'respectability' was much more rigorous than that of the English aristocracy.

Hamilton had early concluded with satisfaction that mechanics and workers would always be inclined, with few exceptions, to give their votes to substantial merchants in preference to people of their own professions or trades; it was a habit of mind that, as Charles Dilke was to bear witness in the 1860s, also operated among the mass of artisan voters in the British colony of Victoria in Australia, who voted into and kept in power solid middle-class moneyed men. Three main factors successfully kept at bay the wilder elements in American life, characterized by Madison as 'an unhappy species of population . . . sunk below the level of men'. One of these lay in the checks and balances inserted into the Constitution itself, which kept the possibility of the direct exercise of power, by anyone, to a minimum; so late as 1913, the federal Senate at Washington was elected not by the people but by the members of the State legislatures. The second was the respect for the Constitution that was early impregnated into American public opinion. Thirdly, the happy chance that the North American continent lay open to a westward march by those who were not contented with their portions in the eastern part of it helped to drain off, and keep busy, many of the unfortunates Madison spoke of. Utopia and Alsatia were for long contiguous and companionable territories in the American West, although neither, fortunately, ever achieved a separate statehood.

In these ways the desired stability of government, the single feature of British practice that Hamilton and his friends so genuinely admired, was achieved without extensive borrowing from either British legislative or social method. The earliest American leaders had developed a habit of authority indeed, but since it was not hereditary it was a habit whose validity had continually to be reasserted by their successors, and whose value had continually to be re-assessed by the sovereign people. Jefferson's devotion to 'rights' was to be overlaid, by Jackson's time, by the popular doctrine of 'the will of the majority'— which might, or might not, be right. There came a time when Virginia's old families, reared on tobacco, retired before the money-power of South Carolina's new families, buoyed by cotton, and when the Adams family of Massachusetts could no longer appeal to their heaven-born right to the franchises of the American people. Many and various were the types of citizen who rose to power in the republic, and, if they were Southern politicians who in the main dominated the executive until the Civil War, that was due more to the fact that their economy was dominant rather than to any exceptional virtue or talent in themselves. Yet, if there was no distinctive caste or class in power, there was a distinctive habit of mind that had to accompany the use of power, and which was essential to popular suc-

THE HABIT OF AUTHORITY

cess. American politicians had to believe in the national experiment; and they had to respect, even if they lacked any inner conviction regarding, that commonsense of the people, to whose existence Tom Paine had originally drawn the attention both of Englishmen and 'Americans' alike.

Moreover, it was the commonsense of all the people that their elected representatives had to consider. Little time elapsed before universal suffrage became looked on as a popular right. Even by 1796, seven out of sixteen states had no property qualification restricting the franchise for the lower house; half of them elected their governors by popular vote. Three 'western' states—Vermont, Kentucky and Tennessee—entered the Union with manhood suffrage. By the time Andrew Jackson was elected president in 1828, there was manhood suffrage (if Negroes are excluded from the calculation) in fourteen out of twenty-four states. It was late in entering New York State, always a Federalist stronghold, and it did not do so in 1821 without much misgiving being expressed by those who had not forgotten the arguments of Hamilton and Madison. Chancellor Kent was their spokesman.[1] The tendency of universal suffrage, he warned, was to jeopardize the rights of property and the principles of liberty. It was 'too mighty an excitement' for the moral condition of man to endure. What might not come of it, not only in America but elsewhere? One-seventh of the population of the city of Paris at that moment subsisted on charity, and a third of the inhabitants died in the hospitals; what would happen to Paris, the Chancellor asked in a tone that was echoed by many Parisians when the barricades went up nine years later, were universal suffrage to come upon it? And in England! There, the Radicals

with the force of that mighty engine, would at once sweep away the property, the laws, and the liberties of that island like a deluge.

How could it be justified, anyway? To qualify the landless would only be to increase the influence of selfish manufacturers, who could buy both the will and the vote of the poor.

[1] See R. Hofstaedter, *Great Issues in American History* (1958), I, 256.

There were none of these arguments that were not familiar to, and heartily supported by, the embattled aristocracy of England, whose suspicions of the potentiality for evil of English Radicals naturally went even deeper than Chancellor Kent's. The Tory New Yorker realized as he spoke that he was pronouncing 'the elegant epitaph of the old constitution' in America. But in England, although menace abounded, matters had not reached that pass. English Toryism was determined that they should not, either in domestic or in imperial public affairs. The old constitution was not yet interred.

II

Indeed, in the English colonial world the old constitution was still in rude health. The rebellion of thirteen of the colonies in North America had not set that continent free for democracy. There were other colonies, and in these English habits of authority remained either firmly settled or were about to be further reinforced. For while the political triumph of American democracy, and the fissures torn in what was one day to be called (chiefly by American historians) 'the old colonial system', saddened English statesmen and officials, these events did not bring them to believe that they had misread the situation that faced them. The errors, if any, were those more of omission than commission. It was not a new colonial system that was needed—only a tightening and strengthening of the principles that had always been applied to colonies. Colonists in America had carelessly been allowed too many constitutional liberties. These they had converted into political licence. This should no longer be permitted to happen. As Grenville in 1790 wrote to Guy Carleton, now become Lord Dorchester and still ruling Canada, 'in former colonial governments, the aristocratical part of our constitution was but ill supplied'.[1] Therefore, the general object of the new Canadian constitution, just then being arranged, was 'to assimilate the constitution of the Province to that of Great Britain'.

Canada and the Maritime Provinces, to which the great

[1] Manning, *British Colonial Government*, p. 330.

majority of American Loyalists had exiled themselves, were indeed places where such an experiment seemed likeliest to succeed. Such men needed a constitutional air to breathe much the same as that they had been bred to. This the existing form of Canadian government was not equipped to supply. On the morrow of the conquest of French Quebec in 1764, an executive body that consisted of two lieutenant-governors, a Chief Justice, a solicitor-general and eight men 'from amongst the most considerable of the inhabitants of, or persons of property in, our said province' had been appointed by the Crown to control it.[1] In 1774, by the Quebec Act, the governor was ensured a revenue and the French Catholics were granted civil rights, thus easing the strain on both the governor and the governed. It was in this same year that the parliament in England abolished the constitution of Massachusetts (when Charles II had done the same thing he used the royal writ) as a punishment for that colony's misbehaviour. A new Massachusetts Government Act gave the governor power to appoint the members of his council, and took from the council its previous power to ratify the appointment of sheriffs. Lord North himself explained to parliament that these steps, among others, were being taken because 'the democratic part' of the colony's existing constitution was too strong. Indeed this was putting it mildly, and the puritans of New England, scenting a Popish wind of change blowing from the north, had things much more vehement to say on the subject, which were in two years' time to be inserted into the Declaration of Independence itself. The Quebec Act was listed among the 'American' colonists' grievances, in that it had abolished the free system of English laws and had established an arbitrary form of government in the neighbouring province. Moreover, the province itself had been enlarged, and now extended down into the Ohio valley—for what other reason save to

render it at once an example and fit instrument for introducing the same absolute rule into these colonies?

This accusation was somewhat too shrill. Absolute rule was not, then or later, the aim of any British government. If in 1787

[1] Martin Wight, *The Development of the Legislative Council* (1946), p. 37.

New South Wales was not granted a Council and was to be governed on the lines of a man-of-war for thirty years, if Sierra Leone in the same year was put under an equally autocratic sway, that was because the original population of the one were convicts and of the other were freed Negro slaves and white prostitutes: paternalism could not well extend constitutional liberties to people it considered outside the social pale. Yet obviously the remaining colonies of settlement in North America were not of such a kind. The representative principle, although its record in the immediate past proved it capable of absurd abuses, was therefore still of value. For without it, how was a colonial government to be financed? American colonial rebellion had not produced any alternative answer to that question, and indeed the United States' own politicians were by the 1790s forced to cope with a similar independence of mind among their own states, whose inhabitants seemed as prepared to assert their 'rights' against an American federal government as they had been against King George. The granting to a colonial governor of a civil list, so that he could maintain both himself and a system of local patronage without being at any one's mercy, took care only of part of the colonial problem as a whole.

The concept of colonial representation in colonial governance was deeply rooted on both sides of the Atlantic. In England Fox's Whigs were always prepared to accuse Pitt's Whigs—known to history as Tories, a fact that bears witness to the successful imperialism of Foxite ideas—of not being willing to extend to it the proper degree of respect. Moreover, as Dorchester pointed out in 1787, it would be very unwise

> to withhold from dutiful obedience, what might have been obtained by tumults and rebellion, or by delay—to let leaders of sedition usurp from government the gratitude and confidence of the people.[1]

He gave twice who gave quickly: and there was, after all, no danger in giving, as the Canadian Loyalists were the least likely of all people to favour sedition, the least inclined to sympathize with those democratic and republican principles which had just

[1] Dorchester to Sydney, November 8, 1787; Manning, *op. cit.*, p. 323.

made such personal havoc of their own lives—relegating them to pioneering communities, and robbing them of all those hopes for a safe and prosperous future which they had had every right to entertain.

Dorchester himself, when in New York and in charge of Loyalist expatriation in 1783, had always been sympathetic to the plight of these unfortunates. He had pointed out to the governor of Nova Scotia that, since many of these Loyalists were men 'of the first families', in their re-settlement in a new land they were 'entitled to be distinguished beyond the ordinary portions which are to be given to mere settlers, considered as such'.[1] The Council in New Brunswick, a colony that speedily pared itself off from Nova Scotia (1784) as a direct consequence of the Loyalist influx, consisted mainly of Massachusetts lawyers, although the majority of the new settlers seem to have come from New York. (Contrary to a traditional New Brunswick belief, there were very few Harvard graduates or gentlemen in the English sense. At any rate, Lord Edward Fitzgerald, who was there in 1788, seems to have met nobody he was prepared to recognize as such.[2]) The right of representation in Assembly, and participation in legislation, could scarcely be denied to such men, who had fought and suffered so severely for their especial interpretation of the rights of Englishmen and the British constitution. Accordingly, in 1791 the Canada Constitution Act divided the governor's Council into two parts, a Legislative Council, or Assembly, and an Executive Council. The latter was intended to become the nucleus for an hereditary aristocracy, a colonial House of Lords. Writing to Dorchester in October 1789, Grenville stated firmly one of the unwritten assumptions of the British constitution. The intention of the British government, he said, was to establish in the Canadian provinces

a body of men having that motive of attachment to the

---

[1] E. C. Wright, *The Loyalists of New Brunswick* (Fredericton, N.B., 1945), p. 53.

[2] The *Cambridge History of the British Empire*, vol. vi, 193, says that the aristocracy went to the Maritimes and the yeomen to Ontario—but these terms need to be defined.

existing form of government which arises from the possession of personal or hereditary distinction.[1]

The fact that, fifty years afterwards, the work of this Tory government had to be partially undone by a Whig successor does not detract from its considerable success in carrying out this intention. The colonial air could not indeed accommodate the idea of a house of colonial lords, but this first generation of Loyalists to whom the British now gave executive power in the Canadian provinces certainly possessed a personal distinction, and by careful instruction of their large numbers of young they themselves ensured so far as they could that this distinction should be regarded as an heirloom both inside and outside the family. The 'Family Compact' of United Empire Loyalists in what was now to be called Upper Canada [Ontario], like the restored Bourbons in France after 1815, entered the nineteenth century convinced of the commonsense of mid-eighteenth century practice. They were naturally hostile to democracy, to political radicalism, and to those many American immigrants into their province who could hardly help bringing these contaminations with them. Moreover, the continuing and increasing presence of the French in Lower Canada [Quebec][2]—yet another group of exiles from the past, themselves as distrustful of democratic principle as they were of their British overlords—helped to congeal these social prejudices into a national mould. Memories of the blank inaction of the Quebec militia in the face of American attack in 1776 were laid aside, and the French as a whole were reckoned to have worked their passage to acceptance, when they conjoined with Loyalist Canadians and British troops to repel the American invasions of 1812–14. But acceptance never grew to affection; nor was a simple factual knowledge of how the other half lived ever to become widespread among either race. After 1825, when the British Government passed the Canada Trade Act to prevent English merchants in Montreal from levying French dues on their Toronto brethren, the English in Ontario combined to forget as far as possible—until

[1] V. T. Harlow and A. F. Madden, *British Colonial Developments 1774–1834*, (Oxford, 1953), pp. 197 ff.
[2] As the provincial names survive today after a series of political changes, I refer throughout to Ontario and Quebec.

English Whigs at home forced a Union of the provinces on them in 1840—the existence of Quebec altogether. Bilingualism was (as it still is) something a Frenchman had to acquire in order to prosper in his Canadian world; it remained a decorative talent only to an English Canadian.

Thus, throughout this vital period of growth, from the passage of Pitt's Act of 1791 to that of Russell's Act of 1840, Canadian Toryism took up an attitude and followed a line far otherwise than that adopted by other Britons struggling to find their footing elsewhere in the world overseas. Toryism in Australia, for example, was to fight its way up from nothing and nowhere, many of its exponents riding to eventual success on the back of the merino sheep. In contrast, Canadian Tories had both their status and their viewpoint presented to them by the British along with their Loyalist-compensation acreage. They subsequently developed ideas about the correct ordering of society that could never have occurred to a squatter in New South Wales, who had simply struck it lucky and was determined to keep it that way. The democratic outlook, therefore, which while it has no time for airs and graces has no objection to riches, took firmer hold in the antipodes than ever it did to the north of the American republic, with signal consequences to the very divergent social histories of the countries involved.

Canada, as Professor Lower has suggested, is as much a child of the American Revolution as is the United States, 'but on the wrong side of the blanket'.[1] This may account for the marked sense of social rigidity displayed in the provinces in their early days. There appears to be an artificial element somewhere, pervading all aspects of social life. More attitudes were struck than adopted: language that ought to have aroused masses of men to violent revolt in fact did nothing of the sort. The activities of two Scotsmen, the one a pillar of the regime, the other its assailant, may be taken to illustrate this point.

John Strachan and Robert Gourlay followed careers respectively more Tory and more Radical than any they could then have pursued in contemporary England—or in Scotland, supposing them to have taken the unlikely course of staying home. Strachan, originally a presbyterian dominie, cast in his lot with

[1] A. R. M. Lower, *Canadians in the Making* (Toronto, 1958), p. 140.

the Anglican Church in Canada and rose to a commanding position in both Church and state—believing however, as no Anglican prelate in England who had not had the benefit of a Calvinist education could possibly have believed, that the Church should be the parent of the state. At his funeral procession in 1867 Hussars lined the route—also an unlikely honour for a clergyman in England. Robert Gourlay, whose background included a stay among the radical weavers of Paisley, arrived in Ontario in 1817, and at once set to work to improve the local scene in a more Utilitarian fashion than any contemporary English Utilitarian. He called for *cahiers* from the inhabitants and issued a piercing questionnaire. The last of his thirty-one questions wanted to know

> What, in your opinion, retards the improvement of your township in particular, or of the Province in general; and what would most contribute to the same?

He wished to pursue this democratic approach by summoning a convention of deputies of all the constituencies, to discuss sending commissioners to England 'to call attention to the affairs of the Province'. The Family Compact retorted to this signal impertinence by refusing to grant land to any man connected with the convention movement, and they saw to it that Gourlay himself, a British subject, and unconvicted of any offence known to the law, was deported from the province under a statute directed against aliens. (It was apparently the judge's view that only a freeholder, and not a tenant, could be reckoned a *bona fide* 'inhabitant'—an opinion even Lord Braxfield in Scotland might have baulked at.) As the *Cambridge History of the British Empire* soberly remarks, the young man

> overestimated the scope and initiative permitted, even to an abler man than he, in an organized colony.[1]

Gourlay certainly overplayed a hand which had anyway not many cards in it; but his noisy and impractical behaviour served a purpose in that it established a precedent for protest in a place

[1] *loc. cit.*, p. 262.

where the authorities had combined to consider protest un-
thinkable. Moreover, he was hustled out of Canada at a time
when many people in England were considering afresh the issues
of emigration and colonization, and the methods whereby these
might best be instituted and controlled. Gourlay's flat accusations that colonial policy was 'abominable', and that colonial
governors were all of them armed with too much power which,
almost to a man, they abused, were certainly relevant to these
discussions. He repeated them in a work of some 1,900 pages,
his *Statistical Account of Upper Canada, Compiled with a View to a
Grand System of Emigration* (1822), and circulated it among
British members of parliament and editors.[1] It was obvious to
him, and to some of them, that no 'grand system' could be
established while the abuses of which he complained, and under
which he had suffered, continued. But a man under the stigma of
deportation could not wield much influence in any English circle
where it mattered, and the Family Compact rightly feared
nothing more from Gourlay. Governor Sir John Colborne
proceeded in 1829 to found Upper Canada College in Toronto
along the lines of an English public school, so that the incoming
Yankee democratic tide might be stemmed by building a repel-
ling wall of aristocrats. These would no doubt, when they came
of age, be ready to deal both with the Gourlays and the Yankees
of their particular day.

Gourlay indeed anticipated some of the views later successfully publicized by Gibbon Wakefield, Charles Buller, William
Molesworth and the self-styled 'Colonial Reformers'. Their
intellectual leader, Wakefield, was also under a stigma, in his
case that of abduction, and none of them, because they were
Radicals, could ever rise to places of power in the Whig party.
Nevertheless they kept colonial questions before the public, and
caused a considerable degree of official re-thinking to take place.
Gourlay had urged that colonies needed other kinds of immi-
grant than paupers, and that the exportation of a cross-section of
English society would at once invigorate colonial life and prevent
the petty tyrannies that at present emasculated it. Wakefield
adapted this idea, although he did not share Gourlay's faith in the
virtues of democracy. Indeed, he disliked it almost as much as

[1] A. J. Harrop, *England and New Zealand* (1926), p. 29.

any of the colonial governors or Peninsular veterans—the two at this time were almost synonymous—of whom Gourlay had complained. Of 'Yankee principles' Wakefield took as sour a view as any United Empire Loyalist. After all, who were the Americans but a people who, although they continually increased in number, had made no progress in the art of living? Was there not to be seen, in the United States, the unpleasing spectacle of a whole people exercising 'the most terrible despotism' over individuals?[1] There must be no place in the British Empire for such principles and practices.

Wakefield doubted moreover, whether there was any place either for the type of emigrant who at the moment abounded. Whereas in old countries, as he pointed out in his *Letter from Sydney*, modes and manners flowed downwards from the higher classes, they must, in new countries, ascend from the lowest class. This was a poor look-out for colonial society in general, particularly as the lowest ranks in it—if one was to judge by the shocking condition of their teeth—came from 'the gormandizing and guzzling classes'. What could cure this state of affairs? Poor men emigrated in crowds—peers, almost never. It was too late in the day to change the habits of peers, but surely more of the middle-classes of the country could be encouraged both to seek their own fortunes in the colonies and at the same time to raise the standards of behaviour there? A high moral tone in society was the natural accompaniment of commonsense in government. To these ends, therefore, Wakefield worked out complex schemes of colonization according to proper principles, with a correct equation made of the relations between the three main elements of the colonizing process: land, labour and capital. Their application greatly influenced settlement both in South Australia and in New Zealand, and their success was to attract the attention of Karl Marx himself, who in his *Capital* railed at Wakefield for attempting the manufacture of wage-earners in the colonies. 'This, he calls "systematic colonization"!'[2] But Wakefield, although often prepared to adapt his 'system' to local circumstances, never saw any reason to alter his paternalist outlook. In his *Art of Colonization*—published ten years after

[1] Wakefield, *Letter from Sydney*, pp. 25 ff.
[2] Quoted in Harrop, *op. cit.*, p. 44.

Durham had advocated local autonomy in Canada—he repeated his view that the imperial government had a right to control the colonial legislature. These legislatures should be what Grenville had wished them to be back in 1791: 'representative, aristocratic and monarchical'—in other words a replica of the British constitution, complete with an hereditary second chamber. Wakefield was, and remained, hostile to the very idea of universal suffrage, and frequently expressed his admiration for the great Puritan emigration to New England in the 1620s: an example of non-democratic 'systematic colonization' if ever there was one.

The Colonial Office's distrust of professional colonial reformers, camped like Mordecai the Jew outside its gates, did not imply that the officials there had some other system of colonization at hand which they much preferred to impose. Throughout the 1830s and the 1840s, officials' ideas of paternal government clashed with the facts of colonial life. The main objection of James Stephen, Permanent Under-Secretary at the Colonial Office, to the plans for a colonization of South Australia, was that they would transfer to Wakefield's 'company'

and ultimately to a popular assembly, the sovereignty of a vast unexplored territory, and erect within the British Monarchy a government purely republican.

Colonies must be governed, but they could only be governed on acceptable, traditional principles. They had no spiritual essence: one did not need either to 'believe in' colonies, or not. They were there—to some, perhaps, a *damnosa hereditas*, but nevertheless part of Great Britain's international equipment and responsibility. Their existence set a challenge to administrative competence, without trenching on vexed questions that involved policy. Accordingly once in power the Whigs, who believed neither in despotism nor in democracy, continued to expand the representative principle, in which they did believe, in a number of areas, many of them minute, all of them far from public sight and popular opinion—Trinidad and St Lucia in the West Indies, Mauritius and Ceylon in the Indian Ocean, Malta in the Mediterranean. 'Crown Colony' government, with a strong

governor and executive council, with a legislative Assembly
controlled by nominated officials, was government as it ought to
be—authoritative, paternalist, free from party strife. This ideal
situation was unfortunately rare. In colonies of settlement where
white men were numerous and opinionated, there seemed often
as much risk in applying the representative principle as in withholding it; and in consequence, questions of policy at once
arose.

Thus, whether British settlers in Cape Colony should be protected against Kaffir incursion, or whether Kaffirs should be
protected against the settlers' incursion, was a point so moot,
then and throughout the century in South Africa that in the end
(1909) the British government shelved rather than solved it.
Whether those Cape Dutch farmers who, despairing of getting
the kind of paternalism they wanted, had trekked out of the
British sphere of governance altogether (1835-7), ought to be
regarded as rebels, or as simple good riddance, was a related
question. Whether law or 'social justice' should govern in the
West Indies was, in contrast, a question answered with a speed
that allowed little time for anyone to reckon how long a shadow
the answer threw; for the Act that emancipated slaves in the
British Empire (August 19, 1832) is as autocratic as anything
on the statute book, since it took men's legal property, legally
acquired, away from them—'sunset for 70,000 white men',[1] all
of whom felt themselves betrayed by an authority to which they
had been loyal. Whether colonists in New South Wales should
be allowed to wander 'like tartars', as citizens of the United
States were doing, out of the 'pales' where government could
supervise them into the 'outback' where it could not, was an
issue so large that in the long run it was to be dealt with less by
government than by the realities both of Australian geography
and the economics of sheep-farming. Whether colonization in
New Zealand should be permitted at all, whether the Maori of
the North Island should be dealt with as a sovereign race, or
'put down' independently as the aborigines in the Australian
continent were being put down, how best the white 'land-
sharking' of Maori lands could be controlled—these were all

[1] 'But dawn for 700,000 black'; R. Coupland, *The British Anti-Slavery Movement*
(Oxford, 1933), p. 146.

antipodean problems for whose solution no system had yet been devised, and which, in the view of the Colonial Office, were all worsened by the impact of the Wakefieldian 'system' upon them.

In North America the tradition of British paternalism, long extended not to colonists only, but to fur-bearing animals, forests, and Indians as well, took blows even more severe. In Ontario, the Radicals finally turned on the 'Family Compact' and brought its government to a standstill (1837). In Quebec, the French had learned how to use their Assembly, given them in 1791, in the old colonial American style, and as a result brought about an equivalent state of deadlock. Whether the new constitution uniting the two provinces, as advised by Lord Durham— which fitted better with the aspirations of the English settlers than the French—should be allowed to go through, was one puzzle, not made the simpler as neither Durham nor any of his advisers, all colonial reformers and including, *sub rosa*, Wakefield himself, were *persona grata* with the Whig government. Whether anything approaching 'responsible government'—a phrase unknown to the British constitution and heartily disliked by so pure a Whig as Lord John Russell—should be granted to persons who had just proved themselves markedly irresponsible, was another. Russell was accordingly prepared to send out Lord Sydenham in 1840 to rule the two provinces in Canada in the style of a latter-day Duke of Newcastle (or George III), and leave him to it—but to go no further along so suspect a road. The Whigs indeed were content to tackle the issues presented by the Canadian 'Rebellion' not so much on their merits as on the memory that the Tory policy of coercing other North American colonies back in the 1770s had led to such signal defeat.

Thus all simple formulae, all such ideas as Wakefield's which took as their premise a condition of commonsible conservatism in colonial life—a condition which the facts appeared nowhere to support—were much distrusted. It was felt that, if the existing guide-ropes in and for colonial governance were to be cut, if some action taken by the government in England were construed as provocation and reacted to as such, there was a strong probability that thereafter no new ones could ever be thrown across the intervening seas. The colonists themselves would make off into a state of independence, as their predecessors in the thirteen American colonies had done. Many in England believed that this outcome would not greatly have mattered, as their booming industrial country no longer had to have the support of exclusive colonial markets, and no longer needed to maintain the eighteenth-century ideal of an empire of reciprocal trade, rigidly controlled. But the humanitarian conscience was awake also, and operated forcefully despite—or perhaps it can be argued, especially because of—the volume of hard-headed argument emanating from the scholars and sciolists of the new 'political economy'.

The third Earl Grey, Whig Colonial Secretary from 1846 to 1852, continued to believe that a representative government must be better than a 'responsible government' in places where men had no other tradition than that of individualism. He reminded the Governor of New Zealand in December 1846, that 'the otherwise inestimable advantages of colonial self-government' were attended with at least one serious danger. This was,

> that the powers conferred by this franchise on the representatives of the people may be perverted into an instrument for the oppression of the less civilized and less powerful races of men inhabiting the same colony.[1]

It was an opinion which, in the local case, since New Zealand had at that time a population of only 3,157 white men, of nearly 3,000 British troops, and of 105,000 Maori, seemed well justified; and whose wider implications were to continue to trouble other generations of British imperial statesmen.

Grey felt, or so said one of his subordinates, that it was practicable to give a colony representative institutions, and then to stop, without giving it responsible government—'something like the English constitution under Elizabeth and the Stuarts'.[2] But it was certainly too late in the day to convince colonists themselves that this was the kind of constitution they deserved. Burke's principle, enunciated when he opposed Fox's India Bill (December 1, 1783), that all power exercised over a native race

[1] J. R. Rutherford, *Sir George Grey* (1961), p. 151.
[2] G. E. Marindin, ed., *Letters of Lord Blachford* (1896), p. 297.

ought ultimately to be used for the benefit of that race, always seemed too remote and intellectual a concept to many an English settler overseas. It was hard for such a man to feel convinced that his own 'power', over whatever native race was his neighbour, was at all secure—as he stood amid the smoking ruins, say, of his farmstead on Cape Colony's eastern frontier. It was very much easier for him to envisage a future wherein the power of the native race would be exercised over *him*—and exercised without regard to *his* ultimate benefit. Only his own efforts, brutal and without benefit of clergy though they might be, could help him stop this future from arriving. Not all the thunderbolts of denunciation thrown at his head by 'Aborigines Committees' of the British parliament, or by the humanitarian sects which had their London headquarters at Exeter Hall; no Liberal, no 'Fabian', could ever convince him that there was anything but the plainest commonsense in his point of view. Argument drawn from the field of Indian governance did not impress him: for in India at least, power was secure in the hands of the British minority. In such circumstances, but in such alone, was there room and time for intellectual conjecture on the nature and aim of governance, and for the practising of a genuinely benevolent and paternal despotism. Three degrees of latitude nearer the Pole, Pascal tells us, reverse all jurisdiction: 'A meridian decides what is truth.' European expatriates, living three or more degrees nearer the Equator, have generally borne witness to the wisdom in this. White men who have found themselves living beside, but not among, a coloured proletariat, have often felt they could not afford to deal in ethical questions, and have resented social analysis because it menaces their own security— preservation of which is their primary consideration.

Men on the frontier thus could not be expected to share the liberal views of such as Burke. But it was Whitehall and Westminster that continued to mould the world they had to live in. To Burke, the whole point of the first 'Regulating Act' for Bengal, which North's ministry had passed in 1773, was 'to form a strong and solid security for the natives against the wrongs and oppressions of British subjects resident' there. The subsequent doings of Hastings in Bengal, of Fox at Westminster, did not change his mind or the minds he influenced. In 1793, when drawing up new regulations for Bengal, the oriental scholar Sir William Jones—who counted himself a friend alike of Burke, Fox and 'of the People'—echoed the American Declaration: the principal object of every government was the happiness of the governed. This happiness was best assured in conditions of tranquillity: thus 'law and order', when related to this principle, was intrinsically a good. With this notion Henry Dundas, who as President of the Indian Board of Control ruled India according to the same Whig principles as he ruled Scotland, usually employing members of the same families to help him do so, would not have quarrelled. The 1793 regulations were optimistically designed as the 'Permanent Settlement' of Bengal, and governors who came out thereafter saw themselves as improving landlords. To Marquis Wellesley, who was one of these, the settlement epitomized the proper distribution of the legislative, executive and judicial powers of the English state. But in the nature of the Indian case the activities of the English state were far more widespread than in contemporary England, and this aroused misgivings among such Tories in the Indian covenanted civil service as Charles Metcalfe and Thomas Munro, 'tent and saddle men' who wished to act as squires to tenantry indeed, but who did not suppose that English institutions bred under far different circumstances were applicable to India *en masse*. They objected to the making of a new Indian aristocracy, staffed by the peasants' main enemy, the *zamindars*.[1] They disliked also, as did the bulk of English Tories at home, the idea that had been promoted by utilitarians and evangelicals, and which had contaminated many Whigs; that a government fired by moral zeal could shape a society, and had the right to shape it, in the way it ought to go—whichever way that was. (It was a viewpoint Durham was to take with him to Quebec.)

Admittedly, language about Indians could afford to be plainspoken, just because British power was so firmly established in their country. At least, no one ever waxed so frank about the Irish peasantry—whose destinies were, for their own good,

---

[1] A *zamindar* was a landholder who paid revenue directly to the Government, and not to any intermediate superior. Under Cornwallis' settlement in Bengal, he became hereditary, like a baronet. The settlement thus gave *zamindars* heritable landed property.

united to the control of the English parliament by Pitt's Act of 1800—as did James Mill in his *History of India*, long the hand-book of the East India Company's servants, on the characteristics of the Indian peoples. They were, by common consent,

> dissembling, treacherous, mendacious, cowardly, unfeeling, conceited and unclean, victims of despotism and priestcraft.[1]

And if this were so, who could doubt that any step the government took, in whatever direction, was bound to bring about an improvement? And, if the greatest happiness of the greatest number was the object, who could doubt also that the less liberty the Indians, burdened with these unfortunate characteristics, were granted, the better for everyone? The great concern of the people of India, Mill argued, was that the business of government should be well and cheaply performed, but that it was of little or no consequence who were the people who performed it. These people must, however, be 'experts', men of an intellectual bent well able to parse and analyse Benthamite theories of government. It was therefore at Haileybury, the English school established in 1803 for the education of prospective Indian civil servants, that the first chair of political economy in England was instituted, with no less a person than the Rev. T. R. Malthus to hold it between 1803 and 1834.

Mill's *desiderata* were never, however, fully attained, as the population of political economists always remained a small one, and a great many of their arguments continued to fall on deaf ears. Yet the application to Indian affairs of the principle of utilitarianism, with all its zeal for efficiency and uplift, established a powerful core to that 'imperialist' spirit on which later genera-tions were to draw. When the Punjab was conquered in 1849 from the Sikhs—a martial race to whom Mill's indictment could hardly be made to apply—the aim of Tory paternalism was attractively summed up in the words of Sir Henry Lawrence, one of the ablest and most high-minded of the Punjab's overlords:

> Settle the country; make the people happy; and take care there are no rows.

[1] James Mill, *loc. cit.* (2nd edn. 1820), II, 195.

Here was an admirable, if simple, guide to political practice—
so long, of course, as men who knew how to carry out such a
programme were in charge. It is not therefore surprising that
Lawrence's philosophy and outlook, Lawrence's standard of
behaviour, became stock ingredients of Victorian (and later)
romantic fiction, whose heroes conformed inescapably to the
desired pattern: upright, courageous, protective, *right*. The
British officer isolated in his district, doing what he had to do
under an alien sun, establishing the tenets of 'the Law' which, as
Rudyard Kipling stressed, bound governors and governed alike
in a community of justice and interest, was for long to impress
the imagination both of the active and the sedentary.

In contrast, the Court of Directors of the East India Company
could scarcely be said to constitute an image for romance; at any
rate they have never been treated as such. But at intervals of
twenty years, when their charter was statutorily due for inspection and discussion by parliament, they proved themselves
anxious to strike the note acceptable to the majority. On one of
these occasions, in 1833, they showed how far these current
principles of governance had impressed them. (They had no
doubt been also considerably impressed by the Reform Act of
the previous year, which had disfranchised thirteen boroughs
which had been represented in the House of Commons by sixteen members of the 'East India interest'; and by the fact that in
the subsequent general election another twenty-one members
had failed to hold their seats.) It was not, the Court declared,

> by holding out incentives to official ambition, but by repress-
> ing crime, by securing and guarding property, by creating
> confidence, by ensuring to industry the fruits of its labour, by
> protecting men in the undisturbed enjoyment of their rights
> and in the unfettered exercise of their faculties, that Govern-
> ments best minister to the public wealth and happiness.[1]

Fifty years later, Sir James Fitzjames Stephen, drawing on his
experience as legal member on the Viceroy's Executive Council,
underlined these same sentiments, in drier language and without
any expectation that their propagation was likely to arouse a

[1] Quoted in P. Griffiths, *The British Impact on India* (1952), p. 195.

flush of enthusiasm either among those who put them into practice or those who saw them practised in their midst. He declared himself unable to define happiness as a public attribute. He doubted whether any set of regulations had ever made any-one gay. He was aware, he wrote, that the Indian Penal Code, the Code of Criminal Procedure, and the institutions which they regulated, were 'somewhat grim presents' for one people to make to another, and were little calculated to excite affection. But they were eminently well-calculated 'to protect peaceable men and to beat down wrongdoers, to extort respect, and to enforce obedience'. Stephen was unmoved by the assertions, then beginning to rise about the ears of the British in India, that it was a valid criticism of the *Raj* that it did not represent the native principles of life or of government. Certainly it did not, and it was right that it did not: that was not the idea at all. It could never do so, 'until it represents heathenism and barbarism'.[1]

Something not far from heathenism and barbarism could be found in England itself. There was accordingly a danger that the principle and practices of democracy would be stained with both. How was this danger to be met? Here again the Indian analogy did not serve. In India the principle of aristocracy, since it expected to meet no local resistance that could not, in the long run or the short, be militarily dealt with, had established a mode of governance well justified by its own success. But elsewhere in the world it was no easy matter to follow Henry Lawrence's precept, to take care there were no rows. The voice of the people was a loud noise, and democracy seemed easily inclined to rowdyism, if it was to be judged by the rebels in Ontario in 1837, or by the 'Eureka Stockade' and the cry for 'miners' right' in the Australian goldfields in 1854. Democrats were quicker to claim rights than to recognize duties. English aristocrats noted how lackadaisically the American democrats pursued the inter-national proscription of the slave trade, and how it took them another thirty years to emulate the Whigs' measure of 1833 that had proscribed throughout the British Empire the state of slavery itself. It was for this reason, that democrats could not be trusted to behave like gentlemen, that Stanley, the Whigs'

[1] Quoted in E. Stokes, *English Utilitarians and India* (Oxford, 1959), p. 288.

'Rupert of debate' held, and conserved, the views he did. (He conserved them so staunchly, indeed, that he became the leader of the Conservative party after 1846.) Sharing in the government, he observed in 1832, was not an abstract right, which any man could claim. But at the same time it was a right no government could withhold from a man,

> except upon this principle, that the class to which he belongs is not capable of being trusted for the discreet exercise of such a right.[1]

But, in what circumstances this principle was to be recognized, to whom it should be applied, in whom lay the right to recognize it and apply it—who was ever going to reach agreement on these points?

The whole idea of service, with its accompanying concept of loyalty, was anyway aristocratic in its origins, deriving from and remaining closely related to feudal ideas of rank, degree, and status, and the corresponding duties that belonged thereto. Here was the implication of Basil Hall's remark, already noted,[2] that American democrats, individualists to a man, did not know what loyalty was—nor did they know, as Mrs FrancesTrollope was prompt to add, what standards of behaviour and good manners were either, despising these when they encountered them as remnants of arrogant aristocratic pretension, and fit therefore only to be heavily stamped upon. The assertion of Tom Paine, that of all political regimes democracy was the nearest approach to a society without government, was reckoned as one of his most menacing. For just in this lay the point whose real significance Paine was determined to miss, Burke's point and Hamilton's alike, that society, in any real meaning of the word, could not exist at all without government. That democracy and a sense of society, of the community, could long remain attached to one another, was already felt doubtful. For what could rugged individualism contribute, save anarchy?

It was already noticeable that, of all emigrants to the United States, they were the English who took with them the deepest feelings of personal grievance and the least durable folk-memory.

[1] W. D. Jones, *Lord Derby and Victorian Conservatism* (Oxford, 1956), p. 24.
[2] See p. 14, above.

They (and their descendants after them) preserved nothing comparable to the attachment shown by expatriate Scots and Irish to the idea at least, if not to the reality, of 'the Old Country'. Irishmen in America indeed always kept their antipathies to England more firmly to the fore than their affections for Ireland; but Lord (Eustace) Percy, who before 1914 served in the British Embassy in Washington, has left on record his considered view that, even so late as that, it was not the Irish, not the European races in the United States, who enjoyed 'twisting the lion's tail' more than did the Anglo-Saxons in America, descendants of an unrecorded emigration, who still loved the name but abominated the power of a lord—a power that had, by then, vanished away.[1] In many American schoolhouses no great distinction was made between George III and George V, whose subjects, after all, spent a large amount of their time shooting down the natives of India. The great demagogue of the 1890s and after, William Jennings Bryan, from whose lips many Americans drew whatever political lore they had, was always convinced that 'the brewers' dominated the Church of England and the Conservative party, and took Lloyd George's 'class budgets' as patent proof that heretofore British dukes had never paid any taxes at all.

From the outset, this apparently easy dissociation of the English people from the traditions and habits of their homeland had troubled the consciences of Whigs and Radicals alike. It drove Tories into a deeper resentment yet that merchants and manufacturers, promoting the march of industrialism for the sake of their own interests, should have wounded so deeply the spirit of the old community of England. If Cobbett in 1829 was right—

If a man have money, and have, of course, a choice of countries to which to go, and if he can hesitate for one moment between the United States and an English Colony, I despise the slave[2]

—it was surely a sad thing that he was right. This, then, was what came of raiding the parishes of England for paupers and

[1] Lord Percy, *Some Memories* (1958), pp. 30-1.
[2] *Political Register*, May 1829.

then deporting them to the antipodes under the slightly more dignified name of emigrant! Men above, even just above, that lowest grade of life were ready to turn their backs, cheerfully or resentfully according to their natures, but in any event finally, and go off to Philadelphia in the morning, to look out for themselves alone under another sky because no one under their own had ever looked out for them. Aristocrats might talk, it seemed, of the virtues of loyalty and service, but since they gave none to those who were not of their own kind they could not expect much to be given them in return. Robert Southey, become a pessimistic Tory, perhaps overstated the case when he wrote in 1831 that the planters in the West Indies were not in more danger from their Negroes 'than we are from our servile population'.[1] The old habit of obedience was destroyed. The poor were poorer than they ought to be: they knew that, and they knew, too, their strength and numbers. But, if this was more than the truth, it also contained it.

Realization of this led Wakefield and his associates to propagate their very different ideals for colonization and settlement. It had also compelled George Canning, no democrat, to adopt policies usually classified under the heading of 'liberal Toryism'. It led Grey and the Whigs to swallow their distaste for the Radicals, to outflank them and take final charge of the movement for parliamentary reform; and it brought the aristocracy as a whole to make common cause with what Disraeli called 'the middling classes', those substantial and respectable persons to whom their betters were now prepared to give political guidance, for the sake of a mutual security. The passage of the Reform Act in 1832 (whose effects will be discussed later) did indeed remove a great deal of the poisons that had accumulated in the English system, but it could not entirely eradicate them. The Liberal statesman James Bryce allowed to stand in the 1915 edition of his *Modern Democracies* the comment that, although the eighty years which had passed since Grey's Reform Act had brought many new ideas with them, the ordinary English voter was still far from feeling, as did the American voter, that the government was his own, and he individually responsible for its conduct.

[1] Quoted in A. S. Turberville, *Lords in Age of Reform*, p. 17.

For if an American voter felt that he could identify himself with his government, that was because there was very little in its executive machinery that entered his life and got in his way. The constitution of the United States was criticized for that very reason, that it was 'all sail and no anchor'. The Federal Government in Washington had no control over policies that concerned land, Church or education. It therefore made no impact on a man's work, on his soul, or on his thinking. Nor did it commandeer his time, for in the 'Age of Jackson'—a president who was, as Tocqueville noted in his *Democracy in America*, a slave of the majority, but a favourite who sometimes treated his master roughly—the American army had a complement of 6,000 men. Its foreign policies did not require the citizen's approval, for American governments prided themselves on needing none; and, because they needed none, they had no wish to establish diplomatic corps on the European style, whose members, dealing in European styles of thought, would doubtless be contaminated with European habits of mind. The majority of Americans were still small farmers, and the presence of free land on the frontiers of settlement kept employed the energies both of the rootless and the ambitious. The only habit of mind an American needed to become acquainted with was his own; of any habit of authority, or of anything in the nature of discipline he knew nothing at all. He had no betters, and could only be coerced by the opinion of his equals: yet he was coerced so often by this that Tocqueville had remarked that he knew no country in which there was so little true independence of mind and freedom of discussion as in the United States, where the majority lived, because they knew not how to live otherwise, 'in the perpetual practice of self-applause'.

Of this way of living Englishmen knew very little. Indeed, of all countries whose history has touched that of the United States, it is England that has remained the most 'un-American' in its activities. In the nineteenth century the English social and political organization was so entirely different from the American that it was not remarkable that Herman Merivale should have summed it up from the depths of the Colonial Office with the remark that, as everyone knew, such countries as the United States and the English colonies of settlement were no places for gentlemen. To be sure, gentlemen, either born or made, could be found in these places, but there they had no *function* as such, as they had in England. They were therefore easily relegated to unimportance in the public consciousness and their sons were allowed no pretensions to gentility at all. John Stuart Mill observed in his *Representative Government* (1861) how the natural tendency of that type of government, as of modern civilization itself, was towards a 'collective mediocrity'. In the American democracy, the highly-cultivated members of the community, except those among them who were willing to conceal their own opinions and judgment in order to become 'the servile mouthpieces of their inferiors in knowledge', seldom troubled to stand for office in Congress or in the state legislatures, so little likelihood was there of their being elected. Mill added, that American institutions had imprinted strongly on the American mind the idea that any one man, so long as he had a white skin, was as good as any other. But this, he insisted, was a false creed, and it was 'not a small mischief' that the constitution of any country should so sanctify it.

For English liberalism had never possessed, and never acquired, any respect for equality. Its exponents disliked its very overtones, and were apt to hear them in unlikely places. Melbourne's Whig ministry coped but feebly with the Scottish Church, when that institution, whose precepts and philosophy were totally unknown to educated Englishmen, was beginning the career of internal struggle that was to lead finally to its disruption in 1843.[1] The very idea that the people should be allowed to choose, and not patrons to nominate, the pastors for their churches, was sufficient to unman the Whiggism of Brougham and to set Melbourne himself quite at sea: lay patronage had not been mooted in England since the days of the Barebones Parliament. Whigs and Tories tended to confuse the evangelical movement led in Scotland by Dr Chalmers with some kind of dissent, and, since the wooing of dissenters was a Whig tradition in England, this further bewildered the whole issue. The General Assembly of the Church of Scotland came something very close to a 'National Convention', robbed of any

---

[1] On May 20 474 ministers quit the Church of Scotland. Within 4 years 650 churches of the 'Free Church' were built.

jacobin tendencies; yet many English peers had the idea that it had been created by the Crown at the Union of 1707. The young eighth Duke of Argyll, one of the Whig leaders of the next generation, percipiently remarked how far from the general Scottish viewpoint the Scottish aristocracy, barnacled to its English counterpart, had come, for it could give no lead in a matter wherein, if anywhere, men of rank should have counted for much. He himself advised indignant Scottish divines, highly-educated men who had done their own historical research and were constantly brandishing authentic documents at him, that it was 'hopeless' to expect Englishmen to accept ideas absolutely new to them.[1]

If it was not exactly hopeless to expect this, a great deal of patience was useful during the period of expectation. In 1867 the Liberal *Edinburgh Review* was still of one mind with the *Quarterly* in its dislike of the doctrines of democracy. They agreed, too, with one of Tocqueville's shrewdest diagnoses, that

> the taste which men have for liberty, and that which they feel for equality, are in fact two different things.

Travellers normally remarked that the normal manifestation of an individual's faith in egalitarianism was boorishness in public. Frances Trollope had reported in her survey of the *Domestic Manners of the Americans* (1832) that she could find no trace in them of what Burke had called the 'unbought grace of life', and she felt, as subsequently did Charles Dickens on his American tour, that 'strong, indeed, must be the love of equality in an English breast' if it could survive a tour through the Union. (The American habit of 'pirating' English books out of their copyright did not, of course, endear the United States to English popular writers.) Moreover, if, as democrats claimed, democratic politics was the art of reaching decisions that were generally acceptable, then the Tory answer was that this was not worth cultivating, as what was generally acceptable might be neither morally right nor in the public interest. Burke's dictum, that the will of the many, and their interest, must very often differ, appeared in respectful quotation in *Edinburgh* and

[1] Argyll, *Autobiography* (1906), I, 176.

Quarterly alike. According to the *Quarterly's* editor, John Wilson Croker, no republican government could last, and there could be 'no steady mean between democracy and despotism',[1] without the ameliorating presence of a landed gentry. The American 'experiment' was, still, in its experimental stages.

It did not serve, either, to point out to such critics that Americans were a nation of small landowners. For so were the French, and could anyone say that it was genuinely in the interests of the French people to 'will' into the imperial power such a mountebank as Louis Napoleon, despite his equipment of *plébiscites* and the like? And had not universal suffrage, of whose virtues more and more was now being heard, been a prop of the tyrannical consulate and empire of the first, great Napoleon himself?

This cleavage of opinion concerning democracy and its habits, the various diagnoses concerning its future, all the arguments *pro* and *con* which were the stronger because they could not easily find a direct form of political expression, kept the English upper classes from arriving at any understanding of either American or colonial conditions. Understanding was the harder in that knowledge was so sketchy. The case was therefore most often put like this, and left like that: American democracy was plainly fraudulent because it perpetuated slavery. Colonial aspirations were obviously absurd because the majority of English colonists were from the lower orders of English society, and therefore could hardly be supposed to know how to reach beyond their immediate grasp. Accordingly, it was less owing to respect for Lord Durham's Radical precepts—or to any detailed information how the two provinces in Canada had fared since their union in 1840—than to sheer indifference, that the colonies in Australasia had so easy and uncommoded a passage to self-governing status. The Radical leader John Bright commented sardonically in his journal on February 7, 1850, when the Australian Colonies Government Bill was passing through the Commons, how great was the agreement among members on the subject—

marvellous absence of prejudice when the objects are 10,000

[1] Turberville, *op. cit.*, p. 406.

miles away. Should like to move that the Bill be extended to Great Britain and Ireland.[1]

It was a comparison he returned to, and one which was weighing with him more deeply fifteen years later, at the height of his campaign for another Reform Bill. It was only in his own country, on his own soil, where he was born, that an Englishman was denied the right which in every other community of Englishmen in the world would be freely accorded to him!

The implication in this, that there was one law, or set of attitudes, for the colonist abroad, and another for the subject at home, was quite correct. One lesson learned by English statesmen from the experience of the American Revolution, and absorbed, however painfully, from the intellectual impact of the French Revolution, was that it was not possible to coerce large numbers of people, with whatever good intentions and desires for their own ultimate good, without resorting to the apparatus of a military state. This apparatus it was not possible to obtain, since no one wanted to obtain it: as Madison had observed from across the Atlantic, the facts of geography and the acknowledged importance of a powerful navy had made it impossible for the rulers of Great Britain 'to cheat the public into an expensive peace establishment'.[2] If colonists, then, could not be persuaded, then they were best forgotten. Their territories still required to be defended, and indeed the Duke of Wellington was always thankful for the existence of colonies, for in these, out of sight of the suspicious English populace, he was able to salt away a large proportion of the British army. But apart from this, little parliamentary attention was paid to them, and in the nineteenth century a dozen or so colonial secretaries were to follow on each other's heels through the Colonial Office without the experience leaving any great mark either on 'colonial policy' or on themselves.

Colonists early learned, amid some chagrin, that it was in this wise that they were considered at home. To ask for liberty or death, in the old American style, was plainly ridiculous when

[1] Trevelyan, *Bright*, p. 176.
[2] No. 41 of *The Federalist Papers*, ed. C. Rossiter (Mentor Books, New York, 1961).

what was most likely to come one's way was oblivion. Here and there a colonial governor of the old school, who considered that a governor's duty was to govern the people, might set his face against a popular tide—as did George Grey in New Zealand in 1845, Latrobe in Victoria, Australia, in 1854. But this was a momentary gesture only, one which, as colonists knew well enough, was unlikely to be repeated by the governor who came to succeed the paternalist diehard, once the latter had been duly called home and retired with honours.

Clearly it was inevitable that, once the principle of colonial self-government had been granted, in whatever pessimistic state of mind, British paternalism should exclude itself from concern with and knowledge of the internal affairs of the colonies of settlement. Canadians therefore confederated themselves and the colonists of New South Wales partitioned their patrimony twice without any initiative from Westminster. But although such things could be permitted in the outer world, it was absurd to think that they could be permitted in the inner, closely-controlled world of Europe—absurd to think, for example, that Irishmen in Ireland might be allowed to decide whether to confederate or to divide themselves according to taste. Home Rule for Australians, among whom there were very many Irish-born, as bitter about the English as their kin in the United States, could be casually accepted, and an eventual independent Australasian republic envisaged; but Home Rule for Ireland was not to become operative until another seventy years had passed. It would not have done so then, had not a great war engulfed and wrecked the entire European state-system and exhausted the capacity both of British statesmen and public for turning their attention once more to 'the dreary steeples of Fermanagh and Tyrone', as Winston Churchill expressed it, as they arose from the floodwaters upon the horizon. In the long, long interim, the Irish remained a problem in English governance. In 1883 the Conservative leader, Salisbury, quoted Gladstone's remark that the Liberals were going to produce a state of things in Ireland which would make 'the humblest Irishman realize that he is a governing agency, and that the government is to be carried on for him and by him'.[1] Salisbury's own comment on this was dry.

[1] 3 H 276, February 15, 1883, p. 33.

He did not like the idea, he said, of the humblest Irishman as a governing agency.

The English people, too, remained a problem in English governance. No one was actively anxious to see the humblest Englishman as a governing agency, either. No suggestion for 'unlocking the land', a process that absorbed the energies of nearly three generations of Australian democrats, ever emanated from a British Cabinet; and Joseph Chamberlain raised the hair on his Liberal colleagues' heads by taking even an oblique glance in that direction. Tocqueville had noted how it was the habit of aristocrats unconsciously to fashion society to their own ends, and to prepare it for their own descendants.[1] Nineteenth-century circumstance made this habit conscious. The fact that this task had, since 1815, become progressively more difficult had not altered anyone's opinion that it was more than ever essential to carry it out. The dislocations of war were followed by the dislocations of peace, and a generation of the ruling class no more anxious than any other to recast and reorient their methods and aims found that this, in effect, was what circumstances compelled them to do. A greater degree of domestic unrest than had ever before been known among the people made it a matter of the greatest urgency to establish an acceptable leadership. It was a period of trial for the ruled, and error for the rulers.

That both survived it, that both at the last coped with the challenge the times presented, that both were able to pass on to their respective descendants a continuing sense of an interlocking society, attests remarkably to the conservative sense of community that was part of the English outlook.

---

[1] 'The English have left the poor but two rights,' he added in 1835, 'that of obeying the same laws as the rich, and that of standing on an equality with them if they can obtain equal wealth'; *Journeys to England and Ireland*, ed. J. P. Mayer (New Haven, 1958), p. 91.

CHAPTER IV

THE DISLOCATION OF
SOCIETY

I

The governors of England were determined after Waterloo to maintain the position they had fought for twenty-two years to preserve. So were their colleagues, the aristocrats of Europe, who in 1815 gathered in Vienna to restore the foundations, if not all the separate structures, of the *ancien régime*. For the moment it seemed that this task in England would not be difficult. That year public attention was not turned on Metternich, Talleyrand, and the Congress: it was riveted on the Corn Law, which added fourpence to the price of the ten-pound loaf.

But the world lay in the lee of what Thomas Carlyle was to call 'the most convulsive phenomenon' that had occurred within the past thousand years. The ground had been rocked beneath men's feet, and what fissures it now hid as a result no one in authority could know. Napoleon paced St Helena, but the forces he had let loose could not be so caged. Yet surely, an England which geography had insulated from the impact of the French Emperor might be protected from the imperialism of French ideas? There was evidence to uphold this hope. Phenomena, by definition, contain an intrinsic element of incalculability, of surprise. The French Revolution was, for the Englishman of its own day and after, a series of surprises; accordingly, from such a puzzle there was little to be learned. George Saintsbury later summarized the general impression of his educated countrymen: the events of 1789 were 'due to the machinations of an entirely unhistorical Committee of Three—Voltaire, Diderot, and Rousseau.'[1] Popular taste fastened on a set of images, all of

[1] G. Saintsbury, *Collected Essays and Papers* (1923), III, 255.

167

them bloodstained, most of them simultaneous. The fall of the Bastille, Marat in his bath, the Terror with its guillotine and its tumbrils (vehicles nowhere else met with in the English language) filled with brave gallants, continued to dominate the average recollection. The adventures of Sydney Carton (1859) and the Scarlet Pimpernel (1905) served to sum up, and give vivid form to, these images.

Of Napoleon himself, there was never to be an accurate English impression at all. His relation to the Revolution, from what situation he emerged, how he did it, what ideas he had, what he accomplished, how he accomplished it and what legacy he left in the minds of Frenchmen, are all matters that have kept their mystery on the English side of the Channel—and this, despite the eager, indeed excited attempts of a host of French scholars to make their nature plain to all the world. In English eyes the adventurer Bonaparte merely fills a part that a more sensible man would have refused to play; and it is not surprising that his Tory contemporary Jane Austen, although with two brothers in the Navy, should have ignored him in her novels. It is the role that Louis XIV had played before him and that Adolf Hitler was to play after him. It is one which a providential, or Whig, history had so far decreed to be ultimately unrewarding: that of a man who, overflowing with confidence and constitutionally incapable of correctly assessing the English reaction to his schemes, seeks to control the continent of Europe, thereby upsetting that 'balance of power' whose equilibrium, ever since the days of Whig William III, it had been at once the interest, the duty, and the honour of England to preserve.

Merely to state this highly aristocratic point of view is enough to raise an echo of the sulphurous comments on English international behaviour that so often enliven the pages of those French and German histories no Englishman reads. During the 1850s the Radicals John Bright and Richard Cobden did their utmost to gainsay it, in order to make the British middle classes realize how their own aristocrats duped them, and wasted their hard-earned money, by playing on their patriotic fervours. But, despite the cogency of their propaganda, the original point of view still stands. There has never been any popular reassessment of it, nor is there likely to be. Even those poets and writers whose imagination were liberated by the first contact with French revolutionary enthusiasm, and who spread this sense of liberation through the channel of their works, did not allow any similar inspirational fire to catch hold of their political opinions: Wordsworth, Coleridge, and Southey all gravitated to political toryism, and what Burns would have done remains a puzzle. For it was one thing to appreciate French hopes for a new dawn for mankind, another to follow in French footsteps towards it. Since French ideas were by definition alien, they were bound to be inapplicable both to British institutions and to the native thought and habit that had for so long kept those institutions in being and of value. Burke, in so strongly emphasizing the importance of tradition and custom in the proper development of society, was pushing at an open door.

French panaceas could never answer, for they centred on the idea of equality. This principle meant little or nothing to the mass of English people, as in their own society they had never been allowed to have any experience of it. Tom Paine's advocacy, made with all the force he had in him, that they ought to set out to *get* experience of it, reacted more acutely on those who opposed the idea than on those who approved it. He repeated and strengthened the analyses of social injustice that had been made by the seventeenth-century Levellers, but with even less effect. For Tom Paine, like 'Freeborn' John Lilburne before him, was an oddity in that he was a genuine revolutionary. His readers, although their imagination was kindled by him as by the poets, were nothing of the kind: at least, not enough of them ever risked proving themselves so. England, the patient under Paine's diagnosis, chose to remain a patient; and the doctrine of equality, a target against which much powerful intellectual argument was to be hurled for the next hundred years, stayed outside the ken of the English people.

Not desire for a new world, but regret for the old; not the hope of equality to be gained, but resentment at liberty lost, underlie the social unrest of the first forty years of the nineteenth century.

In the eighteenth century, all ranks of society had been able to move freely within their own sphere, the boundaries of which were clearly delimited: Burke had had this in mind, when he waxed ironical about 'the British government, loaded with all its incumbrances, clogged with its peers and its beef, its parsons and its pudding, its commons and its beer, and its dull slavish liberty of going about just as one pleases.'[1] The idea of a community of interests in England—in other words, of a national spirit—was well established. Aristocratic politicians whose natural tendency was to distrust every show of popular enthusiasm had not drawn attention to this, or sought to capitalize upon it except in times of war. Even then, they had done so with misgivings: William Pitt, 'the Great Commoner', master of a potentially dangerous brand of demagoguery, was considered employable in war but not in peace. Governing the country was not very different from governing a county: it was the business of those aristocrats who had a taste for it, and whose skill at it was enough to meet some not very exacting tests. The early movement for parliamentary reform did not command any wide popular support, and even Major Cartwright, who in all his plans for reform retained a property qualification for the franchise, did not expect it to do so. Men who were professionally interested in the political process; men of ideals; or men of no ideals who could nevertheless see in reform a road along which they might make better progress, aired their ideas how best to express the spirit of the British constitution—but they did this, unlike their American counterparts, in a vacuum. Before 1815 no public pressure promoted their opinions to importance. If the mass of Whigs, including all the born Tories among them, never became interested in parliamentary reform at all, that was because they had been accustomed since youth to look on it as a crotchet of men, only the rank of some of whom prevented all from being designated as cranks at best and as jacobins at worst. Similarly, the determination of William Wilberforce and a new generation of evangelical, middle-class 'Saints' to abolish the trade in slaves from West Africa to British colonies was also thought a crotchet, one which a generous heart might applaud, but not necessarily vote for. The idea that slavery as a status should be abolished was slow in finding a voice, even among Saints. Slaves were property, legally bought and paid for: this was a hard fact that landed gentry alike with mer-

[1] *A Letter to W. Elliot*, May 26, 1795.

chants, all strong believers in the sanctity of contract, could never overlook.

In time it proved possible for them to allow Wilberforce, under the aegis of a mixed ministry of 'New Whigs' and others, to fulfil his ambition: just in time, however, as the royal assent to the Slave Trade Abolition Act was given (March 25, 1807) half an hour before a solidly Tory government came in.[1] For, after all—if an Englishman examined these questions without bias—the parliamentary reformers were seeking to tamper with an affair of much greater significance to him than the optimum method of regulating the labour-supply of West Indian planters. The Radicals themselves had this impressed on them when in the upshot, in 1832, it was not their own programme of reform but that of the Whigs that carried the day. Philosophic Radicals were, and were to remain, by nature inclined to over-estimate the sway that intellectual argument can wield over an uneducated people. The first generation of Radicals, whose approach to philosophy was pragmatic, had always handled the democratic principle with care. Cartwright and Price, and even Paine when he had a grip on his emotions, had all clearly realized that their chief task and duty was to *instruct* the public, to bring it to full comprehension what was in its own best interest. Inevitably they made their appeals to the mercantile 'middling classes', since there were few outside of these classes whom they could expect to reach, or who, even had they seen the light, would ever be able to bring it into political focus.

The manufacturers certainly constituted a part of the public that was well able to calculate its own best interest. Employers who had no love for theories of philosophic radicalism could see the utility and advantage of forming an 'interest', on the model of the East India Company, in the House of Commons; and they could see, too, that if they wanted to get such a lobby they must first join forces with those who were urging reform of the entire parliamentary representation. They leagued with the constitutional innovators, at the same time keeping as conservative a political stance as any squire. They wanted only a place in the constitutional system—devolution, not revolution. It was a commonsense attitude the Whigs were able to appreciate, and

[1] The Whigs had been in office just four-and-a-half months.

from its continuance the great Liberal party of the later nineteenth century was to draw the main part of its strength: Gladstone himself never lost his distaste for the implications of the
word 'radical'. But inevitably, it was slow going at the outset,
and any success gained was on a narrow front. Even when, in
the 1820s, Radicals could look over their shoulders at a phalanx
of persons behind them, carrying banners for parliamentary reform, the ablest of them knew well enough that this did not
mean that a new degree of political sophistication had suddenly
embellished English minds.

It was true what the Tory Southey said, that the poor were
poorer than they ought to be, and knew it. But they did not
know *why* they were so, and they turned to those who they
thought ought to know, to find out. Politicians had always publicized themselves as men who 'did things' for the country as a
whole; thus, it was only parliament, the home of politicians, that
could be turned to in this extremity. But, since parliament was
also the home of landlords, it was plainly pointless for the pauper
and the tenant, the employer alike with the employed, to look
for help at that address. Parliament must be reconstituted, so
that someone other than landlords could sit in it: hence, the
popular enthusiasm for parliamentary reform. 'And has it been
discovered, at last', Cobbett inquired, 'that England has *always*
been an enslaved country from top to toe?' And he added the
well-worn refrain, 'We want *great alteration*—but we want
nothing new.'[1]

Great alteration indeed was wanted to restore the old mobility
to English society. War, the dislocation of trade, the growth of
population, and the increase of land-enclosures had all combined
to transform the world it had known. It did not seem possible to
return to those 'ancient practices of the Constitution', which, if
ever they had flourished at all, had done so in some long-gone
arcady, in a green and pleasant land. Pitt's domestic despotism
had gone, but the brutality of outlook it had inculcated in
property-owners had not; and even the despotism itself was to
be repeated between 1817 and 1820. The ameliorating influence
of 'New Whigs' had been overlaid by a Toryism which forgot
that paternalism was not only a role for authority but its justifi-

[1] *Political Register*, November 1816.

cation. 'I do believe,' exclaimed the Radical Sir Francis Burdett in March 1808, 'that the House of Commons is the only spot in all the world where the people of England are spoken of with contempt.'[1] Cobbett watched this trend. It was a new notion, he commented in 1817, that it was proper to consider the labouring classes of the country as a distinct caste. Gentlemen referred to them nowadays as the peasantry, or sometimes, the population. It was now being made clear that the interests of the aristocracy and gentry were not only *not* the same as those of the people at large, but also that the gentry had no wish to consider them as even similar. Once this became known, the old solidarity that had based itself on the loyalty owed to a genuinely paternalist authority, threatened to dissolve. Thereafter the need to counter this threat underlies and accounts for all the shifts and changes in nineteenth-century politics, and for all the accompanying efforts of politicians to find an acceptable 'programme'—something that, in the Whig heyday, had never been thought necessary at all.

For the people became convinced, by Cobbett's *Political Register* more than by Ricardo's writings on political economy, and by sorry experience more than by either, that the landlords had deserted the interests of their tenantry. If grain was dear, and the rent of land high, the country was said to be in a state of sound prosperity. For this prosperity to continue, the produce of the land must be made as dear as possible, and foreign competition excluded: hence the bar against any importation of foreign corn until the domestic price stood at £4 per quarter. Ricardo stressed what this meant:

> The interest of the landlord is always opposed to the interest of every other class in the community. His situation is never so prosperous, as when food is scarce and dear; whereas, all other persons are greatly benefited by procuring cheap food.'[2]

Moreover, the long reign of George III had seen the passage

[1] Quoted in M. Hovell, *The Chartist Movement* (Manchester, 1918), p. 239.
[2] E. Halévy, *Growth of Philosophic Radicalism* (Beacon Press edn., New York, 1960), p. 330.

through parliament of some 5,000 enclosure Acts. This locking-up of five and a half million acres of land had gone far to destroy at least one 'ancient practice': the system of open-field farming that had given to a countryman something he could look on as his particular stake in the country. To such a man, the possession of a goose or a cow, and the right to keep it on the common land, had always meant much more than a vote. When the common land was enclosed this right was lost. Ultimately, as a consequence, the vote became more prized than the cow. For what good was it to own a beast, if there was no land for grazing?'[1]

While land was being enclosed, the population was increasing by nearly six millions. The countryman, his stake removed from him, became a labourer on other men's property, working for wages, or else a 'hand' in one of the new factories. This calling of a man by a part of his anatomy was another example of the process of degradation that had already reduced the name of 'the people' to 'the population': and even 'hands' in their turn were to become 'labour'. (A parallel was to occur in the record of the overseas Empire, where Chinese or African servants, perhaps men in middle-age, could be spoken of as 'boys'.) The problems arising from the employment of 'hands' in factories, because of their novelty, attracted the attention of the political economists from the outset; but by 1834, when one in every eighty of the population was employed in cotton-mills, this was still less than a third of the number of female domestic servants, and only an eighth of those employed in agriculture. Even when, in the 1850s, Great Britain was the undisputed workshop of the world, with the textile industry as one of its principal dynamos, 'cotton' still employed only 1·7 millions of a total population of 21 millions.[2] It was therefore the countryside that was and went on being the scene of the greatest hardships, the countryside where the able-bodied pauper, supported by the Poor Law rates, abounded—and, because he was so supported, proliferated. The rates themselves, which cost the taxpayers £1 million in 1770, had risen to £4 millions by 1800, and to £8 millions by 1817.

[1] 'Three acres and a cow', was a critical description of Joseph Chamberlain's 'unauthorised programme' of 1885; see p. 289, *infra*.
[2] J. D. Chambers, *The Workshop of the World* (Oxford, 1961), p. 20.

The taxpayers themselves were, in the main, landowners. Between 1799 and 1816, when they got it removed, an income tax at two shillings in the pound produced £172 millions. If, then, post-war landowners were selfish, it was in part because they felt they had already paid more than their share towards the country's security. The Poor Rates, for ever increasing, seemed to them yet another 'sinking-fund' for the wealth of the nation. Hard times hardened these attitudes. For the post-war dislocation of society, and the fracturing of its perspectives, there were no precedents. The promotion of many to the role of employer, the demotion of many to the ranks of the employed, the consignment of a great many more to the oblivion of the pauper, and the substitution of money for service as the nexus of society—these were all phenomena, dismaying to a point where the use of reason to discover whys and wherefores roused more anger than anything else. David Hume had noted that the rules which come to be accepted by men are determined by their needs, their capacities, and their environment. In this new situation, the needs could not be met, the capacities could not be used, and the environment was being disrupted almost as men watched. It was accordingly unlikely that rules imposed by authority alone would be accepted, given that deference to which authority in England had long been accustomed. Nor were they. A new basis for the rules needed to be established. As in Cromwell's day, a search for 'fundamentals' had to be begun; and, after Waterloo as after the death of King Charles I, men could not agree what these should be.

Men who had positive views on the situation were more often reckoned to be insulting misfortune than aiding it. Detachment was suspect because no one, in a shifting world, could truly be that detached. So Cobbett continued his weekly anathema. For him, Wilberforce, prime mover in the passage of the Combination Acts (1799, 1800) prohibiting Trades Unions, was only a crafty political hypocrite, whose dogged Toryism in domestic affairs[1] merely served to expose the cant in his campaign for the welfare of Negro slaves—people who were not, whatever else might be said about their condition, actually starving. All the

[1] E.g. his dislike of dissenting ministers; Meikle, *Scotland and the French Revolution*, p. 207.

political economists, the men with messages, the social analysts of the day, were empty-headed dupes. In particular were the Reverend Thomas Robert Malthus 'and his crew' hard-headed ruffians, the hardness of whose heads was as nothing compared to the hardness of their hearts.

Malthus was a pioneer of that type of social planning which, while seeking to benefit humanity, cheerfully ignores the sentimental and irrational habits of mankind. His findings concerning the social predicament were impossible for those emotionally involved in it—and these were the great majority—to accept. In his *Principles of Population*, first published in 1798 and in its sixth edition by 1826, Malthus had arrived at certain iron conclusions. The right to subsistence was an illusory right. Man had to fight for whatever recognition he could get. Once this was obtained, then he might put forward some doctrine of 'right', but this was only the name he himself gave to his own estimate of the things he needed to increase his meed of recognition, and with it his sense of self-respect. Nature herself was well accustomed to withholding or withdrawing her recognition, for she used poverty and vice as her means of restricting the numbers of the human race. The regulations of the existing Poor Law, in contrast, merely served to increase these numbers without increasing the amount of their subsistence. The vast sums of money spent from the rates, money the country could ill afford, was simply being squandered for no return. Hard though it might appear in individual instances, Malthus was convinced that

dependent poverty ought to be held disgraceful. Such a stimulus seems to be absolutely necessary to promote the happiness of the great mass of mankind; and every general attempt to weaken this stimulus, however benevolent its apparent intention, will always defeat its own purpose.'[1]

It was a powerful if unattractive argument: and the Whigs' Poor Law Amendment Act of 1834 was to adhere to it. This act had two principles: that relief should not be offered to able-bodied persons and their families, otherwise than in a well-

[1] *loc. cit.*, chapter 5.

regulated workhouse; and that the lot of the able-bodied pauper should be made less eligible than that of the worst-situated independent labourer outside.[1] But, then as later, a starving man was not helped by the opinion that it was an error he was born in the first place, nor a husband and father gratified by having it pointed out to him that a wife and children were luxuries, to which, if he could not support them, he had no right at all.

Malthus' greatest unpopularity however sprang not so much from his cold view of the vanity of human wishes as from his continuing conviction that rights, like other abstract notions, were only a creation of the human intellect, not something granted from on high to encourage and inspire—a view considered the more repellent in that he was, after all, a clergyman. Rights of man, then, seen through the Malthusian prism, were all very well for those who could afford them. They might, for example, be allowed to have their head in the United States of America, where the population was able to double itself in every generation without anyone having to starve, and where the very name of peasant was unknown; but American conditions were peculiar, and by their very nature untranslateable into English terms. In this at least many Englishmen agreed with Malthus, for throughout the nineteenth century they translated themselves to America, the better to appreciate the peculiar conditions to be found there. By the 1860s the average annual emigration from Great Britain had reached a figure of 168,000, three-quarters of which went to the United States. As a result, employers looked on the Republic as a 'pirate' of their own labour force; for as American wages rose, English wages tended to rise with them, though never so high or so far.

Yet the existence of social analysts, whether dupes or ruffians, met a social need. They sprang into prominence in the years after Waterloo, and 'political economy' became accepted as a science, however dismal, because the problems of the time demanded from its best minds—or, at any rate, from the best minds it could get—a close attention both to the assumptions and to the machinery of national governance, of a kind that had never before been called for.

Comfortable mid-eighteenth century squires had distrusted

[1] Hovell, *Chartist Movement*, p. 78.

Whig politicians more because they were politicians than because they were Whig: politics and Whiggism were indeed the same thing. In so far as they had been able to perceive a Whig principle at all, they had identified it with a spirit of self-seeking cupidity, coupled with a love of interference with matters normally best left alone. Sixty years later, Radicals well to the left even of those 'New Whigs' who were keepers of Fox's flame, had plainly made an advance upon this principle. Many of these, Dissenters in religion and professionally disputatious (Pitt's own name for Dissenting ministers was 'black jacobins'), were laying ever broader foundations for 'politics' as a profession. Their very name of Radical, which seems to have become a noun about 1819, indicated a zeal in them for perpetual motion, for a continuous tampering and tinkering with the structure that had weathered so many storms.

But, even if what Radicals were doing repelled a Tory's mind, he could not ignore it. Men with ideas were now able to find an audience which would, in happier days, have been denied them. In the main they were men of what Adam Smith had called 'the middling classes', a term that was to catch Disraeli's fancy; and, not unnaturally, one of the main ideas they promoted was that of the virtue and value of the middle class. It was this class, they declared, that, with its enterprise, intelligence, rectitude and freedom from outmoded practices, would act as the saviour of society. It had already begun its task. A new generation of 'Saints' had arrived, impressing their humanitarian ideas on many spheres of life, and setting up moral standards for middle-class behaviour of a remarkably durable kind. And, while this 'Clapham Sect' of well-to-do Tories was mapping the safest route to the new Jerusalem, philosophical Radicals innocent of religious opinions were blowing up the obstacles that lay in the path of intellectual and political advancement.

In 1815 Jeremy Bentham was 67 years of age. He was by then the high priest of that kind of commonsense which, in love with its own standards, either refuses to recognize the existence of, or remains merely irritated by, the great deal of nonsense that governs the outlook and conduct of human affairs. (In contrast, George Canning, a statesman where philosophic

THE DISLOCATION OF SOCIETY

Radicals were not, always took care to inspect the nonsense as well as the sense of any given situation.) Men who saw things this way, unconscious that their thinking—like everyone else's —was guided by certain emotional assumptions, took it for granted that vice was the product of an error of reasoning. Sin (not a word in favour with them) was accordingly the effect, not the cause, of error. Thus, if the reasoning was put right, all would be well, and Hume's axiom about the acceptability of rules would once again apply. The claims of tradition and custom, so much beloved by Burke, indeed might mean something, or they might mean nothing: it depended what commonsense had to say in a particular case. The Radical Sir Samuel Romilly, for example, on hearing that one of the laws he wanted to amend dated from the reign of Henry VIII and had indeed originated in principle in that of Edward I, demanded indignantly, 'What care I whether this law was made by one set of barbarians or another?'[1]—a view that naturally scandalized the innate Toryism of aristocratic Whigs.

The object of political economy, according to David Ricardo, whose totem it was, was 'to discover the laws which regulate the distribution of wealth.' It was not for the State to seek to *make* these laws; it was only for men, having discovered them, to behave themselves accordingly. This chilly programme did not appeal to a great many of Ricardo's contemporaries and disciples. As John Stuart Mill expressed it later in his *Responsible Government* (1861), 'a person must have a very unusual taste for intellectual exercise in and for itself, who will put himself to the trouble of thought when it is to have no outward effect, or qualify himself for functions which he has no chance of being allowed to exercise.' Jeremy Bentham was certainly not one of those with this very unusual taste. From a zeal for discovery for its own sake, he graduated to an equal zeal for the reform of the absurdities he had discovered, so that by 1818 he had become a devoted Radical, ready to dub and dismiss his old friend Romilly as 'no better than a Whig.'

Bentham had originally been a Tory. He had approved what he called the 'chance-medley' of the British constitution, and had convinced himself that all he had to do was to enlighten the

[1] Russell, *Speeches and Despatches*, I, 21, n.1.

aristocracy by means of his codes of conduct, constitutional drafts, and the like. Once their eyes had been opened by a reading of his works, the scales would fall from them and reform would naturally follow. Of this conviction events disabused him, and thereafter radicalism overtook him. His principle of utility served to express his irritation with those who, perhaps guided by Pascal's advice, refused to obliterate themselves merely because their presence obscured, or in some way deflected, the light of Bentham's pure reason.

For example, he despised the principles of English law. Jack Cade had burned all the legal records he could get hold of: Bentham talked as if he wanted to do the same. He condemned the 'Norman yoke', festooned as it was with legal technicalities, in Tom Paine's tone of voice. What was law but an occult science, full of incantations and runes whose mystery was carefully preserved by lawyers? And who were lawyers, but the paid underlings of the aristocratic system—men who, since they depended on that system for their bread, were never likely to hand down a verdict hostile to it? He shared Hume's belief that the complexity of the political and judicial institutions of England constituted a bulwark not of popular liberties but of aristocratic privilege. With the 'glories of the English common law' school of thought (a school still easily recruited) he had no patience at all. Montesquieu's *De l'Esprit des Lois* (1751), which flattered the storied wisdom of the British constitution, was after all only the work of an aristocratic French lawyer who envied the freedom and the power of his English brethren. Blackstone too— whom Bentham had sat under, and disagreed with, at Oxford— had woven his own fancies so deeply into his *Commentaries* that the two strands could not now be disentangled. Both men were, naturally, defenders of their own guild, but if one sought the truth one did not go to a lawyer in the first place: it was not *that*, that was his stock-in-trade. In the world there was both priestcraft and lawyercraft, and little enough honesty in either. The pity of it was that the law had not yet produced its own Martin Luther.

These robust views were of course more calculated to annoy than to convince: Bentham all his life made no room for any diagnoses but his own. (He found the reputation for wisdom of both Plato and Socrates sadly inflated.) All the current jargon about 'natural rights', on which Blackstone—bemused by Locke, whom anyway he had misunderstood—set such store, was not just nonsense, but nonsense on stilts. What use was the American Declaration of Independence, since it began by assuming the thing it was trying to prove?

To Bentham, as to any English Tory, security was always a more important factor than equality. It was the duty of government to protect the inequality of fortunes—fortunes which, by definition, were bound to be unequal. This task of protection was indeed the *raison d'être* of all governance; and the French in this regard deserved a lot less admiration than they thought themselves entitled to, for with all their high-flying theorizing about rights of men it could not be said that they had had any marked success in protecting property. But, if security was desired, how best was it to be attained? Only by recognizing certain facts of life, and by constructing a government around them. A good government—and by 'good' Bentham meant efficient and durable—must not only recognize the interests of those who had political power, it should also respect the interests of the people. It should be at once responsible to the people and accountable for its actions, and these actions must be open to public inspection. It remained nevertheless a paternalist government wielding all the executive power necessary to paternalism.

To be sure, the ruling few were always classifiable as the enemies of the subject many, but the endemic danger in this state of affairs would be warded off if the ruling few had the sense to grant to the subject many a constitution based on universal suffrage, annual elections, and vote by ballot. This done, the people might be left to pursue their own self-interest, which was what they wanted to do anyway; and while they were doing that there was no need to allow them to meddle with the actual business of governing, which they were unable to understand. There were spheres, indeed, where popular interference did far more harm than good. In courts of law, for example. That great emblem of freedom, the English jury system, Bentham had no high opinion of: for what was it a jury most often did to a plain issue in court? Confused it. The judge with his expert knowledge was of far more value. And it went without saying that, of all judges, Bentham himself was the best. He cast himself in the role of a Rousseautesque ideal legislator: the guardian of an incompetent society, and the codifier—like Macchiavelli for his *Prince*—of its laws. The legislator must act as physician to the body politic, probing into every organ to see if it was essential to health—and, if it was not, turning surgeon and knifing it out. Thereafter the career of this rejuvenated body ought to be closely supervised by various expert bureaux. In Bentham's constitutional code one therefore finds a minister of health, a minister of education, a minister of communications, and a minister of public assistance.

That commonsense, together with the principle of utility, were purges too radical to apply to society, if it was to survive at all, was plain to men who had more perception than Bentham was ever prepared to allow them. Whigs themselves came of the paternalist tradition, but theirs was a paternalism more of presence than of action. Drastic diagnosis, surgery of any kind, they continued to object to. Revolutionaries once themselves, they now, like reformed rakes, condemned such excesses. So ardent a reforming spirit as Lord John Russell's never sought to cross the border into the arena of that kind of radicalism that had at its base a contempt for the British constitution as such. When he looked back to his youth, he confessed that he could not help feeling at that time

> somewhat of a superstitious reverence for a system which seemed entwined with our liberties, and almost linked with the succession to the Crown.

The entrenchment of Tories in power after 1815 seemed so natural, so right; for after all they were men

> victorious in foreign war, fortified in the possession of boroughs which gave a majority in the House of Commons, and apparently invincible from a long possession of Government patronage, spreading over the Church, the law, the army the navy, and the colonies.[1]

[1] Russell, *Speeches and Despatches*, p. 24.

If this were so, then a mere attack on the system of borough representation, such as Russell then had in mind, was unlikely to change England in any profound way. But of course Russell and his Whig friends had no wish to change England in any profound way. They wished only to prevent it from tilting over into social disaster, they wished to return to that old state of balance which their predecessors, easy-going as they were, yet seemed to have caught the trick of preserving. They were prepared to renovate; but Radicals were men of a different stamp, men who wanted to innovate, and not a few of them on the ground that any change would be for the better.

These men were, in the main, of a type new to English politics, men who could make nothing of Burke's *dictum* that a desire for innovation was a sure sign of selfishness and narrowness of mind. Exactly who composed this 'middling' class was then, and is still, a matter for personal interpretation. In 1903 the historian of the peerage, John Horace Round, was to note that the term 'middle class', which had formerly denoted those beneath the rank of gentry, had since been largely applied to those of moderate fortune, irrespective of their birth.[1] It is a serviceable definition: certainly better than that of the radical Henry Brougham, the Whigs' shock-troop commander, who in 1830 laboured a distinction between the 'mob' and 'the people'. The latter, properly defined, were middle-class; below this class was the populace, looking up in admiration to their natural protectors. In the continuing increase of the middle class Brougham, like Malthus and Bentham, saw the best hope for the future.

With this the sonorous Whig organ, the *Edinburgh Review*, agreed—but English Whigs, like some English bards, did not always respect Scotch reviewers as deferentially as they ought to have done. The middle class was assuredly a valuable 'interest' in the body politic, but it was unseemly to fawn upon it. The Tory *Quarterly Review*, founded in 1809 in exasperation at the *Edinburgh's* views, had scant admiration for Malthus and Bentham and Brougham and none at all for the supposed virtues of merchants and *rentiers*, and it was therefore always a better guide to the opinions of the landed gentry, whether peer or

[1] J. H. Round, *Peerage and Pedigree* (1903), p. 35.

squire, New Whig or Old. Melbourne's remark on the cock-sureness of Macaulay, self appointed seer to the Whig party, is well known, and sums up a lasting attitude: middle class persons, forever equating faith with works, appeared to think that intelligence was a key that could unlock all human secrets. In his heyday in the 1850s, the greatest middle-class figure in politics was John Bright, who normally caused less resentment for his radical views than for the intolerably self-confident manner in which he expressed them. His partner Richard Cobden, harmoniously intoning that everything that had been done to elevate the country during the past half century had been the work of the middle and industrious classes, was equally hard to suffer. For surely, the outlook for England was bleak indeed if control of its affairs fell into the hands of employers and traders, into the hands of those whom Walter Bagehot characterized as men with 'no bond of union, no habits of intercourse', men who were capable, like Cobden for example, of describing the British Empire as a collection of counting-houses overseas. An England so transformed and so governed would become something akin to the American republic, whose most obvious hall-marks were materialism and a deep sense of public irresponsibility.

Indeed, England might fare even worse, for American Tories had been wise enough to protect the conservative impulse, and with it the future of their country, by establishing a popular respect for a written constitution, while the facts of American geography provided a restless society with huge areas of 'free land'. England had no such safeguards. In the age of industrialism, English aristocrats learned to grasp a point of Tom Paine's they had either ridiculed, or missed—that the unwritten state of the British constitution might prove at the last a two-edged sword. Parliamentary supremacy as a doctrine had been workable, and comfortable, so long as the same sort of men were, from one generation to another, supreme in parliament. A future in which this was questionable, to put it no more strongly, was dark indeed.

Thus the opinion of Burdett, that every man was entitled to participate in the power of making those laws by which he was governed, made Tory minds thoroughly uneasy. Burdett said that in July 1819; it was still shocking Tories as late as 1864, when Gladstone declared his arrival at the same standpoint. As early as 1812, George Canning had insisted at Manchester that it was not a true view of the British constitution that the House of Commons should be all-important, and in direct touch with all the people. England had 'the happiness to live under a limited monarchy, not under a crowned republic.' It was the task of the Commons to control the governors, not to administer the government. He warmed to the same theme at Liverpool in 1818. The main error of the reformers

is that they argue as if the Constitution of this country was a broad and level democracy, inlaid (for ornament's sake) with a peerage, and topped (by sufferance) with a Crown.

This argument was totally false—and not all the 'political ventriloquism' of all these 'ambulatory tribunes of the people' could ever make it true. The next year Canning strongly defended one of the repressive 'Six Acts', designed to prevent seditious meetings. By this Act, no person was to attend a meeting who was not a resident of the district in which it took place. No emblems, caps, or flags were to be displayed, and both the debating societies and the lecture rooms in which the debates took place were to be closed down. Now it was one thing, in Canning's view, to bring together the inhabitants of a of a particular division, or men sharing a common franchise. That was to convene an assembly, of which the component parts acted 'with some respect and awe' of each other. But to amass a multitude of individuals! It was monstrous to confound such a meeting with the genuine and recognized modes of collecting the sense of the British people. Was it by meetings such as these, Canning cried, that the Glorious Revolution had been brought about? By no means.[1]

Since, then, 'the people' had not only no political identity but no right to obtain one, their claims could not be recognized— and the activities of the Manchester yeomanry on the occasion of a 'seditious meeting' at St Peter's Field on August 16, 1819, although as much regretted by officialdom as 'an untoward

[1] *Speeches of Canning*, ed. T. Kaye (1878), p. 225; H. Jephson, *The Platform* (New York, 1892).

event' as Navarino ten years later, served successfully enough to underline this attitude. What, after all, was public opinion, gloomed Canning's colleague Robert Peel in 1820, but a great compound of folly, weakness, prejudice, wrong feeling, right feeling, obstinacy, and newspaper paragraphs?[1] That it was a powerful force the events of a turbulent decade convinced the very many who agreed with Canning and Peel. It was a force which it was commonsense to accommodate, but traitorous to respect: the *Annual Register* rasped in 1831 that the electors that year, carried away by the popular tide, had not elected men whose understanding they could trust, but had selected 'speaking-trumpets, on whose voices they could rely.'

Now as ever, Toryism was not of course confined to Tory benches. The aristocrats in the reformed parliament, one that was expected—by those voters who had returned 320 Whigs and 190 Radicals to it—to set about reforming society at large, were disinclined to overhaul the statute-book, or to apply Benthamite principles to every institution in sight. Whigs might combine with Radicals to remove certain obstructions and remedy particular grievances, but they soon lost what reforming impetus they had possessed—and in many a case that was little enough. Codes drawn up on Bentham's models might, and did, serve for such an area of governance as the vast properties of the East India Company, places where 'the people' were for all intents and purposes not a political factor at all; but if they were applied to English conditions they would open too many doors to innovation, and consequently to the emergence of revolutionary ideas. It was fortunate for the Whigs that the industrial middle classes as a whole, once they had seen their representatives ensconced at Westminster, and their manufacturing towns given a share of the redistributed seats, had no political ideas of any classifiable kind. They were content to follow Bentham's prescription, and to set out in the pursuit of their own self-interest. The Radical leaders of middle-class origin and outlook thus devoted themselves to the campaign for Free Trade. This was easily construed by the working classes as an employers' movement: in the 1840s, the antipathies that developed between the Anti-Corn Law-League headed by Cobden and Bright, and

[1] *Croker Papers*, ed. L. J. Jennings, I (1884), I, 170.

the Chartist movement for a further parliamentary reform on
Benthamite lines, were bitter indeed.

As early as 1831, at a meeting of the London 'Political
Union', with Burdett in the chair, William Lovett—one of the
future Chartist leaders—had risen to declare that the working-
classes suspected the middle-classes of making them 'the tools of
their purposes': hence the workers' demand for manhood
suffrage and the secret ballot. Lovett's suspicions of the motives
of these political unions were indeed shared by Lord Grey, not
surprisingly for different reasons. Grey was fearful that these
extra-parliamentary agencies might become permanently established, and was accordingly the more strongly convinced that
the surest remedy to this would be the passing of his Reform
Bill. The upshot thus relieved Grey's mind, but not the minds
of Lovett and his friends. Founded in 1829 by the middle-class
banker and iron master, Thomas Attwood of Birmingham,
these Unions 'of the industrious classes for the protection of
public rights' were beginning to break up by late 1832; in
Birmingham itself the Union disintegrated, and by October the
working members of the industrious classes had formed their
own Midland Union of the Working Classes. By May 1833, a
National Union of the Working Classes was talking of holding
a national convention, to the great disgust of so distinguished a
radical as Francis Place. In 1834 the passage of the new Poor
Law broke the last chain of sympathy between the employers,
who could at any rate look forward to dying in their own beds
in their own houses, and the employed, who could not.

Those who signed the various People's Charters were trying
to use the political machinery of the day to attain a social end in
the future. It was just this that alarmed those in the ranks above
them: had Tom Paine returned, with a hydra-head? For
Chartists were looking—as one of them, Gammage, openly
stated—for the means of social enjoyment. This was not something employers were prepared to issue them. Place himself
complained irritably of men's simplicity, that they should think
of asking such a thing: Chartists apparently believed they had
only to be understood to have everything acceded to them! A
weightier voice than Place's struck the same note of bewildered
surprise. Lord John Russell observed reflectively to the House

of Commons in August 1839 that it seemed to him that the complaints of the Chartists, in all their placards and in all their speeches, were against the very constitution of society itself. They protested that society was so constituted that they did not have a sufficient quantity of wealth and means of support, and they were of the opinion that, by a change of the law, some new state of society would come into being, by which their happiness would be increased, and their grievances redressed. But

> I do not think any law can pass that would at all tend to improve their condition.[1]

Their condition, he freely admitted, was sad indeed. Very large masses of people grew up in a state of society which it was lamentable, if not appalling, to contemplate. Yet contemplated it must be, for there were limits to what legislation could attempt.

This was the answer of one of the most humane and progressive of Whig leaders to that condition-of-England question, on which Disraeli even then was turning a more sympathetic eye. The Chartists, themselves disorganized and unsure, had to fight their battle in an atmosphere of blank incomprehension. In their second petition to the Commons, presented in May 1842, they insisted that government was designed 'to promote the happiness of, and ought to be responsible to, the whole people.' And this was described by Peel, indignantly and with perfect accuracy, as an impeachment of the constitution of this country, and of the whole frame of society.[2]

Chartists reiterated their six points.[3] To judge from the success of the contemporary movement, the middle-class Anti-Corn Law-League, this was five too many. John Bright, the League's leader, constantly urged that freedom could only be obtained through the electoral body and through the middle-class. In the election of 1841 only 140 seats were contested, compared with

---

[1] 3 H 49, August 2, 1839, 1157-9.
[2] 3 H 63, May 3, 1842, 77.
[3] They were: equal electoral areas, universal suffrage, payment of members, no property qualification, vote by ballot, and annual parliaments.

227 in 1832, and Bright went about the country urging men to put their savings into a 40s. freehold, and to use the boon of the franchise this would confer on them. Many sympathetic to Chartism seceded to the ranks of the League, which if it promised less performed more. But many, too, saw the agitation over the Corn Laws as a red herring drawn by the employing classes across the path to universal suffrage and social bliss. Save in rural Wales, the strength of Chartism was industrial and urban. Chartists certainly agreed with the landed gentry, that the repeal of the Corn Laws for which the League was campaigning would ruin English agriculture, but they drew a particular deduction unconnected with the gentry's concern for their own rent-rolls. Repeal, and its consequence of ruin in the countryside, would drive thousands of unemployed agricultural labourers to the towns. There they would form a large pool of labour, something that would be very much to the advantage of middle-class employers anxious to reduce wages—or, as they themselves usually put it, costs—all round. That Bright, Cobden and their friends were no friends to factory legislation was notorious. Indeed this dispute between Bright and the Tory evangelical Ashley [Shaftesbury] echoed that between Hamilton and Jefferson in the 1790s: again it was the Tory landowner who took the paternalist position, denying that the devil had a right to the hindmost, and again it was the advocate of industrial expansion who thought that this alone, left free to operate without interference from the State, would allot the greatest benefits to the greatest number. (Bright also made the point that, if anyone's condition of labour warranted inspection, it was that of the rural worker, who, living in cottage squalor, unknown to and unseen by society at large, drew an average wage of six shillings a week compared with the factory worker's sixteen.) But noisy though it was, this quarrel was overlaid, and was seen to be overlaid, by an essential community of outlook. If the middle-classes' representatives and the exponents of an older Toryism had differing plans for arranging England's industrial future, at least they were not plans that made room for the promotion of democracy.

However, that adjustment had to be made, and that tactics had to be devised which would counteract the current fervours for democratic ideas, was plain to both groups. Tocqueville's analysis of the behaviour of *Democracy in America* (1832) was closely scanned in Europe. His conviction, that the advent of democracy was inevitable, carried conviction with it. But he was convinced, too, that it was not too late to guide democracy's steps. America was important, and a widespread knowledge of American conditions was even more important, because it was in the United States that the first experimental laboratory for the democratic process had been set up. It was from that laboratory that other nations must draw their own lessons in social chemistry, and so avoid some at least of the trials and errors that the Americans themselves, working without blue-prints, had inevitably made. The great question, so Tocque-ville instructed his European audience (with a touch perhaps of that 'chill sententiousness' Lord Acton later objected to)[1] was not whether aristocracy on the one hand, or on the other democracy, could be maintained. That was not the point at all. The question was,

> whether we are to live under a democratic society, devoid indeed of poetry and greatness, but at least orderly and moral; or under a democratic society lawless and depraved, abandoned to the frenzy of revolution, or subjected to a yoke heavier than any of those which have crushed mankind since the fall of the Roman Empire.

Tocqueville saw more clearly into this troubled future than his contemporaries could well bear. Once a nation had modified the elective qualification, he declared, it would proceed sooner or later to do away with the qualification altogether. This deduc-tion was shuddered away from by Whigs, Conservatives, Liberals, and Radicals—by English Toryism as, after 1833, it was represented on both sides of the House of Commons. Mem-bers of parliament were conjointly resolved that, if democracy was indeed to arrive upon the English political scene, it must do so only—to adapt Canning's words—'inlaid with a peerage and topped with a Crown.'

Within this framework Tories were prepared to work. They

[1] *English Historical Review*, iv, April 1889, p. 391.

had first to arrive at a correct assessment of the political facts of life, and adjust their ideas in consequence. It was the Tory party, therefore, that emancipated Catholics in 1829, repealed the Corn Laws in 1846, and passed the Reform Act of 1867. Canning and Disraeli were both leaders who taught their followers how to grasp and assimilate a particular situation. In contrast, such a leader as Peel, whom facts took by surprise, was fated in the end to find himself leading only a group of personal disciples. The course of events since 1815, moreover, itself played a part in educating Tory opinion, in accustoming it to the unexpected, even to the undesirable. It was plain that the too severe repression of the post-war period had not preserved the desired *status quo:* both the Peterloo massacre of 1819 and the public delight in Castlereagh's suicide in 1822 were clear symbols of Tory failure. Francis Place considered that the spectacle of the marital troubles of the King and Queen, presided over by the Radical Brougham as queen's counsel, made the middle and working classes stand less in awe of aristocracy and its ways than ever before, and had constituted 'a step towards democracy which can never be retraced.'[1] In these circumstances, Canning sought to identify Toryism with something other than reaction. But positive action was still thought risky: things might be 'ameliorated', but not changed—a viewpoint that has left good William Huskisson at the Board of Trade, busily paring the protective duties, a rather lack-lustre figure in Tory historiography. After Canning's death, Peel brought himself to emancipate the Catholics. But the positive implications of this act upset him as much as it did his party, and he resigned his seat for Oxford—only to be upbraided by his friend Croker of the *Quarterly*, who saw in Peel's voluntary resignation a recognition of the as yet unacceptable principle of 'the mandate': 'a democratical and unconstitutional proceeding, and a precedent dangerous to the independence of the House of Commons.'[2]

Peel, made timid by his own audacity, could not bring himself to stomach any scheme for parliamentary reform, and here his strategy failed his party. His colleague Wellington detested

[1] British Museum, Place MSS. 27789, 123.
[2] January 31, 1829; *Croker*, II, 7.

both reform and democracy even more keenly than he did, but Wellington knew when to retire from a stricken field. Yet his retirement was orderly, a text-book drill: he would not adopt, as Peel was to find himself doing on the question of the Corn Laws, the enemy's colours. Peel's misfortune was that, as an *émigré* from the industrial north, he was trained to, but not bred in, Toryism. It was not with him, as with Wellington, instinctive.

The Whigs left him to take the consequences. In 1845 their leader Lord John Russell refused to form a government, thus handing back to Peel what Disraeli, in a celebrated phrase, called 'the poisoned chalice'—the chalice in question containing the measure to repeal the Corn Laws, maintenance of which was the stoutest plank in the platform of Peel's own party. In fact this exchanging of poisoned chalices was to become a commonplace of nineteenth-century politics: Hamlet and Laertes became practised in the use of each other's rapiers. A rigid inaction was no longer acceptable to Tories, since it was clear it might put Toryism itself in danger. No one overlooked how catholic was the taste for anarchy shown in October 1831 by a Nottingham mob, which burned down not only the castle (owned by the Duke of Newcastle) but several factories as well. When property was in danger, action had to be taken. Authority had now to be accompanied by paternalism, overtly expressed in national politics; and both parties took on themselves the mantle of the 'Friends of the People'. The Whigs felt they were the better equipped to wear it; Tories relied on an instinctive understanding of the national situation, jettisoning the Corn Laws with regret, but admitting the necessity. There was more principle in the manoeuvres of both groups than there appeared —but so little of it did appear that it is not surprising that all that the radicals could see in the performance was an unscrupulous desire to cling to office. Tories with Whig measures, or Whigs with Tory measures, were reckoned equally anathema.

Radicals felt this sincerely, as they were certain that somewhere, if a sufficient number of honest men thought hard and radically enough, lay a 'solution' to all the problems of the day —an article of faith to which no Tory, with his ingrained strain of pessimism, could ever subscribe. Cobbett accurately sum-

marized the Radical view when he remarked in 1830 that the
people had long looked upon the whole political battle as 'one
mass of fellows fighting and scrambling for public money.' He
was echoed by the Radical journalist from Ontario, William
Lyon Mackenzie, a future leader of his colony's republican revolt against established Tory rule (1837). Visiting London in
the spring of 1832, Mackenzie was not deceived even as he
watched Wellington being hooted and pelted, and Tory peers
jeered at in the streets. Whigs and Tories were neither more
nor less than

> two factions of wealthy and influential men who have con-
> spired to plunder the great body of the people time about—
> the Whigs taking the helm when the Tories become too
> detestable to be endured, and going below whenever
> Toryism had got a refreshed character by a few years'
> pretended opposition to misrule.[1]

This damaging assessment many an abler Radical than
Mackenzie, notably Henry Labouchere and Lloyd George, were
later to make part of their stock-in-trade of invective.

That Radicals were firmly convinced of its truth went without
saying: but the very fact of their conviction bitterly alienated the
Whigs. For what a miserable and squalid conviction it was!
—sure proof, to Grey, that Radicals aimed at nothing but 'the
degradation of all public character, their watchword being that
all Ministers are alike.'[2] Grey expressed this disdain in 1810,
but twenty years afterwards he felt no differently. Yet the
Whigs' own conduct was considerably to blame for the continuing currency of the Radical accusation. The fact that it was
the support of the Tory House of Lords under the mute guidance of Wellington, sitting with his hat pulled down upon his
brows, which allowed the Whigs to carry through the third of
Grey's Reform Bills (April 9, 1832), could be quoted against
them. Clearly, the Tories in opposition agreed to let the Whigs
in office have their way, because they were gambling on the

---

[1] W. Kilbourn, *The Firebrand* (Toronto, 1956), p. 103.
[2] Trevelyan, *Grey of the Reform Bill*, p. 169; and 'Is there one among them with
whom you could trust yourself in the dark?', p. 188.

chance that the latter would prove strong enough thereafter to keep their radical allies on a stout chain.

It was a fair risk. Grey had used his son-in-law, 'Radical Jack' [Lord] Durham as go-between and translator, but when, after 1833, this function was no longer considered vital, the Whigs saw to it that Durham was deported to the snows first of St Petersburg and then of the Canadas. In behaving thus the Whigs were true to their tradition of social exclusiveness, which took care to see to it who was and who was not a welcome guest at Holland House, the senior shrine (Brooks's being the junior) where Fox's friends and relatives guarded his flame. A previous generation of Whigs had used Burke, this one used Whitbread and Tierney, Brougham and Macaulay. But none of these men ever found their way into the inner circle; the most significant of them, Brougham, Grey planked down as Lord Chancellor upon the Woolsack to keep him out of the political arena, where he would have continued to cause his betters embarrassment. Moreover, the events of the 'July days' in Paris in 1830, overlaid as they inevitably were on failing memories and hearsay of catastrophe in 1789, had not disposed Whig aristocrats to put their trust in Radicals—for see what had happened to those French aristocrats who did! The Chamber of Peers had been reduced by a third.

But although Radicals were kept at arm's length, everyone saw how pervasive their political influence had become. It is likely enough that it was the decision taken in 1836 to publish the division-lists in parliament—in other words, to tell the public who had voted for what measure, and which of their representatives had not even troubled to be there—that most forcibly affronted members of the reformed parliament with the new conditions under which they must all live. Such a thing brought the hot breath of the people into Westminster. A century before, in the time of Walpole's ministry, Pulteney had expressed the opinion that 'to print or publish the speeches of gentlemen in this House—looks very like making them accountable without doors for what they say within.'[1] It looked very like that still, and many of Pulteney's posterity felt as indignant as he about the idea: Greville grumbled that the

[1] Lecky, *History of England*, II, 58.

existence of a press gallery in the new House of Commons was quite inconsistent with standing orders. In the immediate aftermath of Reform many feelings were bitter, and many fears exaggerated. Wellington confided to his friend Croker in 1833 that power had passed from gentlemen to shopkeepers; and the Municipal Corporation Act of 1834, which put the towns under the rule of elective corporations chosen by the ratepayers, was thought by many a country Tory as a greater blow to the established order than the Reform Act itself. In the Lords, Lyndhurst (who was the son of an American Loyalist) declared indeed that what was aimed at in the Corporation Bill was the destruction of the Conservative Party, the name under which Peel was organizing the opposition. Meanwhile a Tory University member asserted that the Dissenters' cry against the Church of England would certainly have been *delenda est Carthago* had they been able to understand Latin—an attitude also adopted by Disraeli, who remarked that he now had to translate his classical epigrams for the benefit of the capitalists who sat around him. But, as the reformers' zeal eased, and it became clearer that the Whigs were not going to allow the Radicals their head either in domestic or in colonial affairs, these Tory misgivings dwindled.

II

It was, after all, sensible to accept the fact that times had changed. But it was also sensible to take steps to see to it that times did not change all the time, and to do what could be done to decelerate a pace, political and social, that had become too fast both for its own good and for that of the English society as a whole. The underlying idea of a society, of a community, had not been lost. It was still vivid in English minds, and its maintenance was a thing to strive for, the more so because the recent dislocation had made it plain both to the upper and the middle classes at once how precarious, and how precious, were the bonds that held it together. If hopes for the greatest happiness of the greatest number were likely to be swamped by the sheer weight of numbers themselves, as Malthus' doctrines indicated, then the conditions of *laissez-faire* so much beloved by Radicals required a closer examination. An attention to means for social improvement might prove to be not only a crotchet of the humanitarians, but the most serious public duty of statesmen.

Peel approached this standpoint when he set out the attitude of the Conservative Party in his 'Tamworth manifesto', issued at the election of 1834. This was not a programme for action, it was a recognition of the existing trend. The Reform Act of 1832 was to be accepted by Tories as 'a final and irrevocable settlement of a great constitutional question.' In fact, finality, then and later, was a fluid concept, one whose reality depended on the eye of the beholder. The *Edinburgh Review* was right in saying that the Act had made 'reason the recognized standard instead of authority': in just this lay its revolutionary implication. Peel himself knew this, and defined the light wherein the Act should be read. If 'Reform' implied in spirit

> merely a careful review of institutions, civil and ecclesiastical, undertaken in a friendly temper, combining with the firm maintenance of established rights the correction of proved abuses and the redress of real grievances

—then in that case he could for himself and his colleagues undertake to act in such a spirit, and with such intentions.

The recent Whig innovations, then, were to be conserved, so long as no further innovation grew out of them. To adapt Burke's view of the 1689 settlement, here was another parent who could be allowed no progeny. This was a reading of the situation that many Tories could not accept. In whose judgment was an 'abuse' to be proved? What constituted a 'real' grievance? Peel's manifesto gave no guidance either to the heart or to the head. If it appealed to anything, it was only to a Benthamite brand of reasoning with neither grace nor profit in it. If political action was now to deteriorate to a business of tactics, strategy, and manoeuvre, the Radical criticism was well-founded. This was surely a dereliction of duty.

The attack on this 'secular Toryism', based on shifting sands of reason, torn from its ancient base of authority, came in the first instance from the Church of England. This Tory institution had not, like its legal sister, become 'diehard' in outlook. It had continued to produce intellectual enterprise, and was ready to patronize advanced thinkers so long as these did not seek to subvert the doctrines on which the institution itself depended. It was thus able to be sympathetic to Wesley, but not to Newman—to the Radical, but not to the extreme Tory.

From the 1830s onward, John Francis Newman and his friends in the Tractarian movement were fighting to expunge the same kind of pragmatism from the doctrine and practice of their Church as had, in their opinion, contaminated all true political principle. In February 1841 Newman published his objections to 'Tamworth' in a series of letters to *The Times*.[1] To him it was plain that Peel was not merely accepting Whiggism, which was bad enough—he was identifying himself with it, making an advocate's case for it, in much the same style as the Whigs' own 'great sophist', Brougham. Peel had gone to Tamworth anyway to open a reading-room for working-men: but here again, in Newman's judgment, he should not have been doing any such thing. Secular knowledge was not the principle of moral improvement, and it was moral improvement above all else that English people needed. Even on the mundane Radical principle of utility, how would it ever answer any issue, 'to drench the popular mind with physics?' Such a belief was just another example of those 'heathen charms and nostrums' which modern Liberals, seeking utility in all things in the fatuous expectation that utility was to be found in all things, were scattering broadcast—doing more damage in the process than anyone yet could tell. See how Peel himself, although a good communicant of the Church of England, so far forgot his teaching as to refer to the authority of holy doctrine as 'a brand of controversial divinity'! If men, in reading-rooms at Tamworth or elsewhere, gave up their leisure and devoted their curiosity to the things of this world, they would have none left for the things of the next. Indeed, from that position it was no distance to their denying that there was a next world at all. And where was society then? Were men, in the name of 'Liberalism', in the name of the rights of men, to be robbed of that spiritual consolation and protection that was their true birthright?

[1] They are printed in *Newman: Prose and Poetry*, ed. G. Tillotson (1957).

The idea of human progress, to be achieved solely by human effort, was anyway a gross delusion. In Catholic doctrine, for which Newman was here spokesman, the world was a place of suffering and exile. What else, then, could 'the enthronement of unaided reason' lead to, but disaster? Even pagans had never organized their society without having the notion of some kind of a God. For Him, the new idols of Liberalism were not, never could be, substitutes.

In this argument, there was a singular and lasting appeal, but it was not an appeal that could win masses of men. Lord Acton, a Catholic thinker of the next generation who was not beset with Newman's personal problems of self-realization, was to put it thus: 'Liberty is not the power of doing what we like, but the right of being able to do what we ought.' Merely to state this definition is enough to illustrate the formidable difficulty of impressing it on the minds of men who had already by Acton's day become accustomed to the idea that the aim of Liberalism was to promote happiness on this earth. Liberalism and secularization of thought went hand in hand. Jefferson had well understood this; and it was because Gladstone never did understand it that he drew down on himself the intellectual contempt of his political opponent, Salisbury. In the subsequent era of democratic supremacy, men were to speak of the need for a 'New Deal', or for doubling the standard of living within (or every) twenty-five years. But, for Newman and his kind, the human predicament was part of the divine purpose. The facile Liberalism that supposed it could be got rid of by human action had to be fought, in men's own interest. Liberals were false coiners. It was no task for Toryism, or for a Conservative party if there had to be such a thing, to circulate their currency. Tories had to conserve not what was expedient, but what was true. 'There are entails', Newman warned, 'in more matters than parks and old places.'

Religion was anyway a necessary and practical salve for the wounds a democracy was apt to inflict upon itself. Tocqueville, investigating American attitudes, had been struck by this. In the United States the widespread influence of sectarianism, coupled with the entire absence of any paternalist public policy, had left the people more strictly alone to settle their own salvation than was the case with any other society. They had made a remarkable success of it. Americans kept themselves in order, in a situation wherein there were unlimited opportunities for disorder. They believed, with Bentham, that a man would be led to do what was just and good by following his own interest, rightly understood—but they did not believe this because such a belief was useful. They combined faith with works in a style that perplexed Bentham, who did not look for higher moralities amid the machinery of governance, and who left on record his opinion that Christianity, which had at its core the idea of vicarious sacrifice, was fundamentally immoral—remarking also that the expense of the clergy's support ought to be referred to the same branch of administration as justice and police, since the purpose of all three was the upkeep of internal security.[1] But Tocqueville admired the moral codes of Americans, seeing them as the direct result of their religious cast of mind. In religion for democrats, therefore, there was an obvious social value, as well as a plain sign of the divine mercy.

Bentham indeed in his arguments and diagnoses made the same error as Bernard Shaw a century later. Both assumed that everyone had as logical and unmystical a mind as themselves. England as much as America—in the 1830s and 1840s peopled mainly by English stock—was a country whose response to argument was emotional. Social reformers of whatever kind who forgot this, never made much headway. The 'large ironic English mind' emphasized by G. M. Young in his *Portrait of an Age* (1936), when coupled with the English taste for sentiment, did not warm to the lessons of political economists, or later to those of political scientists and sociologists, who arrive late on the English intellectual stage because they could not assemble an audience. For, unlike the kind of history affectionately parodied, but not pilloried, in *1066 and All That* (which assumes that its readership will share its own assumptions), social and economic history was founded and propagated 'on the Left', as a criticism of the *status quo*. It began in the belief that there was something wrong somewhere, which investigation and publicity would put right. But critical analysis demands from a reader a sympathetic intellectual response. It is a

[1] *Principles of Legislation* (1789), p. 133.

minority of readers who will so respond. Smith, Ricardo, Malthus, McCulloch, Senior and their host of successors all diagnosed as they described; yet none of their histories had the gladdening effect of Macaulay's, which was content to explain how things had come about, and to spread its satisfaction that things had come about in just that way, to so desirable a conclusion.

Patriotism has anyway to base itself on the pride that is taken in the things that have been *done*. Since what has not been done can be no part of the national record, no one who draws attention to these oversights and omissions can expect to please. Although Bentham himself disliked history, denying that a lesson could be drawn from it, and declaring that tradition was more an obstacle than an aid, his countrymen disagreed with him, despite their vagueness regarding historical fact. Images that created self-respect were better, more useful indeed, than no images at all. There was more to Elizabeth I than 'Good Queen Bess': but 'Bess' fulfilled a magical function such as that shrewd *politique* Elizabeth, intellectual sister to France's Catherine de' Medici, could never have performed. Moreover, the objection of Newman and others that the liberals' panaceas for social ills, far from being based on observance of fact, brazenly ignored the greatest fact of all—the continuance of man's state of sin, the consequent degree of his folly—was one that could not fail to strike home on a people, whose majority had at one time or another been under the influence of nonconformist doctrine and the Bible. They therefore did not *want* to make a popular hero of the kind of man his critics wished on Bentham as *his* hero: mean sensual man, pursuing the happiness of a good meal.[1] They caught the commonsense in Carlyle's sarcastic insistence that we had no warrant for regarding ourselves as the centre of the universe— as they did, later, in Herbert Spencer's assertions that not all social suffering was removable, that not all education brought wisdom. They could not plan their lives according to such precepts, but it was in some way good to know that these existed, and that there were men prepared to risk 'popularity' to propound them. In them was a message, of a robust and masculine

[1] Disraeli said that even Mormon had more followers than Bentham; Bryce that Rousseau fired a thousand spirits to Bentham's one.

kind that stimulated rather than depressed, like an effective hell-fire sermon on Sunday.

If utilitarian arguments proved to be imaginatively unacceptable to men in streets, they were doubly so to the Romantic intellectuals of the day, of whom Newman was one and Coleridge another. The Church of England, like other institutions, had to endure the scrutiny of the social critics. It was the harder to do so, in that there was much awareness within the Church itself that there was a great deal to criticize. Hooker's celebrated *Ecclesiastical Polity* had set out the proposition that Church and state in England were one society. This, not true in 1597 when Hooker wrote, had become progressively less true to the point of absurdity. The official life of the English state nevertheless continued to regulate itself according to this proposition, admitting to university education and to the offices of state only those who were members of the state church. Paley, for example, both in his *Reasons for Contentment addressed to the Labouring Part of the British Public* (1793), and in many sermons, supported episcopacy because it attracted into holy orders the younger sons of the nobility. From the late seventeenth century onwards, a series of indulgences relieved nonconformists of their various statutory disqualifications from participating in the life of the country, but the proposition itself was not finally discarded until the state took the official action in 1829 of directly emancipating the Roman Catholics from their previous status.

This discarding of Hooker's proposition struck a blow at the confidence of the Church of England. It was left without its pedestal. If one religion was now to be looked upon 'as good as another', why have more than one? And which one? Questions like these lacerated the souls of men who were asked, many of them for the first time, to defend the ground they stood on. From within the Church, Newman and the 'Oxford Movement' sought to parse and to analyse—in true utilitarian fashion, though they winced to have it said so—as well as to explain and propagate by means of their Tracts those elements in Anglicanism that distinguished it from Nonconformity.

In doing so they were led (or misguided, depending on the viewpoint) to take up a hostile attitude to the state. As they set about renovating the Anglican facade, the Oxford Tractarians found beneath it vast stretches of Catholic underworks, all with the ineffaceable mark of Rome on their masonry. Pope Pius IX, himself with a reputation for liberal sympathies, wittily referred to Pusey, who fell heir to the leadership of the Oxford Movement when Newman 'lapsed' to Rome (1845), as a bell ringing to call the faithful to church but itself remaining outside. But in England it was not a matter for wit. 'No Popery' was still a popular sentiment which neither churchman nor statesman could afford to ignore: the Irish invasion of the industrial towns was to make it, and keep it, even more potent. Radical nonconformists therefore made the maximum capital from 'lapses', and rejoiced in the resultant weakening of Anglican ties with the mass of the people. The Anglican reformers, suddenly discovering themselves accused of reaction, were the last of their community to set out on new, but unexpectedly fogbound, paths. Many Anglicans, after the shocks and trials of this adventure in intellectual and spiritual enquiry, were content to enquire no more, into anything at all. They henceforth cultivated their own gardens with a diligence that prevented them from playing their part in ameliorating the effects of industrialism, as it spread ever more thickly over parish and shire. Their Church was still secure, established, subordinate to the state; but in the state itself Church leaders were for the most part unknown. The Church indeed dispensed with the concept of leadership. Critics saw a hard logic in this: since it was not going anywhere, it needed none.

While many religious thinkers sidetracked themselves into what Peel was perhaps right to call 'a controversial divinity', the dislocations in society continued to attract the attention of men of letters. Many of these became pamphleteers and lecturers, in order to attract a wider audience to this issue and to their views upon it. The Church had taken up the question of authority in the modern state, and had fumbled it. The politicians seemed married to expediency, and unlikely ever to seek a divorce. In this situation detached persons looked both for some means of commitment, and for something to which a man might honestly be committed. Of this group, the poet Coleridge was among the first, and he was able to guide the thinking of such Tories as did not choose to leave their political education

exclusively in Disraeli's hands. Coleridge's analytical gifts
were of a kind very different from those of Bentham, who had
dismissed as rubbish the arguments of the German philosophers
in which the poet had steeped himself.[1] Bentham asked of a
thing, only, is this true?—and used his remarkable intelligence
to supply the answer. But Coleridge wanted to know *why* men
thought the truth what they thought it, and considered 'What
is the purpose of?' a better question than 'What is the use of?'—
a distinction Bentham would have been put to it to grasp.

Coleridge could see a use in the Church of England, considered as an institution. But, had it a purpose? Newman had
put this same question to himself and had found no answer.
(More robust Anglican spirits, like those of F. D. Maurice and
Charles Kingsley, were readier to meet its challenge.) Coleridge diagnosed that since Henry VIII's time the Church had
clung to the Court, instead of cultivating the people—and by
this he did not mean cultivating their acquaintance, but educating and civilizing them. The Church had accordingly lost an
amount of popular ground it was unlikely ever to be able to re-
capture. It had had a chance to do so in the mid-eighteenth
century, and had lost it. When it shed Methodism in 1795, the
Church had plainly exposed itself as incapable of dealing with a
genuine movement of reform, staffed by its own men who had
no wish to break their spiritual ties. The Catholic Church had
once served the Franciscans better. Admittedly, Anglicans were
less worldly than they had been. But the evangelicalism they had
developed was often more a personal than a social attribute.
It rescued individuals, and perhaps only a certain kind of
individual. Even the 'deserving poor' deserved only so much:
the situation of the poor, an evangelical tract of 1834 states
flatly, 'with all its evils, is better than they have deserved at
the hands of God.' Thus the paternalism of such Evangelicals as
Hannah More, or of the Clapham 'Saints', was not attractive:
they believed that poverty of condition, like blackness of skin,
was something immutable, part of the divine plan, and they
took for spiritual mentor the apostle Paul, not a man of broad
sympathies for the unfortunate. The Oxford Movement itself,
although its brand of paternalism took as models such kinder

[1] I have used extensively R. J. White, *The Political Thought of Coleridge*.

Fathers of the Church as St Ambrose and St Cyril, saw the poor indeed as natural objects for compassion and benevolence—but Newman told Pusey in 1835 that he looked on Liberalism as a direct attack upon gentlemen of county influence, and seems ever to have thought the world would be well enough if it could be fashioned after the image of an Oxford college. (He was once in Algiers, and reports that he could not bear even to look at a French ship which was flying the tricolour.) If such was the social outlook of a professedly reforming movement, it is not odd that the north-country name for orthodox parsons was 'black dragoons', or that the anti-Reform Bill bishops did duty for Guy Fawkes on November 5, 1831.

Coleridge agreed with Newman, that Liberalism had no aim of its own beyond that of complying with the demands of the democracy. There was no principle in that. His definition of democracy was also Aristotle's: it was a system under which government did not aim at the welfare of the whole, but was warped to suit the interest of a part only—the commonalty. Plainly this (as Francis Jeffrey had just remarked of Wordsworth's *The Excursion*) would never do. Instead, the State should be organized so as to give due weight to the interests of various sorts of property, or to the claims of ability. Here was an opinion that Disraeli later tried to graft to the stock of acceptable political practice, but his 'lateral extensions' of the franchise were damned by Bright, contemporaries, and historians as 'fancy', and the merits of any plan to establish a meritocracy in England had to wait another century for examination.

Moreover, Coleridge opposed Grey's Reform Act not because it extended the franchise, but because it reconstructed the House of Commons on a wrong principle—the principle not of a representation of interests, but of a delegation of men. It was Canning's own point. Because a great many people now lived in the town of Birmingham, was that a reason in itself why Birmingham should have a representation in parliament? The existence of a dozen Birminghams could not alter the fact that the gentry of England were 'the natural officers of trust, with duties to be performed in the sight of God and their country.' There was now, in society, an over-balance of the commercial spirit. A counterweight was needed—and only the gentry could supply one. How they were to do this Coleridge did not know, or did not tell, but he had a contempt as deep as Newman's for the kind of manoeuvring that Peel's new Conservative party seemed determined to pursue, and which Disraeli in *Coningsby* (1844) ironically summarized in Mr Taper's words as a policy of Tory men and Whig measures.

That Toryism must represent something more than the making of the best of a bad job, must advance some principle of authority, must comprehend a paternalist purpose, was the theme of those who saw the political process as part of a larger whole. Disraeli, always in the thick of the daily battle, sometimes confused the two, and his practices were not always easily aligned with what he declared to be his principles. But his inability in the early 1840s to find himself a secure political haven kept him consistent to his declarations. In the preface to the fifth edition of his novel *Coningsby*, he explained that he had written it because he thought it opportune

> to show that Toryism was not a phrase, but a fact, and that our political institutions were the embodiment of our popular necessities.

This is not far from Coleridge—if things exist, they do so because there is a need for them. Far better, then, to find out the nature of that need than to proceed on the blithe Benthamite assumption that, since the institutions have obvious shortcomings, it would be doing everyone a favour to get rid of them.

Disraeli held that the 'new Conservatism' and its Tamworth programme of acceptance was only an attempt to carry on affairs by substituting the fulfilment of the duties of office for the performance of the functions of government. Devotion to routine, unaccompanied by purpose, would neither promote the happiness of great numbers nor even a simple efficiency in administration. The upshot would be the establishment of a state of 'political infidelity'—the precise state wherein the American republic worked out its destiny. One party would borrow the expedients of the other when it became expedient to do so. Peel's own career was a symbol of this process: this point

Disraeli rammed home with venom when ultimately, in 1845–46, Peel threw overboard the Tory cargo of the Corn Laws and brought the Conservative ship into a Radical harbour under the surprised pilotage of Cobden, Bright, and the Anti-Corn Law League. Peel's political life, Disraeli charged, had been 'one vast appropriation clause.' He had, indeed, 'caught the Whigs bathing, and walked away with their clothes'—but he had not got far before he entangled his feet in them and fell into the water himself. A poetic justice indeed. Mouldy potatoes in Ireland, vagrant professors at home—both, it seemed to Disraeli, had weighed equally on Peel's middle-class mind.

The Tamworth manifesto of 1834 had referred to the need to remove real grievances. But Peel never found out what these real grievances amounted to, as his shocked reaction to the Chartists' indictment showed. Certainly he was not willing to sit at Disraeli's feet while the latter, a rejected junior, read him lessons to the general effect that the palace was not safe when the cottage was not happy. Peel's high intelligence was not blessed with imagination. (Nor was that of his disciple, Gladstone.) When he saw that 'Tamworth' could not take him far, he did not have it in his nature to go exploring an alternative way. Social reform he left to Ashley, and to the evangelicals on both sides of the House. With his principal lieutenant, the Home Secretary Sir James Graham, he denounced the Ten Hours' Bill—drawn up by two devoted Benthamites, Edwin Chadwick and Southwood Smith—as an invasion of the rights of property. He did little for railway or marine legislation, and, by continuing to ignore the nonconformists and their opinions, effectively blocked any hope for the reform of education.

Yet, Disraeli's own record is as unremarkable, displaying little interest in policies in what would now be called 'social welfare'. Of course, at that time these were not 'policies' at all: anything done under such a head was designed only to ameliorate a state of affairs whose basic propriety remained unquestioned, by Disraeli as by everyone else of any importance. (What was actually amiss with society, nobody knew. To accuse Peel of lacking imagination is not to accuse him of failing to grasp the obvious.) Disraeli voted against the Education Order of 1839, against Corn Law repeal—'cheap bread'—in 1846, against the Public Health Act of 1848, against the Mines Act of 1850, and against an Act to set up a General Board of Health in 1854.[1] When Chancellor of the Exchequer in Derby's ministry of 1851, he became (as Lord Randolph Churchill was to become thirty-five years later) as diligent a Benthamite as any vagrant professor, speaking of the financial burden of 'those damned defences' and writing of colonies as 'millstones round our necks'. In fact, Disraeli's contribution to the field of constructive ideas is small. His greatest gift was his clarity of mind, which refused to allow him to be beguiled by the incantations of others concerning liberty, democracy, Free Trade, or anything else. He could occasionally be led away by his own: but once he had defined an issue, it was difficult for his opponents to assert that no such issue existed. That he could see farther than the next man was not proven, but it was believed—and here his alien origin was more a help than a hindrance.

For Disraeli never lost his romantic, outsider's view of England and its institutions. Even when his gifts of analysis led him to make as bitter a criticism of idle aristocrats as ever Bentham made, there was in it as much sorrow as anger, and the anger was reserved for the individuals, not their caste. Aristocrats might indeed have pedigrees that sprang from a spoliator of the monasteries, from a mistress of Charles II, from a placeman of Mr Pitt: but, in the aristocracy that they composed, rested and must continue to rest the natural leadership of the people. The Chartists themselves had gone astray here, for they had not realized 'that in a country so aristocratic as England, even treason, to be successful, must be patrician.'[2] In 1381 Jack Straw had been hanged—but, were some deranged Lord John Straw to appear and lend his patronage to the people's cause, what might he not still effect? It was the lack of a positive, conservative leadership *for* the people that Disraeli continually criticized. In the 1780s Major John Cartwright, the Duke of Richmond, and Christopher Wyvill in Yorkshire—who had

[1] D. Roberts, 'Tory Paternalism', *American Historical Review*, lxiii (1958), 352.

[2] W. Monypenny and G. E. Buckle, *Disraeli*, II (1921), 86. Lovett the Chartist leader agreed. He complained in his autobiography (1876) that the working classes were always looking up to leadership of one description or another: to great men (or men professing greatness) rather than to great principles.

actually revived the ancient 'shire moot' (December 30, 1779) —were all of them gentlemen, and all of them had seen in universal suffrage a return to the 'ancient practices' of the Constitution. The French Revolution had expunged universal suffrage from the vocabulary of respectable politics, and Disraeli had no love for it: but he did regret that such Englishmen should have had no successors, men willing to examine the nature of the constitution in order to bind more closely the community of England. Aristocrats had now to be recalled to a sense of their duty. Cobden would often refer in his speeches to those 'barbarous relics of the feudal system' that still littered the English scene. Disraeli declared his regret that there were not more. For what was the fundamental principle of that system? Why, that the tenure of all property should depend on the performance of its duties! It was this performance that was now neglected; and, as he insisted in 1864 to the wool-workers of Bingley in Yorkshire

> if that principle of duty had not been lost sight of for the last fifty years, you would never have heard of the classes into which England is divided.[1]

It was an echo of Cobbett. The people had become a population, and that population was compartmented into a body of sections, a group of hostile garrisons.

Let no one think, either, that the middle-class capitalist was ever likely to play the role his publicists had found for him, that of saviour of society. It was indeed to his interest to divide it, so that the Utopia he hoped to reach would be one consisting only of wealth and toil. Who would have the money and who the work needed no acute observer to divine. Disraeli assured his audiences that, if he upheld the preponderance of the landed interest of England, he did so out of no snobbish love for aristocrats or from any particular fondness for their society or favours —he did so 'not for the advancement of a class, but for the benefit of the nation'. The middle-class thought, and would continue to think, only of itself: there was nothing there to lift the spirit or the soul. Was England to be turned into 'a sort of spinning-jenny, machine-kind of nation'? The true wealth of a

[1] Monypenny and Buckle, *Disraeli*, II, 248.

nation, as Adam Smith, wiser than a host of his successors, had not forgotten to point out, lay in the character and well-being of its people; and in *Sybil* (1845) Disraeli expressed his hope that England might once more come to possess, with a free monarchy, privileged and prosperous subjects.

While he attacked the middle-classes, Disraeli was even less kind to the Whigs who had made themselves their ally, while continuing to keep them socially 'in place'. (Lord Russell shocked 'society' in 1866 when he asked Bright to dine at his house—this, after Bright had been a major figure in English politics for a generation.) Whigs in what should have been vital years after 1832 had never bothered to have the Prime Minister of their professedly popular party in the House of Commons. Their zeal for reform in the future Disraeli discounted. He discounted also their zeal for it in the past. The Whigs as a party, he argued, had only taken up the cause of parliamentary reform after 1819, when it had become plain to them that, under the protective mantles of Pitt, Dundas, Addington, Liverpool and others during the French wars and after, the extent of Tory boroughmongering had become so widespread as to break that grip on the electorate which the great Whig 'Revolution Families' had for so long maintained. Their only way to rectify this had been to reconstruct the parliamentary franchise; and so, they had decided to throw in their lot with philosophic Radicals and all such vagrant professors. Even so, they had taken care in their Reform Act to see to it that while the 'close boroughs' of the Tories were abolished, their own were preserved.

There was enough truth in this reading to make it sting. Certainly they were both Whigs and Radicals, the ostensible promoters of Liberalism, who voted in 1841 to renew the Poor Law Amendment Act of 1834, while Disraeli and a handful of supporters opposed it. It was Richard Cobden, Radical stalwart of the textile North, who discovered 'socialist doctrines' in the humanitarianism of the Tory evangelicals who backed the Ten Hours Bill. Disraeli, presiding in May 1846 over the wreckage of the Conservative party which he and Peel, by steering a collision course, had combined to bring about, made one of his best damaging points. There was no greater opponent of real democracy, said he, than a modern Liberal: and, as to popular principles, I believe they are never more in danger than when they are professed by political economists.[1]

Nevertheless, in all the general consternation that resulted from the disruption of the Conservatives, Disraeli had less difficulty than has sometimes been supposed in leading political Toryism towards a surer assessment of the facts of public life. When Peel retired from the Front Bench he took with him the intellectuals of the Conservative party, the 'Peelites' who before another decade had passed were claimed either by Liberalism or death. This left Disraeli to battle his way forward not against brains but against prejudice, a state of affairs to which a hard life had made him no stranger, and to cope with which he had already perfected a technique. He therefore set out 'to tickle the ears and the fancy' of the Tory gentry. This phrase is Bright's, who, fascinated even as he was repelled by Disraeli, seldom referred to him without hitting some nail on the head. (He was to remark in 1866 that the fact that Disraeli, 'a man of genius', found himself leader of the Conservatives, 'was a proclamation to the world of the incompetence of the Conservative aristocracy and country gentlemen of the United Kingdom'.)[2] Tories were still happiest, it appeared, sitting beneath the wand of the magician. They asked only that his magic, into the elements and mechanics of which they had no wish to probe, should be successful.

For it was well known that 'Dizzy', in an age with its share of prejudice, had no prejudices at all. He was the only man in English politics who would have thought of using both Bright and Napoleon III as barometers of the political atmosphere, and who would have compared the political career with a climb to the top of the greasy pole. His levity was an essential part of his nature, and his playing of the comedian so expert—in the style of King Charles II, with whom he had much in common—that it is not surprising that both his admirers and his enemies should have thought him capable of playing no other part. For example, he might have eventually been forgiven by the intellectual Peelites, Gladstone at their head, for his attacks on Peel, had they ever been able to bring themselves

---

[1] Monypenny and Buckle, *Disraeli*, II, 371.
[2] Bright, *Speeches*, II, 73.

to believe that he really meant them, that he was capable of being shocked by the conduct of Peel, or by that of anyone else. As Bryce, heir to the Peelite tradition, was to put it: 'People did not take his word for a thing as they would have taken the word of the Duke of Wellington, or Lord Althorp, or Lord Derby, or Lord Russell, or even of that not very rigid moralist, Lord Palmerston'.[1]

What Disraeli's ideas actually were, accordingly, was beside the point so far as his political followers were concerned. (One wonders how many of them ever troubled to ask him.) One team of these followers was generally called, not without some amusement, 'Young England'. Its members were Tory Radicals, who unlike other Radicals did not believe in the abolition of privilege, for many of them were aristocrats and all of them were gentry, with Lord George Bentinck and Lord John Manners at their head. The younger men among them (for they were not all young, save in political experience) were strongly influenced by the Oxford Movement, and believed with the religious Puseyites that it was essential to regenerate the society of their day. The dandies in this movement 'wrote as earnestly as they dressed',[2] taking a solemn view of life and themselves which Disraeli never sought to match. Their devotion to 'Merry England', cricket and heraldry was singularly easy to satirize, as Peacock's novels prove. They aimed at loosening the rigid barriers between the different classes (which they said ought not to exist) by the influence of mutual good offices, by the humanizing effects of art and letters, by a common enjoyment of picturesque religious functions, by popularizing the ideas of national tradition and historical continuity, by restoring the merriment of life, and by protesting against the cash-nexus 'as a sufficient summary of the relations between man and man'.

'Young England' thus represented a type of paternalism and idealism that had not hitherto been heard of in English politics. Its very content of Arcadian nonsense—its love of maypoles, for example—appealed to many ironical and sentimental English natures, and the amiable fatheads satirized by Peacock do not leave the same taste in the mouth as Dickens' 'comic' portraits

[1] James Bryce, *Studies in Contemporary Biography* (1903), p. 28.
[2] Saintsbury, *op. cit.*, III, 259.

of the *bourgeois* Pecksniff or Gradgrind. Its presence and brand of argument, if they could not make any great impact on the course of 'politics', had a value none the less, for they served eventually to leaven the Tory lump. The survival of the monarchy, the aristocracy, the Church of England, and (till a very late date) the British Empire, were things that Bentham would have thought impossible, since to all of these institutions were barnacled so many elements of the ridiculous.

As Lecky has pointed out, folly is naturally Liberal, stupidity naturally Tory.[1] Folly implies an original action; and only Liberals, and their motley allies, looked on parliament as an arena for action. Nevertheless, Tories were compelled to admit that there was nothing unconstitutional in a zeal for legislation itself. They reserved their deepest antipathy for extra-parliamentary 'associations', which were not constitutional at all. The aim of all such bodies was to form what they called a 'public opinion', outside of—and because outside of, likely to be hostile to—that of the landed interest. A century of such doings had not made them any more palatable. The Stamp Act Congress, the Irish Volunteers, the Yorkshire Association, 'Wilkes and Liberty', the Corresponding Society, United Irishmen, Daniel O'Connell's Catholic Association, the slavery abolition movement,[2] the penal reform movement, the Colonial Reformers, Methodists 'thinking by batches of fifties',[3] trade unions, co-operative societies, working-men's clubs, Sunday schools (which, like mission schools overseas, were only too apt to give people ideas above their station), 'Exeter Hall', the Oxford Movement, the British Association for the Advancement of Science, and the advent both of the penny post and of the railway—all these at various times were considered to contain enough menace in them to fill the orthodox with doubt and alarm. (Landowners'

[1] Lecky, *History of England* II, 96.
[2] Admiral Lord Rodney, opposing in June 1788 a motion to ameliorate hardship in slaveships, remarked that he knew the West Indies well and had never even heard of the ill-treatment of Negroes there. They were better off than English labourers. Cobbett himself was convinced that 'no black slave ever suffered for want of food'. For the contrary view see R. Pares,' Merchants and Planters', *Economic History Review supplement*, No. 4, 1960, p. 40.
[3] Matthew Arnold's phrase. Dr Chalmers, leader of the Scottish Disruption, retorted that it was better to think in batches of fifties than not think at all in mobs of thousands.

suspicions of the railway proved ill-founded, since their physical control over vital stretches of line put more authority in their hands and gave them cast-iron stakes in the country far more quickly than the normal processes of enclosure ever could.) Many looked upon the Anti-Corn-Law-League in particular, assiduous users both of the penny post and of the railway, as a seditious conspiracy against the established statutes of the realm, a conspiracy moreover whose tactics—mass meetings, banners, nonconformist ministers, Bright, and all—were deplorably vulgar. But even the League was hardly less alarming than the experience of 'the vile touch of Whig Commissioners', eight of whom on a board of thirteen were laymen, in the affairs of the established Church. This last was comparable, or at any rate was said to be, to the Tudor inquisition that resulted in Thomas Cromwell's *Valor Ecclesiasticus*. Life for the Tory, in fact, was sown with tares, and his resentment towards a political atmosphere of Liberalism that seemed better geared to foster than to prevent this state of affairs grew accordingly.

The Tory attitude to the use of Royal Commissions was however ambivalent. It depended very much on what was exposed to the light. The Commission on the industrial employment of children (1842) caused a great shock to run through all ranks of Toryism, on whatever parliamentary benches these happened to sit, and allowed Ashley to put through his Mines Bill without exhausting his arguments or himself. The Royal Commission, although dubbed by *The Times* in 1838 as 'a Benthamite fad', was clearly a useful instrument for doing the detective-work in society, for twenty years of social upheaval had made it clear even to the most a-political of Tories that an accurate knowledge of what went on in England was fundamental to any policy of successful conservatism. Social reforms might indeed prove to be necessary, for the security of all: there was, perhaps, something, if not of course very much, in what Puseyites and 'Young England' kept repeating. Tories were to find thereafter stronger ground from which to combat both the middle-class zeal for *laissez-faire* and the middle-class hope that the authority of the state in England would grow progressively weaker.

A habit of mind that preferred to maintain a *status quo* in domestic issues naturally looked to preserve a similar inertia abroad. War had closed Europe, and put an end to the 'grand tours' of young English aristocrats. As a consequence, a generation of English statesmen arrived at maturity knowing nothing about the thinking of Europeans. The Vienna settlement of 1815 was a valiant and on the whole successful attempt to return to the *status quo ante Bonaparte*. But Castlereagh's Toryism was not of the actively authoritarian kind professed by Austria's Metternich and Russia's Tsar Alexander I, and non-involvement was never a policy that could win Britain many friends. There was general agreement in English governing circles that the Austrian Empire and the Ottoman Empire were both institutions that ought to be preserved. Englishmen with vague memories of Greek particles at Eton developed a half-hearted philhellenism that supported Greek national aspirations against the Turk, but they did not interest themselves in the hopes of the Slav Christian peoples of the Balkans, also subjects to the Turk. The presence of Austria in northern Italy ensured the continuance of peaceful conditions in the Mediterranean and served also to keep French ambitions at bay. Englishmen continued to suspect Frenchmen of an ingrained zeal for political adventure. This was a charge hard to bring home to Louis Philippe, who presided over France in the style of a George Washington, and whose affairs were mainly conducted, somewhat to Disraeli's contempt, by a *professeur* and a *rédacteur*, MM. Guizot and Thiers. But it was much more plausible when levelled at his eventual successor. Thus, although the Emperor Napoleon III always did a good deal to win the friendship of successive British ministries, whether Whig or Conservative, he found them all ineluctably Tory because they were unable to overlook the simple fact that he was, after all and before everything else, a Bonaparte—and therefore, it went without saying, *capable de tout*. The remaining buttress of the European system was the Russian Empire, whose attachment to autocracy was too devoted to attract even the most rigid of English Tory sympathies, and whose mysterious moves in the direction of Hindustan could not fail to arouse Tory hostility. But his disapproval and suspicion of Russia did not imply that rebellion of Russian subjects in Poland, notoriously an event in which the Powers of Europe had long interested themselves, to the detriment of everyone's stability, was a business that a Tory Englishman could officially encourage, either in 1830 or in 1863—whatever the indignant democrats of Newcastle or Manchester had to say. ('We were fighting abroad upon the same principle,' insisted the editor of the *Manchester Times* in 1831, 'as we were fighting the borough-mongers at home. Poland was only one of our outposts.' Poland had its liberation to win, 'and so had we. We have both of us fallen among thieves.')[1]

Some irredentists, if not the irredentism they promoted, could sometimes wring an unwilling approval. Yet the activities of the heroic Kossuth, and the whole movement of Hungarian nationalist aspiration against the domination of Austria, plainly endangered the equilibrium of Europe—even although it was hard not to applaud, unofficially, the London draymen who in 1850 mobbed one of the punitive Austrian generals. Moreover, although the Italian chieftain Garibaldi became a lion of London society on his visit to England in April 1864, this was homage paid more to romance than to *risorgimento*. Palmerston's Whig government did not consider it politic to allow the hero to wander at large in the north, where he would doubtless have stirred to an unpredictable pitch democratic emotions that had always run deeper than those of the more docile south. (Conversely, Kossuth on an American tour made little impact south of Richmond, Virginia.) That Garibaldi's visit to England was potentially inflammatory was proved by its effect on the emotions of one whose waywardness was slowly becoming more obvious, and more disturbing, to his Whig Cabinet colleagues: for Gladstone in May, 1864 delivered himself of the conviction that everyone not personally incapacitated had a right to come 'within the pale of the Constitution'.

On American affairs, the Tory outlook was always predictable. General opinion at first favoured the Northern cause, seeing it as that of humanitarianism and liberty. But as the North itself, for domestic reasons, was unable to publicize these latter aims, it had to fall back on its desire to preserve the Union—and this was not something that could expect to command support

[1] J. H. Gleason, *The Genesis of Russophobia in England* (Harvard, 1950), pp. 127, 132.

from the English ruling classes. If the democratic American Union was at last breaking up, that was a sure sign that the 'great experiment' had been based on faulty premises. The more Americans who became convinced of this the better. Why, after all, in the name of liberty, should the Union be preserved if a great many of its own citizens, some of these highly distinguished, believed that it should not? Was there not a close analogy here, between the thirteen colonies of 1776 and the eleven Confederate States of 1861? Were not these latter fighting for their liberties? How then could a distinction be drawn in the North between one brand of liberty and another? Lincoln's insistence, that the Union was the living symbol of the social contract made by all citizens at the time the Constitution was drawn up, made no appeal to the Englishmen who had not read the Constitution, and who were impatient at any argument that defended republican principles. English journals therefore joined in the Southern lampooning of Lincoln, as a hayseed in the hands of wily men determined to extend the northern empire: both *The Times* and *Punch* contrasted the plebeian Yankee with the 'aristocratic' Southern planter—a figure largely invented by the Northerners themselves, to their own cost—and found in favour of the latter. What was democracy worth, if the only leader it could produce at a time of desperate crisis was a country attorney with a chequered political career behind him, a man no doubt with a gift of homespun repartee, but with no other ascertainable asset? J. L. Motley, the United States' ambassador in London, noted how pleased upper-class Englishmen felt at the news of the rout of the Northern army at Bull Run in July 1861. The real reason for this, he added acutely, was their enmity not so much to the United States as such, as to democracy in England itself.[1]

Moreover, British commercial interests had no objection to make when American rivalry on the high seas was suddenly stopped—for already the great clippers had taken the 'Boston men' to China and Japan and the Pacific Islands, thus troubling the future of Britain's emporia at Singapore and Hong Kong. The Whig ministry, admitting the validity of Lincoln's blockade of the Confederate ports, had logically to admit that the South

[1] Trevelyan, *Bright*, p. 304.

was a belligerent. It did so—and thus put the infant Confederacy on the same juridical plane as the American Republic itself, now seventy years old. To stay neutral while the Confederate commerce-raiders swept the Northern marine from the seas was plainly in England's interest. But intervention in the struggle was not seriously considered by anyone in authority. That the opinion of the lower classes, even in a Lancashire dependent on supplies of Southern cotton, supported the North was well known: Cobden and Bright lost no chance to insist on it. James Bryce underlined it when, looking back forty years later, he recalled that whereas the meetings which were called in London by the friends of the North were open to the general public, admission to those summoned to advocate the cause of the Confederacy was confined to the holders of tickets, because it was feared that in an open meeting resolutions of sympathy with the South could not be carried.[1]

Yet even the hardest-grained Tory was able to appreciate that a popular interest in foreign affairs, although its expression and ideals might differ from his own, was a sign of social health. It proved that conditions of prosperity were able to alleviate rankling discontents at home, and to distract men's attention to matters which they could not, in the long run, directly affect. Men who between 1855 and 1865 made a popular hero of Lord Palmerston, a statesman who never bothered to profess the slightest interest in the 'condition-of-England' question, were plainly not men who were planning to subvert society. Chartists were absorbed invisibly into the community as Cromwell's Ironsides had been absorbed, partly because the conditions of the 1850's allowed them to be better fed. One of their banners had been 'More Pigs and Less Parsons', and although the population of parsons did not diminish, that of pigs certainly increased. In 1845 under 5 million cwt of corn had been imported into the United Kingdom: but the figures for 1847 were 18 million cwt imported into England, and another 15 million cwt into Ireland. Chartists had been frankly amazed at Peel's repeal of the Corn Laws, and Peel's courage established for him a grip on the popular imagination which he never lost. Bright had stated his conviction in 1843 that there was no institution in

[1] Bryce, *Modern Democracies* II, 275.

England—monarchy, army, Church, or any other—whose fate, if attached to the Corn Laws, could not be predicted. But now the Corn Laws had been thrown overboard, these institutions had a new lease. This was a state of affairs which even those Tories who were most exasperated by Peel's conduct could appreciate. (Some, like Wellington, could not: in 1851, when the Great Exhibition was drawing great crowds of the populace into London, he thought it a sensible precaution to ring the city with troops, just in case.) The rising general prosperity naturally increased the self-confidence of the Radicals, who lost no chance to point out that it was their own policies—the repeal of the Corn Laws and the abandonment of the Navigation Acts (1849) —that had opened up this path to social peace beneath the benign banner of Free Trade.

But, now as before, the Tory gentry paid little heed to these middle-class assessments. Even if the pressure of social discontent had eased as economic circumstances improved, its nature had not changed. However peaceful the immediate conditions, so long as the population continued to increase, and the class-structure to solidify, and the Utopia of Wealth and Toil to be hailed as daily more possible of attainment, to thoughtful men the future looked no brighter than the recent past. Conditions were still in flux: affairs had no centre. By the 1850s and 1860s the ranks of 'Young England' were growing more portly and sluggish, but their diagnosis of social dislocation remained as valid as it had been for the 'Hungry Forties'. One thing plainly exposed by the work of the various Benthamite Royal Commissions was the sunken condition of the mass of the people. This had not changed, and it attracted the attention and aroused the comparison of all foreign observers—such as Taine, who emphasized in his disgust the 'fouled hindquarters' of the fair-seeming English society. In 1840 one-third of the men and half of the women marrying in England and Wales signed the register with a mark—although Taine, quoting the opinion of *The Times*, pointed out that this may have been a statistic more of intoxication than of illiteracy.[1] In 1870 these proportions were still 20 per cent and 27 per cent respectively. The Tory stand against any encouragement of the democratic principle in politics had

[1] Taine, *Notes on England*, p. 217.

thus its commonsense basis. Could uneducated men—men who, since they were unable to help themselves, were not likely to make a success of helping others—be allowed to have any further degree of political representation? To shore up the power and influence of the educated classes seemed to Tories a better policy than to set about to level the walls of 'the pale of the Constitution' on a numerical principle alone.

Bright always denied that this was the principle he was steering by. He rebutted the fretful Tory charge that the middle-class capitalists for whom he spoke wanted to usher in the age of a democracy of numbers. This was an 'imaginary apparition', nonsense on the face of it. Surely it was plain that any disturbance or violent action 'of a democratic nature' would prove more dangerous to the industrialists than to the gentry? A burned hayrick could be replaced: it was not so simple to replace and restock a wrecked factory. Industrial England had a great future before it—and since this was so, it could afford neither to have Luddites in one generation nor Chartists in the next, nor any subsequent successors to these anarchic, emotional movements. The proper, commonsense policy was to establish a durable alliance between the middle and the upper classes, and to encourage under this joint leadership all movements that opened up for the mass of the people better paths of opportunity. The people would willingly co-operate in this—if the people were given their security under the Constitution. It was just this, Bright insisted, that they did not have; and it was because they did not have it that they thrilled to the presence of, at best, dubiously 'democratic' heroes like Garibaldi. Aristocrats had once had the sense to diagnose the danger in just such a situation: Grey and Fox had urged household suffrage in 1797. But now, sixty years later,

> if you ask how free popular institutions are working among your own countrymen on the American continent, you are denounced as unpatriotic, and charged with treason to the House of Lords![1]

Tories who refused to see that the future of the country, and with it their own, lay with the forces of industrial capital, and

[1] Bright, *Speeches* II, 49.

with a sane political constitution that allowed for the free play of these forces, were men with their heads in the sand. 'I profess to be,' Bright exclaimed, with accuracy,

> as Conservative as you—I believe, infinitely more so, if you look forward twenty or thirty years into the future.

It was not because of the actions of malevolent Gradgrinds, but because Tories continued to petrify political action that the English had been separated into 'two nations' (an idea of Tocqueville's Disraeli had adapted as sub-title for his *Sybil*). Bright wanted the constitution to be restored to the people— thus once again promoting the old theory that the constitution had at some time, by someone, been taken from the people. Ten men owned half Scotland, 150 men half England—and this, under what over-sanguine Radicals had hailed in 1833 as a 'reformed parliament'! The House of Commons was perhaps no longer entirely a 'parcel of younger brothers', but it was not short of such: in 1860 108 M.P.s were either sons of peers or heirs to peerages. The House accordingly represented not the people, but 'the prejudices, the privileges, and the selfishness of a class'. Any good that parliament had managed to do since 1833 had been the work of those members sent to Westminster 'by the great and free borough constituencies of the kingdom'. And its most disastrous error had been entirely the work of aristocrats —for what had the Crimean War proved, save that the governing classes could not even efficiently carry out the tasks they had monopolized? W. H. Russell's despatches from the front of war to *The Times*, and a subsequent official investigation, had compelled the admission that the British Government and the British Army could neither feed, shelter, nor medically minister to a force of 25,000 men only eight miles distant from a port securely held. No wonder, therefore, that the publication of Russell's despatches had been considered by Tories inside the army and out of it as an impertinence, an adder in *The Times'* own bosom!

Thirty years after the Reform Act it had certainly become very clear to the middle classes that they had not, whatever Grey's generation of Whigs had led them to believe, inherited the kingdom. Their inferiors had got this point almost immediately. As early as 1836 the London Working Men's Association published a pamphlet, *The Rotten House of Commons*, which showed how one-fortieth of the adult male population of the country made laws for the rest.[1] It was thus the power of the landed interest—and not, despite Coleridge, that of the 'commercial spirit'—that needed a counterweight. The gentry themselves were brought to a realization of their own advantageous position by the constant complaints of Bright and others on this very point. The Reform Act had increased the number of knights of the shire, county members, by 65. The forty-shilling freehold franchise had been retained, and to it had been added copyholders and freeholders. All these, together with those tenants-at-will who paid £50 a year in rent, had continued to respect in their votes the candidate favoured by the great landowners. Although some 455,000 voters had been added to the electorate, thus more than trebling it, Bright was right in his assertion that it was the 'unfair' distribution of these votes that held the middle class back from the exercise of real power. Before 1832, 262 boroughs had returned 465 members; after 1832 257 boroughs returned 399 members, of whom 115 represented electorates of less than 200. The ten counties of the agricultural south and west still returned nearly a quarter of all the 658 members of the House of Commons. In 1858, Buckinghamshire, for example, returned eleven members from its boroughs, which had a total electorate of 164,000. Birmingham had two members for its 260,000 voters. Bright reckoned that 330 members were returned by less than one-sixth of the electorate, a situation not improved by the fact that in the average general election, only 10 per cent of the voters exercised their franchise. Moreover, elections were still so costly that only a rich man could afford to put himself forward for a contested seat. (One Chartist demand was that election expenses should be defrayed out of an equitable district rate.)

Passage of time had only accentuated these anomalies. By 1865, five out of six males had no vote, in a population of 29 millions—a figure that represented an increase of 40 per cent

[1] In a population of 6,023,752 males, only 839,519 had a vote, one-fifth of whom elected a majority of M.P.s: i.e. 331 M.P.s were elected by 151,492 voters. Hovell, *Chartist Movement*, p. 63–4.

since 1832. There was no representation for the workers of the country, who earned five-twelfths of the national income. Bright campaigned not for universal suffrage, still universally distrusted, but for household suffrage and the use of the ballot, whose secrecy was the only safeguard of the voter against his landlord, his creditor, or his customer. For it was not the landowner only who exercised social pressure on the voter, the middle-class capitalist did exactly the same thing: Lord Palmerston's fellow member for Tiverton for twenty-four years was one John Heathcoat, a lace manufacturer who gave the borough its principal means of employment. 'Go into any borough like Stockport, or Bolton,' said Cobden,

> give me the names of the large employers or labourers, and I will tell you the politics of the men employed by these capitalists, by knowing the politics of the capitalists themselves.[1]

The Times might reiterate in tones of pained shock how 'mean and unmanly' it would be for an Englishman to vote in secret, 'lurking within some shuttered booth'—but on what grounds did *The Times*, with its long and dubious tradition of anonymous 'thunderings', take cover behind so specious an argument?

Many Tories, with these facts and figures before them, saw no reason to be dissatisfied with the constitutional arrangements as they were. They readily supported Disraeli, who declared his wish to put the country on a firmer institutional basis, and to see to it that any subsequent reforms were not based on democratic principle. But this was more than anyone could do. The principle had already, in 1832, been given away, as a Tory who was never of Disraeli's stamp pointed out in a series of pessimistic articles in the *Quarterly*. Lord Robert Cecil insisted that the precedent of 1832 allowed the constitution henceforth to be altered according to the democratic principle. It had then been established, although even now this truth was burked, that the people could decide questions of policy by their votes at a general election. The 1832 Act itself had been inspired by the idea that an individual had a right to the franchise, and 'not by the principle of balance in which its authors themselves believed'.[2] What right was this?

---

[1] December 4, 1851; Cobden, *Speeches* II, 505–6.
[2] Cecil, *Salisbury* I (1921), 141.

It was one which, Lord Robert sardonically observed, made scant appeal to middle-class agitators for further parliamentary reform. Cobden himself in 1847 had denied that there was such a right, and had to ground his case on the argument that since the franchise was at that time a legal right for 800,000 Englishmen—512,300 of whom were county voters, and therefore heavily influenced by the landed interest—a further unspecified number of Englishmen, who presumably would not be so influenced, deserved to be granted its benefits. For this kind of thinking Cobden and Bright were severely castigated by John Stuart Mill in his *Representative Government* (1861): in maintaining (even although they denied that they maintained) that the franchise was a right rather than a trust, the Radical 'school of democrats' perpetrated a 'moral mischief', the results of which would probably prove irreparable.

From behind his aristocratic emplacements Lord Robert Cecil made Mill's point again. Whoever had first connected the words 'freedom' and 'progress' to the word 'democracy' had done an inestimable service to the democratic cause. The equation thus made was an easy one to read. Ignorance coupled to numbers bred passion, and this passion would prove easily exploitable by demagogues, men who would seek political power 'for the pay and the journey-money'. For what was happening among the professional democrats on the other side of the Atlantic? There the leaders of the federal government had turned the sword on their own subjects, men as freeborn as themselves; and could anyone really say that, however the professed aims of those concerned might differ, the effects of Sherman's harrying of Georgia in 1863 were different in kind from those of the Russian armies in Poland the same year? Here surely was tyranny: of an autocratic Tsar in the one case, of an autocratic majority in the other. Political equality, like every other kind of equality, was a chimera; but the actions of democrats who professed to believe in it made this even plainer than did the actions of autocrats who had never had any truck with the idea. The Conservatism which Peel had steered into a Radical harbour, and which Disraeli was now trying to find an alternative course for, had no answer to this state of affairs. The year 1832 had admitted the £10 occupier. What argument could then be levelled against the claim of a £9 occupier? Or against that of those below?

Disraeli's own Reform Bill of 1859 sought less to answer this question than to swamp it among a host of similar problems, on the principle that the best place to hide a leaf is in the forest. The Bill was designed to add appreciably to the political weight of the landed interest, and therefore included devices of 'lateral extension'. These were dubbed 'fancy franchises' and railed at as undemocratic by the Radicals, who clearly had not read the constitution (1855) of the extremely democratic colony of Victoria in Australia, where such franchises were not thought fanciful. They included a vote for a man who had £60 in savings or who had invested £10 in the funds; for lodgers in £20 houses; for graduates and professional men. But the Bill did not lower the qualification for the borough franchise, and, since the boroughs were strongholds of Whig-Liberalism, Russell marshalled his party to kill it. This action committed the Liberals ultimately to further democratic reform, of a type wherein, as Lord Robert Cecil warned, 'the rich would pay all the taxes and the poor would make all the laws'.

Whigs meanwhile winced at this thought, and in consequence Reform was to be passed only over Palmerston's dead body. Palmerston, who took many things lightly, took the interests of England very seriously. He saw both Bright and Gladstone as conspirators against those interests, and developed a genuine animus: it was owing to these men, he remarked acutely, that the governing classes were faced with 'something more difficult to handle than Chartism'.[1] He rebutted Gladstone's assertion of May 1864 that every man had the right to come within the 'pale of the Constitution'.[2] He reiterated the sentiments of Cromwell, Charles I, and Burke: what every man had a right to was 'to be well governed and under just laws'. But when Palmerston died in 1865 Gladstone succeeded to the leadership, and was constrained to fulfil the pledge he had made. It was no very valiant effort to breach the pale. His Reform Bill of March 1866, which included Disraeli's scheme for a savings-bank franchise, was a measure that would have added some 144,000 men (the £7-£10 householders) to the electorate. It was carried by five votes in

---

[1] Trevelyan, *Bright*, p. 354.
[2] The phrase appears to have been coined by John Wilkes in March 1776.

the Commons but defeated in committee, after a stirring session in which Robert Lowe emerged as the chief opponent of the democratic principle. In May a Redistribution Bill was lost. With Derby's Conservatives back in power, Gladstone wintered in Rome; but Bright stumped the country and whipped up enthusiasm for reform in the great cities. It was left to Disraeli to deal with the consequences of this, and after complex manoeuvring, he produced a Reform Bill in 1867 which added some 938,000 to the electorate, the mass of whom were not householders (at whatever rental) at all, but lodgers. The number of borough electors was doubled, but the number of borough members in the Commons was reduced from 323 to 286 while the number of county members was increased from 144 to 172, thus maintaining Disraeli's principle that the landed interest deserved a lateral extension. But what other principle of his it maintained, was a problem that both baffled and antagonized his contemporaries.

In his Bill of 1859 Disraeli had rejected household suffrage, arguing how dangerous it would be to introduce democracy and its ways into the English polity, dangerous alike to property and freedom. In 1865 his tone had been the same: he assured his constituents in Buckinghamshire that for him democracy implied 'the tyranny of one class, and that one the least enlightened'— and this was the argument, polished till all its facets caught a baleful light, that Lowe made such effective use of in the great debates of 1866. (Bright caused Lowe's most famous passage to be printed in a pamphlet, to arouse the indignation of the working classes 'If you want venality,' Lowe had rhetorically enquired,

> if you want ignorance, if you want drunkenness, and facility for being intimidated; or if you want impulsive, unreflecting, and violent people, where do you look for them in the constituencies? Do you go to the top or to the bottom?)[1]

But, in 1867, Disraeli made the Tories his accomplices in 'dishing the Whigs'—the phrase of his leader, Lord Derby—by passing,

---

[1] 3 H 182, March 13, 1866, 147–8. Cf. Alexander Hamilton's speech of June 21, 1788—'Look through the rich and the poor of the community: the industrious and the ignorant. Where does virtue predominate?'

as Grey in similar circumstances had done in 1832, a Reform
Bill far more radical than anything that the Radicals themselves,
hemmed in as they were by their Whig overlords, could ever
have passed. This action confirmed Disraeli's reputation for
slipperiness, which he never lost thereafter. He had attacked
Peel for 'political infidelity': now, Lord Robert Cecil wrote
bitterly of 'the atmosphere of pervading falseness' which, due to
Disraeli's own behaviour, enveloped the public scene. Elder
statesmen of a later day, some of whom had greatly profited
from Disraeli's perspicacity, all agreed, when they looked back
to the events of 1867, that these constituted the great watershed
of the century's political life.

Professionalism in politics was now become a virtue. Tactics
took precedence over policy. Electors had to be wooed, 'plat-
forms' and programmes had to be constructed, party organization had to be perfected and individualism disciplined; and the
great men of the day, if they wanted to remain great men, had to
find the common touch, make the broad appeal. As it turned out,
Tories found this less hard to do than Liberals, for on Liberalism
was laid the added duty of perpetuating a programme that would
epitomize their doctrines. This was not simple, more especially
since the amount of constructive ability within the Liberal party
was always small. The single Liberal who had both a programme
and the capacity to maintain it against odds was Joseph
Chamberlain—who was never granted elbow-room by his
colleagues. But Tories had no need to convert and commit themselves to action. Their Toryism retained its magnetism. It
guarded the social codes and conventions of the time, and its
authority remained unquestioned. Its effect on the most lately-
arrived of 'new men', the rich commercials who wished less for
political power than for social acceptance, was especially marked.

These were the men who were now most to insist on the distinctions between 'classes'. Such an insistence had been unknown
in the pre-industrialist times when people had known and kept
to their stations; but it inevitably added a new lustre to the
position of the man of rank and birth. The very separateness of
aristocracy and gentry, the confidence of their caste, the glamour
of their tradition, were things of great political and social value.
This prestige was stronger in the countryside than in the towns.

In the country the squire, whether as Master of Fox Hounds or as Justice of the Peace, was still respected for his especial skills —although incompetence on the bench was more socially permissible than incompetence in the saddle. In the towns the member of the 'ruling class' was now a less identifiable figure. In the previous century a duke wore his orders in the street, and placed his armorial bearings on everything he owned. But in 1806 the House of Lords thought it in poor taste when the Marquis Wellesley, who had laid aside the trappings of his Governor-Generalship of Bengal but not their psychological effect, addressed them in his full regalia. Perhaps Louis Philippe, the Orléans prince who after the 1830 Revolution in Paris was called 'King of the French' and walked the streets carrying an umbrella, was thought to be taking this democracy of appearance a little far: a nobleman, did he actually find himself in the street, should surely have been impervious to rain. Yet there was now a tacit consent among aristocrats that they should be publicly invisible, and they modified their social behaviour accordingly: Melbourne and Palmerston remained incorrigibly eighteenth-century in their outlook, and owned cheerfully to sexual indiscretions, whereas Lord Hartington, a Whig grandee of the next generation, did a languid best to conceal his. But this self-effacement did not imply any loss of self-confidence. Aristocrats lived in a new world, but it was one they were determined to control. In the title of the 1832 Reform Act the reference to 'the people'[1]—who had never previously had such statutory recognition—was correctly taken by the ruling class as an omen that there were to be new conventions, new gradations, in the ranks of society.

'Society' was anyway a more closely-knit concept than that of 'the community' at large, composed of 'the people', who had now a political name but no social habitation. It was time, then, for the aristocrats to close society's ranks, for whoever 'the people' were, their opinions would remain self-centred, their outlook narrow, and their culture incommunicable. It was time to harden rather than weaken aristocratic codes of behaviour, in order that the value and utility of these codes should at least penetrate the consciousness, even if they never reached the full understanding

[1] Its title is: An Act to amend the Representation of the People.

of, these *arrivistes*, and shape their future political behaviour accordingly. It was time—to borrow a term describing the authoritarian aspect of Anglo-Irish history—to re-establish an 'Ascendancy': in this case not one of a particular religion, but of caste, and of the authority which is its natural accompaniment.

CHAPTER V

THE SURVIVAL OF
THE ASCENDANCY

In 1846, while in the throes of repealing the Corn Laws, Peel made a point with feeling. It was no easy matter, he declared, 'to ensure the harmonious and united action of an ancient monarchy, a proud aristocracy, and a reformed House of Commons'.[1]

A generation later, when the House of Commons had been reformed once more, this problem had intensified. After 1867 (the year Stanley Baldwin was born), Great Britain entrusted its future and its fate to the impulses of a single chamber in a democratic system.[2] Nor was democracy in Britain, like its elder brother in the United States, checked and balanced by formal regulations. Its freedom of movement was unhampered by constitutional safeguards, on whose utility Hamilton and Madison had laid such stress. There were rules governing the succession to the throne, the use of royal prerogative, and the privileges of parliament; but these, together with the statutes of the realm, had been promulgated by men of property during centuries when 'the people' was a patient, and never expected to become an agent, of governance. When the 'third estate' of the realm invaded the arena wherein the rules of play and the habits of authority reflected the interests of the other two estates, it was plain that here was an emergency that no unwritten constitution could cover. There remained only a series of precedents and conventions, based on an assumption of continuity. On the power of these to bind and fix both public and

[1] Quoted in A. Ponsonby, *The Decline of Aristocracy* (1908), p. 106.
[2] Bryce, *Modern Democracies* I, 32.

private action, the political and social stability of the country was henceforth to depend.

This was plain, however, only when attention was paid to the matter. But Peel's interest was not reflected at large. The mass of the people did not wish to involve themselves in political action at all: 'united action' was beyond both their means and their grasp. Tocqueville had pointed out that the affections of men generally lay on the side of authority—and he had added that, because this was so, patriotism did not survive (as the Normans could have confirmed) in a conquered country. In England these affections had not altered. Disraeli's Reform Act of 1867 had changed neither the habits of the authoritative nor those of their subordinates.

For all the heirs of the utilitarians—whether Radicals, socialists, or imperialists—were as convinced as Bentham himself had been, as any Whig had always been, and as every natural Tory still was, that 'the people', now politically identifiable, living within the pale of the constitution, were to be *led*. To be sure, they could not be led, any longer, by the nose; but, as Bagehot insisted in his *English Constitution* (1867), 'we have not enfranchised a class less needing to be guided by their betters than the old class; on the contrary, the new class need it more than the old'. There was, then, still work for paternalists. The task of governing the people had become more complex. A challenge now faced politicians, how at once to give to the people what was good for them, and how to get them to agree to it. Around the ways and means of doing this, disciplined parties came to be formed, each with its serried ranks of Tuscany that could scarce forbear to cheer the sway of political fortune from one side to the other, provided they were assured (as they were) that it was not they but the various courageous heroes in the van who were expendable. For, however they set about it, and whatever difficulties and anomalies they met along the way, men with the habit of authority were still convinced that the tried and obvious merits of 'government for the people' clearly outweighed the problematical claims for 'government by the people'.

In holding this conviction, and in acting according to it, they were singularly fortunate—for the majority of the people agreed with them.

This majority shared one long-standing Tory opinion, that 'politics' was beside the point of life as they had to live it. The interests of the average man, whether enfranchised or not, continued to revolve around his job, his family and friends, his religion, and his amusements. What time remained to him he devoted to his civic duties, if he felt he had any. He had no wish to rule the country, or to involve himself in problems of administration. It was singular, Sidney Low remarked in his *Governance of England* (1904), how little the advance of democracy had led to the actual control of affairs 'by persons belonging to the most numerous classes of the population'. But it was not really so singular. The voters were compelled by their circumstances to leave these matters to the attention of those who had the time to cope with them—in other words, to the leisured class, the class with leisure to claim and exercise ascendancy.

This no longer consisted of an aristocracy of birth, although it included that aristocracy. The moneyed men now bought the time to wield the power that had till then been the monopoly of the landed class. But time to govern was more easily found than the knack of governing. As an excited crowd had found out in July 1866, it was one thing to push over the railings of that aristocratic enclosure, Hyde Park—but another, to know just what to do next. The rich, who had earned their leisure by trusting to their own wits, were baffled by a point of view which admired neither money nor dexterity; yet, since politics was an occupation with inescapably aristocratic traditions, they were compelled to bury their resentment and to borrow from their social superiors the latter's forms of habit and behaviour. Middle-class members of parliament had to catch a 'tone of the House' that they had not invented. A later generation of Labour party members had to do the same: and some, like Maxton, were to master the craft so well as never to do anything else.

The governance of British India displays a microcosm of this process. This, originally a mercantile venture, never wholly emancipated itself from its past. The aristocratic viceroy was the sole representative of his class. John Stuart Mill thought this a very proper state of affairs: for, if English aristocrats were once allowed to invade the Indian arena in strength, he with the best connections would advance the farthest. Reward by reason of merit alone had certainly never been a fetish of the aristocracy.[1] But the civil servants who ruled India—at any one time, never more than forty seniors—were not from those ranks. They were the 'competition wallahs',[2] a meritocracy drawn from the middle classes after the introduction of the examination-system in 1855. They were either unlanded gentry, or sons of tradesmen or of the manse (whose brothers were tradesmen), but they formed an unchallenged élite, and developed an aristocratic hauteur towards those of their own kind in India who were actually engaged in trade there. More money was made in jute than was ever got in government service; but the Scottish jute magnates of Calcutta never attained the social prestige of their immediate overlords in Dundee. They were looked on as 'box-wallahs', and kept below the salt. In India the 'tone of the House' was translated as the tone of the viceroy's entourage: but the result was the same.

Thus, Lord Robert Cecil's prediction that a horde of professional democrats, Tom Paines to a man, would invade the English political arena 'for the pay and the journey-money', was not fulfilled. Malevolent jacobins did not reign. The intellectual forebodings as to the nature of democratic behaviour turned out to be too high-flown. Whig, Liberal or Tory, the government of the country remained in the hands of an 'Ascendancy', self-confessed 'Friends of the People', who were determined to use their authority to command the confidence of their *protégés*, the electorate among the people. It was not an easy task, but it was a possible one. It was doubtless from 'the heavings of the democratic deep', so deplored by the *Quarterly*,[3] that there gushed up the torrent of gin and beer which in 1874 washed from office those friends of the people who were Liberals, while a receding tide caught complacent Conservatism by surprise in 1880; but these events were accurately construed to be less symptoms of revolutionary changes brewing below than of an insufficient attention paid by the rulers to the rules of the game they were

[1] Whig Lord Holland laid it down that a sinecure was an evil, but one grossly overrated: it was simply a bad, uneconomic, and uncertain method of rewarding public services; Davis, *Age of Grey and Peel*, p. 267.

[2] *Letters of a Competition Wallah* (1864), is the title of G. O. Trevelyan's early novel, much disliked by Haileybury men.

[3] *Quarterly Review*, 1849, v, 85, 291.

now playing. Salisbury was to complain in the 'eighties that Liberal ministers had too much a habit of appealing 'to the streets', too great a tendency to 'legislation by picnic',[1] and here he echoed William IV's objection to the 'itinerant speechifying' his Whig ministers had indulged in: but his own Conservatives were compelled to do the same thing. It was a necessary activity, and it brought dividends. In the election of 1885, 522 seats were contested, and the Conservatives captured 118 industrial seats to the Liberals' 100, Manchester choosing the singularly un-Cobdenite figure of A. J. Balfour, Salisbury's nephew, to represent it. If this was a sign that the ship of state was, as Sidney Webb expressed it, 'drifting before a nameless undercurrent', the ship none the less appeared to have learned the trick of drifting where its masters wanted it to go.

The political skill of the Ascendancy, married to its social self-confidence, thus ensured the continuance of its régime. No one successfully challenged it, not even the Irish, who were never able to enlist the sympathies of the English people in support of their cause of Home Rule. Anglo-Irish history had always presented a harshly-lighted reflection of the assumptions of the ruling classes of England. As Lecky points out, in the early eighteenth century the phrase 'the common enemy' was the habitual term by which the Irish parliament described the great majority of the Irish people.[2] By Grattan's time manners had improved, but a spade remained a spade: one of the first things his Protestant landlords' parliament of 1782 did was to reject a Reform Bill (December 1783). He argued that,

if you transfer the power of the State to those who have nothing in the country, they will afterwards transfer the property.[3]

He added in 1792 that he was certainly a friend to liberty for the Roman Catholic, 'but it is only in as much as his liberty is entirely consistent with Protestant ascendancy.'[4] His English

[1] Speech at Sheffield, July 22, 1884.
[2] *History of Ireland*, I, 166.
[3] *Ibid.*, III, 19.
[4] *Ibid.*, 222.

contempories applauded; and even his Protestant Irish contemporary Wolfe Tone, Ireland's first modern nationalist and a
man resentful of the whole pattern of ascendancy, stopped
somewhat well short of democracy. Tone demanded in 1791
that the Catholic £10 freeholders should be granted the
franchise; but in granting this, the parliament should

> on the other hand strike off the disgrace to our Constitution
> and our country, the wretched tribe of 40s freeholders whom
> we see driven to their octennial market by their landlords, as
> much their property as the sheep or the bullocks which they
> brand with their names.

But it was, of course, the English who were responsible for this
disgrace; their ascendancy, and those of their Irish lackeys, had
fashioned these chains of ignorance upon the country.[1]

Tone in Ireland, like Paine in England, had to be dealt with;
and thereafter the democratic principle filtered rather than
fought its way through. Eighteenth-century aristocrats had long
been bemused by the idea that the vote was property: a nineteenth-century democracy found out that, even if it was, no
social asset attached to it. Social privilege was still, as the
Normans had known, the best charter of political power: Reform
Acts might grant new political rights, but they supplied no
'right of passage'. The 'genius of English liberty' so often
appealed to by publicists meant more to an individual Englishman, accustomed to his 'place', than it did to the community at
large: Dicey summed up in his *Law and Custom of the English
Constitution* (1885) that 'the securities for personal freedom are
in England as complete as laws can make them', without considering the question of the limits of legislative competence in a
nation wherein one-ninth of the inhabitants enjoyed one-half of
the national income. The *Edinburgh Review* in October 1899
commented how the scheme for compulsory insurance against
old age was 'generally felt to be repugnant to the genius of
English liberty', and doubtless this was true, if the principle is
accepted that the governing ideas of a generation are the ideas
of its governing class. English ideas were still 'colonized' in this
way.

[1] *Ibid.*, 13.

Jefferson in one age and Mazzini in another had insisted that democracy was a creed of itself, with a code of its own, but in England those who had weighed (or even heard of) the writings of Jefferson and Mazzini, which were not curricular texts, were never more than a handful. To the new Civil Service, recruited after 1870 by examination, 'pay and journey-money' were certainly granted, but never in such quantities as had come the way of the eighteenth-century sinecurists. Reform of the Civil Service, begun in the 1850s, reform in the Universities of Oxford and Cambridge put through following the Royal Commission of 1861, the investigations into the curricula of the public and the grammar schools, and the new-found zeal for examining the talent available in all these places, were none of them based on any popular 'mandate' or interest. But, taken together, they at least assured the governing class that, if democracy did come, it could not seize hold of the administrative bureaucracy in a 'spoils system'; and also, that intelligence would be available to it. A general bureaucratization of English government is a feature of the last thirty years of the nineteenth century, invading even the oldest precincts of squirearchical rule: county councils were established in 1888, parish and rural district councils in 1894. But the *rapport* between the higher ranks of the Civil Service and ministers of the Crown, because it was one founded on both training and attitude of mind, remained close: and in the public service at large aristocratic influences were still powerful, if only because there were still a great number of offices which were either not at all or insufficiently paid.

At the dawn of this new age, Gladstone's ministry of 1868 set the tone by including a number of middle-class men in it, such as Lowe, Childers, Goschen, Forster, and of course Gladstone himself. But a careful observer noted at the time that this did not go too far, that the only middle-class men who got a 'real lift' were men who were 'both regular "county families" and steady-going fellows with no turn for revolution'.[1] Membership of the House of Commons tended to follow this pattern: in 1885 the Liberal whip, the Whig Sir Richard Grosvenor, estimated that of 333 newly-elected members 232 were moderates and

[1] December 20, 1868; Blatchford, *Letters*, p. 276.

only 101 Radical.[1] Harold Laski once calculated that between 1867 and 1884, 60 per cent of Cabinet ministers were aristocrats by birth, 67 per cent were graduates either of Oxford or Cambridge and 60 per cent were products of public schools. Between 1885 and 1905 the picture did not greatly change: 58 per cent were aristocrats, 83 per cent were graduates and 65 per cent were from public schools.[2] Of the House of Commons itself, sitting beneath this aegis, 'perfumed by the presence' of aristocracy, Bagehot remarked in 1870 that it represented the plutocracy, just as the Lords represented the aristocracy, of England. The main interest of both these classes, he added, was identical: they wished to prevent or mitigate the rule of uneducated members. 'Sensible men of substantial means are what we wish to be ruled by.' Bryce, taking a view of the Commons in 1905, noted that although many of the members were middle-class by origin, they belonged practically to the upper class by sympathy. A very different state of affairs prevailed in the United States, where Bryce had been astonished, both in 1870 and in 1881, to find how small a part politics played in conversation among the best educated classes and generally in the cities. In England, it appeared in contrast, the leftward Liberal movement in politics had been successfully 'counterweighted' by the aristocratic factor, even as Coleridge would have wished.

What the people chiefly required of this governing class was a particular kind of perception, an ability as it were to read the runes of the general will. Labour leaders were later to pay respect to this when they spoke of their party as a 'Movement': they surf-rode a groundswell they had not created and did not (as many of them painfully discovered) ultimately control. In the German Empire, where there was manhood suffrage between 1871 and 1913, the skill of Bismarck and his aristocratic successors was made manifest in their appeal to the people over the heads of the Social Democratic party—many of whose natural leaders, the professional intellectuals, they had already wooed away by means of glittering prizes—by instituting more far-reaching 'welfare schemes' than could ever have been carried by

---

[1] J. L. Hammond, *Gladstone and the Irish Nation* (1939), p. 399.
[2] H. Laski, *The Personnel of the British Cabinet, 1832–1934* (1928), p. 176.

the Social Democrats who did not command the confidence of the industrialist class. Always, it was a question of confidence; the politician was expected by the voters to perform the duties of the professional letter-writer in Spain, who was employed by the illiterate lover to set down on paper a grammatical passion. The task of government was not only to remove popular grievances, but to prevent their formation. This needed acuity, training and skill. Paternalism in England, therefore, far from suffering marked defeat as a sturdy and independent democracy came pouring through the gaps in the pale of the constitution, took on a new lease of life.

A politician had now to be, or at any rate had to seem to be, a man of good will, who wished the people well. An aristocrat who had neither gifts nor inclination for playing this role could still prove acceptable if he elected to devote his time and attention—as did Robert Cecil [Lord Salisbury] himself—to the field of foreign policy. This was an arcane area of diplomatic negotiation, conducted in secret and in the French language,[1] where the public did not tread: in 1904 the Anglo-French *entente* was signed at Clouds, George Wyndham's country house, by Balfour, Lansdowne and the host. The judicious public use of the phrase 'British interests', or reference to the necessity of maintaining a 'balance of power', gave assurance that the national welfare of the people, and their continuing freedom from foreign interference, had not been lost sight of. Palmerston's popular reputation in foreign policy as a forthright John Bull, making the voice of England ring in the affrighted ears of unconstitutional despots, did him less than justice, but this was in the main his own fault: as Bagehot pointed out, Palmerston was 'not a common man, but a common man might have been cut from him'. But by making such an appeal he successfully counterweighed the effects of his entire disinterest in domestic policies of a reformatory kind. Cobden and Bright, endeavouring on the people's behalf (or so they always said) to show him in his true light, could never make much headway. 'Our only instrument for regenerating other nations.' Bright darkly reminded the Commons, 'is a Cabinet purely aristocratic, whose

[1] But not by the Liberals' Foreign Secretary, Sir Edward Grey, who could not speak French.

love of liberty has never yet been proved'.[1] That the people should allow themselves to be beguiled by such aristocratic legerdemain was sad indeed; it was this that Cobden had in mind when he stated that democracy formed no element in the materials of English character. There was no genuine republicanism in it.[2]

Foreign secretaries subsequent to Palmerston, although less brusque in their international tactics, were equally aristocratic in rank and outlook. Here they could always count on the warm support of Queen Victoria, who continued to consider foreign policy as one of the royal prerogatives, and who bitterly complained when anything in the nature of 'party' invaded any of its problems. Gladstone, in bringing foreign affairs into the public domain—in particular during his Bulgarian and Midlothian campaigns (1876, 1879–80)—offended very gravely against the accepted official canons of conduct. It was fitting therefore that it should have been Lord Rosebery, Gladstone's successor (although hardly his heir) as head of the Liberal party, who prided himself on establishing the doctrine of 'continuity' in foreign policy. The people wanted security of hearth and home, and a foreign policy that obtained this for them was something they were prepared to take on trust. All that was required of the aristocrats in charge of it was that they should know what they were about.

Owing to the inevitable party bias in the writing of political history, very much less has been heard of the doctrine of 'continuity' in domestic policy. It was, and has remained, a doctrine with few preachers. Politicians whose electoral stock-in-trade consisted of diatribes against the fatuous opinions held and the appalling blunders committed by members of the opposing party in power, preferred to strike a note of contrast, not comparison. Only those who stayed aloof from this fray—elder Whigs beached on cays while the Liberal tide swept forward, or Tories who continued to despise the entire political process—could afford to stress the similarities, and to insist that what was held in common was a lot more significant than what was held in dispute. For these last Lord Robert Cecil can speak again. He

[1] Trevelyan, *Bright*, p. 195.
[2] [And see title-page]. Cobden, *Writings*, I, 102.

had stated in the *Quarterly*, in the disheartened days of 1867, that it was the duty of every Englishman and of every English party to accept a political defeat cordially, and to lend their best endeavours to secure the success, or to neutralize the evils, of the principles to which they had been forced to succumb. It was the language of Peel's Tamworth manifesto: the duty of the Conservative party was to act as a brake on heedless action, and to gain whatever time was necessary to repair the damage that had been done by non-Conservatives. This must be done so well that in future Conservatives would be forced to 'succumb' as little as possible to further radical errors of commission.[1] Here was a line of continuity laid down for domestic policy, and following it was to bring Conservatives remarkable success. The aim, as in foreign policy, was security. This was also the popular aim—and Tories who did not forget this fact were very often able to exploit the mistakes of Radicals who did. Radicals who were genuinely devoted to progressive principles were often to get so far in front of those they hoped were following them as to forfeit all claims to leadership at all.

That, if a choice was forced upon them, democrats would prefer security to liberty, was something that had been prophesied alike by the aristocratic Tocqueville and the middle-class Bentham. In America, the truth of this had been made manifest by civil war. A majority had imposed their political and social systems on a minority; and, in order to maintain the sanctity of the constitution, a president destined to everlasting fame as a democratic hero had sent armies marching throughout his own country to stamp out the doctrine of self-determination, bred among men as freeborn as himself. From such passion and paradox the English record was free—and it would stay so, it was argued, so long as democrats, who were inevitably men who would never be able to gauge the consequences of their enthusiasms, were kept in their place. Moreover, to keep them in their place was to do them a service: for of what value, either to society or to himself, was a displaced person? See how France had suffered, so many times, at the hands of her *déclassés!*

The calculation that a revitalized Conservative party would

[1] Cf. W. L. Burn, 'The Conservative Tradition and its Reformulations', in M. Ginsberg, ed., *Law and Opinion in the 20th Century* (New York, 1955).

make a broader appeal to the expanded electorate than the
Liberalism which put so high a value on *laissez-faire*, was made
in advance by men so dissimilar as Disraeli, Engels and Herbert
Spencer. English Tories, under Disraeli's guidance, geared
themselves to adopt one of Bentham's master-rules: so to act
that the people, as far as was possible, got what they wanted.
The success of the Conservatives at the election of 1874 therefore gave a tonic both to themselves and to Disraeli's reputation
for political prescience, and made him undisputed master in the
house he had so laboriously built. In the Commons in March
1867 Disraeli had stated his hope that it would never be
England's fate to live under a democracy; but when, after the
Liberals' victory in the election of 1868, his ministry resigned
before parliament reconvened, he made it plain that he accepted
the view that members of parliament were in fact, despite the
disgust of Lord Robert Cecil and his friends, 'delegates of the
people'. He continued to believe, nevertheless, in government
for the people, and was highly gratified when 1874 seemed to
prove that the people believed in this too. It now appeared that
persons happy in their cottages were antipathetic to the shop-
keeping outlook; were in fact, as Disraeli's crystal ball had told
him, loyal to throne, empire and the other aristocratic institutions of the day. People permitted to prescribe the ends of
government would not interfere in the means; and, as the problems of administration became ever more complicated, it was
less and less likely that they would ever want to. There was
therefore a long future ahead of the ruling class, so long as it
followed this creed and observed its code. As Anthony Trollope
had presaged in *The Bertrams* (1859)

Let the people want what they will . . . the Tories will carry
it for them if the Whigs cannot.

The creed, however, was always more easily grasped by those
not bred in it than the code. 'It is a great advantage,' Pascal had
written, 'to be a man of quality, since it brings one man as
forward at eighteen or twenty as another man would be at fifty,
which is a clear gain of thirty years.'[1] This 'clear gain of thirty

[1] Quoted by Tocqueville, *Democracy in America*, ed. H. Reeve (1862), p. 293.

years' was the most powerful weapon in the aristocrat's armoury, particularly since most of the middle-class members of parliament found the leisure to seek election and a political career only when they were well past middle age anyway. Use of this weapon by the aristocrats themselves was a potent agency in keeping England, socially speaking, a 'colonial society', with habits and conventions imposed from above. This was done not, as the Normans had done it, by methods of tyranny, but by the magnetic attraction of English aristocratic attitudes themselves. In the countryside, 'the *quality*' remained the term in common use to describe the gentry. The wish of the people, as everyone agreed, was to be governed by gentlemen. Those desirous of obtaining political power, and of maintaining themselves in it, had therefore to become indistinguishable from gentlemen. To succeed in doing this, they found it was necessary to build a new stockade in society, to enclose in security the 'upper middle class'. This constructive work was to occupy the last thirty years of the nineteenth century. In 1869 Matthew Arnold gave his opinion, in *Culture and Anarchy*, that the middle classes had a distrust of themselves as an adequate centre of authority. This handicap they were determined to lose; and one of the best agencies available to them for learning the necessary degree of confidence was the public school.

This was, as it has remained, one of the most powerful Tory institutions in the kingdom. From it, and from the universities of Oxford and Cambridge that it nourished, were to emerge into public life a solid body of 'pass-men', instinctive Tories, uneasy with theory, unhappy with ideas, pillars of society. But it was to be expected that public schools, like other institutions, should pass under a keen Liberal scrutiny, to discover what was needed in the way of renovation: no one of any consequence, of course, wished to explore possibilities of reconstruction. The type of renovation recommended by the Whig Lord Clarendon, who headed the Royal Commission of 1861–4 which investigated the seven leading schools,[1] was utilitarian. Clarendon, who was not himself the product of a public school education, thought that the existing system placed the upper classes in a state of

[1] These were: Eton, Harrow, Rugby, Winchester, Shrewsbury, Charterhouse and Westminster.

inferiority to the middle and lower classes—a functional inferiority, since the kind of education provided was inadequate if they were to meet, as they must meet, their future responsibilities. The same line of approach was taken by the subsequent Taunton Commission which examined the grammar schools; in its report, stress was laid on the needs of the professional classes, 'who have nothing to look to but education to keep their sons at a high social level.' But it was, in the main, from the public schools that the future officers both of the military and the civil services were expected to come; and, as Clarendon noted, the public schools had been failing their function. Between 1858 and 1861, of 375 Army candidates for Sandhurst, only twenty-three were public school men, and of 1,976 entrants for the Civil Service, only 122.[1] Of the schools examined, only Rugby taught the natural sciences—and, as an indirect consequence of this, both the Army and the Navy for the next forty years were to find it increasingly difficult to decide what social status to allocate to indispensable officers who were also engineers and who, *ipso facto*, had no 'background' of public school training.

Thus the gentlemen of the Clarendon Commission recommended a certain liberalizing of the curriculum, the introduction for example of French and mathematics. But they showed no tendency 'to drench the popular mind with physics', in Newman's phrase. Eleven out of the twenty hours of instruction in the week were still to be devoted to divinity and classics. Even this amount of reform affronted the instinctive Toryism of Gladstone, who insisted that the study of Latin and Greek was the key discipline of Western civilization, the *alter ego* of Christianity itself. Although few could follow him through an intellectual labyrinth that connected Homer with Dante, there was a general agreement. *The Times* felt it close on treason to make any changes at all at Eton. Nowhere else in the world could be seen the spectacle Eton presented

—a continuous body of gentlemen of all ages, having one common centre at school, and only leaving it for active life, to return to it, as it were, in their sons.

[1] See E. C. Mack's important book, *Public Schools and British Opinion since 1860* (New York, 1941), p. 35 and throughout.

Fraser's Magazine thought it as little easy to found a school such as Eton, or Harrow, or Rugby, as it would be to call into existence a nation.[1] Etonian members of the House of Lords accordingly saw to it that the railway line, together with the touring American evangelists Moody and Sankey (all three of these adjudged as deleterious democratic influences) were kept away from college bounds. What went on inside these bounds was beside any point that mattered. Dean Farrar, author of *Eric, or Little by Little* (1858) was one of those who did not greatly care what the boys learned, so long as their characters were purified. He feared that, as public schools were at present constituted, boys were threatened with moral menaces not dissimilar from those their elder brothers met with in the night-hells of the Haymarket. To Radical critics, too, curricular questions were beside the point. Henry Labouchere predictably saw in the schools what Cobbett had seen before him, 'hotbeds of social exclusiveness and aristocratic prejudice, where people sent their sons to pick up what they called gentlemanly connections'. This was true, but Tories wondered why such a truth should foment such indignation.

Two views of the system were based on commonsense. The *bourgeois* view was that a boy met at school other boys who would in after life be 'of use' to him. The aristocratic view (scarcely worth formulating) was that a boy met there his natural equals, his future colleagues in public office, his future relatives by marriage.

As Dr Thring of Uppingham pointed out, education is a long process. Only the few, therefore, would have *time* for it, just as only the few had time for cricket and, later, for golf. Mid-Victorians who bought time with their money were accordingly deeply interested in the best education money could buy. Their sons did not inherit this interest. Little is heard in late-Victorian times of the need for reform in the public schools, for the reason that the sons were well satisfied with what their fathers had wrought, and happy to pay a higher fee for the selfsame instruction. Of course the world of education still had its critics. T. H. Huxley remarked, in his *Science and Education* (1894), that if the education of the richer classes had been such as to fit

[1] Mack, *op. cit.*, 20, 44.

them to be the leaders and governors of the poor; and, if the education of the poorer classes had been such as to enable them to appreciate a really wise guidance and governance, the politicians would not have needed to fear mob-law, nor the clergy to lament their want of flock, nor the capitalists to predict the annihilation of the country's prosperity. But gloom of this kind was not spread at comfortable dinner-tables. The upper middle class felt it could afford to dispense with the outlook that had contributed to its making. Once, the 'middling classes' had aspired to programmes of social equality, of broad educational opportunity; but, in their prosperity, these ideals passed naturally, by a process of social imperialism, to the class below, which was already borrowing from above such public-school paraphernalia as badges, mottoes, school colours, slang, and organized games.

The most zealous of Eton's utilitarian headmasters, Dr Warre, openly set out to produce 'the best baronets . . . honest secretaries of state, open-handed village squires, broad-minded bishops'.[1] If these were fashioned more by the playing-field than by the classroom, what did it matter? In organized games there was at once an innocence and a discipline. Innocence—since, as a subject of conversation, games were morally preferable to those other topics that Dean Farrar for one thought only too prevalent. Discipline—since on the playing-field the eccentric and rowdy republicanism of school life was transmuted by the team spirit. 'Playing the game', 'not letting down the side', were the ideals that fired the individual, who subordinated his innate ruggedness to these tasks; and that personal sensibility which, at least as Rousseau had argued, it was the grand task of education to foster, was eradicated in the process usually recognized even by those who endured it as having one's corners knocked off. The voice that Henry Newbolt was to hear rallying the ranks at a moment of peril was that of a public schoolboy—grown slightly older, but no different. It was the sense of paternalism, responsibility for others, inculcated in him from early youth, that stopped him from joining in with any democratic spree of *sauve qui peut*.

If this was stereotyping, as critics of the public school system and *ethos* so often complained, at least it was of a utilitarian kind.

[1] Mack, *op. cit.*, p. 130.

The aristocrats supported a system that inculcated their own outlook into the sons of the middle classes because it was to their interest to do so. The system did not allow for the parsing and analysis of principle: it was not designed to do so, but to uphold a culture, a habit of life, that did not primarily depend upon intellectual values at all. Those who believed, like Thomas Hughes' *Tom Brown at Oxford* (1861) that it was very desirable that the young should make good connections, were therefore seldom caught off-balance by Radical criticism. A system that recruited and maintained the Ascendancy was self-evidently sound. So it did not wound, when Bernard Shaw sneered that at a public school the rich governing class 'passed from juvenility to senility without ever touching maturity except in body'; or when H. G. Wells described the schools as 'beautiful shelters of intellectual laziness'; or when both insisted that pouring a jelly into a mould did not necessarily 'develop' it. Such men seemed to want the schools to produce a horde of incisive social critics like themselves. But, to what end? If every educated man set up as a destructive agency, there would soon be no social system left to complain of, only a state of anarchy. (Something of this kind of thought seems indeed to have inhibited the work of John Galsworthy, a social critic who spent his life trying to fight his way, but most often not hard enough, out of his Harrow jacket.) Fortunately, however, the risk seemed small. As Bryce pointed out, for every man who could think his way through a difficult question of ethics, there were ten who could remember what they had been taught to believe.

Over-intellectualism, therefore, was held by the Ascendancy to be in poor taste. Paine and Godwin, Shelley and Bentham, Newman and Owen, Marx and Hyndman, forever grinding axes, parading *idées fixes*—all of them were, if a Tory was honest about it, *bores*, schoolmasters of society whose first reaction in the presence of Sir Robert Walpole's sleeping dog was to kick it awake. Shaw indeed was certainly not a bore, but all his paradoxes fitted into one another like a series of Chinese boxes, and anyway, since he was Irish, he might be forgiven a national taste for farcical exaggeration, something he could not very well help. But enemy agents within one's own lines made definition a harder problem. Galsworthy's uneasiness of spirit was uneasily communicable. 'Could a man,' a character wonders in *The Island Pharisees* (1908), 'suffer from passion, heart-searchings, or misgivings, and remain a gentleman? It seemed impossible.' Indeed it did. Such menaces lay on all sides, and even the introduction of the study of English literature into the curricula at the Universities of Oxford and Cambridge was thought by many to be dangerous,[1] to be likely to lead impressionable young men down strange paths into the undisciplined areas of other men's minds. The shadow Swinburne threw was always longer than himself.

But the cultivation of doubt and misgiving, like that of liberalism itself, was a product of an assured position in society, of an imagination not fully occupied with problems of getting and spending. Only a minority was in this position; and the majority of the others who were born to leisure, spent it more often in enjoying it than in questioning themselves. Their education successfully reinforced their self-confidence. The Etonians whom Warre had hoped would act as a 'general staff' to the community were not educated for citizenship, an unEnglish concept anyway, but for leadership. They were not urged towards intellectual eminence, they were encouraged in practical commonsense. At Harrow, for example, one was 'licked into shape for the big things—diplomacy, politics, the Services':[2] and it was to remain an axiom among those directly involved that one fairly well-educated and capable Englishman who had forgotten his classics was as well able to perform the duties of a public department, any public department, as another. W. S. Gilbert made play with this notion in *H.M.S. Pinafore* (1878); but Gilbert's satire was misconstrued, then and later, as good-humoured fun.

Aristocracies, since they do not have to live by their wits, have a natural distrust of ideas. (The English exception to this rule occurred in the period of the Restoration, when the grandees were, because hard times had taught them to be, remarkable for acumen and agility.) In Victorian times, on a high plateau of security, the Ascendancy did not expect life to catch it by surprise; and it did not. Accordingly, despite the Clarendon Commission's recommendations, science, mathematics and

---

[1] Cf. C. H. Firth, *The School of English Literature and Language* (Oxford, 1909).
[2] Mack, *op. cit.*, p. 250.

languages made only halting progress in the public schools, for the reason that the pupils there, particularly those who were eldest sons, did not expect to need these things in the culture of which they were part. If there are 'two cultures' in English society to this day, that is the direct result of careful planning to that end. Salisbury's gibe at 'experts' is well-known: expertize of any kind was looked on as ancillary to the tradition of authority, but in itself it gave none. In contrast, the Clarendonian advice to establish a 'common entrance' examination, which in effect abolished the rights of the poor in what had originally been designed as establishments for poor scholars, was briskly taken. 'Common entrance' demanded a standard few common boys had. One way to rid a school of problems of class-distinction was, plainly, to get rid of every class but one's own. 'Scholarship boys' whom it was not possible to reject could always be brought to realize their own privileged position the more keenly by having to wear, for example, boots where others wore shoes.[1]

No emphasis needed to be placed on knowledge, since for all practical purposes gentlemen might count on always knowing more than the 'players' whom they would captain through life. In England primary education was not instituted until 1870; and the Education Act of 1902 did not provide the general secondary education which the Bryce Commission had recommended, but contented itself with authorizing the use of public funds to assist it. In fact, of boys born between 1910 and 1929, less than one-fifth (17·6 per cent) reached a secondary school: one-seventh (14·3 per cent) went to a university.[2] In this situation, the gap between the educated and the rest, and accordingly between one kind of opportunity and another, one habit of life and another, remained a wide one. In the primary schools themselves there was no compulsory attendance for children who had reached the age of ten. In 1893 the leaving-age was raised to eleven. In 1918 it was raised to fourteen, and stayed there for another thirty years. The main business of these schools was to teach the three R's and some degree of social discipline. What else went on in them few comfortable persons troubled to find out: the one public issue that reverberated outside of the schoolroom was

[1] As, say, at Fettes College, Edinburgh, in the 1930s.
[2] Laski, *Personnel*, p. 113.

that of religious instruction, an issue on which dissenting opinion stirred fervours that few Anglicans (Balfour an exception) sought to understand. Dissenting quarrels on this matter had helped the Liberals lose the election of 1874, and thereafter cost the middle-class nonconformist W. E. Forster the party leadership, which passed to the Whig grandee Hartington, who did not have, and never wished to attain, any views on national education. Yet there was general agreement that education was a good: and 'high schools' in India, 'board schools' in England, became accepted parts of these landscapes—'beacons of the future', as Mr Sherlock Holmes rather unexpectedly remarked to Dr Watson as their railway-carriage passed above the roofs of London schools sometime around 1895. Approval of these beacons was properly paternalist, but the future they heralded was still distant. H. G. Wells was always to speak of the 1870 Act as one that was designed to educate the lower classes on lower-class lines.

The upper classes did not think this verdict unjust, but they objected to the note of complaint in which it was issued. If rich people were expected 'to pay for the education of other people's children'—and why stop there, fumed *The Times* in 1889, why not clothe them too and set them up in business?—then they felt that they had a right to be assured that these other people's children would not eventually usurp the position of their own off-spring. One of the Chartists' most exasperating habits had been their insistence that they saw life more clear and plain than their betters: as one of their petitions to the House of Commons had put it, 'Heaven has dealt graciously by the people—but the foolishness of our rulers has made the goodness of God of none effect.' This kind of perception was not to be encouraged in the commonalty. Thus the warnings of Mill, that the division of the human race into two hereditary classes of employers and employed could not be permanently maintained, fell on uneasy ears. And outrage greeted Joseph Chamberlain's 'Radical Programme' of 1885, which frankly admitted to 'legislation with a socialist tendency', but asserted that this was no novelty, as the path of legislative progress in England had been for years distinctly 'socialistic'. The following year Karl Marx's *Capital* was translated. Was it possible, then, that the English lower classes—unlike their American counterparts, who had already mythologized the path that led from the log-cabin to the White House, from the tar-paper shack to the board-room—would come to look on 'capitalism' not as a ladder up which they might climb, but as an obstacle to their own emancipation? An exchange from the minutes of evidence taken before a Royal Commission on Education (May 3, 1887) speaks for itself:

> Q. You say the board schools are likely to favour socialism . . . what do you mean by socialism?
> A. I mean the state of things in which there is not the respect for the classes above the children that I think there ought to be.[1]

The young, ever a potential menace to the established order, were the people to be watched, far more so than their elders, who constituted the deserving poor, and by their labour properly contributed to the system that maintained them. Hence the insistence from pulpits in churches which the poor did not attend, and in journals which the poor did not read, on the moral value of 'savings', the blessings of thrift. Hence, too, the fact that poorhouses were made as disagreeable as could be contrived without actually making them indistinguishable from prisons.

No self-made man was able to look at such people without forming a grim determination that his children should not be classed among them. Sending a boy to a public school insured his future as a potential member of the Ascendancy, and segregated his existence for ever. Samuel Butler remarks in his *Way of All Flesh* (1903) how education at a public school cut off a boy's retreat; H. G. Wells in his *Mr Britling Sees It Through* (1916), that as soon as the manufacturing class prospered and sent its boys to Oxford, it was lost. The manufacturers thought this criticism totally irrelevant, but could not deny its truth. Barriers were placed behind such a boy. There were places he could not go to, things he could not do, thoughts he could not entertain—and remain a gentleman. Even if he turned out to lack the character required to make his way in the society to which he had been given so expensive a passport, he could not

[1] Helen Lynd, *England in the Eighteen Eighties* (1945), p. 97.

slide back into the outer darkness without disgrace to himself and shame to his family and friends. (This dark area included the colonies, always regarded as a convenient oblivion by the Ascendancy, which as a consequence never lent itself to any vulgar jingoism about the glories of the British Empire.) Yet within these barriers a man was free, to make his way or lose it. He had the privilege of freedom, both of will and of movement. This was the privilege, perhaps best appreciated when lost, which, according to the unanimous testimony of late-Victorian autobiography, made life 'before the War' [i.e. 1914] so sweet, so rare. No other freedom, whatever democrats might say, could ever capture its magic.

The orthodoxy that served middle-class society as a stockade was the hallmark of people to whom this aristocratic privilege was and ever would be unknown. Striving after 'respectability' does not permit of freedom of movement. It was common to speak of a respectable tradesman: but to speak of a respectable duke, entirely worthy and virtuous though that particular duke might be, was to misuse the language, and mistake a tone. The morals of eighteenth-century aristocrats had been loose, but their manners strict. Their posterity, having breathed the evangelical air in their upbringing, insisted on the essence as well as the rules of good behaviour. But there was still room for personal eccentricity. A gentleman's soul was more his own than a tradesman's, as George Brummell freakishly underlined when, as a hussar officer, he sent in his papers rather than be posted to Manchester. In observing that Dissent was no religion for a gentleman, Charles II had passed an accurate social observation as well as a sneer at piety. Time did not blur its accuracy: in the nineteenth century Dissent was often taken as 'the religion of the cad'.[1] Bright had perhaps been more perceptive than he knew when he spoke of 'the remorseless aristocracy of Britain'—for remorse was more publicized in nonconformist circles than among Anglicans, who thought all emotional 'enthusiasm' in bad taste.

The blank incomprehension on both sides of this barrier made communication difficult. During a parliamentary enquiry into a

[1] 'The cad on the omnibus' is a late-Victorian equivalent of 'the man in the street'.

railway bill, a peer asked a shopkeeper, 'Can it be of any great importance whether the article [of merchandize] goes there in five or six hours, or in an hour and a half?' Cobden quotes this exchange, to ridicule it: but the peer might as justly have returned the ridicule on Cobden. This illustration of the fact of Disraeli's two nations, looking out upon different worlds, was seen as sad, funny, or infuriating, according to temperament. In Conan Doyle's *The Crime of the Brigadier* (1898), the horror of Wellington's officers when the dashing Frenchman sabres the hunted fox is the point of the joke. In J. M. Barrie's *What Every Woman Knows* (1918), designed for middle-class entertainment, the woman who plainly knows nothing worth knowing is the aristocratic Lady Sybil. In *Lady Chatterley's Lover* (1928), this same lady is forcibly educated, with a solemn fervour. Popular novels and comedies had endless recourse to the stock and simpleton figure of 'Lord Algy'; and for long in American folk-lore, which had a more bitter taste to it, the Englishman could be distinguished by his eye-glass even before he opened his mouth to utter his incomprehensible vowels.

But ridicule damages only those who live in uncertainty. English aristocrats, untroubled by problems of status, could afford to admit with equanimity that they on occasion produced noodles: yet even such were mindful in an emergency of *The Code of the Woosters*. This self-confidence had its many admirers. The historian of the peerage, J. H. Round, 'confidently and boldly' asserted that the reason that England had been saved from much that was beyond dispute deplorable in the public life of the United States, was due to the existence of a social standard other than that of mere wealth.[1] A government of gentlemen might have all kinds of defects, Lecky added, but the standard of honour common to the class at least secured it from the grosser forms of malversation, while the interests of its members were indissolubly connected with the permanent well-being of the country.[2] This view underlined Tocqueville's, who had pointed out that although aristocracies were capable of very tyrannical and inhuman actions, they rarely entertained 'grovelling thoughts'. 'An aristocratic body,' he went on,

[1] J. H. Round, *Peerage and Family History* (1901), p. 33.
[2] Lecky, *History of England* I, 220–1.

is composed of a certain number of citizens who, without being very far removed from the mass of the people, are nevertheless permanently stationed above it; a body which it is easy to touch, and difficult to strike; with which the people are in daily contact, but with which they can never combine.

The composition of the English aristocracy had since changed and expanded, but the principle underlying its existence had not. The landed classes did not possess such an exclusive stake in society as before, but they still looked on the middle classes as essential props of the society over which they themselves continued to preside, a society which certainly needed its producers, distributors and professional servants. They agreed with Dr Johnson, that trade could not be conducted by those who conduct it if it presented any difficulties. Success in business had none of the moral trappings Samuel Smiles and Horatio Alger found in it: it required only application, a high degree of selfishness, and a worship of success itself. The world in which these qualities were prized must necessarily be a narrow one, unlikely to produce broad-minded men of vision. It would, at worst, throw up that 'robber baron' individualism which a similar world in the United States was at that moment bringing in to the light; and, at best, the crack-brained *rhodomontade* of Cecil Rhodes. The robber barons, from their own day to this, have never lacked for admirers in America; but in England, the prestige of a millionaire who is a man of money only, has never stood high. Harold Laski, staunchest of left-wing intellectuals, declared when he looked back at the record, that he would rather have been governed by the Tory evangelical Lord Shaftesbury 'than by Mr Cobden, by the gentlemen of England than by the Gradgrinds and Bounderbys of Coketown'.[1]

It was not sufficiently considered, Mill wrote in 1861, how little there was in the ordinary life of most men to give any largeness either to their conceptions or to their sentiments.[2] But many ordinary men instinctively knew this themselves, and the religious fervours that mingled with the fumes of Coketown, or rose into the clear air of an American frontier settlement, bore

[1] Laski, *The Dangers of Being a Gentleman* (1939), p. 29.
[2] In *Responsible Government*, c. 3.

vivid witness to the realization. The oriental imagery and often incomprehensible language and thought of 'King James's Bible' were more likely to light an imagination than instruct a mind— and so many men, thankful at least for the illumination, were content to look on the Bible as their main source for knowledge and guidance. This habit of so many, of setting their hopes on the next world instead of buckling down to reform and repair the one they lived in, was always infuriating to better-fed Radicals who trusted to their own intellectual weapons to carry all before them. Cobbett once complained that it was 'really a stain upon the national character, that [the Methodist preachers] should find such multitudes to follow at their heels'. That these same people, when they did turn their eyes to secular matters, should resign themselves to what could not be mended in the station in life wherein it had pleased God to place them—that they should even admire many features of the system that so confined them —was even more galling to Radical politicians of independent means. For it was plain that popular admiration was not with- held from the monarchy and the nobility. These 'relics of the feudal system' were looked on with a genuine sense of wonder, as figures larger than those of common life, and all their doings and habits had a fascination, precisely because they were so far removed from the ordinary run of things. (It is a fascination that has yet to die.) From this admiration a good deal of aspira- tion, as well as a great deal of snobbery, was to spring.

That men may often be happier looking upwards than side- ways, and that the ability to recognize and respect genuinely superior attainments is not at all uncommon, are sentiments that lie outwith the sphere of democratic argument. Only in wartime is reference made to 'qualities of leadership', and even then accurate definition of them is avoided. But it has yet to be proved that a man's ability to respect a person or an ideal harms his character and attests to his innate servility. If the imperialism of manners and behaviour was to become the most successful and prolonged of all those invented by the gentlemen of England, that was in the main because the core of these conventions— debased though they had been from a chivalric code, itself more the product of clerkly imagination than of baronial practice— centred on courtesy towards others and respect for oneself.

There is in these things a direct appeal to the spirit; and where, as in professionally democratic societies devoted to the doctrine of equality, this appeal cannot be publicly answered, the inability to do so may leave a sense of rancour. It can sometimes be as false to call one man an equal as to be compelled to believe another man superior. If snobbery has no commonsense in it, neither has the determination to equate bushes with trees. But a man was less inclined to do this, who lived in an old society where the trees had in time grown tall and plain in sight.

For the strength of the 'Norman yoke', as the Plantagenets, Jack Cade, Levellers, Diggers and Tom Paine had understood, lay not in its oppressive force, but in the acquiescence of the English people that it was a useful yoke, under which useful work was done. Middle-class men had not, as yet, worked their passage to this popular acceptance. Rich employers might stress the social utility in the very fact that they employed people: but since plainly they did not employ people from altruistic motive, the argument never lost its hollow ring. Whether examined from above or from below, middle-class morality had this deep stain of selfishness in it. Hence both aristocrats and commoners were able to find a better level of human understanding in the world of sport, an arena that middle-class money and morality was slow to invade. The common verdict of praise, 'a real sport', or 'a real gentleman', meant much the same thing, since the rules of play in sport had been drawn up by gentlemen in the first place.[1] That was the kind of thing that gentlemen, with their knowledge and assurance, were *for*. The lower middle class whose outlook this was has remained an isolated class, with few admirers. It drew its picture of the world from such writers as Hall Caine and Ouida and Marie Corelli, who were themselves the progenitors of 'True Romance' magazine fiction, and who were never so much as mentioned by middle-class literary critics. But theirs was the picture of the world that was wanted: it lighted the imagination.

This English 'genius for deference' has drawn down on it severe criticism, since it leads so easily to servility and flunkey-

---

[1] E.g. the Marquess of Queensberry; or the third Duke of Dorset—'an ignorant, illiterate debauchee' (Turberville, p. 381), who drew up the original rules of the Middlesex County Cricket Club.

ism both of mind and of manner. It opens a wide window into the world of the snob, whose boundaries were first traced by Thackeray, and whose possibilities for malice were most heavily exploited by *Punch*. But in some sub-sections of this territory both Thackeray and *Punch* trod softly. Thackeray tilted at one kind of social conformity, but himself displayed another. He was a writer in the realistic tradition of Swift and Fielding, but, since neither would ever have found a publisher in the nineteenth century, he had to make shift to conceal it. The respected Victorian critic George Saintsbury was to note it as a fault in the work of Balzac and Zola that they made everyone feel uncomfortable. His own creation of Becky Sharp made Thackeray uncomfortable. She has ten times more life in her than his gentleman-hero, Colonel Newcome; and Henry Esmond's moral rigidity would assuredly have got him nowhere in the age of Queen Anne wherein his adventures are set. Writers with a middle-class readership, who wished to retain that readership, were allowed to satirize the aspiration, but not the achievement; to poke fun at those who aspired, but not at the habits of those who had arrived.

It was of course best to arrive unnoticed, without fuss, in an age when display was classed as vulgar. Dissenters who agreed with Charles II continued to migrate from chapel to Church, an institution which, because in 1893 it claimed only $1\frac{1}{2}$ million communicants in a population of 38 millions, was dubbed by the Radical John Morley as 'the church of a class'. Rich men began to graduate into the peerage, although not without opposition from Queen Victoria, who refused Disraeli's request in 1868 to elevate the banker Lionel Rothschild: she 'could not think that one who owed his wealth to contracts with foreign governments for loans, or to successful speculation on the Stock Exchange, could fairly claim a British peerage'.[1] But her son the Prince of Wales had no objection to gambling or to the gilt-edged security which the Jewish financiers of his Marlborough House set epitomized, and with his aid Lionel Rothschild's son Nathaniel was successfully equipped with a peerage in 1885. Disraeli did however manage to get one brewer enobled, a member of the Guinness family—an action that would have grieved the

[1] W. D. Jones, *Lord Derby and Victorian Conservatism* (Oxford, 1956), p.110.

Queen's revered 'ancestor' Charles I, who when granting a charter to the borough of Colchester had not permitted brewers to enjoy even the franchise.[1] Between 1876 and 1886, another four commercial peers added their weight in gold to the aristocracy; and between 1886 and 1896, another eighteen. Still more rich men sought a seat in parliament. Being an M.P., like being a professional beauty, ensured a certain degree of social recognition: influence in politics, and prominence at dinner-tables, had long been intimately connected.

Further down the social pyramid the same hopes and attitudes could be observed. In the servants' quarters behind the green baize door of the English country-house the social hierarchy repeated itself: the butler ruled his empire, the housekeeper managed a harem, and the niceties of 'place' were fined down to the subtlest degree of accuracy, spoilt only by the difficulty of knowing how to treat the governess who educated the master's children. Yet the certainties of this private world of 'upper servants' were perhaps easier to accept than were the ravages brought about in many a middle-class household by the war between mistress and maid over the question who, precisely, had the 'right' to the usufruct of candle-ends, half-bottles, and cold joints—questions never raised in country-house life.

A determination to have both place and privilege respected was common to all ranks of society. As democracy crowded the streets, and public transportation became more widespread, 'the man in the street' came into his own. But the very anonymity of democracy diminished its appeal. Even when the sturdy common-sense of the man in the street was being praised, no one was content to cast himself *only* as such. He had other parts to play, other places to play them in. A tinge of vulgarity, by definition, coloured the things that went on in public: in her time Fanny Burney had declared herself as shocked by public weddings as by public hangings. Accordingly the 'Royal Enclosure' at Ascot racecourse had many private parallels.[2] People who wanted to be correctly 'placed' built their own enclosures, behind the walls of

[1] J. H. Round, *Peerage and Pedigree* (1903), p. 36; H. J. Hanham, 'The Sale of Honours in Victorian England', *Victorian Studies*, No. 3, March 1960, pp. 278–9.
[2] E.g. the Glyndebourne opera in Surrey, attendance at which entails wearing full evening-dress on the platform of Waterloo Station at 5 p.m.

which they were able to enjoy their privileges, and where the only unalarming kind of equality—the equality of equals—could thrive. A serjeant's mess had an etiquette different from, but as rigorously respected as, that of a gentleman's club. In 'clubland' itself both the company and its opinions were always deliberately predictable. As one might be sure of finding a traveller at the Travellers', so one would expect to find a bishop at the Athenaeum, racing men at Boodles', politicians of one's own way of thinking at the Carlton or alternatively at the Reform, writers and actors at the Garrick, and men about town at the Savage. Jockeys would not be found at the Jockey Club, solicitors among barristers, or Household Cavalry among the Royal Engineers. Persons not readily identifiable at all, like the involuntary companions of a railway carriage, were best ignored. 'Unable to judge at once of the social position of those he meets,' Tocqueville observed, 'an Englishman prudently avoids all contact with them.' In P. G. Wodehouse's *Ukridge* the narrator makes the same point. This pleasant stranger, he muses, may be a Snooks, or a Buggins. Best not enquire.

The most substantial private stockade, however, was built around the home itself, which became more like the Englishman's ideal of a castle than ever. The ramparts of suburbia, the middle classes' own particular empire, were thrown up much farther away than was convenient from the areas where their daily work was actually done, but convenience was not a priority. Distance was expected to lend the enchantment now thought necessary to mask the harsh reality of the office, the works, and the working-class 'districts' alike. It was in fact an additional barricade, built of materials always hard to come by: more time and more money. But, by encamping behind it, middle-class owners, employers, and managers made it difficult for themselves to play that effective paternalist role in society which had been open even to the Gradgrinds of the original, compact Coketown; for it was assuredly hard to co-operate with and know the mind and thought of men who were never seen at leisure, off duty, out of 'time'. More and more, those who might in fact have acted as genuine 'captains of industry' found themselves becoming observers of a process only, dependent on various theories of what was awkwardly to be called 'labour relations', and apt therefore to be caught off-balance when the value of any one such theory ran out. No amount of philanthropic effort under the name of social work by the 'boss' and his womenfolk was ever to counterweigh the handicap of social segregation.

Thus every city of the world-wide industrial democracy had its class map, on which there were always ghettos allotted for the latest comers, whether Irish in Glasgow or Poles in Pittsburg. There were accordingly parts of town, where the other half lived, where the child of a middle-class business or professional man never went; only when the working classes made *their* Sunday forays, promenading dressed in their best into the places where the other half lived, would he be likely to see the type and style of the majority of his fellow-citizens. His own style was likely soon to be stereotyped. It must always have been difficult for a travelled stranger, who found himself amid a maze of avenues, crescents, and drives (seldom a street), and among a welter of Scottish baronial or Abbotsford gothic 'hatters' castles' to feel quite certain whether he was in Liverpool's Sefton Park, Glasgow's Kelvinside, Toronto's Forest Hill, or Melbourne's Toorak. That passion for physical comforts, which Mill had noted as being peculiarly middle-class, was everywhere in evidence and everywhere the same: the Crystal Palace of 1851 was to mirror down a vista of time the marble halls of Chicago's Exhibition of 1893. Cushioned from austerity by looming furniture, barricaded from necessity by greenhouses and pianos, secured from thirst and hunger by China tea and joints of the best beef, transported by carriage and encompassed by dutiful women, the upper middle classes the world over set up their bastions of privacy.

In the shadow of these, they bred up their sons: either, depending on whatever genetic trick nature had played on them, to copy what they themselves had done and to improve on it, or else to reject their legacy of complacent conformity and to seek some alternative, rebel ground, bare of all the household gods. For the bounds of a society where conventions of respectability were of more significance (because they were of more use) than any play of ideas could ever be, wherein people of an independent turn of mind were suspect almost as agents of some alien and hostile power, proved too constricting for many to endure. Hugh

Dalton, spending his childhood in a Windsor canonry, with a good view of Eton across the meadows thrown in, remarked that an irreverence for authority was in his case inevitable.[1] It was from such homes—and from homes less comfortable whose prisoners nevertheless dreamed domestic dreams of Belgravian ease, or imperial dreams of dominion over palm and pine—that many were to emerge determined to obtain once more the confidence of 'the people'. This body was now inevitably enclosed in quotation-marks, since the long middle-class quarantine had ensured that no one was now quite sure who 'the people' were and what it was they were likely to want. From such homes, graduated also the sisterhood of the 'New Women'—the first of the twentieth century's assertive 'colonial nationalists', rejecting the assumptions of a society they had not made, and no longer content with a form of 'indirect rule' within it that received a personal, but no public, recognition.

The middle-class intelligentsia (forced to borrow this Russian name for something the English language baulked at), critical both of their surroundings and of the assumptions that fashioned these, were necessarily a minority. But their chief weapons were tenacity and a sense of righteousness, weapons in fact much the same as those that had brought success to their fathers. This similarity of temperament gave the family disputes a content of venom they might otherwise have lacked. It was a widely-held attitude, much encouraged by the writers and draughtsmen who staffed *Punch*, that an artist of any sort was a licensed clown (the licence was of course revocable), and that writing-fellows and scribblers were persons on the fringe of polite society, court jesters whose eccentricities might amuse, but which could hardly affect 'real life'. But although these hacks of Grub Street, now known as penny-a-liners, remained as despised a race in the nineteenth century as in Samuel Johnson's time, leisured middle-class writers, for ever asking awkward questions and pointing out anomalies, could not be so easily ignored. These were men secure in their bank balances, however uneasy their minds; they had 'connections', they knew all kinds of important people. When Matthew Arnold lectured his audience on their shortcomings, he was, if not eagerly listened to, at least accepted as

[1] Hugh Dalton, *Call Back Yesterday* (1953), p. 14.

someone who spoke with a measured authority. Moreover, he was catholic in his distastes, and everyone who winced could enjoy the sight of someone else doing so a few moments later. Aristocrats, for example, were only 'children of the established fact'; their country-houses, marching across the land, were the 'great fortified posts of the Barbarians'. The middle-classes were Philistine (like Macaulay, whom Arnold disliked), lost to philosophy and wonder. Nonconformists 'thinking by batches of fifties' were incomplete and mutilated men, for no man, who knew nothing else, knew even his Bible. Electors in a democracy were bound to exercise not reason, but their natural taste for bathos. Matters were even worse in America, a country without aristocratic barbarians, composed of narrow Philistinism almost entirely—'A whole nation touched, amidst all its greatness and promise, with that provincialism which it is our aim to extirpate in the English Nonconformists'.[1]

In England dogmatism, if delivered ironically, has often won general respect. Thomas Carlyle, a social critic with a deeper range than Arnold's, was less effective because his irony was so heavy-handed. Although, unlike Mill and Morley, Arnold never had to air an opinion in the House of Commons and hear how it sounded aloud, he struck a responsive chord. He did not attack the capitalist system as such, only the narrow outlook of its operators, insisting that because they did not think hard enough, and did not seem to be interested in thought anyway, they would assuredly be caught by surprise. It was a shrewd line of attack. Industrialists who watched the growing competition from the United States and Germany from the 1880s onwards could not safely reject the criticism. Nor was the 'condition-of-England' question, which even the most blinkered Bounderby was coming to recognize as a factor in the continuing prosperity of Coketown, showing any marked improvement. It was true what Arnold said, that never had a people believed anything more firmly than nine Englishmen out of ten believed, that the national greatness and welfare was proved by 'our being so very rich'. But other nations were rich, and getting richer; and one of Carlyle's *dicta* was also believed, that the cash-nexus by itself made no very firm bond for society. The older ties had been

[1] See his *Culture and Anarchy* for these views.

shredded away, by a process which, disguised under the reasonably innocuous title of parliamentary reform, was now found to
have its revolutionary implications. Arnold emphasized that as
feudalism, which with its ideas and habits of subordination had
for many centuries supported the whole concept of the British
Constitution, died out,

> and we are left with nothing but our system of checks . . . with
> [our] notion of its being the great right and happiness of an
> Englishman to do as far as possible what he likes, we are in
> danger of drifting towards anarchy.

This was thought something worth saying, and worth listen-
ing to. The danger was certainly there. But, it might surely be
controlled? Even if feudalism of the old authoritative kind, bind-
ing fast loyalty and duty and service in an instantly recognizable
whole, had gone for ever, the memory of it had not, and the
habits of authority and of deference to authority were still very
well marked in the mutual relations of the English. Was it not
possible, then, that a kind of 'sublimated feudalism' might still
continue to underline the assumptions of the British Constitution, and to prevent the anarchic tendencies of individual men
from finding any channel of influence?

It was indeed possible—so much so that the possibility was
never even seriously threatened. The chief danger of social
criticism is that it points out alternatives to men who might
otherwise not have thought of these for themselves. But in
England the danger was minimal. Social critics had to fight
against the deep grain of Toryism in the people, and many
were compelled to adopt barnstorming methods to get any
attention at all. Foreigners of course had even less chance:
English gospellers according to Karl Marx were never numerous. The aspirations of 'Labour', and the concepts of Socialism,
were later to make a hurried because necessary wedding in
England: but between idealistic Fabians and the rank-and-file of
'the Movement' there was always an abyss of incomprehension,
and members of the intelligentsia who attached themselves to
the emergent Labour party found themselves acting as its public
relations officers with the middle classes, a useful role indeed but

not the one they had supposed they were destined to play. Life in England continued to react far more strongly to events than to ideas. This was a disillusioning truth that drove many middle-class 'rebels' out of politics and out of English life—or the English death, as Lawrence Durrell has called it—altogether, as Arnold's Philistines continued to grow in number and power.

Yet, even if the area in which ideas made an impact had its definite limits, the intellectual empire where the doctrines of sublimated feudalism were successfully distributed was still extensive enough. The young make the best captive audience; and the young could be very easily beguiled by fairy-tales at an early stage in life and, at a later, by history books of the 'Little Arthur' variety. Middle-class fairy-tales were written, although no one matched the skill of E. Nesbit; but the greater number were inescapably aristocratic, with a cast of kings, princesses, and loyal peasants, in which the knight who rescued the maiden from the dragon took over, to the sounds of popular applause, the dragon's lapsed *droits de seigneur*. The most influential histories produced in the nineteenth century were those of Hallam, Macaulay, Froude, Freeman and Stubbs. All of the often contradictory findings of these men of firm convictions were to filter, unacknowledged, into school textbooks—and often into the *same* textbook—for another four generations. Taken together, their books explained how it had come about that England had reached its apogee in the Victorian epoch, and readers in the long afternoon of that epoch were content with the explanation. George Bancroft had once performed the same service for his fellow citizens in the United States, and was rather put out when the German historian von Ranke assured him, by way of intended praise, that his history was 'the best ever written from the democratic point of view'.[1]

English historians took no such view. Their tone was pater-nalist, and they approved the successive paternalisms of English governments. England had the right to expect every man to do his duty. The price of liberty was, as Pitt would have agreed, eternal vigilance. If the medal had another side, it was not shown. That England's aim was to hold the balance of power was made an axiom, despite the fact that England had never

[1] Gooch, *History and Historians*, p. 406.

managed to do any such thing, and that all her major wars had been fought in alliance. Military failure, in a notoriously peace-loving nation, could be excused, and the grand old Duke of York be given a consolatory niche in a nursery-rhyme. Unsuccessful admirals, in contrast, seldom reached the printed page. Biographies of great men were decently reticent concerning any lapses from greatness that these men may have known, and adequate biographies of persons in a high place of whom it was the accepted opinion that they had, in one way or another, failed—such as Bolingbroke, Bute, and North—were not written at all. The greatest problem of this kind in England's history, whether or not Oliver Cromwell was an English worthy, was not resolved. As a result, no axiom covers his case, and no one is sure even yet whether he succeeded or failed.

Historians are always to a serious extent the masters of the past they are evoking. The danger of this was clearly seen. The materials for writing recent history were therefore kept from the merely curious, or from those thought likely to make some mischievous use of them. Cabinet ministers were apt to look on the departmental correspondence of their own term of office as their personal property, and to go home with it on their retire-ment, sometimes to sift it with a view to some future official biography. The archives that remained in the public departments of state were, as they still are, held incommunicado until fifty years had elapsed. It was more than likely that a reputation for political mastery would not survive investigation: and even if the policy-maker himself was dead, his descendants would still be alive, and sensitive. It was also very likely that some of these would hold public office.[1]

---

[1] Cf. Lord Chandos' *Memoirs* (1962), pp. 324–5, on the composition of Churchill's 'Caretaker' government, May–July 1945: 'The Prime Minister was the son of a Chancellor of the Exchequer [Lord Randolph Churchill]; Anthony Eden a descendant of a Governor-General and Viceroy of India [Lord Auckland]; Lord Salisbury the son of a distinguished Minister and grandson of a Prime Minister; Lord Rosebery and [Richard] Law were both sons of a Prime Minister; James Stuart a descendant of James V of Scotland; Oliver Stanley the son of a Minister and descended from a Prime Minister [14th Earl of Derby]: 'Rab' Butler the son of one of the most distinguished Colonial Governors; Harold Macmillan was allied by marriage to the Cavendish family, his father-in-law had been a minister and Governor-General of Canada; I was the son of a Secretary of State for the Colonies [Alfred Lyttelton].'

In these circumstances, the historical education given to the young has always had shortcomings. In the University of Oxford in the 1930s the curriculum still stopped at 1878, when Disraeli imported peace with honour into England from Berlin. Many other spheres of public life in England have only an ill-recorded history, since their content was never encompassed in the outlook either of the Ascendancy or of its historians. As a result, no one can yet safely assume that his definition of 'middle class' corresponds with anyone else's. There is no comprehensive study of English Dissent, and 'Nonconformity' itself is still more a generic than a descriptive title. The public schools have been analysed by friend and foe alike, but the Dissenting academies lie in unknown country. How the professions arrived at respectability, in a society that looked askance at 'experts', still wants thorough investigation. How the missionaries took Christianity into the British Empire, who they were and how much of it they took, needs it also. Few Englishmen were ever taught anything about India under British rule, or for that matter anything concrete about Scotland, Ireland or the United States. Since the history of large business enterprises is difficult to describe, but easier to describe than to discuss, only a minority of such enterprises have ventured to take their chance in this difficult field of public relations. (The Hudson's Bay Company, for example, still closes its archives at 1870.) Histories of English local government deal always with measures, not men; and in consequence, the history of graft in municipal administration belongs peculiarly to the United States, whose nineteenth-century sense of self-confident magnitude—'Come and show us up', urged the citizens of one community to the diligent muckraker who had just published a blistering *exposé* of another, 'We're worse than they are'—was large enough to meet even this challenge. One beneficial result of this has been the spread of the notion in England that corrupt practices among bureaucrats, like cowardice under fire, have always been exceptional. A distinguished American historian of the British colonies in the eighteenth century, C. M. Andrews of Yale, once remarked in a footnote that the history of corruption in the British Navy required to be written.[1] The need was never obvious to the Admiralty.

[1] Andrews, *Colonial Period of American History*, IV (New Haven, 1938), 315 n.

If the kind of history likely to disturb the equanimity of the educated was unlikely to be written—or if written, read—so too many works of fiction, whose authors well understood that critical themes were unpopular in the fullest sense of the word, must have been stillborn. That more people went to the theatre than read history-books is not proven, but may be taken as probable. In that enclave, suitably festooned with plush and gilt and statuary, reassurance was again the keynote.[1] The author of the play—whatever the name of him and it, for these were not matters of any great importance—was expected to please the stalls, while at the same time throwing in material sufficiently 'strong' to hold the easily-lost attention of the gallery. Since the ability to write just this kind of play has never at any time been common, the Victorian theatre did not recruit either many new plays or any new ideas. There were many revivals of long-popular melodramas dealing with the conflict of vice and virtue, and also many presentations of the 'classics', always cut to a supportable length. In these life was seen as from a high place; tragedy belonged to the court, not in the kitchen. The chronicle-plays of Shakespeare particularly emphasized this aristocratic tone: as the repertory-actress heroine of *The Solid Gold Cadillac* (1946) remarks ruefully, playing in Shakespeare 'you never get to sit down unless you're a king'. The stage, peopled by star-crossed noblemen, Restoration wits or drawing-room comedians, was not expected to reflect the English scene as a whole, and it did not do so. If the lower classes appeared on it at all they were cast as figures of fun, whose whole lives were one long, light-hearted predicament, brought about mainly by their own fecklessness: preferably Irishmen or Cockneys, and thus easily identifiable as heaven-born wags,[2] but always faithful to 'the Guv'nor', their own particular *sahib*.

The awakening of some people's social conscience was

[1] Charles Kingsley wrote in 1873 that few educated persons either went to or wrote plays, 'Finding that since the grosser excitements of the imagination have become forbidden themes, there is really very little to write about': J. L. Hammond, *C. P. Scott* (1934), p. 55.

[2] Erskine Childers, in his *Framework of Home Rule* (1911), p. xv, speaks of the 'systematic defamation' of the Irish character since the Union. Cf. the books of Somerville and Ross which take, from the standpoint of an Irish 'Resident Magistrate', a firmly colonialist view of the natives.

reflected in the plays both of Ibsen, the cartographer of the distortions caused to the psyche by its being too tightly laced into suburban respectability, and of Bernard Shaw, who made game of this constricted society. But these plays were too startling to be popular. Very many, including the drama critics of the respectable newspapers, asserted that these men's works were not plays at all, and denied that the unpleasant series of *fracas* on family battlegrounds, which Ibsen loved to depict, were suitable matter for drama anyway: people, as his own Judge Brack remarked, did not do such things. Sir Arthur Pinero's maps of the moral issues that beset the upper middle classes, well-dressed and gracefully articulate through the severest crises to the final curtain, were much more to the general taste. The 'well-made play', such as *His House in Order* (1906) presented the spectator with a soothingly finite view of life: things had indeed a beginning, a middle, and an end, just as they ought, and one was free to put in order as one saw fit one's own house, the existence of which could be taken for granted. The writers who stocked the shelves of Mudie's Library agreed with this. One of their major themes was 'sin', implying adultery, an activity which can only be pursued by those with money and leisure. In time this theme was rivalled by that of murder, for the lovers of twentieth-century detective stories were normally circumstanced as to be able to take an academic view of violence. Most of them had never met a policeman who did not say 'sir'.

Anthony Trollope did not trench on these themes, but he admitted in his *Autobiography* (1883) that he wrote partly for money and social position, and he therefore put a great deal into his books about money and social position. This frankness lost him the posthumous respect of a large part of his following who had been entranced by his earlier anatomy of the clerical world of Barchester. These stately gavottes of deans and chapters threw light into yet another of the private enclaves of society, the Church of England itself, an institution on which attention was always focused and whose public attitudes had accordingly been brought to a high pitch of professional ease, and this despite three bitter pills Liberalism had forced it to swallow: disestablishment in Ireland, together with the abolition both of church-rates and the Test Act qualifications for entry into Oxford and

Cambridge. The private motives of churchmen, however, lay in unknown country, and a traveller who brought back news of fascinating rites and customs was sure of attention. Even politicians welcomed anything that cast light on this dark field, for many a Prime Minister found out that appointment to bishoprics was a very chancy affair, since 'the Evangelical appointed today might become the Ritualist of tomorrow or the Papist of the day after'.[1] They were of course Oxford men, who had dreamed too much under the spires, who were most likely to give this particular trouble: for it was always difficult, remarked a Regius Professor of Divinity at the University of Cambridge, to think of Cambridge men as bishops.[2]

But it is not odd that the popularity of the aristocracy should have been always much wider than that of these Forsytes (to borrow Galsworthy's name for the *genus*). Forsytes took themselves seriously, to the point of solemnity. Aristocrats inclined, in contrast, to the opinion that life was not so stern and earnest as all that, since they had never had any need to find it so. Even the pessimistic Salisbury, from whose character gaiety was absent, spoke with a freedom of satirical wit beyond the compass of most of his own party. He believed that there was the world of God, and the world of man. The two interpenetrated but slightly: for, as he pointed out to Liberals in 1886, their great doctrine of freedom of contract, even that of Free Trade itself, was 'not on a level with the Ten Commandments'. Men were, and would always be, capable of any folly: the democratic system was merely likely to give them fuller scope for its exercise. But there was no need to take their secular preoccupations as if they were matters of life and death, for they were not. The aristocratic predilection for sport was now filtering down into middle-class modes by way of the playing fields of the new public schools, but Forsytes could never approve the idea that a grown man should spend his life in the pursuit of frivolity. The lure of the Turf, however, both for the nobleman who owned a racing stud and for the plebeian who gambled on the horses it produced, was strong enough to hold its own against this

[1] Dudley Bahlman, 'The Queen, Mr Gladstone and Church Patronage', *Victorian Studies* iii, No. 4, June 1960, 351.
[2] *loc. cit.*

middle-class distaste. Racing was neither a virtuous nor a useful activity; therein lay its attraction.

The attraction itself could be put to good political use. Wilfrid Blunt reports that Lord Rosebery told an enquirer that he continued on the Turf

> because it was the easiest way in England to be accepted as a statesman—and he had appealed to Gladstone, who had quite agreed with him.[1]

Although Gladstone's agreement was never so profound as to make a racing man of him, he was right to agree. The intellectual Rosebery made his title to the premiership secure when his horse won the Derby. In March 1894 the Russian Ambassador in London, Baron de Staal, wrote to his chief at St Petersburg, commenting that in a recent despatch concerning the likelihood of the Rosebery Cabinet's remaining in office he had omitted *'une considération majeure. Si* Ladas *gagne le Derby, son propriétaire est maître de la situation'.* When *Ladas* did so in June, Staal reported *'les feuilles les plus sérieuses . . . supputaient déjà le nombre de voix que cette noble bête ferait gagner à son maître'.*[2] Aristocrats lost no face appearing at, and profiting from, the democratic jamboree of a race-meet. They did not mind, as their social inferiors did, if people 'talked'. Racing slang indeed became a modish way of talking, and even those who lacked any lore of the stable came to understand, in a highly organized society, what an outsider was. But many terms, of racing as of other sports, remained recondite, the hallmarks of a particular caste. Whatever their newly-acquired acreage in the home counties, merchants were not particularly welcome on their hired horses at the meet, and were not invited at all to the *battues* of pheasants at the country-seats of the great. Consequently they never learned to go *down*—as opposed to *up*, the geographical direction—to Scotland for the Twelfth [of August],[3] or indeed to look on that country as North Britain, a preserve of birds, stags and ghillies.

[1] Blunt, *Gordon at Khartoum* (1912), p. 237.

[2] A. Meyendorff, ed., *Correspondance Diplomatique du Baron de Staal* (Paris, 1928) II, 240, 245.

[3] Grouse may be shot after August 12, pheasant after September 12.

Travelling first-class *down* to Scotland, there to debouch, laden with rod and gun, under the sardonic eye of the villagers, the English sporting gentry were unlikely to meet many Scotsmen who would have helped broaden their view of the Scottish scene. Ghillies who answered back were cast as 'characters', and promptly forgotten. Highland Scotland had a tradition of respect for rank, but in Lowland Scotland, centre of the country's industrial wealth, a gentleman was seldom seen, and there were even fewer to be met within the towns and cities. But not being a gentleman was never the lacerating thought it was in England. The middle classes of Scotland, makers of the national prosperity, had a higher opinion of themselves than their English counterparts, and did not insist on copying the manners and customs of their betters—since, disciplined from youth in the aristocratic doctrines of Calvinist theology, they were apt to maintain that their betters, on this earth at least, did not exist. Hence they exported the ablest of their sons as cheerfully to England as to India, and were not at all surprised when these successfully colonized the governments of both. They had their own codes and customs, and particular groups looked on their own as the most commonsensible. In the early nineteenth century the advocates of Edinburgh, guardians of the social tone, set the pattern for dining at 4 or 5 p.m., but Glasgow continued to dine at 3 p.m.; later, Glasgow would have 'high tea' at 5 p.m. and Edinburgh would dine at 7 p.m.; and when Glasgow learned that dinner was an evening meal, Edinburgh sat down at 8 p.m. Glaswegians therefore continued to look on the citizens of the capital as finicking people, chained by habits of genteelism they ought to have had the sense to do without. But these were minor distinctions. In Scottish society as a whole the right of passage was freely admitted, as it was not in England. One was expected, as in the American democracy, to 'get on' if one could —the fact that one had, was nothing in particular to boast about. A boaster could anyway be crushed with the remark that 'we were a' Jock Tamson's bairns', or a prominent person socially relegated with the dry reminder, 'I knew his feyther'. The protracted unease of middle-class Scots in regard to the admittedly 'immortal memory' of Robert Burns has developed from the fact that Burns, although given his right of passage and capable of fully exploiting it, chose to turn his back on a society which would have been glad to make him its own.

The Scottish independence of attitude was reflected in politics, often to the mystification or annoyance of English observers. Scotland in the nineteenth century voted Whig and Liberal. 'Whigs' had originally been a Scottish product, and indeed, as one of the Scottish leaders of the Whig party, the eighth Duke of Argyll, reminded Edinburgh's burghers, Whig heads on pikes had often embellished the walls of the town, reminding all how dangerous was the struggle for liberty.[1] The formation and maintenance of Dundas' phalanx—forty-three out of the forty-five Scottish M.P.s in 1802, the year that the Whigs' own *Edinburgh Review* was founded—acclimatized the few Scottish voters, and a great many of the voters' needy kindred, to the custom of loyalty to the government, a loyalty Dundas always took care handsomely to reward. While English Radicals, although perforce allied to the Whigs, continued to upbraid them as timeservers and of course hailed Pitt and Dundas as outright traitors, founders of a new Tory party without any ascertainable principles at all, Scottish Radicals continued to adhere to the intellectual brand of Whiggism promoted by Sir James Mackintosh and by the argumentative zealots of the *Edinburgh Review*. Bentham's name was not one to conjure with in the 'new town' or at the University, where Dugald Stewart held that 'philosophic radicalism' was a contradiction in terms. Scottish educated opinion supported the southern movement for parliamentary reform on the commonsense principle that, if the English found their own parliamentary representation full of anomalies, then that of Scotland was plainly ridiculous.

Accordingly in 1832, Grey's reforming Whigs won forty-three out of the fifty-three Scottish constituencies, and set the pattern for the next fifty years. Its value was obvious as early as 1837, when it was Irish and Scottish votes that kept the Whigs in power; and in 1841, so secure was Liberalism in Scotland that only twenty-two seats were contested. The Scottish burghs were the principal strongholds, but even in the counties until 1865 an almost level balance of the Liberal and Conservative interests was kept. In the 1840s Bright's Anti-Corn Law-League

[1] Speech at Edinburgh, April 1, 1863; *Autobiography*, II, 196.

made a powerful impression on Scottish opinion; on one occasion he convened 801 ministers, the better to denounce 'the sinfulness and injustice' of the Corn Laws. Disraeli's Reform Act of 1867 shrewdly set out to woo Scotland by giving her another seven seats, but his immediate return was bleak, as Scottish votes overwhelmingly swept in Gladstone and the Liberals in 1868. Gladstone, a Scot himself and devious in the ways that Scots were devious, was a man North Britain could understand, and as his career waxed his name, always prefaced with 'Mr' even forty years after his death, became a heroic talisman in middle-class presbyterian households. Disraeli's deviousness, in contrast, was his own highly individual kind, not one appreciated in manse or farmstead. His romantic attachment to institutions that were purely English, and to a monarchy which the Scots, romantic in their own way, continued to look on as German, was not translateable across the Border, and a contemporary opinion summed up the policy of his Conservative party as 'imprecise, frivolous, or opportunist'—adjectives of doom in Scottish politics. The election of April 1880, the climax of Gladstone's campaign in Lowland Scotland, won for the Liberals fifty-three of the sixty seats. The many troubles of the Gladstone ministry between 1880 and 1885 were excused by the Scottish electorate, which, having been awarded another twelve seats by the Reform Act and Redistribution Acts of 1884–5, expressed their confidence yet again by giving the Liberals sixty-two out of the seventy-two seats, in the election of November 1885.

This marked, however, the zenith of Liberal dominance in Scotland. In the election of July 1886, the consternation caused among Liberals by Gladstone's belated and concealed conversion to the principle of Home Rule for Ireland, was felt in Scotland also; the party split ran the length of the United Kingdom. Only fourteen of Scotland's seventy-two seats remained in the Liberal camp, nine of the burghs returning Liberal-Unionists. Thereafter fluctuation set in. By the election of 1892 the Liberal strength was back to fifty seats; they were Scottish and Irish voters who combined to negate the Conservatives' English majority, and to ensure the formation of Gladstone's last ministry. But the situation was reversed again in 1895, when the overall Scottish Liberal majority stood at only six. The Unionists—the name by which the Scottish Conservatives still prefer to be known, long after anyone can remember why—continued to gain political ground: Glasgow, more versed than many a country burgh on the social aspects of the Irish question, was voting solidly Unionist. The 'Khaki election' of October 1900 saw the Scots reflecting the patriotic fervours of the English, actually going to the extreme of giving the Unionists an overall 4-seat majority. Like the English, however, they regretted this conduct in January 1906, when once more the Liberals held fifty seats, and Scotland returned to Westminster her first two Labour members —for Dundee, and the Blackfriars division of Glasgow.

In their outlook Scottish Liberals preserved a certain independence. Lowland Scots, suspicious of any Celtic strain even in themselves, were accordingly disinclined to make a hero of Lloyd George, and if they did not approve of dukes they did not look on them as a public menace: no landed grandee of Scotland owned a great deal of urban property anyway. In the Highlands, people were accustomed to the presence of gentry, Scottish in title and English in upbringing and outlook. Highland Scots, bred to the most closely-knit of all paternalist systems, the clan, still admitted that aristocracy had a role to play: what was in dispute was the method of playing it. In the eighteenth century Scottish highland chiefs, like their contemporaries in Africa, had kidnapped and sold men to the American plantations, but they preserved as long as the English allowed them to the aristocratic code of honour: they were Lowland Scots in the Edinburgh Parliament who had sold Charles I, with the blessing of the kirk, to the English republicans, but they were highlanders a century later who protected his great-grandson, whatever the price on his head, from the English redcoats. In the nineteenth century, however, although the high hand was still carried, the honourable code was not so much in evidence. It is doubtful whether any English peer ever experienced so public a rebuff as the Duke of Sutherland, who, seeking to raise volunteers for the Army at the time of the Crimean War, was thus castigated by a citizen of his own county seat at Golspie:

I do assure your Grace that it is the prevailing opinion in this county, that should the Czar of Russia take possession of

Dunrobin Castle and of Stafford House [the Duke's county and London residences] we could not expect worse treatment at his hands than we have experienced at the hands of your family for the last fifty years.[1]

It was a line of argument whose possibilities for political exploitation were clear even to so urbanized a Radical as Joseph Chamberlain, whose unauthorized programme made an instant appeal in rural Scotland thirty years later. Speaking at Inverness in September 1885, he asked his audience whether it was not time to submit to careful examination and review a system which placed 'such vast powers for evil in the hands of irresponsible individuals', and which made the possession of land 'not a trust but a means of extortion and exaction'.[2]

It seemed so indeed. In the six crofting counties of Scotland between 1883 and 1903, land given over to deer forests increased by close on a million-and-a-half acres, and the argument put forward by the Duke of Argyll, that sheep reclaimed waste land but did not expropriate arable, was neither welcome, credited, nor statistically proven. In an article he wrote for *The Nineteenth Century* on 'The Economic Condition of the Highlands' Argyll pointed out that emigration from the Highlands had preceded the introduction of sheep, and insisted that Sutherland in particular, whose population in 1881 was very little more than in 1801, had had 'three generations of affection' lavished on it.[3] It was perfectly true that the glens of Scotland had once maintained, amid frequent famines and with occasional assistance from unwilling Lowlanders, a population which lived in idleness, ignorance and poverty: Bailie Nicol Jarvie of Glasgow had noted of the Highlanders (in Scott's *Rob Roy*) that they worked 'as if a plough or a spade burnt their fingers'. It was true, too, that these glens were now tenanted by perhaps five farmers, if as many. But that was only saying that at last change had come to the Highlands, the same change that had come long before to the Lowlands and to English shires and which everywhere in the country had been the one indispensable condition of an improved

---

[1] A. Mackenzie, *The Highland Clearances* (Edinburgh, 1883), p. 106.
[2] *loc. cit.*, p. 264.
[3] *Nineteenth Century*, February 1883, p. 194.

and improving agriculture. Argyll remarked also that of the great capitalist class of graziers, who were vulgarly supposed to monopolize the Highlands, he could identify only seven.

The island of Lewis in the Hebrides, for example, supplied a sufficient comment on the evils wrought by *laissez-faire*, when that principle was applied to the land. The population of Lewis in 1801 had been a supportable 9,000: but by 1881 it had reached an unsupportable 25,000, people living in conditions of extreme poverty. An empty glen might indeed have a history of eviction, and therefore of human suffering—but consider the suffering in the present day that had been avoided.

This argument, which would not have convinced the Indians of North America either, could never win many adherents. In 1883 Alexander Mackenzie published his *History of the Highland Clearances*, a book which brought together documentary evidence on the motives and methods of eviction, and which fuelled Highland memories thereafter, in Scotland and in Nova Scotia alike. Argyll himself was answered in the *Nineteenth Century* by an Edinburgh professor of Greek, who set out to show, in his own phrase, 'the copper side of the duke's silver shield'.[1] The characterization of Highlanders as a feckless and idle race of dram-drinkers, who made their women do all the work and who were themselves useless for anything other than fighting, was thought impertinent by a nation whose Lowland educators, forgetful of the verdict of their own ancestors on Highlanders, were now beginning to look at their own national history through a romantic tartan haze; and Argyll, the Campbell chieftain, was sharply reminded that the name of Campbell was no talisman anywhere in the Highlands outside of Argyllshire. Once, in the glens, had lived a contented, happy, and well-behaved peasantry. But now the crofters had vanished, either behind the shopcounters of *parvenu* townships like Oban and Dunoon, or into the stokeholds and boiler-rooms of the Peninsular and Oriental Steam Packet Company: their sons were to be found distributed among the slums of Glasgow or the shellfish of Prince Edward Island. The Scot, heir to a land that could not support him, had already become the professional exile of the world. When Lord Sydney sent to Pitt in 1784 a list of

[1] J. S. Blackie: *loc. cit.*, April 1883, p. 605.

field-officers in India, he remarked that he could only find three who did not have a Scotch name: a diligent student might be set to find out how much, if at all, this state of affairs had altered by 1850, or by 1900, or by 1930.

Whatever the truth of the various arguments and analyses, by airing them the Scots compelled official attention to these processes of displacement. The condition-of-Scotland question, although a late arrival on the stage of British politics, drew down on it at least as much limelight as did the long-familiar social problems of England, and each generation of twentieth-century Scottish members of the House of Commons, irrespective both of their political parties and of the fact that they were not the best men Scotland could produce, continued to ensure that this was so. Their own ignorance of the Scottish background was one that English political leaders were prepared to admit to, since they were, if pressed, unable to argue that 'North Britain' was not an insulting appellation or that shooting was other than a frivolity. It was therefore with respect that they listened to the early Scottish pioneers of the Labour movement, who spoke often more in sorrow than in anger, but always colourfully, and always in excellent English delivered in what was, after all, a foreign accent. But, to confess to a like ignorance of the social conditions of his own country was a bolder step than most English politicians were prepared to take, since it argued some-how a dereliction of duty somewhere: and the same degree of attention was often withheld from representatives of the English working classes, the more so since they spoke in 'un-standard' English and were not always free from a truculence of attitude indicating that they themselves knew of the enormity of their own conduct in setting up to criticize the social order. Gentle-men whose business it was to select candidates for the Indian Civil, the colonial or the home services were happier dealing with the unknown than with the half-known. They were often prepared to grant an indulgence to the candidate who was a Scottish crofter's son, assuming that his dourness of mien con-cealed that natural integrity which was the most highly-publicized feature of the Scottish character. But they might be less sympathetic to the merits of the son of a Bradford wool-worker, since his future official life would have to be passed among people he himself would look on as his social superiors. (As a consequence, intelligent youths from the north of England rarely presented themselves for this ordeal, and the Severn-Wash frontier divided the administrative services of the country until well after the Second World War.)

The Scots were thus able to exploit their alien background, and the opportunities which were either given them or which they got for themselves, without social hindrances. They imposed their own image, often with considerable malice afore-thought: J. M. Barrie for example stressing a fey Celtic insight, and Harry Lauder making a life's career out of flattering the vulgar preconceptions of English music-hall audiences. Even in less sophisticated *milieux* like Ontario and Nova Scotia, the exiled Scot set up his own standards of puritanism—originally designed as a defence against the devil, a potent character in Scotland's history—and compelled other immigrants, less trained to insight into their own souls, to conform to them. The Englishman in contrast migrated with far less personal and national publicity, and in his homes overseas St George's day never rivalled St Andrew's day in nostalgic celebration, while few met to toast the immortal memory of William Shakespeare. As has already been noted, English migrants to countries already settled by their own kind were very quickly absorbed into the local society: it is only the name of the *Mayflower* in 1620, not that of any of its thousands of successors, that is com-memorated. Similarly, Englishmen at home who throughout the nineteenth century migrated from the country to the towns, severed their links with the life of the countryside, the older women's herbal lore being a last reminder in many homes of another way of living.

Unlike the Scots, too, a great many Englishmen did not remove themselves from the rent-rolls of the landed gentry by physically transferring from the village green to a back street under the railway bridge. Scottish grandees owned vast tracts of land indeed: among them three dukes, a marquis and an earl owned $2\frac{1}{4}$ million acres of their own country, and Buccleuch's annual rent-roll of £217,163 was the highest in the United Kingdom. But land was more valuable per acre in the south than in the north of the kingdom: the dukes of Bedford and Westminster had great and profitable estates in London itself, and although the Duke of Northumberland held only 186,000 acres in comparison with Sutherland's 1¼ million acres, the lesser acreage was the better property. Dukes and earls were not typical of the landed gentry as a whole, since they were by definition, and were regarded as, a privileged minority. In 1876, of the 209,547 landowners, only 874 owned more than 5,000 acres. But it was the minority at the heart of this minority that drew the most attention. Amid this 874,525 noblemen owned 15 million acres, rather more than half the country. Forty-nine peers held an acreage of over 50,000 each, and fifteen held over 100,000. Forty-five drew an annual rental of above £50,000, ten of above £100,000. Bolingbroke had been fond of remarking that the landed interest were the true owners of the political vessel: a writer in 1882, presaging *The Coming Democracy*, observed how everyone 'naturally thinks of a Cabinet minister as a landlord *in esse* or *in posse*'.[1]

The former type set the pattern for the latter. In 1908, for example, Lord Derby—the head of the house of Stanley, and the great magnate of Lancashire—still owned his 70,000 acres, had eight houses to live in besides his principal seat, 'the large taste-less hotel' of Knowsley, and still spent £50,000 a year on house-hold expenditure. On his property at Bootle, a working-class suburb of Liverpool, there were eighty-seven houses to the acre, as Lloyd George took care to point out: Derby countered this criticism by observing that 'property development in the area had followed the normally accepted pattern of similar estates'[2]—which was of course Lloyd George's point in the first place. With so great a man pervading by his influence both the social and political scene in Lancashire, it was not surprising that he had no need to monger boroughs, or to fear the intrusion of carpet-baggers. Looking back over a life in politics, Bryce recalled how the tendency of the electoral vote in any constituency to shift from Tory to Whig or Whig to Tory had used in England to be 'deemed to indicate the presence of a corrupt element. It was a black mark against a borough'.[3] Of these black marks Lancashire

[1] G. Harwood (1882), p. 174.
[2] Randolph Churchill, *Lord Derby* (1959), p. 110.
[3] Bryce, *The American Commonwealth* (1915 edn.), II, 332.

boroughs were refreshingly free. Accidents had happened, of course. In 1830 a Radical had defeated a Stanley, and the Lord Derby of the day had made his attitude known by discontinuing racing and blocking up the windows of his house in Preston. Again, in 1906, when the democratic tide was running high, another Stanley was defeated by a Labour carpenter in one of the divisions of Liverpool; and when the Conservative leader Bonar Law was defeated in Manchester in 1910 Derby attributed this disaster to the influence of 'the foreign Jew quarter'. But despite the occasional nefarious intrigue, it remained true that there was

> hardly a Conservative Association in Lancashire or Cheshire which, confronted with the necessity of finding a candidate, did not instinctively wonder whether there was any member of the Stanley family available to carry their banner.[1]

The principle of the *quid pro quo* had never been expunged, Reform Acts notwithstanding, from English electoral practice. A member was still expected to 'nurse' his constituency, or, more accurately, his constituents: 'against the average M.P.', remarked Sidney Low in his *Governance of England*, 'especially if he be a Conservative, there can hardly be a more injurious imputation than that he 'does nothing' for his constituency— that he spends no money there'.

That a nobleman of great estate could still wield more personal influence than a man made merely of money was obvious to the gentry, to capitalists and to radical socialists alike. Aristocracy was still a feature of the British Constitution. Lloyd George himself seized on this when he attacked the 'dukes' in his Limehouse campaign, not so much because they were dukes—something which, given the original absurdity of the English social structure as seen through Welsh eyes, they could not very well help, as no one chose his parents—but because they fulfilled no function. In 1493 Henry VII had demoted a duke because he did not have enough land: modern dukes, bred to respect the rights of a great deal of property, apparently respected nothing else. During the political row over Lloyd George's budget of 1909 the House of Lords came under attack

[1] Churchill, *op. cit.*, p. 274.

for this same reason. If a second chamber was required, as the majority of those who were interested in the matter at all were prepared to admit, were hereditary peers, a group of their fathers' eldest sons, the best people to sit in it? The Toryism of hereditary peers, whatever might be their party label in a passing day, was bound to be constant. It was ingrained into them, like the blueness of their blood stream. They would forever act as a brake on progress, because all their influence stemmed from the conditions of the past.

While stressing these points, no Radical in England, certainly not Lloyd George, could afford to consider something that would never bring him any political dividend: the fact that it was just in the Toryism of the House of Lords that its genuinely representative character lay. The peerage did not represent any-one by the direct means of the franchise—but it reflected a way of life, and an accompanying attitude of mind. It represented not the exclusive detachment of the Conservative party only, nor the social superiority of the landed gentry only; it represented also the traditional conservatism of a large body of English public opinion, propertied, professional and working class. This opinion preferred to see the Lords remain above the political mélée, since by doing so they represented best those things in English life which could not expect to, and indeed did not want to, find expression in 'politics'. There would always be a great many people who, wanting something in particular at a particular time, would vote for one party or the other, causing now a Liberal triumph, now a Conservative 'swing', now a Labour landslide. These were people who saw the political process as a process of exchange. They cast their votes, thus issuing a mandate to the delegates they elected, who then set about to grant their desires. Were these people in the majority? Fervent party-men, as much as men who instinctively distrusted all politicians, hoped not. Burke's letter to his Bristol constituents, denying that in being their representative he was also their delegate, still struck a receptive chord. A Conservative who declared his conviction that 'the heart of the country was sound' was thinking of a different set of citizens than was the Radical who proclaimed he could hear 'the voice of the people' before it spoke—but they were both appealing to the social instinct that kept the nation together as a whole, as a community, despite the divergent political allegiances of its members.

For, whatever notions were held by individual peers, the idea of aristocracy did represent an ideal in the English community. Men acknowledged that standards had been set, and respected the authority that had set them. In contrast, 'social efficiency', 'social justice', were unknown factors, which avoided accurate definition. No popular enthusiasm hailed them, no tradition hallowed them; for, if the doctrines of utilitarianism had been thoroughly comprehended and accepted by the people, then surely the peerage, and the monarchy with it, would have vanished in some great explosive revolution of the 1840s. No one disagreed that the House of Commons should remain the dominant instrument of the Constitution, the position it had held since 1867; but there were many, not instinctive Lord Eldons or Lord Halsburys, who also believed that the House of Lords should continue to exercise a restraining influence on movements that might be rapid, but had not yet been proven progressive.

This consensus of Tory opinions was interestingly reflected in the daily mirror of the penny press. Newspaper magnates who, not having any constituents, could if they chose so contrive their lives as never to meet anyone who was a subscribed reader of the papers they published, used their capital resources to form their own empires of influence; but they soon found out that they could never venture too far out from lines of orthodoxy, since they would lose their unseen readership if they did. The most successful newspapers were therefore Tory in tone and Conservative in political colour, as admiring of the institutions of England as Disraeli had been. Even on Sunday, a day when, if ever, a disgruntled citizen might be expected to have the time to formulate plans of sedition and to welcome assistance in doing so, no newspaper was printed which was not Tory to a point of complacency. The Fleet Street magnates found out ultimately, and not without experiencing great personal disappointment as they did so, that their true role was that of the entertainer. Their power lay not in initiating anything new, but in reflecting the assumptions of their readers, and in flattering them that no other assumptions could properly be held. Different kinds of newspaper were aimed at the different enclaves of society: the

Morning Post mirrored a world other than that of the *Daily Mail*, but the readers of both preferred to remain undisturbed at breakfast. The rise of the headline and of the 'human interest' story on the front page were both part of a programme designed to save a reader mental exertion, and to keep him safe from the menace of abstractions. The policies of statesmen could be properly identified as the essential requirements of John Bull or Britannia: J. A. Hobson's comment that the 'jingoism' of the popular press had kept the people quiet for a generation, itself in line with Cobden's assertion that appeals to the sanctity of the balance of power in Europe were designed to bemuse the masses, was exaggerated, but it was an exaggeration with point.

Security, always the Tory aim, was highly prized, in particular by people whose own destinies were on the move.

For where it was possible to gain much, it must also be made possible to conserve the gains; and even where a man had nothing but his own wits to help him, the thought of 'glittering prizes' which, could his wits win them, would always be his, put an even higher value on security and made radicalism the hallmark either of unsatisfied youth or of failed middle-age. Radicals seldom had any other kind of promised land in view but the one whose comforts and privileges were already obvious to all. They wished merely to make a better distribution of these comforts and privileges: the new Jerusalem would be only a larger conurbation than the old. Doors of opportunity into it should be opened, rights of passage leading to it should be secured. So it came about, that even the intelligentsia who took up rebel ground fought in fact under the same banner as that which flew over the ranks of the society from which they had, or believed they had, seceded. They wanted to broaden the horizon for the people: only a few of them thought of getting them to look in some different direction entirely.

For English society, despite the dislocations that the processes of industrialism had caused, was still close-knit. There was such a thing, although never so publicized as its fellow in the United States, as a national outlook, a generally accepted method of dealing with life, even if it was most often defined in terms whose negative aspects had an easily-exploited comicality: 'not playing the game', 'not cricket', 'not done', all of them implying the existence of some aristocratic code of action and doing. Society still had its ranks; but these were marshalled not, as formerly, in feudal array, but grouped horizontally in platoons, the separate garrisons of the institutions of England, where all public action originated. The excellent system of communication between them ensured a unity to that action. Ideas and purposes were easily interchanged, in a society wherein the leaders of the court, the Church, the services, the bench and the stage came from a similar background, and spoke the same language: indeed a large Victorian family was often able to supply sons to grace all these professions at once. These leaders were all of them actors in the public sight, the bishop as much as the judge, the general as much as the 'matinee idol'. They set the social image. The lawyers and the doctors, men whose services were essential in a time of trouble, were the most insistent on the dignity of the professional code. Out of it they made a *mystique*, and borrowed from the clergy the category of the laity, to describe all those who did not know what they knew; and with its aid they elevated themselves, not in their own eyes only, to the aristocracy of the middle class.

General acceptance of this social structure, based on the conviction that everyone either had or could get a function of value within it, made life in England in fact easier than was often supposed by foreigners, who were able to see the distinctions between the classes more clearly than the unity of the society these classes composed. Unity allowed a genuine sense both of leadership and of public spirit to develop, and kept at bay dangers which both Burke and Mill had foreseen in too rigorous an application of the principle of representative government. A saddened Burke had written in May 1795 that

if none can be got to feel that private persons may sometimes assume that sort of magistracy which does not depend on the nomination of kings or the election of the people, but has an inherent and self-existing power which both would recognize,[1]

then he saw nothing in the world to hope. Mill had warned, with the United States in mind, that where a school of public spirit

[1] *A Letter to W. Elliot*, May 26, 1795.

did not exist, it would not occur to 'private persons, in no eminent social situation' that they owed any duties to society except to obey the laws and submit to the government. The concept of public service would be entirely absent. Every thought or feeling, whether of interest or of duty, would be absorbed in the individual and the family. A man would not think of any collective interest, or of any objects to be pursued jointly with others. A neighbour, not being an ally or an associate, could therefore be only a rival. Hence the 'melancholy' that Tocqueville had seen pervading the American democracy: the alertness of the average American citizen expressed his state of mental tension, a sense of oppression under the perpetual competitive struggle. The twentieth century was to provide further illustration of this, when it became necessary for the United States to turn its back on the past and maintain a standing army. The officer, unfortified by any tradition of authority and therefore with no habit in its conduct, was often at a loss to know how to deal with his men, while men were at a worse loss to know how to deal with their officer; and as a consequence, very many post-World War II novels dealing with American army life from the point of view of the enlisted man found it possible, even in some 600 pages, to omit the official enemy, whether German or Japanese, entirely. But fortunately, from these grimmer consequences of the doctrines of free enterprise and rugged individualism—which American citizens themselves showed an eagerness to avoid, as they formed and joined every kind of association from Rotary to Alcoholics Anonymous—English society was ultimately, though not without effort, to escape.

Imperturbable British Toryism, Henry James noted in his *English Hours* (1905), might be said to be the very style of the landscape. James, an American gentleman of leisure who had averted both his gaze and his life from his national scene, was not thinking of Radicals and Socialists, persons he was unlikely to encounter: but his diagnosis included them nevertheless. They too wanted only that more of the British people should be enabled to fit into that Tory style. It was because they wanted this, and did not want a revolution that would blast away for ever the last shards of that Tory landscape, that they and all the Social Democrats of Europe were to fall under the lash of paternalists more extreme than themselves. As Josef Stalin put it, if 'socialists' of that sort got power they would maintain the old *bourgeois apparat*—which was of course, as it had ever been, only a screen devised to hide the ulcers of imperialism and capitalism.

English socialists were not extremists: yet they went much too far for some stomachs, and the tone of their constant criticisms made them, in a Tory landscape, marked men. Kin to the comfortable, they knew best how to unsettle them: Forsytes and Pharisees were driven resentfully on to the defensive, convinced that the world they lived in was being betrayed—and for what, in heaven's name?—by its own clerks. Gentlemen deprived of their assurance in life forgot the style of a gentleman. As Shaw pointed out, such a one was far happier and more useful while he accepted the standards of Horseback Hall than he ever could be trying to find out how to cope with life at *Heartbreak House* (1919), where the stables were empty and where people came and went in socialistic-aesthetic dress—'the badge of those who read Turgeniev's novels, scorn current fiction, and think of higher planes'.[1] To many such gentlemen, the outbreak of war in 1914 came as a relief, by giving them something positive and exciting to do.

But many others, whose energies were fully employed making a profitable business more so, stayed unmoved by intellectual attacks on *bourgeois* mentality and morality. Matthew Arnold, in filial respect for the educational system that trained the governing class, had allowed that it had, with all its faults, 'a high magnanimous governing spirit'; but he had doubted that this spirit was easily communicable to those not bred to it. Many good *bourgeois* shared his doubts. They despised their brethren who 'put on airs' and apparently welcomed a future wherein an expensively-educated son would disdain his father. Only after a hard, indeed a cruel battle, does F. Anstey's middle-class worthy, Mr Bultitude, allow his son to go to Harrow (*Vice Versa*, 1882). For fifty years Frank Richards wrote public-school fairy-tales designed for the lower middle classes, allotting the aristocratic names of Ponsonby and Vavasour to 'Highcliffe cads', poking fun at drawling 'swells' like Mauleverer and D'Arcy, while at

[1] H. G. Wells in *Kipps* (1905).

the same time epitomizing 'Bounderdom' in one Vernon-Smith, son of a rich *parvenu*. The heroes of these stories have Service fathers, not above the rank of Colonel. The stress is not on 'gentlemanly connections', but on gentlemanly conduct: the code, in other words, had been learned, at least by these fictional characters. In real life, however, the *bourgeois'* social position of solid respectability was satisfactory in his own sight and, it was even more satisfactory to know, in that of those below him. He knew he was not the same as a peer of the realm, but he did not suppose he was worse. In the north of England in particular the industrialists prided themselves on a sturdy independence of out-look, and shook their hard heads at anyone who became too con-taminated with 'soft southern ways'. They did not think their conventions restrictive, they thought them commonsensible—for outside of them, sometimes through them, could be seen the depths below. Like Charles Dickens, they feared a relapse into the blacking-factory: but they knew, too, that a man who climbed higher than his ability to maintain himself was nearer to, not farther from, such an abyss.

Accordingly, no accusation that they were stuffy and narrow and dull could wound them. Rigidity was the price they willingly paid for what they had. That they had a great deal, so fierce a critic as Marx's friend Friedrich Engels, always fascinated and repelled by the mysterious English, could see. He was to pay a sufficient tribute to the strength of *bourgeois* morality by marry-ing his deceased mistress's sister.

They spoke therefore of social critics as 'agitators', and relegated them and the poor for whom they were agitating to a lower moral order. The poor were always with us, as the New Testament insisted: indeed, the emphasis placed on the environ-ment as a cause of poverty was, in its way, un-Christian, as it removed the moral responsibility for his own fate from the individual. That was the path to anarchy, not to social better-ment: socialism, as Lord Rosebery exclaimed, was 'the end of all, the negation of faith, of family, of property, of monarchy, of Empire'.[1] Socialists were always impersonalizing, dealing in large and cloudy concepts. Thus, the problems of poor men became the Problem of Poverty—well characterized by Henry

[1] Lord Crewe, *Rosebery* (1931), II, 623.

George's book *Progress and Poverty*, the English edition of which (1882) sold over 60,000 copies in three years—and as a consequence a collective blame was summoned up from somewhere and charged against men who were not poor. The notion was propagated that there was in existence a 'system', of which this state of 'poverty' was a standing criticism; and for this system, 'the capitalists', another sinister collective, were responsible. This, it appeared, was the kind of thinking by numbers in which the 'democracy', itself an undefinable term, liked to indulge. It was certainly regrettable that in the 1890s a quarter of the population over sixty-five years of age were paupers, and that over half died in workhouses. But it was even more regrettable that Radicals and Socialists should regard the poor, simply because they were the majority (as was inevitable), as the rightful inheritors of other people's wealth. Here another abstraction did duty: one was told that something called 'social justice' demanded this and that. Again this was nonsense: for, if one cleared one's mind of cant, it was clearly as unjust to rob a millionaire as a beggar. (The words of Winstanley the 'Digger', that it was impossible to amass a lot of money by honest means, had never sunk very deep into anyone's conscience.)

But to such passes, it seemed, the modern type of radical thinking had come. To the middle-class opinion that had been bred to respect the memory and continue the principles of Cobden and Bright, both of whom had detested state-action and socialist doctrine, the very use of the adjective 'radical' seemed an insult. (The confusion was well illustrated by Gladstone, when he told Argyll in 1885 that he 'radically' disapproved the leaning of both parties to socialism.) Cobden had declared that he knew it was easier to please the people by holding out flattering and delusive prospects of cheap benefits to be derived from parliament, rather than by urging them to a course of self-reliance; but, he had added, while he could not be the sycophant of the great, he could not become 'the parasite of the poor'. What else were these socialists, but parasites of the poor? Cobden had also pointed out that, while the rich alone were not qualified to legislate for the poor, on the same principle neither were the poor alone qualified to legislate for the rich. But what else did Socialists advocate, but this? The temperance movement, although it of course lurked under a moral cover, was a case in point: and upper-class Tories looked with particular venom on this movement, one staffed by nonconformists, since it attacked a private enterprise on the excuse of doing someone a 'social benefit', whatever that meant. In this view they were supported by a great many on whom the social benefit was presumably intended to fall: as has been recently acknowledged, 'it is certainly true that at every level from the Guinnesses and Grettons down to the poorest tied-publican there has historically been an agreeable association between the purveyors of the national beverage and the Tory Party'.[1]

It was however clear that interference of emotional people in matters that, since they were not exclusively their concern, ought not exclusively to concern them, was a trend of the times. It was a trend which, as the nineteenth century closed, alarmed many Tories whose political interests were not centred on the distribution of beer, and who were anyway to be found in the ranks both of the Conservative and the Liberal parties. The philosopher Herbert Spencer complained that the Liberal party was confusing the elimination of evil, which was its proper function, with the achievement of good, which lay out of its province. Indeed, once it had stopped removing restraints and performing various acts of emancipation, and had set out to attain some mysterious 'justice', it was no better than Toryism: in his *Man versus the State* (1892) Spencer listed the series of state enactments regulating the lives of the people that had been made since 1860, and found that the blame for most of them could be laid at the doors of the Conservative party. The true task of modern Liberalism, he asserted, was 'to dispute the assumption of unlimited party authority'.

But this was not a diagnosis likely to appeal to the Liberals' principal Radical, Joseph Chamberlain, who had been a prime mover in the founding of the National Liberal Federation (May 31, 1877), and whose fondness for party 'machinery' on the American democratic model was distrusted by his Whig colleagues and by such independent Radicals as Leonard Courtney. Chamberlain moreover, far from believing that the achievement of good lay outside of the Liberal party's province, was

[1] Churchill, *Derby*, p. 43.

convinced that therein and nowhere else lay its kingdom: a conviction that was in the short and the long run to prove unassimilable both by the Liberals whom he left in 1886 and by the Conservatives whom he joined in 1895. He was a genuine Radical, and the English party system was unable to make room for him.

In 1880, when Gladstone had included him in the Cabinet— and, not to many people's surprise, in a minor post—the *Manchester Guardian*, the Liberal organ of the north, welcomed the appointment with an agreeable condescension. 'It will be surprising,' it intoned, 'if the experience of power and the admission to the intimate counsels of men vastly more versed in affairs does not have upon him both a sobering and stimulating effect.'[1] In the upshot it was the *Guardian* that was surprised, as the company Chamberlain was forced to keep stimulated more than it sobered. In 1883 and 1884 he welcomed the forthcoming Reform Bill, on the grounds that the extension of the borough franchise to the counties would, by doubling the power of Liberalism, make it synonymous with Radicalism. At best it was a doubtful prophecy to make about peasants; times had perhaps changed since Thackeray's Lady Southdown in *Vanity Fair* (1846) would order 'Gaffer Hodge to be converted, as she would order Goody Hicks to take a James's powder, without appeal, resistance, or benefit of clergy'—but they had not changed to the extent of making the sons of Hodge and Hicks politically-minded citizens, abreast of the latest Radical thought. The countryside voted with care. Tenants, ballot or no ballot, always did their best to find out how their landlord wanted them to vote, and if the small tradesmen of a country township were Liberals, they disguised it with success. The Radical farmers of Scotland had no English counterpart, and there were those in Scotland who preferred to ignore their existence anyway: Sutherland's ruling Duchess informed Disraeli in 1880 that she had let her tenantry know 'that I expect them to give their votes according to the principles always held by my house'.[2] In England the tenantry generally did not have to be told this, and

[1] Hammond, *C. P. Scott*, p. 62.

[2] H. J. Hanham, *Elections and Party Management* (1959), p. 18. Sutherland had only 325 electors anyway.

the gift of the franchise to the peasantry did not widen their horizons. The passage of the Small Holdings Act in 1892 made no change in the habit of dependence. 'In England more than in any other nation,' J. L. Garvin remarked of this, 'a primitive instinct had been too badly broken'.[1]

Thus, although the Reform and Redistribution Acts of 1884 and 1885 abolished the difference between the borough and the country franchise, making single-member constituencies the rule, and bringing into the House of Commons, for the first time, more commercial men and manufacturers than landowners —although Manchester voters retained their confidence in Arthur Balfour—Radicalism made little rural progress. According to Robert Giffen's statistics, the average agricultural labourer in 1881 was consuming five times more food than in 1840; since his present was plainly better than his past, he saw no point in gambling with the future. Moreover, since the issue whether or not the Irish should be allowed to govern themselves or not exploded in the faces of Liberals and Radicals alike almost immediately after the general election of 1885, Chamberlain's 'unauthorized programme' had no chance of acceptance. It included a reform of local government, land for the labourers, free education, a revision of taxation on more equitable grounds, manhood suffrage and the payment of members of parliament. But Chamberlain knew well the shock this would give the shires. The farmer, he remarked in August 1885, was a hard man to serve, since he chose to confide his interests to the landlords who represented him—'which is very much like, in the words of a homely proverb, setting the cat to guard the cream'.

Chamberlain's conviction that the urbanization of English life called for a reconstruction of the attitudes of the governing class was bound to alarm all members of that class, whether in office or out of it. The Whigs were scandalized by Gladstone's Home Rule Bill into recognizing their own Toryism: Lord Randolph Churchill was exaggerating, but not excessively, when he exclaimed that the 'old Whig gang' was more mischievous to democracy than the old Tories themselves.[2] Whigs thought it no time therefore to encourage Radicalism, or to reconstruct

[1] J. L. Garvin, *Joseph Chamberlain* II (1932), 423.
[2] *loc. cit.*, 434.

anything at all. Their distrust of democracy and its ways had a long pedigree: the views of the Whig martyr, Algernon Sidney, were no distance from those of Lord Hartington, the Whig leader in Gladstone's ministry of 1880–5. Sidney had laid it down that

> those governments in which the democratical part governs most, do more frequently err in the choice of men, or the means of preserving that purity of manners which is required for the wellbeing of a people, than those wherein aristocracy prevails.[1]

A century later self-styled Whig 'Friends of the People' agreed with him; in 1831 Grey's Home Secretary, the amiable Melbourne, had suppressed popular disturbances with a severity that surpassed the performance of the Tories' Sidmouth in the post-Waterloo years; and the Whig bard, Macaulay, never lost an occasion to assert that the people were to be governed for their own good—'and that they may be governed for their own good, they must not be governed by their own ignorance'. Hartington had developed no other ideas, and did not encourage those who had. As a result, and as Chamberlain himself gloomily recorded, the legislative work of a Liberal administration was always decided by the maximum which the moderate section was ready to concede, and the minimum which the advanced party would consent to accept.[2]

It was Gladstone himself who forgot this. He was not a Whig and not the kind of Radical Chamberlain recognized as such. He remained an unclassifiable phenomenon, a kind of Merlin. To Tory minds, this very unpredictability made him more alarming a foe than Chamberlain, whose confessed Radicalism certainly made him capable of any folly, but at the same time removed in advance the element of surprise. Salisbury from the Conservative benches characterized the Liberal party as an inclined plane—a plane 'leading from the position of Lord Hartington to that of Mr Chamberlain, and so to the depths over which Mr Henry George rules supreme'. Even on this

---

[1] *Discourses concerning Government*, c. 2. S 519.

[2] Chamberlain to Gladstone, February 7, 1885, *A Political Memoir 1880–95*, ed. C. H. D. Howard (1953), p. 116.

slope Gladstone could find no footing. But fortunately, from the Tory standpoint, his obsession with Ireland destroyed both his own political influence and, what was much more important, that of the Liberal party for close on a generation. In this new situation, it was not the Tories who had to cope with Chamberlain, but Chamberlain who had to cope with them. 'Jack Cade' vanished behind orchid and eyeglass, taking his Radicalism with him. For, once he had allied himself with the Unionists, he was compelled to export his zeal for social betterment to the colonies. The 'condition-of-England' question was thus shut off from the attention of the best Radical mind in politics. Rosebery spoke correctly of the period of Unionist rule, the imperialist heyday between 1895 and 1902, as 'seven years lost for all social and human causes'.

If official Toryism could thus neutralize Chamberlain, it augured well that it could also adapt itself to that world of which Chamberlain's Birmingham was symbol. So act, Bentham had advised all governors, that the people, so far as possible, get what they want. It was still sensible advice. To the task of finding out first, who the people were, and then, what they wanted, twentieth-century governors had now to apply themselves.

CHAPTER VI

BONAR LAW'S DYNASTY

In making a defence of the rotten boroughs which were the ornament of the unreformed parliamentary system, the Duke of Wellington had used one argument whose implications were wider than he knew, and whose application to circumstance he could not foresee was remarkably apt. He approved of members for rotten boroughs because they were Tories. He approved of Tories because, it went without saying, they were men—'*I don't care of what party*'—who would preserve the state of property as it was; who would maintain by their votes the Church of England, its possessions, churches and Universities, together with all the great institutions and corporations; the Union with Scotland and with Ireland;[1] the dominion of England over its foreign colonies and possessions; the national honour abroad and, at home, good faith with all the king's subjects, whose prosperity was bound up with the perpetuation of all these things. In Toryism,

> I see men at the back of the government to protect individuals and their property against the injustice of the times, which would sacrifice all rights and all property to a species of plunder called general convenience and utility.[2]

It would always be the clear duty of Tories to stem such a tide, the purifying effects of which would be exaggerated by people whose own property, did they chance to have any, would not lie close to shore.

[1] This involved keeping the Catholics at bay. In 1868 the Tory Gathorne Hardy spoke of the union between Church and State, under which 'it is the glory and the privilege of the State to uphold the light of the Reformation in Ireland'; 3 H 191, 598–9.

[2] Quoted in Davis, *Age of Grey and Peel*, pp. 225–6.

Rotten boroughs disappeared. Wellington's creed survived. But his Tory posterity was also committed to making money, to a degree 'that would never have done for His Grace'. Could both programmes be carried out simultaneously? Was money-making itself an example of 'the injustice of the times', which 'sacrificed rights to a species of plunder'? Some said so. In January 1898 C. E. Montague wrote in the *Manchester Guardian* that, although the United States was still a political democracy, an oligarchy of wealth had got hold of the representative institutions there. 'The power of organized capital,' he deduced, 'is the standing danger of democracy.' English Tories, whether in or out of the Conservative party, had been brought to realize after 1867, and even more forcibly after 1885, that political democracy had itself become one of the institutions of England.[1] It must therefore, like other such, be upheld. But another such institution was capitalism itself: and it, too, needed its warders.

Capital, moreover, had an advantage that talent always lacked—it was easily transmitted from father to son. Society was already geared to the idea that a man had a title to importance who was in possession of some kind of power over others. Just what kind of power, was thought beside the point by those who held and entailed it. Walter Bagehot had diagnosed that the people wanted to be ruled by sensible men of substantial means. But, what if a man's means became too substantial? Did his senses leave him? Or betray him? It was certainly hard for the people to believe they were in good hands, who were compelled to live 266 to the acre in the Deansgate district of Manchester, or 428 to the acre in the thirteenth ward of New York City.

Questions on the nature of the society wherein the English democracy found itself—politically recognized, but socially and economically unprivileged—were now being put. But *fin de siècle* threw a haze of inertia over politics as well as literature. The Conservatives' leader, Salisbury, grown more detached than ever, lost himself in the intricacies of diplomacy—'putting out boathooks' to avoid collision with other ships of state, but never finding a course to a chosen harbour. The imperialists in

---

[1] After Reform and Redistribution in 1884–5, 'for the first time the number of commercial men . . . in the House of Commons exceeded the number of landowners;' Hanham, *op. cit.*, p. xvii.

his party meanwhile encouraged a large part of the electorate to listen to the magic of distant drums. The Liberal-Unionists, themselves bewitched by these imperial rhythms, finally discovered that their leader Chamberlain had entrapped them in a South African impasse. When in 1902 Balfour's Education Bill released them from it, by bringing forward the denominational controversy with which they had long been familiar, their nonconformist consciences were thankfully cleared, and thereafter Liberal-Unionism lost its dynamism and shredded itself away. Unhyphenated Liberals fell heir in 1906 to an authority that had lost its self-confidence. Those on the left who admired Lloyd George looked on their titular leader Asquith and his kind as 'Whigs', a name now loosely applied to the type of Tory in the party who had no plans for social reform.[1] Indeed, political labels were beginning less to describe than to mislead: for Lloyd George was himself a 'Radical' whom Cobden could not have recognized as such.

The solicitor from the Welsh countryside had elements in him of both Disraeli and Chamberlain, who were also born strangers to the preconceptions of the governing class. He was to have less luck than either; yet, with fewer principles than both, he had also a deeper insight into the weakness of what had become an unprincipled system. As he looked at England, its lands and its leaseholds, he saw little either of democracy or of liberty. In the celebrated speech at Limehouse (July 30, 1909) which rang an alarm-bell among the comfortable, he declared how hard it was, that

an old workman should have to find his way to the gates of the tomb, bleeding and footsore, through the brambles and thorns of poverty.

Disraeli is echoed in one comment, that the ownership of land was not an enjoyment, but a stewardship; Chamberlain in another, that no country however wealthy could permanently afford to have 'quartered on its revenue' a class which declined to do the duty it had been called upon to do 'since the beginning'.

[1] Cf. Wilfrid Blunt, *My Diaries* II (1919), p. 129: 'The new Cabinet [of 1906] is a Whig Cabinet'.

But the tone, a mixture of ridicule and venom, was new. Chamberlain's attacks had grown rancorous, but with the rancour of the ego, not that of a class. New, too, was the paraphernalia of paternalism for the people that Lloyd George borrowed from industrial and imperial Germany: labour exchanges, the sweated trades wages scheme, the details of his Insurance and Unemployment bills.

But, like Chamberlain before him, Lloyd George had to accommodate his pace to that of his colleagues. It was now agreed, both among those who administered it and those whom it controlled, that the old Poor Law system was inadequate. The long enquiry, Who are the poor? had propagated the related question, Why are they poor? without more than a muted Tory rumble about vicious idleness. Yet, just as the old Poor Law had rested on a paternalist assumption how people ought to behave, so too did the amelioration that was made to it. The Old Age Pensions Act of 1908 withheld pensions from those 'who had habitually failed to work according to ability and need and those who had failed to save money regularly'. The National Health Insurance Act of 1911 gave the same payment in sickness benefit, ten shillings a week, to the single worker as to the man with a family, and forty years were to pass before this idea was reassessed.[1] Physic had to be administered to people who did not know what was good for them: it was the 'Crown Colony' *ethos* of government, at that moment successfully building the country to be known as Nigeria. Here was a paternalist role that a school of social reformers at home, and a generation of colonial civil servants, was eager to play. Winston Churchill mused in 1911 on the condition of the people, wondering what it was they were mostly interested in. Ignoring a dry answer that they were interested in earning their living and in football, he went on to paint a picture of happy days coming when all the working-classes would live in municipally-owned flats, centrally cooked and catered for[2]—proving thereby that a residue of the ideas of Robert Owen, the pioneer English Socialist, had lodged in unexpected quarters.

Paternalists were able to recognize the challenge to them in

[1] R. Titmuss, *Essays on the Welfare State* (Allen & Unwin, 1958), p. 18.
[2] Lord Riddell, *More Pages from my Diary 1908–14* (1934), p. 22.

the plight of the democracy. They saw it as part of their imperial mission overseas to disseminate law, order, justice, education, peace and prosperity: they could not burke the same tasks, different only in degree, at home. 'Protection', a new enthusiasm among many imperialists, threw a clear shadow beyond the arena of commerce. But, while seeing this, they saw no need to change the social structure. The very concept of 'social welfare' summoned up, as 'liberty' itself had always done, the image of its necessary guardians, whose task it was by their influence to impel fellow-members of the Ascendancy to a deeper study of their duty. There was useful data for this in an area an imperialist might have been expected to look. Social reformers could have found in the self-governing colonies a set of tools for their work which had been well tested in societies lucky enough to breathe an air at once uncontaminated with revolutionary doctrine and free from the deadweight of assumptions inherited from privi-leged persons long dead. (There were, however, some parts of the British Empire that could have given no help: the index to the *Cambridge History of the British Empire's* volume on *Canada* contains neither 'Socialism' nor 'Labour'.)

The self-governing colonies—'Dominions' after 1911—had long been protectionist in trade. They had applied the protective principle further. In 1890 Charles Dilke had presaged in his *Problems of Greater Britain* that

> as the future of the English Liberal Party may lie in the direction of that European Socialism which I have called Revolutionary or Democratic, the future of the English Conservative Party, in the increasing strength of Socialist opinions, may lie . . . in the direction of State-socialism of the Australian type.[1]

A Liberal himself, Dilke was wrong about Liberals, right about Conservatives. In the Australian colonies in the late 'eighties he had seen a pioneer for England's good, a pattern for the English society that was yet to emerge, but which would preserve its innate Toryism. Australians enjoyed the eight-hour day, uni-versal suffrage, death duties, nationalized railways, and a mania

[1] II, 278–80.

for football and racing. In its earliest days, the site of the race-track at Melbourne had been decided on before the township itself was surveyed: now, 'half the city's population lived in houses of its own, every [sic] suburban house had its lawn-tennis court, and all the citizens patronized the municipal "Six-penny Restaurants" '. Chartists translated to and mellowed in a southern sunlight had fashioned their society as they wanted it.

Yet the newspapers in Australia, moulders of opinion, were as Tory in tone as those in England. Since they were commercial enterprises (something that English journals often forgot to admit) they naturally reflected the non-radical opinions of the advertising classes. They reached a public whose energies were not absorbed in the promotion of grievance. Australian farmers, better read than their English counterparts, were also better off. In the wealthier colonies one could not distinguish one class from another by its dress. They were all State-socialists: but they kept clear of far-ranging philosophy, and were 'as impatient of the doctrine of natural rights as is the editor of the *Quarterly Review*'.[1] Other predictable views to be found regularly in that journal they were prepared, at so safe a distance, to forgive. As one Melbourne citizen had put it, in May 1859 on achieving the eight-hour day, things were thus different in the colony of Victoria because the colonists were not content, as were 'the poor docile working classes of England', to labour on and permit the upper classes to think and act for them.[2] Yet independence of action was one thing, independence of attitude was another. Australians did not want to take the latter too far, and the leisure was used oftener in sport than in thought.

There were of course exceptions. William Lane of Queensland —'a kind of Australian Mahomet',[3] out of Bristol via Canada and the United States—was the first man to challenge Australian Labour whether it stood for socialism or social reform. The answer he received caused him to quit in 1893 in order to form a Communist Utopia in Paraguay. Socialism was proclaimed as a dogma among a few of the faithful, but it was suppressed before

[1] Dilke, *loc. cit.*, II, 239.
[2] R. Gollan, *Radical and Working Class Politics: a Study of Eastern Australia* (Melbourne, 1960), p. 72.
[3] *Cambridge History of the British Empire*, vii, i, 373.

the electors, and the Labour 'platform' of 1891 had no hint of it. Agitators or enthusiasts, as another observer put it, were no more representative of the aims or methods of Australian Labour than were the cranks who gesticulated in Hyde Park of a Sunday representative of the British working man. Even the Republican Lane himself, whether in Paraguay or in Brisbane, retained his stout stand on the menace of Chinese labour: in 1888 his journal *Boomerang* carried a hair-raising serial of Chinese despots grinding down Australian helots, in a future that lay only twenty years ahead.

Sir Keith Hancock has characterized his country's Labour movement as 'a search for equality of attainment, not of opportunity'. It needs sometimes a considerable equipment to seize an opportunity; and it is an equipment which in any one generation only a few will be likely to possess. It may then seem to the majority better to sacrifice the opportunity itself, since it can only promote inequality. The Australian Labour Party, says another of its historians,

> grew out of a movement that was implicitly directed against the basis of the capitalist system, but it became a party whose function was to modify the capitalist system and to make it acceptable to the movement of which it was a part.[1]

This could be said of British Labour, as Dilke foretold. In Australia he saw a householding urban democracy, whose voters did not insist on returning 'working-class men' as their representatives to the colonial parliaments, and who did not issue mandates for the conduct of these representatives. Indeed, Labour parliamentarians in Australia often stood well to the right of the Trade Unionists, a complete reversal of the English pattern. The reason for this was that the middle classes, again in contradistinction to the behaviour of their kind in England, backed the aspirations of Labour: they had no call to ape their betters, since they had no betters to ape. As Dilke declared, it was the English civilization with the upper class left out.[2] It was therefore like the form the English civilization would probably,

[1] Gollan, *op. cit.*, 153.
[2] Dilke, *loc. cit.*, II, 229, 236 ff.

one day, assume, when the upper class had been overwhelmed on the one side by 'new wealth' and on the other by increasingly powerful Labour. Australian experience thus provided a springboard into the twentieth century: one confident leap was all that was needed—a leap this time not 'in the dark', but into the light of common day.

But English, Scots, Irish and Welshmen at the antipodes had not reached this happy state without working for it. Dilke took his ranging view a little too early, for it was not until the 1890s that Labour made its final breakthrough. Capital was as formidable a foe to the aspirations of Labour in Australia as elsewhere: against the militant trade unions were ranked the pastoralists and the mining and shipping magnates, whose efficiency and common interest had already established a strong intercolonial unity among the employers' organizations. The trade unionists went down to defeat in a series of strikes between 1890 and 1894. Beaten on the industrial front, they regrouped their forces for an invasion of the political arena, and even at the first try Labour, with a mass vote behind it, won 28 per cent of the seats in New South Wales. The large capitalists might for a time be able to rule the industrial roost, but as the results of this became even more clear to an educated and observant electorate, they were never able to muster enough support to make the political arena safe for their operations. In a country without an aristocracy, a State Church, or a denominational school system; without a standing army, a navy, a foreign policy, or a millionaire *class*, the main task of politics was to cope with economic and social questions. Herein only the voice of the democracy counted. The Australians were luckier in their generation than the Americans, for in the United States social and political equality had preceded industrialism, and it had thus laid down no rules for industrialism to follow: rich Americans, able to say that they were 'as good' Americans as anyone else, were able to combine industrial with political power, manipulating men's aspirations to the sound of men's applause. In Australia ideas of equality and techniques of industrialism grew up together. The social and the industrial condition were as one, and those who locked up the land, capital, or enterprise were looked on not as the makers of society, but as its enemies.

Down over in New Zealand an even smaller society with this same outlook gained even greater dividends. (The parliament there in 1890 did not contain 20 per cent of the members of London's County Council.) Education had been free, compulsory and undenominational since 1877, but under a Conservative régime that lasted from 1870 to 1890 the legal protection of the working classes was weak. But thereafter, a Liberal-Labour government stayed in power from 1891 to 1912; and even within its first decade agitated for, and finally got, legislation and taxation to break up the great landholdings, a protective tariff to assist local industry, labour laws to ensure reasonable working conditions, a tribunal to fix a fair level of wages, government loans to establish small farmers on the land, State experiments to compete with trading monopolies, and government relief of poverty in old age.[1] The single session of 1894 passed the Compulsory Arbitration Act—based on the theory that it was legitimate to use the power of the State to protect the workers' standard of living—a Lands for Settlement Act, a Shops Act and an Advances to Settlers Act. In this world where experiment seemed to the majority better than stagnation, women had the vote, and a factory was defined to include every workshop that employed two men. After 1912 the Conservatives predictably returned to consolidate the position, significantly under the new name of the Reform party, with the small farmer as their principal prop.

Here was news of social evolution, not revolution, heartening to that minority of Tories in England who had heard of New Zealand at all. For small farmers were certainly not socialists. Capitalism was still firmly entrenched beneath the southern cross, the land was not nationalized, and the single-tax panacea Henry George had advocated was not in operation. Moreover, the Liberal-Labour stalwarts who had fashioned this comfortable world 'did not know what Socialism was, and if they had studied it would not have agreed with it'.[2] They had wanted 'justice': and by their own efforts, on which they could congratulate themselves, they had got it, supported by what Jefferson might have described as 'the commonsense of the business'. New Zealand

[1] J. B. Condliffe, *New Zealand in the Making* (Allen & Unwin, 1929), pp. 161 ff.
[2] Pember Reeves, *The Long White Cloud* (Allen & Unwin, 4th edn. 1950), p. 282.

thus basked pleasurably in her reputation as the experimental laboratory of democracy, naturally continuing to believe, as the twentieth century wore on, that the reputation would never wear out.

Yet 'social justice' was still as suspect a term in England as it had ever been. Who could be trusted to define it? From what bench of magistrates was it to be meted out? Who were these magistrates to be, and from whom were they to derive their authority? If an 'experimental laboratory' was to be set up, who would elect, and from what constituency, the white-coated figures within? Those who put their trust in the English political system as it had been handed down to them were more frightened than stimulated by such imagery. That the attainment of social justice was a task for Liberals was an idea that had in their day irritated Lord Palmerston, the *Edinburgh Review* and Herbert Spencer alike. Leading Liberals, bred in the Whig principle that political liberty was all-inclusive, did not make that cause their own. They were content to clear the ground of encumbrances: they did not build on it. Gladstone's view of political economy, like Adam Smith's, never took him far to the left. Budgets had to be balanced; expenditure had to be cut. He became too absorbed in his quest for justice for Ireland to notice there was some call for it the hither side of St George's Channel. He saw England as a community, and believed that the interests of the rich were fundamentally identical with those of the poor. (Disraeli in contrast thought they ought to be, but did not suppose they were.) It was a valiant belief—and in propagating it with all his great personal authority, Gladstone did all his countrymen, rich and poor, a signal spiritual, if not a political, service. But his successors in the Liberal leadership were at once more realistic, less optimistic, and less 'guided' than he in their daily political action. They could not share his belief, since the facts were so militantly against it. Chamberlain, their best champion, was lost to the Tories early in the day, and all his guns spiked. Rosebery was an instinctive Tory who could not bring himself to take a consistent interest in the political process. Campbell-Bannerman came to power too late in life to leave a domestic mark; and Asquith, if not the Whig he was dubbed, by his second marriage promoted himself into the ranks of that 'upper ten thousand' whose influence Gladstone himself had thought so mischievous, and was content thereafter to ornament his generation.

It is an embittered view that sees the twentieth-century heirs of Gladstonian Liberalism, whatever their party, as hard-headed, hard-faced diehards capable of treachery and violence if they saw their own ease in danger.[1] But in Edwardian England ortho-dox Liberals on the Government Front Bench, well to the right of Radicals and Labour members behind them, were indeed short of passion and principle. Dukes on the other side they saw as fair game for attack, but never the plutocrats on their own. As the Radical Josiah Wedgwood expressed it, it was a great disaster to have a Liberal Government—because then no one dared to criticize the policy of the Front Bench from a Liberal point of view.[2] In foreign and imperial affairs Liberals appeared equally devoted to expediency. Sir Edward Grey as Foreign Secretary followed a policy the Conservatives would have heartily approved, had they known what it was. In their 1905–06 election campaign, and before it, Liberals had made a great uproar over Milner's introduction of Chinese labour into the gold-mines of the Rand in South Africa. The Conservative Colonial Secretary who sanctioned it, Alfred Lyttelton, had foreseen what would come of all this as early as April 1904. 'When the other side come in,' he wrote Milner, 'they will be confronted with their dishonest and insincere utterances about Chinese labour by the ignorant and sincere of their followers, and I am convinced that they will extricate themselves from a painful dilemma by grant-ing self-government to the new Colonies *sans phrase*.'[3] When the Liberal Government did just that in 1909, they thus could not expect applause from the Tories, who anyway objected to handing over valuable portions of the British Empire to two governments composed of recent rebels to the British Crown, and who did not fail to note either that the Chinese Labour Ordinance was retained 'word for word' until 1910, or that the long-established tradition of a paternalist supervision of the welfare of the Bantu races in southern Africa was thrown over-board at the same time.

[1] It is Stephen Spender's, in his *Forward from Liberalism* (1937), p. 73.
[2] Cf. A. P. Thornton, *The Imperial Idea and its Enemies*, p. 116.
[3] April 26, 1904: '*The Times' History of the War in South Africa* (1909), vi, 158.

Zest in Edwardian politics was therefore the monopoly of embattled Conservatives who designated His Majesty's Government as His Majesty's enemies, and who considered that in such circumstances the true duty of a 'loyal Opposition' was to circumvent, by constitutional means if possible but anyway to circumvent, the misguided policies put forward. They formulated a programme of obstruction accordingly, insisting on a larger Navy, a less radical budget, less powerful Trade Unions, and the right to abet militant Ulstermen (who objected to Home Rule for other Irishmen) in resistance to the forces of the Crown —with varying degrees of success.

Both the gusto and irrelevance of these tactics of the party game angered men who were seriously concerned to find some solution to the 'condition-of-England question'. While politicians fought for advantages, the British people remained at a disadvantage. Crusading publicists drove this point home. At present, the socialist Robert Blatchford insisted in his *Britain for the British* (1908), Britain did not belong to the British. It belonged to a few of the British, who employed their fellow countrymen as workers or servants. This vast majority was kept 'below the salt', like the contemporary population of India—a land also ruled by a handful of British Tories, themselves the cousinhood of the upper middle-class that now maintained the *Raj* in Britain itself. Blatchford's argument followed that of Winstanley and Paine. The land did not belong to the people, for either

> it had been won from the Saxons by William the Conqueror, or by him given in fief to his barons, or it had been stolen from the common right and 'enclosed' by some lord of the manor or other brigand.

Brigandage was still abroad, although it lurked under the name of unearned increment. Of every 1,000 persons in the country, 939 died without leaving any property worth mentioning; and 90 per cent of the producers of the nation's wealth had no home they could call their own beyond the end of the week. In such a situation the current party labels were meaningless. Liberals and Conservatives, cut from the same cloth, made up the privileged classes, an Ascendancy, an Establishment—the kind of people Wellington had in mind when he praised those who sat for rotten boroughs, whatever their party. Political Liberalism still propagated its doctrines of democracy, individualism, and the free market. The relevance and morality of these were becoming progressively harder to justify, at a time when one half of the national income went to one ninth of the population, and more than a third of it to a thirtieth.[1]

Then why was the situation not more dangerous than it was? Why was Disraeli's 'second nation' not gearing itself for the battle? Because, as Blatchford recognized in sorrow, the people knew no better. They could not even make a tally of their own wrongs. They did not experience life fully enough: people of the surface, they had no powers of penetration. They had made deference and loyalty a vice, and now lived at second-hand, taking their opinions on and views of the world around them from parsons, journalists, lawyers, and members of parliament—all of them men with an interest to protect which they did not declare, all of whose attitudes were governed by that interest. No wonder, then, that one of the real evils of the time was a 'baseness of popular ideals'. On this a fellow socialist, H. N. Brailsford, agreed. Since the basis of a leisured class was rent and law, it was inevitable that the majority 'must grow up deaf to music and blind to beauty'.[2] Blind also to political insight, for it was not likely that out of this heavy dullness of spirit any strong light could emerge. Another radical, Lowes Dickinson, winced at what he saw in the United States, and echoed Arnold once more. 'Radically and essentially, America is a barbarous country', he wrote. 'The life of the spirit is, not accidentally or temporarily, but inevitably and eternally, killed in this country.'

It seemed, indeed, as if yet another of Tocqueville's predictions had come to pass. He had foreseen the ultimate establishment, in the democratic system, of

> a kind of virtuous materialism, which would not corrupt the soul so much as enervate it, and noiselessly unbend its springs of action.

[1] Asa Briggs, *Seebohm Rowntree* (1961), p. 51.
[2] H. N. Brailsford, *Socialism for Today* (1925), pp. 40, 44.

Political freedom would ally itself to a system of productive industry, and the resultant general devotion to the spirit of commerce would breed its own dangers. Men bemused by that spirit, the better to look after what they called their business, would neglect their chief business—which was, to remain their own masters.

The point was underlined by the Tory Alfred Milner, the Liberal-Imperialist proconsul lately arrived in the Conservative ranks. He warned them that their party was becoming merely the embodiment of upper and middle-class prejudices and alarms. It was also emphasized by Winston Churchill, a Conservative lately arrived in the Liberal ranks, when he complained that his new colleagues were still bent beneath a deadweight of Cobdenite principles. Both verdicts were just. In power for a generation (1886 to 1906, with an 'interregnum', 1892 to 1895), the Conservatives had prided themselves on detachment —and as a result their Cabinets were referred to, by the middle-class lawyers and industrialists who made up the majority on both sides of the House of Commons, as the 'Hotel Cecil'. They did not have a social programme, and were glad to keep Chamberlain—who came over to them in 1895 and who would not have been at a loss to produce one—imperially employed in the Colonial Office, giving him his head there since they could not risk the impact of his Radical presence anywhere nearer home. A Toryism that neither carried the banner of a cause nor worked for the popular good lost touch not only with the people, but with its own sense of justification. When after 1906 Balfour had become the leader of a Conservative Opposition only 100 strong in the Commons, he was forced to pretend that this traditional Tory role of paternalism had passed to the House of Lords. The duty of that House, he remarked to members of the Junior Carlton, was 'not to thwart the will of the nation—but to see that its will was *really and truly* carried out'.[1]

The Lords reckoned themselves good judges of the real and the true; and to their tasks of diagnosis peers applied themselves with vigour. They reached their apogee in 1909, when their 'Osborne judgment' declared that all political action by trades unions were *ultra vires*, and thus prevented the unions either

[1] Quoted in J. A. Hobson, *The Crisis of Liberalism* (1909), p. 38.

from putting forward their own candidates at national and local elections or from subscribing out of their funds to any political party. It was their last successful attempt to purify the political system.

But in just such conduct lay the *Crisis of Liberalism*, as described by the Radical economist and publicist J. A. Hobson that same year. He pointed out that, ever since they had crushingly rejected Gladstone's Home Rule Bill in 1885 (by 419 to 41 votes), the Lords had been mounting first a concealed and then an overt attack on the aspirations of the democracy—until, by 1909, they were now ready to take a stand against the principle of representative government itself. And the House of Lords itself represented only the first line of defences on this battlefield. Behind it were ranged in depth other powerful institutions, all bound by custom, all demanding deference and loyalty; some of them visible, some of them not, but all of them equally determined to maintain the *status quo*:

> a whole row of defences, represented by the laws and the judiciary, the bureaucracy, the Court, the electoral machinery (favouring at every turn the power of the purse), the secret unrepresentative character and working of Cabinet Government, the manipulation of electoral opinion through the public house, the Press, the pulpit and those other instruments of popular instruction which depend for their financial support upon the charity of the propertied classes.[1]

No wonder, then, that freedom and equality of access to public justice did not exist in Great Britain, that not 5 per cent of the children of the working classes got anything beyond the barest rudiments of education, or that the English land system was the worst in the civilized world! Hobson set out a new charter, with six points more revolutionary than those of the Victorian Chartists. He called for the nationalization of the land, for the nationalization of communications, for the nationalization of credit and insurance, for free education, free justice and for the 'popular control of future monopolistic tendencies'. This would entail, no doubt, a certain socialization of government—but it

[1] Hobson, *loc. cit.*, pp. x–xi.

was not Socialism, as it would not give to the State all the instruments of production, distribution and exchange.

But could such a programme ever make a wide appeal? Would a myriad signatures ever appear on a petition for such a Charter? Hobson doubted it. This was an age of money—and worse, of the love of money, that root of all evil. Money had power: and it appeared that, the more democratic the system of government and the arrangement of society, the more power it had. Like C. E. Montague, Hobson looked across to the United States for examples; and, like Bright before him, amid that kaleidoscope concentrated on the things that would best support his critical case. There were scarcely any great American fortunes into which corruptly-obtained charters or tariff-aid, illegal railroad practices, land speculation, over-capitalization, Wall Street gambling, and all such ploys, did not enter largely as ingredients: California's railroad king Leland Stanford, for example, had done it all on land speculation and cheap Chinese labour—this last a commodity that had only just been prised from the hands of the millionaire magnates on the South African Rand. That a great many Americans admired these confident buccaneers was, to Hobson as to contemporary American 'muckrakers' themselves, the most dangerous factor of all.

For these money-barons were only average Americans, inflated; and, to a critical English observer, an 'average American' was still only a transplanted member of the English working class. Young America in 1900 read the works of Horatio Alger, young England those of G. A. Henty. Henty took a hero to dangerous places under a call of duty, where he earned the esteem of his colonel, or possibly of a prince of the blood. Alger's heroes, by exercising their innate American virtues, arrived at worldly success. Accordingly, very many in the United States believed that, since wealth was the reward of virtue, poverty was clearly the fruit of indolence. The pursuit of happiness, under a government devoted to principles of *laissez-faire*, brought more glittering prizes within the reach of a few than ever state enterprise could do; in the American democracy, Everyman strove to become one of those few. Opportunity was part of the equipment of that time and place. In the forty years since the civil war, the American people had settled half their continental domain, laid down a vast railroad system, and risen to power on their huge resources in coal, minerals, oil, and land. In this 'Gilded Age' a magnate could easily come to believe that, since it was his enterprise that had built much of America and would build more, he was owed as much out of America as he could get. He was a convinced utilitarian. Exploiting workers, buying Congressmen, spying on competitors, hiring private armies, intriguing, threatening—these were all necessary tools of his job. Some of his kind were men born comfortably, like Edward Harriman and Leland Stanford, but most were in the approved American tradition of being up from nowhere—Andrew Carnegie from a cottage in Scotland, Philip Armour and Marshall Field from the farm. They appealed to evolutionary doctrine, which they assumed explained that in the battle of life the weakest went to the wall, and deserved to go there. Herbert Spencer's philosophy made him a visiting hero in the United States in 1882. Millionaires vied with one another in dining a man whose opinion it was that natural economic processes must be allowed to proceed without hindrance from self-styled 'reformers', impractical men with impracticable ideas, who would never be able to build that better mousetrap which was the emblem of a commercial empire on the march. John D. Rockefeller, believing that 'God gave me my money', believed also that evolution was on his side. This position was flanked by one of simple piracy. Jim Fisk, who attempted to 'corner' the nation's gold, was a contemporary of Jesse James, whose greatest exploit was a raid on the Kansas City Fair, when he made off with $10,000 in gate-money.

Where great enterprises are afoot, great rascals abound. British critics were quick to comment on American rascalities; but very few assessed American achievements, which were not of a kind they had any experience of. Among other things, the history of the United States is a history of transportation. Thus the engineer, the maker of things, had a role and a status in American society that his kind never attained in England. Britain produced one railway king, a contemporary of Commodore Vanderbilt's—but George Hudson does not rank as an English worthy, and has left his name only on the history of stock-jobbing.

Yet by the turn of the twentieth century the nature of the

American achievement was forcing itself upon the attention of the world. What happened to American capitalism was to happen later to American foreign policy: it outgrew its bounds, and drew the world into its orbit. In the earlier era the money-barons, however rich they grew, remained personally interested in their own businesses. In mentality they remained the small-town, small-time operators they had once been, and this of course accounts for the major part of their appeal. Andrew Carnegie held 58 per cent of the stock of his own steel company. Such a man published a balance sheet with reluctance, and took care that the minimum of information was printed on it. He dispensed with stockholders' meetings, and if government probed into his affairs, government got a dusty answer on the lines of 'mind your own business and I'll mind mine', the point being that the business was indeed his. It was in this spirit that railroad companies were frequently thrown about either from hand to hand, or on to the garbage heap, like paper cups. Capital, like a dollar bill, was personally negotiable. But in the later age the great capitalists, having been geared to the traditional American notion that competition was healthy, sat up nights thinking up ways how to get rid of it. Hence the formation of 'trusts', which could charge what they pleased and force competitors out. A corporation could be formed to buy the stock of various companies, and, acting first as a holding-company, go on to control all their operations. The greatest of these corporations was United States Steel, formed in 1901, at the head of which sat men who had never previously had any deal-ings in steel, or knew one end of an ingot from the other. The banker and the corporation lawyer became the really important men of the day, since it was they who had the credit and the know-how that others were prepared to pay for. And not Americans only, for the house of J. P. Morgan was as prestigious in Paris and London as in New York.

Now Morgan was only Cobden projected and magnified, the admired representative of a rich industrialist middle-class. In 1900 the American government was still Cobdenist, spending as little as possible (roughly half a billion dollars annually, about one-eightieth of what it spends now). If it wanted to raise money, it had to apply to Morgan and his Wall Street associates;

it had no federal reserve of its own. If it interfered in labour disputes, it got itself a bad name: Theodore Roosevelt was the first
president who took action to settle a strike, in 1902, and many
heads were shaken at this unconstitutional behaviour. But
Roosevelt was a Tory paternalist who disliked the way his
country was tending, believing that while the plutocracy ought
certainly to have its place in American society, it ought to keep
to that place, and not usurp any other position to which it had no
right, and to which money could not give the right. He made no
bones about calling highly-placed politicians who had manipulated public money *thieves*—a word not heard in democratic
politics for years. In his era 'reform' became acceptable. It was
now that Carnegie and Rockefeller established their charitable
foundations, and that the New Jersey Democrats, a hard-bitten
school of professionals, chose Woodrow Wilson of Princeton
University as their candidate for governor. Magnates emerged
who wanted money as much as Rockefeller, but thought of more
popular ways of making it—like Henry Ford. It was in 1913,
when Wilson had become president, that a federal income tax
was at last introduced; and the moral justice of its imposition
was admitted, or at least not fiercely rebutted. Thus the
American democracy, even as Hobson pilloried its excesses, was
amid all its materialism reasserting its puritan sense of virtue
once more.

British public life was enlivened by no such progressive
figures as the Republican Roosevelt and the Democrat Wilson:
the fractured hopes and largely irrelevant career of Joseph
Chamberlain, the lost ideals of Lloyd George, speak for themselves. The British people produced no such figure as that 'man
of the people', William Jennings Bryan, a Democrat as unlike
Wilson as anyone could well be, and of whom it has been said
that 'he spoke for the people so perfectly that he never spoke to
them'.[1] But he and they held a simple republican creed, the 'good
old Cause' the monarchical system of England could not accommodate, and which the unwritten British constitution did not
include. Bryan saw himself as the heir of Jefferson and Jackson,
although he was always less devious than both. With Jefferson,
he believed in the virtues of the 'yeoman', distrusting the

[1] Hofstaedter, *Great Issues*, II, p. 132.

capitalist and the merchant. He had faith in the dignity of man, in his commonsense, and in his ability to recognize all political questions, as, at base, moral questions. (It was Gladstone's own stance.) With Jackson, Bryan believed in equal rights for all and special privileges for none, and that it was the duty of government to protect all from injustice, without partiality to any one class. He saw no need to change the American constitution, which had been designed to ensure just these things. If something had gone amiss, that was only because the constitution had been misinterpreted, or because good democrats had grown lazy. There is no socialism in one of Bryan's most famous addresses, the New York Speech of 1896:

> Our campaign has not for its object the reconstruction of society. We cannot ensure to the vicious the fruits of a virtuous life; we would not invade the home of the provident in order to supply the wants of the spendthrift; we do not propose to transfer the rewards of industry to the lap of indolence.

Property was, and would remain, the best stimulus to endeavour, and the compensation for toil. The Declaration of Independence assuredly asserted that all men were created equal—

> but that does not mean that all men are or can be equal in possessions, in ability, or in merit; it simply means that all shall stand equal before the law.

With much of this any English Tory could agree—indeed, his publicist W. H. Mallock was writing books on this very theme. But both Bryan and his audiences shared an assumption: American society did not need to be reconstructed, because that task had long ago been tackled. To be an American at all was to be a subscriber to certain principles concerning society, its aims and its ideals. To be an Englishman implied no such thing. An American who demanded justice saw himself, and was seen by others, as an individual litigant only: he accused someone of trespassing on his rights, but he did not level any charge against society itself. But in England a cry for justice was taken, and

311

correctly taken, as just such an indictment. Socialists shocked
the gentlemen of England, as once Jack Cade and John Lilburne
had done, when they asserted that in England men were not in
fact, whatever they were told, equal before the law.

The American politician Bryan, the English economist Hobson, were both social critics, Radical Liberals. They both
believed in the worth of their own national systems, which
needed only some purification to be the best of all systems.
Hence when Bryan looked across the Atlantic he could see only
the corruption of aristocracy, and when Hobson looked at the
United States he could see only the corruption of democracy.
Bryan could rest easy, for the United States at this late date was
not likely to be further influenced by unsightly British practices.
But Hobson felt he could not—for Great Britain, slowly develop-
ing within itself the opinions, if not as yet the self-confidence of
democracy, was more than likely to become contaminated with
American ways, just as Arnold had foreseen and deplored.
Disraeli's 'third-rate republic' was well on its way to becoming
a first-rate power, which would ask, and be paid, respect. The
American democracy was no longer a 'great experiment', it was
a great success. The British democracy, still looking for a leading light, could not fail to be attracted, as the Chartists had been,
to the land of Goshen, to the beacon in the west. Comfortably-
placed English intellectuals might sneer at the American pursuit
of the dollar, but there were many other Englishmen who did
not consider an equation of money with happiness as absurd, or
even degrading. Henry James and George Meredith, close
observers of Ascendancy *mores*, came to agree with the average
worker that money is freedom, the key that unlocks; and that
even if it cannot buy happiness it can at any rate buy time,
culture, and privilege. This practical outlook was to clash with
that of the social reformer from that time to this, and to make
conservatism the natural politics, Toryism the natural attitude,
of the man who had made his pile.

Hobson saw this plainly. It was bad enough that money
should contaminate democratic politics, but it was worse that it
should influence democratic education, the only resource by
which a people could gain a genuine freedom. What else did a
successful college president in the United States need to be, but

a skilful mendicant? Doubtless the rich men who patronized
schools and universities steered clear of the intricacies of the
curriculum, but those who were in charge of the curriculum
could not choose to steer clear of them. It was not the past
patron, or even the present, but the patron of the future whose
influence curbed liberty—'the unknown prospective donor whose
goodwill must be conciliated, or, what comes to the same thing,
his ill-will averted'.[1]

Nor was this a menace peculiar to America because some
Americans had grown richer than was good either for them or
their society. There was such a phenomenon in England as a
'South African millionaire', modern counterpart to the eighteenth-century's East or West India nabob, who, on leaving the
Rand with his pile, attached himself to that part of society that
was glad to have it, if not him. Here Hobson directed a baleful
glance at the University of Oxford. There, the teaching of
imperial history had recently been endowed by Alfred Beit. This
subject, as defined by the donor and accepted by the university,
gave prominence to the history of the South African colonies, in
whose recent record Beit and his associates had played a very
significant part. Did any thoughtful person believe, Hobson
asked, that if historians appointed under this trust applied themselves to an accurate analysis of the precise influences exerted
upon politics in South Africa by the financial combination of
which De Beers, Wernher, Beit and Company and the chartered
British South Africa Company were the chief constituents, the
trust would be renewed at the expiration of its term of probation?
Did anyone think so, he should make a careful study of the
educational propaganda conducted during recent years by Beit
and his friends throughout the press and in the Conservative
party, and enlighten himself accordingly. This kind of thing was
part of the tacit conspiracy set on foot by the possessing classes
against disturbing thoughts: its consequence would be the
breeding of an 'intellectual quietism', a mortal enemy to the
cause of democracy.[2]

'This kind of thing' was not the kind that English politicians
thought it their business to deal with. The Conservatives learnt

[1] Hobson, *op. cit.*, p. 227.
[2] *Ibid.*, 229.

nothing from their defeat in 1906. Balfour as leader lost a general election three times, and his lieutenants Bonar Law, F. E. Smith [Lord Birkenhead] and Sir Edward Carson had assuredly no message of any kind to deliver to anybody. In 1911 Bonar Law succeeded him—and thus the Tories of England found themselves under the political direction of an ironmaster from New Brunswick via Glasgow, who had no knowledge of their traditions, no sympathy for their habits, no interest in their ideas, and no plans for the future at all. Pitt alike with Peel, Wellington alike with Disraeli, would have stared in disbelief. If it really was the political task, according to Bentham's nostrum, so to act that the people, as far as was possible, got what they wanted, it was plain that the Conservatives, Toryism's official spokesmen, had no idea how to cope with it. Bonar Law and the business fraternity of which he was the very adequate representative had no notion what the people wanted, and were not disposed to find out.

Tories had not produced a capable economist since Pitt. They did not produce one now. They could not even attract a capable adventurer to do them service, in the style of Canning or Disraeli. Early death removed from them two likely leaders, Alfred Lyttelton and George Wyndham. Their aristocracy of birth, its dukes pilloried by Lloyd George and the Radical press, its property threatened by taxation meted out in the name of a social justice which drew the hitherto unperceived moral distinction between earned and unearned incomes, closed its ranks; but they found neither a banner to wave nor a cause to exploit. They could complain, as they did, against the taxes on the people's food which would have been a concrete result of their businessmen colleagues' policy of Protection: it was this that Lord Derby had in mind when he damned the Chamberlains, father Joseph and son Austen, as the curse of the party and the country.[1] (Ultimately it was the other son, Neville, who brought this policy into harbour.) But they could not discover Tocqueville's 'springs of action'; they could not find a function that anyone was ready to respect. The upper and middle classes, similarly beleaguered, attacked as the upholders of an unjust social system, pilloried as dull Philistines, railed at for their lack of insight,

[1] Churchill, *Derby*, p. 160.

denounced as exploiters, received no rescuing inspiration from their own politicians. These were men who, although happy to make off with the 'glittering prizes' (the phrase is F. E. Smith's) of public life, did not comprehend that even a glittering prize had its price, and that something was owed in return: the real scandal of 1912's 'Marconi scandal' lay not in its details but in the haste with which, by common consent, it was buried.

The educated classes continued to send their sons to govern the territories of the British Empire; but the paternalist rule of distant natives attracted little attention at home, the Empire was more often referred to than thought about, and no one was of less significance in public life than the retired colonial official, as the great proconsuls Milner, Cromer and Curzon all found out. 'If we personify the Empire', Lord Hugh Cecil noted in his book on *Conservatism* (1911), 'our imaginations recoil like Frankenstein from the monster that we have made, the monster of a heterogeneous personality'. H. G. Wells' comment was more incisive. Nineteen people out of twenty, the middle class and most of the lower class, knew no more of the Empire than they did of the Argentine Republic or of the Italian Renaissance.[1] English workers did not care to concentrate on such facts as the lack of Factory Acts in Egypt, the twelve-hour day put in by women and children in the cotton-ginning mills there, the £1 a month pay-packet which the Calcutta jute-mill worker took home, or the kind of home he took it to.

If what went on in the British Empire seemed an irrelevance to the British democracy, so too did the Ulster problem and the ultimate destinies of the Irish, another native race that appeared, from all the evidence, to be ungovernable anyway. Workers in Glasgow, Liverpool and other areas into which the Irish had poured had reason to look on Irish labour as 'black', and therefore stayed resolutely unsympathetic to catalogues of the wrongs of Ireland. Politicians who wanted to concentrate their attention on possible solutions of the condition-of-England question were equally inattentive to the condition of Ireland. Indeed, they saw no need so to attend, for if one's ears were determinedly shut to the stream of Irish propaganda on the subject, it was plain that Ireland was socially healthier than John

[1] Wells, *Mr Britling Sees It Through* (1916), p. 212.

Bull's principal island. Ireland after 1903 had more tenant-farmers than England, and few of its problems of urbanization—one of which was revealed that year by the report of the Royal Commission on Physical Deterioration, itself a product of alarming medical evidence from the Army during the South African war. The report claimed that between 16 and 20 per cent of the school population in England and Wales suffered from malnutrition. In these circumstances, reformers in England felt they had more to worry about than 'Home Rule for Ireland', a purely political matter, and one that anyway lay at the end of an impasse, as the Irish were obviously never going to agree among themselves about it. Ireland lay, a red herring, across the path of the English political process, and plagued in particular Liberals who resented having to deal with it to the detriment of other, and more important, duties.

The Irish irrelevance was followed hard upon by the irrelevance of a war with the German Empire. This, indeed, was an unfortunate generation, whose few crusaders had to leave their mounts in the stable, while they fought on foot, in a gathering mist. Those who were always anxious to do their best for the democracy were at the same time fearful of the worst democracy might do. Over-fearful, as it turned out: for the outbreak of war in 1914 was not attended with the social horrors that some at least had presaged. Charles Masterman reports how one of his Cabinet colleagues, 'in those awful twelve days in which the world broke under our feet',[1] assured him that, if the country went to war, within a fortnight every mill and factory in the north would be closed, and hunger-maddened multitudes would sack every rich man's house and break into civil riot in their need for food. Here was one diagnosis what the people of England—who, as G. K. Chesterton had dourly reminded his middle-class readership, 'had not spoken yet'—were likely to say when they did speak. Similarly, when the war was well under way, the people of England were expected to speak out loudly against conscription; and thus the Military Service Act was long postponed 'through fear of systematized revolt'.[2]

But, if the people themselves had not spoken yet, there was

[1] C. F. G. Masterman, *England after War* (New York, 1923), p. 8.
[2] F. J. C. Hearnshaw, *Democracy at the Crossroads* (1923), p. 195.

no lack of idealists to speak for them, men equipped with and ready to use a keener perception to point out the horizon towards which the people ought to begin to march. 'The march of democracy', of which much was to be heard, was always a significant metaphor: for it argued the presence of intellectual sergeant-majors, whipping in democracy's flanks. Robert Blatchford objected that the people took their ideas at second hand; but what he really complained of was the type of ideas they absorbed, not the process of absorption itself. There were many of his kind, who felt that more had to be done for the mass of the people at large than would ever suit the book or even catch the attention of an orthodox, paternalist Toryism.

The hope of the Chartists not merely to amend the political constitution, but to alter the social structure in the name ot justice, had never been forgotten. The idea that 'rights' could be made to apply to a community of men, however damned by Burke, Pitt, and circumstance, held in it something too valuable to be let die: the heart remembered it. Were ideas of a wider life, of broader opportunities, forever to be confined to those who went off to Philadelphia in the morning? Was the American republic to remain forever a comment on, a criticism of, the life most Englishmen lived? Was nothing ever to be done about England, in and for England, by Englishmen? Tom Paine's pleas for 'commonsense' had gone largely unheeded, for he appealed to what was not in his day, or in any day, a common quality. But other social critics arose with more constructive ability, men who made plans and drew maps for the future. The earliest English Socialist, Robert Owen, neither a Chartist nor a parliamentary reformer, devised a philosophy (seen by some as an unpleasant mixture of Calvinism and Benthamism) which included the belief that character was entirely the product of environment and education. He was sure that the working classes could be regenerated if they lived in co-operative settlements, or 'colonies'—a notion which, dismaying to Tories, was equally anathema to two such dissimilar Radicals as Cobbett and Marx. Yet Owen's own Toryism was deeply rooted. He did not believe in rule by the working classes, only in rule for them. It was the clear duty of any government to consider the territory it governed as an estate, and the population on it as a family. This opinion was no distance from that of 'Young England', which believed in a domestic equivalent of 'Crown Colony' government. But since Owen also held some eccentric views about the family itself, and despised religious doctrine, he was attacked by churchmen, who condemned his New Lanark community as illegal, and his writings as revolutionary, blasphemous and obscene.

Yet Owen's ideal of a healthy community, which could be fashioned by forethought and planning, challenged the goodwill and imagination of paternalists. The Tory Southey approved it, with the proviso that it must be a Christian social order that governed and educated the new society. To young churchmen of the 1850s the challenge was compelling. It was one of these, Charles Kingsley, whose novels *Alton Locke* (1848) and *Yeast* (1850) filled out in detail the picture of national poverty presented in Disraeli's *Sybil*, who complained almost in Marx's own words that the Bible had been made into 'an opium-dose' for the people. To these 'Christian Socialists' democracy was not a menace to be feared and fought. Democracy was, or could anyway be made, representative of 'the giant self-control of a nation, ruling itself as one man, in wisdom and righteousness'. But first, false standards and values had to be abolished. Here was a programme that jarred their colleagues and their congregations, who were unable to understand what was meant by this charge of falsity. The world wrought by the *entrepreneur*, approved of by political economists, upheld by free trade, liberalism, and self-satisfaction, was to remain devoted both 'to the Good Book and to the keeping of good books'.[1] The minor virtues—efficiency, reliability, punctuality, thrift—certainly flourished in the new industrial society. What else was needed? Perhaps these virtues were not essential attributes of the 'new Jerusalem' that the poet Blake had had in mind—but, after all, did it really matter what the poet Blake had had in mind?

Thus the Christian Socialists made their brave sortie, but too late, over a darkling plain. Comfortable Anglicans anyway preferred the ministrations of non-polemical parsons who did not seek any limelight; and all the devoted work of the Christian Socialists, as their own historian admits, could never rid the other kinds of Socialist of the opinion that the Church of England

[1] The phrase is Asa Briggs': *Age of Improvement*, p. 27.

had ever been, and remained, 'a body of privileged hypocrites valiant only in defence of their emoluments, the bond-slaves of vested interests, offering to starving souls the consolations of an antiquated mythology and to starving bodies the crumbs of a rich man's charity'.[1] Hobson himself characterized the Christian Socialist message as a 'sentimental utterance'.

The English Victorian trade societies or unions were composed indeed of Christians. But they were seldom either Anglicans or Socialists. Their membership of skilled workers was drawn from the nonconformist majority in the country; they believed in co-operation with the unskilled no more than 'poor whites' in South Africa believed in co-operation with the unskilled black, or the Australian miner in healthy competition from the Chinese. They kept clear of the First International [Working Men's Association] between 1864 and 1873, causing Karl Marx to exclaim that the English were incapable of making a proletarian revolution, and that foreigners would have to make it for them. They kept clear, too, of all such 'syndicalist' and subversive doctrines as animated their *confrères* in France; and they were almost as suspicious of the pioneer English Socialists. In these they saw emissaries from the employing classes, different in function but not in essence from the new factory inspectors, whom many a 'hand' wrote off in advance as men who came armed not with a benevolent governmental authority but with a bucket of whitewash, for employers' use only. The unions were themselves the pioneers of 'Labour' representation, but they left the movement for social democracy to be started and kept going by middle-class men, as they could see no stake in it for themselves. They felt they had more than enough to do to put forward, and to get attention paid to, their immediate claims. The trade unionist's dream was to fix wages, to get a 'rate' for the job—and this, of course, was always denounced by those with whom he had to treat as a limitation of the great doctrine of freedom of contract.

For the forces of British Labour, unlike their kin in Australia and New Zealand, had to wage their battle with capitalism on ground that had previously been chosen for its advantages by the capitalists themselves.

[1] C. E. Raven, *Christian Socialism 1848–54* (1920), p. 1.

Authority in England, although lapped by peace and prosperity, had not yet lost sight of its original motivation, self-preservation; and, since flexibility had always been found to be an asset to this policy, its rigid doctrines were accordingly few. Those it did hold to were reckoned self-evidently just. Freedom of contract, for example, was one of those 'natural laws', or laws of the universe, which had been handed down in a chain from one Ascendancy to the next, from Locke to Burke, from Jefferson and Ricardo, from Macaulay and all the schoolmasters of society who spread the word among the people, on both sides of the Atlantic. In his *Thoughts on Scarcity* (1795), Burke had reached the conclusion that 'the laws of commerce are the laws of nature, and therefore the laws of God'.[1] Darwin had since illuminated still other laws of nature, which ruled that if one was more successful than one's fellows, one deserved to be. Complacency at this astronomical level can seem a more thwarting foe than tyranny itself. It so struck English Socialists. Some educated men with humanitarian views, and with a contempt for the ideas of their comfortable contemporaries, the dullards they remembered from schooldays, had perhaps in consequence a keener wish to *épater le bourgeois* than to rebuild Jerusalem. Yet the one process might speed the other, for if the Ascendancy was forced to examine its own assumptions, it might be brought to recognize that these had no rational basis at all. It would then lose its confidence and its will, and the day would pass to the opposing forces. Some others among these educated men, although never many of them, were attracted to harder and faster measures: to revolution itself, as the only way to resolve society's ills. But the rest preferred to set to work on the stuff of human nature itself, an even grimmer (and certainly longer) task.

Of H. M. Hyndman, for example, who was a product of Cambridge and who had in his time played cricket for Sussex, it was said that there never was a more arbitrary leader of a democratic movement: he himself, however, was to live long enough to be shocked by Lenin's ruthlessness. The organ of his Social

---

[1] This verdict drew down upon him one of the most ferocious of Marx's gibes: 'No wonder that, true to the laws of God and of Nature, Burke always sold himself in the best market!', *Capital,* ii, 786.

Democratic Federation (1884) was *Justice*, and the organization itself was a latter-day Chartism that demanded the reconstruction of society. The Social Democratic Federation's programme included compulsory secular education, free justice, the eight-hour day, the taxation of the rich, the nationalization of railways and public utilities, the repudiation of the National Debt (that old Tory bugbear), adult suffrage, the nationalization of the land, the disestablishment of the Church of England, and a comprehensive pensions scheme. In other words, it aimed at the overthrow of capitalism, and drew its inspiration from Marx's attack on that system. Working-class rioting in London's West End in February 1886, and 'Bloody Sunday' (November 13, 1887) in Trafalgar Square seemed to presage to many a capitalist that the overthrow was upon him. But the total membership of Hyndman's movement that same year stood at 689, and its atheistic content could not be accommodated by the nonconformist conscience of Labour. Whatever else it was, the Social Democratic Federation was not a 'friendly society'; it did not believe in co-operation. But even its zeal for reconstruction was surpassed by another middle-class organization, the Socialist League, whose journal *Commonweal* was edited by William Morris. This body was distinctly hostile to the parliamentary system altogether, bringing a cold commonsense to bear on it that Tom Paine would have approved. It assumed, as a matter of course, that

a government of privileged persons, hereditary and commercial, cannot act usefully or rightly towards the community: their position forbids it.

This language, like Tom Paine's, frightened more people than it convinced. There was something too austere, too remote, in this intellectual brand of Socialist paternalism. If England were to be reconstructed as a clean, well-lighted place, those who preferred a life of cosy disarray would inevitably suffer. There were limits, as there always had been, to English radicalism. It was the Fabian Society that set about to define these; and, because of this very moderation, that was to throw the longest shadow.

Fabians, among whom (according to Bernard Shaw, their

most attractive publicist) there were 'no born rich men and no born poor men', believed in a policy of gradualism and of permeation. They filtered into the ranks of Liberals, Radicals, trade unions and co-operative movements. Unlike the Whig 'Friends of the People' of a century back, they charged an annual subscription of half-a-crown, and only the non-payment of this could warrant a member's expulsion. Sidney Webb, who acted as the society's intellectual dynamo, was a disciple of J. S. Mill. He believed in the gradual limitation of the sphere of private property, and he could see already how things were going his way. Mines Acts, Passenger Acts, Truck Acts, Factory Acts, Adulteration Acts all showed the power of the state at work: it had only to press on along these same lines. In his Fabian tract *The Progress of Socialism* (1888) Webb rejoiced at the steps already taken by a state whose leaders still insisted on considering themselves the exponents of *laisser-faire*. The state now registered, inspected and controlled nearly all the industrial functions which it had not yet absorbed, and the inspection was both detailed and rigidly enforced. In most large industrial operations the state prescribed the age of the worker, the hours of work, the amount of air, light, cubic feet, heat, lavatory accommodation, holiday and meal times; where, when and how wages should be paid; how machinery, staircases, lift-shafts, mines and quarries were to be fenced and guarded; how and when the plant was to be cleaned, repaired and worked. Even the kind of package in which some articles should be sold was duly prescribed, so that the individual capitalist should take no advantage of his position. On every side this capitalist, more beleaguered than most of his kind had yet noticed, was being confined to strict bounds—

eventually he will be superseded by the community, and he is compelled in the meantime to cede for public purposes an ever-increasing share of his rent and interest.

The policy of gradualism and permeation had thus won so many victories already that there was no need to suppose that it would not go on doing so.

It was a good diagnosis. The spectacular dockers' strike of

August 1889 saw the first alliance of this middle-class socialism with the forces of unskilled labour, and paid a dividend: for the assistance given in this 'class struggle' by the Fabians was not forgotten by the workers, who contrasted it with the lack of assistance or even sympathy given by the skilled trades unions. On the other hand, the knowledge that they had actually done something positive in the workaday outside world, that they were some use even when they left their armchairs, gave the Fabians a brisker self-confidence. The Independent Labour party established in 1893 was the product of this new solidarity; this group was to cast itself ever afterwards as the true keepers of the socialist flame, a piece of pretension for which it was of course denounced at the outset by the Social Democratic Federation. For Independent Labour party leaders such as Keir Hardie were neither economists, atheists, nor Marxists, and they had no gigantic revolutionary plans. Their journal had a quieter title either than *Justice, Commonweal,* or Blatchford's *Clarion* (1892): it was, simply, *The Labour Elector,* and its aim was the practical one of making more and more workers who now voted for the Liberals transfer their support to the Independent Labour party. Ramsay MacDonald so transferred in July 1894. The party put up twenty-eight candidates in the general election of 1895, seven of these being middle-class men, the rest trade unionists; while the Social Democratic Federation put up four, including Hynd-man and George Lansbury. But all were defeated: the imperialist heyday was not the time for the 'permeation' that the Fabians had in mind.

But the pattern for the Labour party of the future was already set. The socialist movement of the 1890s was staffed mainly by young men, and, as young men will, they valued the assistance of women more than their elders: women henceforward were to be of great importance in 'getting the vote out' in working-class districts. Every socialist address was called a lecture, the pamphlets produced were collectively referred to as literature: an example of that upgrading of language to which democracy is always attached.[1] (Dilke had noted how among the Australians

---

[1] Some upgrading was perhaps needed. Canon Raven remarked that 'Socialism, as anyone who has ever been to a Fabian Society meeting will know, has been especially cursed by its fatal fascination for the degenerate and the eccentric.'

wages had become salary, servants employees and poorhouses benevolent asylums.) The atmosphere of revivalism was never far away, hymn tunes were much in use, and even 'The Red Flag' could be sung to *Maryland*. On January 8, 1924, when the Labour party assembled in the House of Commons to admire its own leaders sitting for the first time as His Majesty's Government on the Front Bench, its members sang hymns, the *Marseillaise*, and the 'Red Flag' too, 'which may have puzzled some who were not previously acquainted with the diverse sources of Labour's inspiration'. Nor was 'The Red Flag' so ill-at-ease in this company as was generally supposed, since the 'red' referred to the workers' blood that had flowed, not to the *bourgeois* blood that was about to be spilled. MacDonald was a Presbyterian, Arthur Henderson a Methodist lay-preacher, Lansbury an Anglican; and when Philip Snowden made a visit to his birthplace after becoming Chancellor of the Exchequer, he was met by the local Temperance brass band, and escorted to the United Methodist schoolroom by the whole population.[1]

Moreover, the Labour movement, like all English movements which are capable of success, had its solid Tory core in the trades unions, which could not deny the socialists some virtues so long as they continued to support the strike-principle, as they never failed to. The Independent Labour party programme for an 'industrial commonwealth' was anyway plainly one that, if ever it succeeded, would promote the importance of trades unions, and of skilled workers in general. That was an agreeable horizon for even the most suspicious of hard-headed craftsmen to look at. The Trades Union Congress therefore voted for 'collectivism' in 1894, and thereafter lumbered in the rear of socialist scouting-parties. The Labour Representative Committee, with MacDonald as its secretary, was the product of this solidarity (1900), electing two members in the general election of that year. The agreed aim was social reform, for at the Labour Representative Committee's first meeting, a Social Democratic Federation resolution declaring that the objective to strive for was 'social democracy', was defeated. The Labour movement was henceforward to be commanded by social reformers, who used the name of socialist without ever clearly

[1] R. Lyman, *The First Labour Government 1924* (1958), pp. 9, 96.

defining it, and in a later generation avoided using the name at all, preferring the more definable public image of 'Labour': from the 1920s onwards Lord Beaverbrook's newspaper chain made it a duty continuously to remind the public of the facts as he saw them by referring to all Labour members always as Socialists, with the capital letter. Aneurin Bevan seems to have agreed with him: he told a friend before the election of 1950 that what he hoped for was not the return of another Labour government, but of Britain's first socialist administration.[1]

At the general election of January 1906, the Labour Representative Committee—which the following month adopted formally the title of the Labour party—put up fifty-one candidates, and thirty were elected: fifteen socialists, fourteen Independent Labour party and one from the Social Democratic Federation (Will Thorne). The chosen thirty thereafter worked a passage to working-class acceptance by busying themselves with trade union matters, their most signal achievement being the reversal of the Osborne judgment in 1913. MacDonald in particular displayed a marked aptitude for politics and became a trade union favourite: 'no generous outburst of wrath disfigured his public utterances', remarks one ungenerous critic of his activities at this period. Such outbursts of wrath continued to come from the Social Democratic Federation, which objected to the Labour alliance in parliament with the Liberals, and from the Independent Labour party, which continued to dislike a doctrine that forbade any positive move in any direction at all until a class-conscious proletariat should have given a clear majority. The most militant of the Independent Labour party men were naturally the Scots from Glasgow, where there was (or where it could at least be plausibly argued there was) such a thing as a class-conscious proletariat.

This dispute, between the tacticians and the doctrinaires, was never to be buried: it was the trade union stalwart Ernest Bevin who, become Foreign Secretary in the Labour government after 1945, most bitterly complained that his tactics were being hampered, that he was indeed being stabbed in the back, by woolly-minded and vindictive colleagues in the movement, intellectual socialists who could never grasp the hard fact that

[1] Leslie Hunter, *The Road to Brighton Pier* (1959), p. 22.

the world had to be dealt with as it was, and not as it ought to be. But the socialist *pur sang* who continued to believe that internationalism and the general will of a concert of the nations could purify even so poisoned a matter as that of the Palestine mandate, continued also to propose in domestic affairs the abolition of poverty, which was to be brought about by substituting national for private ownership of land and capital. The social reformers, of whom Bevin was one and Attlee another, were content to propose the abolition of destitution (not the same thing) by using taxation as their chief weapon, and by distributing more equitably the portions of the national 'cake'. But they had no wish to bake another cake: they did not tamper with any revolutionary principle, and did not eagerly look forward to a coming struggle for power. From the outset the true socialist had claimed that in the future, when society had been made over according to his pattern, state action would dwindle to nothing, as there would be nothing for the state to do. The more pragmatic social reformer, borrowing socialist aims but not socialist techniques, foresaw that the state would need to act in more and more spheres of the community's life, as it would always be the duty of a government to ensure that the welfare of the people was what it should be. He was sure that it was he who, amid a crowd of false suitors, was the true 'Friend of the People', the kindly overseer of the estate of the realm, the paternalist who would use authority as a trust, in Burke's sense of that word.

Nevertheless, for both socialist and social reformer, idealist and pragmatist, there was always a common enemy: Toryism, upholder of the system of privilege, dynamo of the Ascendancy as it was at present constituted. William Morris had seen in parliament a mere committee of landlords and capitalists. Keir Hardie had admitted there was 'a conflict of interests', while denying that these interests would have to clash one day on a battlefield. In France a more logical conclusion was more readily reached. French trade unions were not legalized until 1884, and thereafter their members remained cynically unconvinced that any support would ever come their way from a *bourgeois* Chamber of Deputies. Georges Sorel accordingly promoted a type of social democracy designed to sabotage the *bourgeoisie* entirely.

It did not seem an impracticable programme. As Jean Jaurès put it (November 21, 1893), these *bourgeois* masters of the Third Republic, who called themselves Radicals, had in their self-centred attack upon the Catholic Church, in their laicisation of education, interrupted the old lullaby that had long cradled human poverty. They had awakened the disinherited, who

> would demand their rights with more urgency in this world if they had lost hope of a future world in which the balance would be redressed.

Even in America there were signs of an awareness that an eighteenth-century constitution did not interpret all twentieth-century problems. The Socialist party of America, a counterpart of England's Social Democratic Federation, polled close on a million votes in the presidential election of 1912. It would have done even better had the trade unionists who controlled the American Federation of Labor seen a point in allying themselves with something so unAmerican as socialism—but they were men, as Ramsay MacDonald sighed, 'whose political genius is of a low order'. And in 1914, when Britain's Independent Labour party had some 30,000 members, the Social Democratic party of Germany could muster more than a million.

Thus, even if the workers of the world had not united as Marx in his manifesto of 1848 had urged them, at least they had become collectively conscious and resolved, in one form or another, to take political action. The times were poised for their success: the dawn seemed near. But alas for these hopes, *der Tag* found for itself a different connotation. It was therefore not surprising that, on August 2, 1914, every section of the British socialist and Labour movement demonstrated in Trafalgar Square to oppose the idea of British participation in a dynastic, militarist struggle in Europe. For clearly, whatever else it was, war on a European scale, involving every country's industrial and spiritual potential, would be blank denial of mankind's best hopes.

Every Liberal mind felt this shock. In October 1912 Field-Marshal Lord Roberts, the empire's most distinguished soldier and the propagandist for the National Service League, had declared his conviction that the German Social-Democrat, that representative figure of all the European socialist movements, would make war on his English and French 'comrades' if his superiors ordered him to do so. Events proved this military appraisal of the situation quite right, and saddened many minds who had wished to think all military thinking outmoded.

The Regular Army, with all its aristocratic appurtenances, returned in 1914 to the position of prestige and authority which it had squandered in South Africa; but unhappily, like the civilian Tories, its officers threw up no leader of even more than average competence. For this misfortune, popular memory had not forgiven them even fifty years later: the war memorials to be found in every town and village were construed to commemorate not only the loss of brave men, but their 'sacrifice' at the hands of 'donkeys'. The inaction on the Western Front—it was significant that the German name for what was, after all, the Allies' Eastern Front should have been so universally adopted— wore down the sense of patriotic excitement: certainly the Gallipoli campaign of 1915 was a failure, but, as H. G. Wells pointed out in *Mr Britling*, 'forcing the Dardanelles was historically British', and exhilarating for that very reason. 'Seeing it through', in contrast, was a process that was bound to make very serious calls on men's accumulated stocks of endurance and courage.

The outbreak of war had come as a surprise, a climax which did not seem to fit a decade of domestic political infighting. But this unexpected lightning helped to illuminate the barrenness of the scene, and it was perhaps the shocked realization of this that held English society together. The appeal of the balance of power had more strength in it than Cobden would have supposed, or wanted; and the Gladstonian principle that small nations had as much right as great nations to be free found now its followers *à la Belge*. Moreover, war, whatever else it did, called out more qualities in men than those of Tocqueville's virtuous materialism; it reminded, or instructed, men that they possessed energy and resource and courage. It certainly reminded Conservative politicians in opposition that martial qualities were traditionally Tory, and were accordingly unlikely to be found among the set of pacifist Radicals on the Government Front Bench.

In a nation gearing itself to wage war, gifts of leadership were no longer suspect: indeed, Asquith's downfall in December 1916 was brought about from the reverse cause, that too many suspected he had no gifts of leadership. Thereafter a coalition government under Lloyd George was able to employ in its Cabinet such non-democrats as Milner and Curzon and Carson without any popular outcry. A precedent had been established by Asquith when he installed in his Cabinet as Secretary for War the extreme non-democrat, Kitchener, who did not believe in conscription but made it clear that when a man had his duty to king and country plain before him he had no excuse not to see it. And it was he who became the true hero of the populace. 'Daddy, what did you do in the great war?' was one of the recruiting posters of 1914—making a deep appeal, since it recognized the principles of 'loyalty' and tradition so peculiar to English society.[1]

Kitchener's first 100,000 volunteers, the Old Contemptibles, were the only figures of romance to emerge from the war, and the memory of that comradeship was to soften the no less bitter hardships of the peace. Yet even by 1915 it was clear that above 650,000 eligible men had not volunteered, and that some other principle than the voluntary had to be found.[2] Other methods were indeed adopted, but no other principle ever emerged. Patriotic fervour ran out as it became clear to those present in Flanders, at Gallipoli, at Kut, that courage alone was not enough to win a field, and that the leadership available was not going to be granted the gift Napoleon had decreed as essential, luck. The popular symbol of sacrifice thereafter was 'the unknown soldier' —some shattered Atkins for whom even the authorities could not find his own name.

For the slaughter on the Somme in the summer of 1916 marked the end of an era. On the wire died, with the many men, many of the assumptions that held society together. The searchlights that played over the shattered landscape of what had been

[1] It would not have made any appeal at all in the United States, where in the century's two world wars married men tended to think the fact of their having families was warrant to avoid military service altogether. Nor was 'military service' a concept of American speech. Cf. Samuel Goldwyn's award-winning motion picture, *The Best Years of Our Lives* (1947), with its underlying note of resentment and betrayal.

[2] Churchill, *Derby*, p. 201.

a pleasant, well-watered farmland illuminated the 'journey's end' at which the nineteenth-century's hopes of progress had, at long last, arrived. The casualties of 1916 fell most heavily on the non-regular, volunteer regimental officers, the future leaders of their civilian professions, men whose absence from the post-war scene was never to be absent from anyone's mind. The United States' ambassador in London, Walter Page, had a sorrowful vision of the Europe-to-come as 'a bankrupt slaughterhouse inhabited by unmated women'.[1] If it was never as bad as that, it was never good. One casualty that could be read even between the close-set lines of the official casualty-lists was the popular belief that 'the Government', that remote but paternal entity, knew what it was about: that it could be trusted to do its best, and that its best was to be trusted. Lloyd George's battle with the services, his refusal to give his commander-in-chief, Haig, the reserves asked for because he feared Haig's strategy would kill them, went generally unperceived at the time and had to remain unconfessed later.

The disasters of 1916 animated the 'war aims' campaign of the Union of Democratic Control, staffed by Radicals—left-wing Liberals and members of the Labour party. The democracy, controlling nothing, held on to what it knew and rejected what it could not rely on, like the jingo press, whose magnates thereafter were permitted to entertain the people, but not to instruct them. They set their hopes on a better future, and in the meantime sporadic objection—the miners' strike in South Wales of August 1915, the Clyde munitions strike in March 1916, the engineers' strike of May 1917, the decision taken by the Labour Conference at Leeds that month to set up workmen's and soldiers' councils to work for a 'democratic' peace, and all those odd tales from 'the front' that no one ever printed in regimental histories—illustrated the general discontent. The people now knew more of matters of life and death than the politicians did, and henceforth distrusted politicians. The Labour party itself suffered under this awareness, for 317 out of its 376 candidates were rejected by the electorate in the election of December 1918, an electorate which at last represented the old Radical principle of universal suffrage. On this unpalatable fact was founded the

[1] Masterman, *England after War*, p. 4.

Tory distinction between Labour and labour: the Labour party was obviously, in Churchill's celebrated words, 'not fit to govern', if the forces of labour themselves had so thoroughly rejected its leadership. On it, too, was founded the socialist animus against the habits of a *bourgeois* democracy, and against workers who had not seen, because they refused to look in the direction of, the dawn. Hence such diatribes as that of G. D. H. Cole in *The World of Labour* (1913):

> In this country at least it is useless to invoke public opinion because it is selfish, unenlightened, and vindictive. . . . The great British Public is marked by narrowness, egoism, and intellectual indolence.

In this mood it was not hard for a middle-class visionary to concede to Lenin and the Bolshevik paternalists a point, at least. Lenin was quoted in *The British Citizen* of March 9, 1918 as frankly admitting that, just as 150,000 lordly landowners under Tsarism had dominated 130 million Russian peasants, 'so 200,000 members of the Party are imposing their proletarian will on the mass, *but this time in the interests of the latter'*. It was a sentiment Robespierre would have applauded: it was he, after all, who had used the expression 'government of the people, by the people, and for the people' seventy years before it occurred to Lincoln on the field of Gettysburg.

The society that survived this war, like that which had weathered Napoleon's, had a clearer view of what it had lost than of what to do next. 'Back to normal' was a natural enough aim for Tories; but no one knew how to trace the road to normality across the wasteland the war had made. The normality of pre-war England lay anyway in the eye of the beholder, largely depending on his income; it was not of the kind that anyone who had not been in possession of 'some form of power over others' wanted to conserve. If the future was to be made to reflect the past, the majority had a poor lookout. Yet it was plain that leadership of a positive kind, towards some definable goal, was called for. In the bright glare that beat down upon the political scene it was often impossible to make out what Lloyd George was doing, but to begin with there was a hope that he would prove the man capable of winning the peace as well as the war. The hope grew fainter, however, as his Conservative-supported coalition government found itself, often to its own bewilderment, passively presiding over industrial troubles at home, but actively meddling in the affairs of Russia, licensing guerrilla warfare in Ireland, and laying the foundations of a new empire in the Middle East. Lloyd George now occupied a position whose existence he had divined well in advance. 'You often see,' he told a friend in 1912, 'that a man who has attained a position by the exercise of certain characteristics ceases to display them in his new circumstances, and then becomes a failure.'[1]

Pitt had remarked in 1800 that there might be occasions, but they would ever be few, when an appeal to the people was one just mode of proceeding on important subjects. One hundred and twenty years later, it might have been supposed that such occasions would have become more frequent and their significance more readily recognized; but this was not the standpoint of His Majesty's Government under Lloyd George's premiership, which after December 1918 conducted some very startling policies in the apparent assurance that no appeal to the people was necessary. (Their ultimate failure introduced the other extreme: between 1922 and 1925 there were five general elections.) The politicians who stood behind Lloyd George, such as Bonar Law and Austen Chamberlain, were men who had no popular following at all; while the figure of Stanley Baldwin, emerging from behind an arras, was something hardly recognized even by his own chiefs. These lesser men were regarded as interchangeable; they so regarded themselves, and continued to do so, being quite content in many a Cabinet 'reshuffle' to change places, so long as they were not excluded from the seat of power altogether.

They were men with the air more of the bureaucrat than of the statesman—and this, too, was fitting. The facts of war had acclimatized men to the idea of the State as an agent that ordered both their lives and their deaths. Joint recognition of this by both governors and governed bred general assent to the proposition that a man who would die for his country must, in the liberal tradition, be allowed to vote for it. Hence all the new

[1] Riddell, *More Pages*, p. 38.

nations that emerged on to the map of Europe after 1918 adopted the principle of universal male suffrage, thus putting 'democracy' on a new kind of trial. But the definition of democracy still varied from person to person. Mazzini, in the humanitarian tradition of European liberalism, had defined democracy as the progress of all, through all, under the leadership of the best and wisest. But this raised formidable questions, and betrayed an attitude alien to that of the working politician. What person, or what group of persons, possessed virtue and wisdom, and how could a hastily-enfranchised democracy be expected to know the answer to this in advance? Suppose the candidates who presented themselves for the honour of representation were themselves neither good nor wise? That the House of Commons between 1918 and 1922 had more than its share of fools and scoundrels was certainly a popular, if unproveable, assessment.

Any system that set out to provide security in a dangerous age was bound to attract its admirers. Bolshevik authoritarianism had its admirers from the outset. Oswald Mosley, elected as Conservative member for Harrow in 1918, emphasized the duties of 'socialistic imperialism', and appeared to many in his party and outside it as a coming man. Some of his ideas he had got from Milner, who had for long inveighed against 'the waste of human power through bad social and industrial arrangements' in England, drawing attention to the vast output of half-trained young people, with no definite skill in anything; declaring that it was the 'race' that had made the British Empire and must continue to govern it for its own good, and remarking (this in 1907) that England was far more socialistic than it had been fifty years back, due in the main to the social action of Conservative governments.[1] There were other young Conservatives who felt the problems of the time as a direct challenge to paternalist ingenuity: George Lloyd and Edward Wood published their *Great Opportunity* pamphlet in 1919. But these views lay to the left not only of their own party but of the Labour voter also, who was mainly concerned with getting higher wages for shorter hours. For eighteen months after the war ended he enjoyed both; but in 1921 there were $2\frac{1}{4}$ million workers unemployed (1913's figure had been $\frac{1}{4}$ million), in 1932 the

[1] See his *The Nation and the Empire* (1912).

figure rose to 2¾ million, and at no time did it drop below 1 million until the outbreak of the second world war of the century. The unemployment figures constituted the peace-time casualty lists. They might have been expected to galvanise the workers to a consciousness of their predicament, and to a resolution 'to do something' about it. Yet on the whole, as Cole irritably noted, instead of being encouraged by the growing difficulties of capitalism, the workers were frightened by them. Hungry men had no appetite for barricades. Capitalism was the only thing they had their bearings in. They did not wish to destroy the system, they only wished it to protect them effectively.

Labour solidarity certainly increased under the hammer of economic hardship, polling 6½ million votes—although returning only forty-five members—in the election of 1931, and over 8 million in that of 1935. The Labour programme which was to be carried out between 1945 and 1950 had been lying 'on the table' since 1918, its merits admitted, its idealism praised. But not enough people in the British democracy, in this post-war and pre-war era, were magnetized. In the main they were still disinclined to believe that any ordering of the political system was likely to obtain for them 'the good life'. They still identified the pursuit of happiness with the things that money could buy. The things that money could not buy, they were too cynical to suppose would be given them *gratis* by politicians.

A similar detachment manifested itself amid the democrats of the American republic, where nearly half the voters could not be bothered to vote in the presidential elections. In 1926 Walter Lippmann, in an article entitled 'Is Democracy a Failure?', remarked that the common man (that unknown soldier of the peace) lived in a world which he could not see, did not understand, and was unable to direct.[1] Clemenceau found the world *en pleine incohérence*. Others claimed they had perceived the gas escaping, at long last, from the democratic balloon that had been floating tantalisingly above the heads of men since 1789. The Irish provided, for many Englishmen, an excellent test-case: for the first thing the Irish did with their 'freedom' from Great Britain was to start a civil war. Thus the Fabian stalwarts, Sidney and Beatrice Webb, decided to drop the question-mark

[1] In *Harper's Magazine*, October 1926, p. 558.

from the second edition (1927) of their *Soviet Communism: a New Civilization?*, while H. G. Wells observed that in Russia and Italy one did not find haggard peasants wandering around in search of a polling-booth.[1] Shaw added that a country governed by its people was as impossible a notion as a theatre governed by its audience. The apathy of the 1920s became notorious, even among the apathetic: Cyril Connolly reported later that at Oxford a fashionable undergraduate would as soon have gone to Church as attended a political meeting.[2] The Socialist R. H. Tawney did his best to recognize this fact in one of his replies to the Royal Commission on the Coal Industry (January 24, 1926). 'The fact is,' he explained,

> that in all large communities the majority of men are not thinking about public questions. But, on the other hand, the majority of men trust the ballot and elect persons who *are* thinking about these things; and what you have to consider is the judgment of that minority who command the confidence of their fellows.

The implication of this was that if the judgment of the governing minority was at fault, the confidence of their fellows would very speedily evaporate. Possibly aware of shortcomings in their own powers—'a low-spirited lot', is Lord Eustace Percy's comment on his own generation of the ruling class[3]—the minority were never certain whether to lead the people or to follow the people in the direction they thought the people wanted to go.

In the great days of 1906, Liberal leaders flushed with victory had proclaimed that the will of the people, as expressed through their elected representatives, would be made to prevail. But in the post-war era an odd situation faced these representatives, for it did not appear that the people willed anything in particular. England, Charles Masterman wrote, was 'not interested in anything at all'.[4] No wonder socialists were mortified, who were forever trying to stimulate an interest in politics among 'the

[1] Wells, *Democracy under Revision* (1927), p. 91.
[2] Connolly, *Enemies of Promise* (1938), quoted in Neal Wood, *Communism and British Intellectuals*, p. 103.
[3] Lord Percy, *Some Memories*, p. 188.
[4] Masterman, *op. cit.*, p. 23.

masses', only to find that it could not be done at all in prosperous times, and done only spasmodically even in times of the severest hardship. There were sixty-one Labour members of parliament in 1918, 142 in 1922, and 193 in 1923. But what shades of opinion they represented only the individual member could tell. A study of Labour's public attitudes does not clarify the question. In June 1919 the party conference voted for 'the unreserved use of industrial power' to keep Winston Churchill, Secretary of State for War, from sabotaging the Russian Revolution. In July 1920 the Trades Unions Council confirmed this, and added a veto on interference with the Irish republicans for good measure. George Lansbury urged the weapon of the strike, Tom Mann advocated revolution, as did all the 'Red' Clydesiders, brandishing their journal *Forward*. (In the election of 1922 the Conservatives were able to hold only fifteen of the seventy-four Scottish constituencies.) A general strike threatened in April 1921, but the railway and transport workers broke the 'triple alliance' with the miners and scotched whatever hopes for social revolution the Communists may have nursed. It was J. H. Thomas, the railwaymen's leader, who made an appeal to the middle classes in his pamphlet *When Labour Rules* (1921). He asked only for 'a more reasonable share in the decencies and comforts—not luxuries, note—of life'. He asked in fact for fair play: a shrewd appeal at any time. And it was a genuinely representative view, reflecting the attitudes of those who knew nothing about Russia, took no interest in Ireland, agreed in secret with their wives about strikes, looked on the Scots as weird wild men from the north, and had no intention of going *Forward*.

What the mass of the people wanted, as Bentham had known, was economic security, and they looked to the government of the day to get it. After 1922 Lloyd George produced many ideas on national rehabilitation, most of them good, all of them worth considering: but they were not considered, since everyone knew that there was no likelihood, amid the ruins of the Liberal party, of his ever getting into power again to put his ideas to the test.

The Labour party saw itself as the natural successor to disintegrated Liberalism. Young intellectuals like Stafford Cripps and Hugh Dalton—'nonconformist English gentlemen', was J. M. Keynes' description—joined it, in order to rule paternally over the next major revolution, the next 1906 when it came. But there were not enough of these. Not enough to reassure the middle classes, who had to get what reassurance they could from the presence of elder Liberals and detached peers in the first Labour government of 1924. Not enough, to convince the Labour rank and file that these invaders, scouts from the ranks of Tuscany, were potential leaders, worthy of trust. They brought ideas with them, a suspicious currency at best. The party preferred the ideas it had got used to, and Fabian gradualism was still the mode, and still presided over by an ageing Sidney Webb, translated as Lord Passfield. Hyndman in his old age was still on the left of the Independent Labour party, but he outdistanced Churchill himself in denouncing the Bolsheviks. The Independent Labour party itself showed the soothing Fabian influence when in 1921 it decided not to affiliate with the Third International. These were signs of staleness. There was a lack of fire somewhere: and the route was already open that was one day to take Glasgow's Jimmy Maxton, the Robespierre from Bridgeton, to his role as 'the most beloved member' of the House of Commons, and Davie Kirkwood from Clydebank to a seat among his peers as Lord Kirkwood of Bearsden.[1] This path was one that led sideways and upwards, rather than *Forward*. In 1930 G. D. H. Cole published *The Next Ten Years in British Social and Economic Policy*. In its preface he remarked that twenty years back, in 1910, socialism was still in the main an exercise in fantasy. He might have added that in 1930 it was that still. A year later, in the aftermath of Labour's electoral catastrophe, the fantasy took on the quality of nightmare. In the Commons a 'National' government, with Ramsay MacDonald as its honorary colonel and Stanley Baldwin as its active commander, was able to count 536 supporters, of whom 472 were Conservatives.

But this phalanx found that leadership, to which Toryism had always been accustomed, was lacking. A blight had fallen on the Conservative party. Educated young men who had, greatly to their own surprise, survived the war, showed no keenness to

[1] Glaswegians who know the difference between grimly-tenemented Clydebank and douce suburban Bearsden will best appreciate the irony of this translation.

start waging the political battle at Westminster. They disappeared into the City, into the shires, into the Drones' Club, into the highlands of Kenya and the tobacco-farms of Southern Rhodesia. Those with a taste for administration took themselves overseas into Crown Colonies still largely unaware of the elective principle, where the habit of authority was still taken for granted, and where 'politics' was another word for subversion. The Indian scene was clouding, but Gandhi and *swaraj* [Home Rule] was more a problem for the viceroy than for the average district officer, dispensing high, middle and low justice beneath the peepul tree, among villagers who were yet to hear the name of the Congress party. The scene in the Sudan, always the most innocent of all the imperial properties, was not clouded at all. Life in Malaya moved at the pace of a golden afternoon. What Great Britain lost in talent and ideas to its own empire cannot be computed, but that there was a loss is sure. The absence from the home front of these the living, together with the absence of the dead, necessarily left authority in the hands of elders who regretted the world that had gone. Many lacked the confidence to exercise it; and the best of them, like Baldwin himself, knew that they lived in a society to which they had not been given a passport. They were therefore left to soldier on, under the general accusation that they were deliberately clinging to power, jealous of potential successors, and through a mixture of envy and malice, 'taking it out on' the young. But, if Captain Anthony Eden rose high and fast in the Conservative hierarchy, that was because his elders could not find many of his kind to promote: and none that were better.

This negation at the top caused a new generation, too young both for the war and for the society of their elder brothers and sisters, the Bright Young Things, to turn to political questions, although not to the political parties. Many of them turned their heads in the direction of, and some of them took the step that brought them to join, the Communist party.

In 1920 this organization in Great Britain had 2,500 members. This number had risen to 15,500 by 1938, and was to reach its peak of 55,000 by the middle of the Second World War. It was therefore not a significant political group in itself, but its voice was always to be heard in the new, professional 'Left

Wing' clamours that arose to combat the conditions of the iron 1930s. Cyril Connolly's apathetic Oxford was replaced by an Oxford that had a Communist party 400 strong. This Left Wing directed the intellectual strategy of political protest, and it was staffed by committed poets and writers, angry men who (unlike a subsequent generation) did not trade on their extreme youth. They were a new generation of Tractarians—or, to use Raymond Postgate's phrase, of Encyclopaedists; their principal organ, the Left Book Club started in 1936, had by 1939 distributed over a million and a half tracts for the times.[1] Poets equated Communism with liberty, socialists who found themselves trapped in a Labour party too pragmatic and *bourgeois* for their taste shouldered their way out of it. The 'Popular Front' in the government of the French Republic became a Left ideal: the struggle in Spain between one group of fascists and another became a symbol of the proletarian struggle towards the dawn, thus constituting—the pun is Anthony Eden's—a 'War of the Spanish Obsession!' The insurgent Spanish Republicans, the friends of Soviet Russia, were simple heroes to the British Left, and simple Reds to the Tories. Toryism, now as ever, was well represented on both sides of the House of Commons, since the trade union wing of the Labour party, strengthened by the secession of the Independent Labour party in 1932, constituted 'a sub-governing class'. On September 9, 1936 the National Council of Labour—comprising the Labour party, the parliamentary Labour party and the Trades Union Council—voted to support the government's policy not to intervene on either side in the Spanish struggle. Those who wanted to go crusading were not to expect to be equipped from any central armoury.

The crusading Left, in publicizing its international conscience, gave its utterance moral force. Left-wingers were often told that their ranks, like those of the Mexican Army, were composed principally of officers—but this in itself, in a community habituated to the authority of a governing class, was not a drawback, and may well have added to their influence. They drew strength, as other 'Friends of the People' had done before them, from their family connexions, and more than a touch of aristocracy in their movement made professional radicalism what Charles Fox had

[1] Neal Wood, *Communism and British Intellectuals* (1959), p. 61.

also made it, *à la mode*. They despised the *bourgeoisie* (a phrase they used constantly) with a hauteur Wellington himself might have admired. But they carried no concealed weapons. Their plans for these *bourgeois*, so benighted in their impasse, so blandly unaware of the coming struggle for power, so entirely devoid of soul, were much less vicious than Sorel's or Stalin's. For it was clear even to a harsh critic that Marx's picture of the *bourgeoisie* as a crafty, hard-headed class, constantly calculating with dividers its exact political position, issuing secret orders to its unseen forces to be ready to combat the proletariat, in fact flattered the British middle classes—many of whom at this time were delighted to see themselves represented by the truly appalling figure of Strubé's 'Little Man' in the *Daily Express*. The aim of the intellectuals was therefore still *épater le bourgeois*, to make him blink and stir. But they would not use the tactics of Guy Fawkes.

Stephen Spender, the poet son of a well-known Liberal publicist, did not, like Hobson before him, discover any crisis in Liberalism. The crisis was over: Liberalism had died.[1] Liberal democracy had always been 'a dishonest pair of scales heavily weighted in favour of industry'; now, in an era of acute economic depression, more and more people were grimly assimilating the obvious. The confidence-trick of the past was now exposed. The law did not help the people, political rights did not serve them,[2] in a world where economic opportunity and its accompanying social status were 'open to all, like the Ritz hotel'. The laws, originally designed to protect a landed gentry, now expressed the will of another Ascendancy, the capitalist class. Henry James was right: only money bought the key that unlocked the magic of living. But *A Room of One's Own*, in which alone, as Virginia Woolf pointed out (1929), a life could be lived at all, cost £300 a year. How many had a spare £300 a year? It is not odd that the democracy, encouraged by its thinkers to realize the ineffectiveness of its political power, was inclined to go looking for a ruler who would promise them the moon; no wonder, too, that dictatorship had a prestige; no wonder, either, that shrewd

---

[1] See his *Forward from Liberalism* (1937).
[2] E.g. in Gwyn Thomas' stories about South Wales in the depression, the characters are collectively referred to as 'the voters'.

capitalists in many countries felt that they could use a dictator to mask their own activities, which might go on uninterrupted behind a screen of bread and circuses, pageantry, imperialism, and anti-Semitism—'the socialism of fools'. In the irrationality of fascism lay its appeal: the true enemies of Hitler and Mussolini were not the leaders of the liberal democracies, but such men as Einstein and Jung. Fascism made a fetish of efficiency—and efficiency, to all those who were suffering under ineffectuals, seemed indeed a prize worth having.

The pall-bearers of capitalism were often out of step with one another, but they were all certain they were on the right road towards its grave. John Strachey's *Coming Struggle for Power* (1932) mapped the route remorselessly, and gave other social critics who had not found the Marxist path short shrift. Freud, for example, was after all only one of the last great theorists of the European capitalist class, content to analyse its behaviour without trying to change the conditions that would continue to give rise to that behaviour. H. G. Wells, who had caught a glimpse of the true dawn in his youth, had now retreated into a kind of reactionary prophecy, calling (at a Liberal Summer School at Oxford in 1932) for the recruitment of 'Liberal Fascists'. What was Marcel Proust's vast anatomy of society but an odyssey of snobbery? Whom did Lloyd George now represent but a set of big-business Philistines? Sir Clifford Chatterley, impotent and crippled since the war, was indeed a fitting symbol of the governing classes—no wonder his wife, representing the life-principle in the community, looked to the virile worker for rescue. T. S. Eliot had mapped the waste land, but had provided no route for a pilgrim to take across it, as once Bunyan had done. The dwellers in this waste land had been described by Evelyn Waugh in his *Decline and Fall* and *Vile Bodies*—after which, Strachey felt, Waugh had only three courses open to him: to commit suicide, become a Communist, or immure himself within the Catholic Church.

Those who tried to provide a map were as suspect as those who did not. All kinds of schemes were produced for shoring up the system, when what was really needed was a wrecking-crew. Some called for empire free trade, some wanted to 'do business with' dictators, others wanted nothing beyond a bit of peace and

quiet. Younger Tories sought efficiency: such men as R. A. Butler, Robert Boothby, Alan Lennox-Boyd found much to admire
in Mussolini and in Franco. Captain Harold Macmillan, who in
1932 published a memorandum on *The State and Industry*, next
submitted a *Middle Way* (1938)—but the very idea that there
was a middle way was anathema to the Left. Yet even these
Tory ruminants, tampering and tinkering, seemed less despicable
than the present crop of social democrats who abounded everywhere in Europe. 'The workers' were in office, but not in power.
True socialism had accordingly been relegated to the hereafter.
It would be got in heaven, with other rewards for virtue. The
British Labour party itself was hampered by this kind of double
vision. Its socialist phraseology was strongly counterbalanced
by the sturdy, the rigid conservatism of its actions. According
to Strachey, in 1929 when Labour had very nearly obtained a
clear majority, Ramsay MacDonald, that 'very valuable servant
of British capitalism', had been very gravely worried, for had it
done so he would have lost his alibi: that since Labour held
office but not power it could not put through the proper
socialist programme. Everyone was now busily 'erecting the
umbrella of the social services', but umbrellas only deflected,
they could not stop, the deluge that was coming. Social democrats were in their own way paving the way to Fascism as much
as were the Tory planners, and the mass of the workers seemed
ready to follow them along that road. Strachey noted how the
very idea of the community, 'the national interest', was exploited.
The long-continued expansion and the incomparable stability of
British capitalism ever since 1850 had undoubtedly established
traditions of class collaboration, which were only gradually being
broken down by the repeated shocks of the present governing
class offensive against the workers. Conditions such as these
allowed those trusted allies of the capitalists, the members
of the Labour party, to convince themselves that Communist
methods were useless for the purpose of appealing to British
workers.

Clearly Strachey was right: so they were. There were many
who counted themselves as 'Left Wing' who were glad he was
right—among them J. B. Priestley, then as later an accurate
emotional barometer of the time. He was sure however that

Strachey was not right about anything else. It was not true that
a struggle for power was on its way: it was also dangerous to
propagate such an idea. But he was prepared to agree that the
Labour party of the 1930s was not fulfilling its function, or any
function at all. It did not appear to want to: 'an unscrupulous
determination to achieve power at any cost is not a fault with
which the official Labour party could be charged.'[1] Its trade
union basis was to blame, for trade unionists were by definition
men who did not take the initiative. They supervised the initiative of others: they were the self-appointed minders of the
capitalist machine, which for all they cared could go on running
for ever, so long as the hours and wages were all right. Priestley
represented, as he freely admitted, that *bourgeois* social democrat,
intent on social reform, who was the stock target of the extreme
Left. But it was plain commonsense to insist on social reform,
what else was needed? One wanted to clear away the derelict
area of Rusty Lane, West Bromwich: the amenities would not
be improved if the spilled blood of the *bourgeoisie* went coursing
through it. But apathy was the likelier enemy. Perhaps the
British people in fact deserved the government they had got,
perhaps they were satisfied with being mere inheritors, 'like
useless young men waiting for rich uncles to die', invalids themselves, without energy or volition, content to breathe a stale
atmosphere, intent on triviality, worthy of Hitler's sneers at the
decadence of the pluto-democracies? For it was certainly true
that the country was not a democracy. It was true too that a
plutocracy masqueraded as an aristocracy, whose children had
hardly heard of the dark towns from which the money came. All
real government was done, all matters of political, social,
economic, and judicial importance were controlled by, the
'Right People', still staffing the institutions Hobson had listed:
men with the 'right background', which normally included a
private income and the outlook that went with it. Priestley
would have reckoned that Hobson had little enough to complain
of, for in his view 'the England of 1914 was superior, in every
important department of national life, to the England of today'.

Since, in this reading, it was these Right People, Tories born
or made, who both did all things and permitted some things,

[1] J. B. Priestley, *Rain Upon Godshill* (1939), chapter xiii, for these views.

there was a case for saying that the Labour party itself existed on Tory sufferance. There was room in the English political system for a Labour party: the Liberal party had shredded itself away, and it was necessary, after all, to have an opposition, an alternative government. It was Stanley Baldwin, the Midland ironmaster who succeeded the Glasgow iron merchant as the Conservative leader in 1923, who instructed his following in these tactics. The presence of Labour in politics must be accepted: it was commonsense to do so, since they held 287 seats between 1929 and 1931. In 1925 Baldwin had declared that he was anxious to form a government of which Harrow should not be ashamed: but his sympathies were always wider than such remarks gave warrant for. In educating his own party he wanted also to educate Labour, so that, if ever it achieved power, it would not behave in the corrupt and frenetic fashion of Lloyd George's coalition between 1918 and 1922—an example of *arrivisme* that had left a deep mark on Baldwin's mind. He was thus able at a time of acute economic depression to attract the trust and confidence of a large part of the electorate, including many who voted Labour. But this was not a gift he could bequeath to his lieutenant and successor, Neville Chamberlain. The latter was sincerely active in the fields of housing and local government, and accomplished much; but his Labour opponents were never able to rid themselves of the conviction that he despised them, even while admitting their right to be there. It was a comparable prejudice that prevented Chamberlain in the dangerous summer of 1939 from hastening the negotiations with the Russians for an anti-Hitler pact—for he had never been able to convince himself that the Soviet system had any right to be there, either.

Chamberlain thus well represented the brand of Toryism which allowed that there must be an alternative government, but could never face the thought of an alternative system of government. Tories who were able to accept some aspect of trade union obstinacy about hours and wages with a shrug of what-else-can-you-expect made no similar allowance for the intellectual arguments of Socialists, whom they colloquially damned as parlour pinks. Elementary school teachers were notoriously left-wing, but this did not alarm, since these schools were looked on in the first place as finishing schools for manual workers. The pupils on becoming adults would vote Labour, but would also remain impervious to Socialist propaganda. But the minds of middle-class children needed to be protected against this, and governing bodies tried to ensure that no teacher with a Socialist tinge ever invaded a secondary-school classroom. The same political tabu affected polite letters. A place might be found for *Lady Chatterley's Lover* under the sofa-cushions in a respectable home, since sex was not thought of as a sociological issue; but *The Coming Struggle for Power*, which plainly had an even more marked tendency to corrupt and deprave the young, was not allowed in a Tory household at all. The books of Victor Gollancz's imprint in particular needed careful scrutiny, in case the library subscriber, seeing but not reading the distinctive type-face on the yellow jacket, brought home not the latest Dorothy L. Sayers or A. J. Cronin but something entirely different. A servant could be allowed her *Peg's Paper*, *True Romances*, or regular visits to the local cinema—the 'picture palace' was, significantly, the last place social comment was to enter—but not a subscription to *The New Statesman and Nation*. That no girl was likely to spend a small wage in this fashion was beside the point—because, for every educated and subversive agent, were there not likely to be ten dupes? In A. G. Macdonell's *England, Their England* (1933), the aristocratic heroine's chief nightmare is that one day the family's model butler will turn round and tell her to go to hell. Then again, there was such a thing as 'Moscow gold'. Marx's verdict that the English proletariat would have to have a revolution made for them by outsiders, since they were so obviously incapable of making it for themselves, had not been forgotten. Amid all these menaces, foreign and domestic, bulwarks against Bolshevism had to be found: and it was the opinion of the Liberal H. A. L. Fisher, in his influential *History of Europe* (1936) that Hitler's National Socialist dictatorship was one of them.

The atmosphere in which such thoughts could be expressed, such fears confessed to, ultimately exhausted the generation that had to breathe it. As a result it produced little clear thinking either on domestic or on international affairs. What was not done remains more significant than what was. The 1930s constitute a period of omissions, the number and nature of which no historian will ever fully identify, for no record will help him. Men will confess to a conventionally mis-spent youth, but they will not reveal the extent either of their errors or their apathy. For there were many who, in that iron decade, chose to concentrate on immediate ends. Among the young were those who did not heed the praises either of the Communist system or of the Fascist, because they had not the inclination to find the time. Many an educated man who was quite capable of assessing the arguments of Strachey, Spender, Auden, and of *Mein Kampf* as well, was also quite capable of deciding that a job on the *News of the World* was preferable to hawking unwanted brushes from door to shabby door, or that marketing his looks and presence on the stage was better than tutoring someone's stupid son. Those whom economic hardship forced to live among the proletariat lost patience with the fortunate who preferred to make their discovery of the masses safely between the covers of a 'Left Book'. For every George Orwell who went to see for himself on the road to Wigan Pier there must have been ten, if not more, of these others: and how the Spanish peasant regarded the foreign intellectual who came to assist his 'cause' (however he assessed that) no Spanish peasant has left record. In the Earl's Court world delineated in Patrick Hamilton's dispiriting novels, set in a zone lying somewhere between the frontiers of middle-class society and the sea-coasts of Bohemia, no political consciousness, no awareness of anything beyond the self, enters at all. In this no-man's-land everything is felt, nothing thought: and since nothing is thought, not much is felt. At the other end of the social system could be found something equally instinctive, the equally a-political and anti-social world of aristocratic or 'Swinbrook man'—the world of the fifth Earl of Redesdale, at least as he and it have been displayed for public appraisal by his daughters, the Misses Mitford.[1]

This inertia in the community diminished any sense of purpose that remained on the Right, and helped reduce the anger on the Left to a railing petulance. The Nazi-Soviet pact of August 1939, devoid of all principle, indeed provided a fitting tombstone to

[1] E.g. Nancy Mitford, *The Pursuit of Love* (1945): Jessica Mitford, *Hons and Rebels* (1961).

the era it interred. Only the professionally committed Left, who had taught themselves to believe that a declared ideology meant what it said, were cruelly dismayed and shocked at its occurrence: they had on consequence henceforth to endure a galling reputation for gullibility. The majority had never made much distinction between foreign dictatorships, and, since it was not inclined to put much stock in what politicians said, was not taken aback either by a Nazi or a Soviet *volte-face*. (This attitude had its serviceable aspect. When France 'fell' in 1940 a common reaction among the British was the recollection that they had never trusted the French all that much in the first place.) In September 1939 war was visited upon the people rather than declared by them.

It took a major military disaster to stir the British into life. Dunkirk was an 'appalling defeat'—but, unlike the Somme and Passchendaele, it had a quality of exhilaration, overtones of hope. One whose nature expressed both these things thus came into what was not his own. In the summer of 1940 the leadership of the National Government, and thus of the Conservative party, was usurped by Winston Churchill, who without benefit of election stood forth from the ranks of the gentlemen of England, as leader of the people. It was not a secure position. He found himself at the head of a party whose parliamentary representatives, elected in 1935, had generally disliked and distrusted him—less for his defects than for his qualities. War put him into office, and kept the Conservative party in power, thus prolonging the rule of the dynasty established in 1911 by Bonar Law. But in July 1945, when victory in Europe had been attained, Bonar Law's dynasty fell at last—and took the usurper with it.

CHAPTER VII

AGENTS AND PATIENTS

Long accustomed to leadership, it was in a state of resentment that the British people had endured its absence since 1919. Peace had been mishandled, and prosperity never came. Too many existed rather than lived in a Britain whose rulers gave them neither a 'New Deal' nor any hope that it would ever arrive. In many who lived above the level of the dole and despair, this resentment had bred a mocking spirit, whose ridicule wounded the confidence of the Ascendancy more deeply than an active, even subversive, radicalism would have done. As a direct consequence of the futilities of 1914–18, the Army suffered its onslaught first, and no Army officer existed who was presumed to be other than a blimp or a dug-out. Simultaneously the prestige of the gentry, the class from which officers were traditionally supposed to spring, declined, and less was heard of the values of the gentleman's code than of the mutual admiration society conducted by those who wore the same 'old school tie'. The politicians, exposed to more open criticism than either the Services or the inhabitants of clubland, winced under a like attack, and accordingly Baldwin's ability to convince a majority that it could, in fact, trust him was to them an asset the more highly prized since it was so rare. But Baldwin's lease on the popular affection ran out, and his party produced no similar figure. Nor did it produce a policy whose success would have brought it adherents, if not admirers. Authority was left unaccompanied by any efficient paternalism, and the Conservatives, under fire for this omission, could not recover their habit of aplomb, or successfully refute the indictment of 'Guilty Men' that was soon to be brought against them by Left-wing publicists.

The second war against the Germans therefore provided many Conservatives with a release from a political treadmill, a grant of a 'second chance'. They felt that, since war cannot be waged without authority and discipline, their talent in exercising both, their ability to control and accomplish a task with a traditional appeal, could be given full scope. All charges of self-seeking could easily be countered in the presence of the foreign foe: and guilt, if there was any, would be expunged by patriotic action. They were right about this only in a very short run—in fact, for no longer than 'the duration'. The British people took an official euphemism closely to heart, and looked on the war as an 'Emergency'. In times of emergency, things are given which men will not normally give. Among these things were now numbered a trusting allegiance to official, and unofficial, Toryism; to the idea of an Ascendancy, and to the habit of its acceptance. The impact of war rallied and marshalled the ranks of the people under an inspiring leader; but, as it turned out, they had no intention of following him beyond the bounds of the battlefield. He kept too dubious a company.

Yet although the Conservative party was not to profit from it, the war served at least one essential purpose. It rekindled the national sense of community, a sense that had been dissipated amid the stumblings of the inter-war years. Those in authority indeed had some excuse for misreading the signposts to the future, since the enthusiasms of the present were so encouraging. In wartime the paternalism of the governing group was necessary, was seen to be necessary, and so was popular. The responsibilities of the government were great, and were seen to be great. The difficulties of administering the affairs of a nation under fire could only be guessed at by the people at large, but they made no bad guess and accorded their sympathy also. In these times of emergency, the men in authority were not thought of as a junta of conspirators, whose major purpose was to stay in power, anti-democrats instinctively seeking to gull the people. They were seen, instead, as men with a vital task. They were in charge of the national security—both the condition and the aim. Security had long been prized by the people, since it was not, in its essence, political: that party politics, Left or Right, would certainly not have survived a German victory was clear even to the citizen who had never troubled to vote for either. All that was required of the authoritarians was efficiency—and some enjoyment in the exercise of their authority, since enjoyment was a sign of confidence that the task was not impossible. For this reason, in the period of 'phoney war' between September 1939 and May 1940, it was Churchill alone as First Lord of the Admiralty who commanded an enthusiastic popularity since it was he who, in a grey and dispirited Cabinet, plainly warmed to his work, and was able to communicate a sense of gusto in the challenge of great events. Churchill was a romantic: war to him was 'strife', 'battle', 'struggle', all terms with an evocative and exhilarating content. This attitude was a tonic to people whose hearts had not been lifted this long time. In the first years of the war, therefore, official exhortations to the people to 'Go to It' (this one devised by the Home Secretary, Labour's Herbert Morrison) were not countered, as they would certainly have been in peacetime, with raucous queries as to the destination intended, or for whose benefit the journey was to be made.

The unknown, long distrusted Army was suddenly replenished, as in Kitchener's day, with men without ambition to be soldiers, but with much ambition to serve—with the result that, unlike its predecessor of 1914–18 which wore itself out, it became a symbol of the national community itself, ultimately obtaining leaders (all of them of junior rank or no rank at all at the outbreak of war) of a high competence. The Navy, always a symbol of the popular zeal for security, increased its prestige. The merchant navy worked its courageous passage to a similar status. The Royal Air Force's Fighter Command both epitomized, in a fine hour of 1940, the courage of the individual, and finally shed the Cinderella status that had dogged the Force since its beginnings in 1917. The realization that 'the services' were not enclaves of stupidity controlled by Tory brasshats, but were public instruments actually capable of serving the public, and able to illustrate the resolution of a nation in arms, spread throughout the community. Trade union leaders learned to allow that there were matters of more moment than the computation of hours and wages, and the peaceable introduction of industrial conscription bore witness to their larger vision. The Home Guard tapped the martial qualities in those no longer young.

The self-importance that had long been attached to social status was now converted to the self-respect that naturally attached itself to social function. Even the irretrievably comfortable drew extra comfort from the reflection that at least they were the countrymen of a host of indomitable East End charwomen whom no bombs could dismay. The barriers of reserve between classes, pondered on by Tocqueville, were, if not removed, at least sufficiently parted to allow new channels of communication to flow: if the presence of an American soldier was often still needed before the involuntary companions of a railway-carriage could be got to talk to one another, still they very often continued to talk after he had left.

After June 1940 the British people 'passionately attached themselves to the war'.[1] The conditions of the battle itself made it inevitable they should do so: as Peter Fleming underlines in *Invasion 1940*, had the Germans chosen to ignore the continuing British defiance after their Army was dispersed and scattered at Dunkirk, a sense of stalemate might well have drained away both the passion and the commitment. But this did not happen. Behind a stockade, outside of which an active enemy continued to prowl, and over which he continued to hurl explosive missiles, the British cohered their persons and their purposes. And although, as more than one American observer noted, the war was never talked about except as a joke, for once it appeared that the notoriously frivolous approach of the British to great affairs had its point. It engendered a sense of security.

Accordingly, that 'living sense of the State' which Wells had singled out as an integral part of the national outlook, became more profound.[2] The isolation of 1940–1, which to outsiders looked like the beginning of an inevitable end, was fashioned into a positive asset. At that time the British Empire—the name Commonwealth, never popular in Tory circles but long publicized by South Africans and Irishmen, seemed in these circumstances to lose what symbolic meaning it had—reached the zenith of its moral influence in the world; and Churchill, with his sense of drama, loved always to refer to 'our island'. as if geography itself was leagued with these few battalions that con-

[1] W. K. Hancock and M. M. Gowing, *British War Economy* (1949), p. 209.
[2] H. G. Wells, *The Future in America* (1906), p. 233.

tinued to fight for the right. Critical voices died from the air. Since it was not possible to trek beyond the confines of the stockade, the best had to be made of conditions within it. 'Committed' poets and publicists of the pre-war era found they could also commit themselves to the Royal Air Force or to fire-fighting. But, if idealism suffered in patriotic silence, and roughened its hands on material tasks, materialism too took heavy blows. For materialist aims also had, in the midst of this storm, no immediate chance of fulfilment; and thus fewer and fewer people confessed to having any, and made a positive virtue of austerity, until matters reached such a point that the visible presence of an unreconstructed materialist, such as a 'black marketeer' or even a determined inhabitant of a 'safe hotel', became an issue of public scandal and concern.

The waging of modern war

> presupposes and imposes a great increase in social discipline; moreover, this discipline is tolerable if—and only if—social inequalities are not intolerable.[1]

The social inequalities of pre-war Britain were still there; but life in the stockade masked them. An orderly people with a revivified sense of community thus accepted without demur the necessity for the queue and the ration-book, for a shortage of consumer goods and for a commonsense system of 'reserved occupations'. (The white feather, as an emblem of social dis-respect, did not reappear in society.) The concept of 'fair shares' was no longer the monopoly of earnest socialists, it had now become the stock-in-trade of popular opinion. The main prin-ciple of the non-socialist had ever been 'every man for himself'—but it was clear this could take nobody far in wartime. Conditions of struggle and interdependence made better Levellers of more men than ever John Lilburne could, and ideas like his concerning the existence of a 'public weal', with the corresponding need to plan for its continuance, took root in Tory minds which considered the apparent burial of party politics as a silver lining to the war cloud. 'Defence of the Realm' Acts could, as experi-ence proved, be made to cover many things otherwise difficult

[1] R. Titmuss, *Essays on the Welfare State* (1958), p.15.

to legislate for, and from which more general application might later be made: the first free 'health service' in Great Britain dates from 1917, when prophylactic treatment was granted to soldiers who had contracted venereal diseases.

But a government that assumed that, since so little criticism was voiced, none existed, was badly mistaken. Men in wartime do not think much about the present. The present is dangerous, and it may at any time be brought to a stop. It is therefore dangerous to think about it. This leaves the more time to think about the future. This they will be lucky if they live to see—but, if this luck is coming their way, they ought surely to take care to invest it wisely. What are we fighting for? or even, Why are we putting up with all this discomfort? are questions not encouraged by politicians. That the propagation of 'war aims' was a dangerous practice, the record could show: a programme of declared policy depended for its accomplishment too much on circumstance, on the unpredictable notions of one's allies, and on economic conditions not yet shaped. The whole matter demanded a concentration of thought which war-leaders had not time to give to it, and whose implications might well take them down a route they had no wish to explore. The various interpretations of the Atlantic Charter of March 1941 greatly embarrassed the British Government, whose members did not care to assume, as American statesmen assumed, that the clauses in it concerning political freedom for all might be applicable to the inhabitants of British colonies. But individual Englishmen who did not have to cope with these nice questions of international policy continued to scan the future and to demand much concerning it. A man who sees his life dislocated, his family disrupted, likes to be sure there is some point to these misfortunes, and wants to know what that point may be. The least reflective dislikes to be killed for nothing ascertainable. He is not satisfied to be told, as Neville Chamberlain told him, that he is fighitng against evil things. Evil has sometimes an enviable identity: in the personality of Hitler's Nazis there was certainly a positive quality. Could the same be said of the officially 'democratic' forces opposing them? *That* combatant is plainly evil—but does anything make *this* combatant as plainly good? If Hitler's proclaimed 'New Order' is a tyrannous sham, what other kind of 'New Order' should be substituted that will never prove so? These anxieties could not be allayed by the issue of brisk slogans by the authorities, slogans which indicated to a questioner that his leaders, although stoutly patriotic, were not thoroughly aware of the nature of the struggle to which they were committed, and to which, as a matter of administrative course, they committed others. 'Take One With You'—a grim Home Office poster prepared for circulation during the invasion-season of 1940—was exceptional, having to it a commonsense, positive quality that 'Britain Can Take It' patently lacked. Had Britain perhaps been good at 'taking it' rather too long for Britain's own good?

Moreover, memories of a promise made in the 1918 election to build a land fit for heroes to live in had died very hard (as the Labour party was going to underline in 1950 when it exhorted the voter, 'Ask Your Dad'). Heroes were again going to be produced in this present war—and where were they going to live? In what conditions? Under whose control? With what purpose in view? Here were unanswerable questions, which nevertheless fashioned a formidable agenda of public business for a government to cope with in the future, of whatever party it might be composed. *The Times* itself, in a leading article published on July 1, 1940—at an hour of the day when the future of Great Britain seemed highly problematical, to all observers, friendly, neutral, and hostile—called for a future wherein 'social justice', that old goal long seen in the distance through a radical haze, would at last be attained.

Political leaders, engrossed in each day's formidably difficult task of waging the war itself, no one part of which went according to anyone's plan, did not think such thoughts or think it likely that those they led were thinking them. As governors of the country their own duty was to think about the present, the very subject their subordinates instinctively avoided. They had to think about the present all the time, since a moment's inattention might dissolve the present, and with it the future of the country, entirely. So preoccupied, they grew isolated from public opinion. They met the people only in order to give them words of encouragement, and were themselves encouraged by the people's praise in return. The occasions were transient, and so were the sentiments expressed. The leaders were therefore not equipped to cast the horoscope of the coming age. 'Blood, tears, toil, and sweat' were plainly means, not ends, however heart-catching the rhetoric; and 'victory', the only end officially aimed at, was equally plainly a meaningless symbol if it symbolized nothing except the enemy's defeat, as the events of 1919 stood clear on the record to show. These things might be plain, but were not the common political currency. The system as it was, not as it might be, was what the Tories of the coalition government were striving to preserve. The publicized 'war effort' was an effort in the here and now, an exercise in present ingenuity and fortitude, and too much advice concerning it was as likely to hinder as to help. 'Committees,' Churchill wrote soon after becoming Prime Minister and Minister of Defence, 'are an encumbrance from which I am sedulously endeavouring to free our system.'[1] At times, too, parliament itself seemed to him an obstacle to the efficient prosecution of the nation's business, which was war.

Taking charge in the summer of 1940, Churchill never lost the outlook the events of that climactic time bred into him. In his mind the state of siege was never lifted, and he could not concern himself with the petty issues of a safe domestic future. What post-war plans he did devise had a Palmerstonian colour to them: they concerned British interests, the safeguarding of Britain's imperial and international position. He was aware of the shadows that hung around the future of Europe, and could assess the nature of the balance-of-power problems that would inevitably arise when Germany, the fulcrum of any European balance, was destroyed—as it had to be. But here, as in related issues, he was hampered and finally checkmated at Yalta by his friend Franklin Roosevelt, who throughout the war looked unfavourably on anything in the nature of a post-war plan. A care for the balance of power was historically Tory, part of that 'great heritage' of the English tradition to which Churchill so often paid tribute in his speeches; and he was never able to understand the view of this heritage which was held by those who had not been remembered in the will that the possessing classes of the past had entailed on their own posterity. The

---

[1] Hancock and Gowing, *op. cit.*, p. 218.

American judgment on this, although less emotional than that of the British Labour party, was no great distance from it. Churchill's deputy in the coalition government, Labour's Clement Attlee, was later to condemn this same heritage, in an unexpected flash of Tom Paine, as 'the mess of centuries'. To Tories this was a scandalous remark. To Churchill and his kind war against fascism involved not the death of the traditional world, with all its virtues—but their rejuvenation, and indeed their justification.

But beyond the confines of the Ministry of Defence and Admiralty House, Radicalism was once more germinating. Attlee and other Labour ministers would on occasion allow their Socialism expression at, say, meetings of excited West African students in London, where what they said was reported by their party's *Daily Herald* and by a school of colonial newspapers, but not by anyone else. Junior ministers among the Conservatives such as R. A. Butler, even senior men out of the public eye such as the Colonial Office's Oliver Stanley, devoted themselves to matters of planning and welfare, which inevitably cast a long shadow: 1944's passage of the Education Act and of a consolidatory Colonial Development and Welfare Act are two of the most remarkable achievements of the war period. In 1942 Sir William Beveridge published his 'Report' recommending a comprehensive scheme for social insurance, based on the conception that it was the state's duty, in collaboration with the individual, to provide income-maintenance for all those families whose normal incomes had been interrupted, or were likely to be interrupted, by events outwith their own control. This map for the future was disseminated throughout the ranks of the Army— at that time a body that had no fighting to do nor much prospect of any—by the Army's own Bureau of Current Affairs, an organization which as a result came to be looked on with suspicion by orthodox Tory officers. But although new ideas were spreading, no popular newspaper reflected them, and throughout the war the principal oracle of public communication, the British Broadcasting Corporation, expressed nothing about anything but the official 'line'—displaying also, as J. B. Priestley and other analysts found out, the irritability natural to an oracle when its views were called in question. The newspapers, reduced to four pages, reported what they were allowed to print by the authorities, and dispensed good cheer sometimes to a point of fatuity when there was little cause for it. (Nevertheless it was the Press which converted Dunkirk from a total military disaster to a triumph of national skill and endurance; and, in retrospect, this was certainly a remarkable public service.) But men in the armed services who had themselves been present at Dunkirk—or, later, at Crete or Dieppe or Tobruk, or over Hamburg and Berlin—learned to discount what passed for factual reporting, and the general cynicism as to the integrity and the adequacy of the Press which had been a feature of the inter-war years continued to grow, until in 1945 the electorate was able to prove to itself how right its estimate had been of this, since it voted in a manner not one social commentator of standing had predicted.

This lack of a barometer to reflect accurately public opinion was no new thing: writers in the quarterlies had commented bitterly on its absence when caught by surprise both in 1880 and in 1906. But since 1906 the Tory middle class had come to rely on its own reporters, and had extended its dynasty with Press approval and support. Moreover, it was easily assumed that in the storm of war the patriotic umbrella could afford to shelter all divergencies of opinion. These represented only an acceptable grumbling, the right to which had long been accorded to Englishmen who asked no other outlet for their disgruntlement. Among the mysterious 'other ranks', enlisted from Disraeli's second nation, were now many middle-class observers, many of whom formed their observations into best-selling books. In these they depicted the novel experiences they had endured, although usually for a short time only, among the able-bodied seamen, privates, or aircraftmen; and they all agreed that in these democratic circles there was now as ever no shortage of salty, rumbustious 'characters', who had no patience with 'politics', no love for 'barrack-room lawyers', whose hearts were in the right place, whose courage was unquestionable, who would soon put paid to old Adolf and the Eyeties, and whose message was, in sum, that life in the services was rather a lark. The British serviceman, unlike his articulate American counterpart who saw the Army as an embodied denial both of the principles of the constitution and the rights of man, was prepared to follow any officer, provided he was efficient, although he still preferred his officers to be gentlemen. Indeed he worried about officers a lot less than his sergeant-major, whom he saw a lot more of—and the non-commissioned officer of the British Army, by a long tradition in the Ascendancy, looking downwards, was the backbone both of the Army and of the class from which he came. All this was comforting. Much of it was true; and it heartened that middle-class readership which had long been content to take a tourist's eye-view of England, and of an England south of the Trent at that.

But many middle-class men who became war-time officers, who deepened their tourists' views as a result and who preferred not to write agreeable books but to stand as Labour candidates in the 1945 election, were irritated rather than relieved at the continuing lack of political interest among 'the men'. This factor had caught Marx's attention. It had angered the Webbs and infuriated Wells. It had been deftly exploited by Baldwin. But it still took men with a social conscience by surprise to find out what Fabians and others had found out before them: that what the 'other ranks' wanted, and all they wanted, was security. They wanted someone to look out for them. They did not want to do this for themselves, as they did not know how to. They lived in a Tory society, in a state of Tory acceptance. They voted, when they voted at all, 'Labour', since they reckoned themselves 'working-class': those who had stopped so reckoning themselves aspired a further step and voted Conservative. But the majority did not belong to 'the Movement', in any sense of emotional commitment. They had little knowledge of and put less stock in socialist theory, although there was no lack of schoolteacher sons and brothers in their midst very ready to spread the old Chartist doctrines once more. When in depression and doubt, they spoke darkly of 'the system', which had always ruled, always would, and which you could not beat. Beveridge's *Report*, which envisaged another 'system', dealt also with bread and butter, and shelter, and provision for accidents, sickness, and old age—and this was language they understood, as their grandfathers had understood the language of Joseph Chamberlain and Jesse Collings about 'three acres and a cow'. It is arguable that the shape of the welfare state that was to come was discernible in the atmosphere of acceptance that was a necessary part of service life. The services fed, clothed, sheltered, repaired, pensioned and buried, as a matter of course. Since 'They' did not encourage radical ideas, and indeed made it unpleasant for anyone who insisted on having any, it was better to accept this restriction too, and not have any. The welfare promoted by the services served a utilitarian purpose. So did that put in train by Labour when it reached power. Both had to cope with a similar attitude in the people they governed, and both had to extend their paternalist authority to get the latter to function with any efficiency.

Yet the Labour party was still the only place wherein a social conscience, looking for a political home, could come to rest. Since most of its ideas were fifty years old, it lacked the capacity to surprise. Passage of time indeed had made its programme, even its political jargon, respectable. Labour men had governed many a city council without ruining the city, and the image of 'a good Labour man' conjured up a certain down-to-earth solidity, well personified by Ernest Bevin. The party had never been as 'popular'—it had certainly never polled as many votes—as the Conservative party; but there it stood, the alternative party, the only party into which new ideas might yet be inserted. Moreover, for all its chequered history of trade union Toryism and of a political leadership with a tendency to political Toryism, it had never shaken itself free of its original reputation as a zealot for social reform, and as a repository for social idealism. It had also been lucky enough to have a few men either in it or on its fringes whose genuine passion for social justice was clear to a point of menace: the Independent Labour party in one era, Stafford Cripps in another, Aneurin Bevan in another, were all outright socialists for whom Labour could not find houseroom. Furthermore, it was true what both orthodox and unorthodox said—that 'the Left' had never held effective power, since Labour had held only office. It had never been given its 'chance'. Many now felt the time had come to give it its chance. In the 1930s it had not proved an effective, or even sensible, Opposition —but at least it had not been 'the Left' who had led this generation into doldrums and then disaster, it was not the Labour party that had a roll of 'Guilty Men'. Accordingly, many people who

359

knew very little about the organization of the party and less about its leadership were prepared, by 1945, to vote for it, and did so. Some leaders they did know and were ready to trust, since these they had seen working throughout the war as members of Churchill's Cabinet for the good of the country as a whole.

Embattled Toryism having won the war, Labour won from a wearied electorate authority to control the peace. It won this authority by default. The Conservatives were reckoned untrustworthy still. War had doubtless purged them of their 'guilt', but it had given them no new image. They had proved able warriors, but then, they had always proved themselves so, and had always had a great deal to fight for: that heritage to which they so warmly referred. The image that had emerged burnished bright was indeed not that of any party, but of the State itself—paternalist, effective, addicted to fair shares and social justice as epitomized by the ration-book and the clothing-coupon. The State, in its peacetime action, could now be made to embody the will of the people that this type of paternalism should continue. Who could make it do so? Plainly the Socialist, whose whole theory of government was bound up with an active State paternalism. Plainly the committed Radical, the Left-winger whose moral drive would supply the necessary dynamo for the mechanism of the State, and prevent its entanglement in the red tape of a vastly-expanded bureaucracy. Plainly the Labour party, which had always represented 'the workers', the broad mass of the population, who were all fit objects for rescue by the State. Thus 73 per cent of the electorate, voting Labour into office and power for the first time, did not by this action fall into closely-disciplined ranks such as Rousseau and Robespierre would have been pleased to inspect. If 'the march of democracy' now meant more than it had, it did so because those who were marching wanted their leaders to take them to what they considered a right and proper destination. They did not know where it was, but they would know it when they got there. These leaders, set in authority by the will of the majority, faced a problem Lenin had not troubled to encounter—how to convince that majority, and maintain its conviction without using force, that socialism was good and just, and that a true democratic government cared not only for the democracy that supported it, but also for the democracy that did not.

People who now decided to give Socialists their 'chance' did so because they felt they deserved it. If by their behaviour the latter turned out not to deserve it, they would not be given a chance again—not, at least, by this generation of voters. Labour, given its opportunity, was also given a moral challenge. The care of the community was the first charge on a paternalist authority: and there were *frissons* on both Left and Right when one Cabinet minister served notice in the House of Commons that 'We are the masters now', and another declared in his constituency that the Tories had always been in his estimation 'lower than vermin'. This was not the exercise of moral authority—this was merely Buggins, enjoying his 'turn'. More was to be heard of this tone of spitefulness than was good either for the community or for, in no long run, the Labour party itself, since it endangered the very principle, social justice, of which the party was meant to be the especial guardian.

Individual guardians at once camped themselves on the party's Left, and kept up an enfilading fire on officialdom's flanks to ensure that it kept strictly to the right route. The right route of course was to *Keep Left*—the title of a pamphlet issued by these guardians as early as March 1947. They constantly attacked Ernest Bevin for the pragmatic Toryism of that trade unionist's foreign policy, who appeared to have inherited a care for 'British interests' not only from Eden but from Castlereagh. While Richard Crossman appointed himself as Bevin's warden, Aneurin Bevan saw himself as keeper of the socialist flame at home, refusing to be cast merely as janitor to the institution known as the National Health Service; but when he resigned over the charge placed on 'teeth and spectacles' in Hugh Gaitskell's budget of April 1951 he was unable to convince the majority of the party that there was any principle involved. These were men who, since they lived on a plane of idealism, lived also in a state of indignation. They were not content to preside paternally over a bureaucratic administration, allocating 'fair shares', with a minute attention to detail. Fair shares of what? they asked: and although they themselves gave no clear answer, and their sketch-maps for a 'new society' were always vague, there was about them and their plans something exciting—something which certainly could not be said of Attlee and Bevin and all the party veterans. For a time the austere figure of Stafford Cripps, whose integrity was plain even to the most critical eye, gained almost the status of a public hero, as the inhabitants of the welfare state groped their way through the dispiriting shortages, including bread-rationing, of the late 1940s. Cripps could convince people that austerity was a moral virtue, where his colleagues had an unfortunate knack of making it seem a result of their own inefficiency. But he founded no school, and not surprisingly found it difficult even to make friends.

As their five years of power neared their close, Labour found itself in exactly the same position of any other political party that wanted to retain office, and could claim no higher stance. Its election literature for 1950 did not map any new society: it merely insisted that life with Labour was better, was bound to be better, than life with the Tories. *'Ask your Dad.'* It had to get its own vote out, drum its faithful to the polls. It could no longer rely on attracting that 'floating' middle-class vote, whose size could not be accurately known but which could be guessed at as considerable, which had so signally aided it to power. Labour rule had not knit society together, and given it a new purpose. It had cushioned hardship, but in doing so it had also accentuated the old class distinctions and jealousies. The 1950 election thus saw the party scrape together a parliamentary majority of six. The 1951 election put it into the wilderness for thirteen years, years of individualism and materialism during which political radicalism and idealism could find no sure footing anywhere.

Yet, if a new home for society had not been built, what was it that had been done? The old home had certainly been extended, and its façade renovated. The Britain of the 1950s was different in appearance, in attitude, and in aspiration from that of the 1930s. How fundamental were these alterations? Even as early as 1948, after a prolonged bout of nationalization and the application of controls—to the Bank of England, 'Town and Country Planning', the coal industry, civil aviation, road and rail transport, gas and electricity, cable and wireless—private industry still employed 80 per cent of the people. The land had not been nationalized, but 'further provision' had been made for it, so that 75 per cent of the produce of the average farm was now sold at a guaranteed price and in a guaranteed market. By 1957, when the Tories had been in power for six years, it was reckoned that only one-fifth of the economic structure had been 'socialized'. The State now played a greater part than it had ever done in education. The universities, 80 per cent of whose students were receiving grants from public funds, were themselves receiving about three-quarters of their incomes from parliamentary and local authority grants. But the graduates they produced were dismayed to find that the world outside was still operated by a set of Tory assumptions, which surely by now should have been relegated to the history-books. The concept of social welfare had indeed been spread broadcast, and the principle that it is

> the duty of the state to maintain the wellbeing of all its members by guaranteeing them a minimum of income and services, and insuring them against the hazards of sickness, unemployment, and old age[1]

had been widely accepted. In fact acceptance had reached the stage of assumption, since children were being born into the system, who in turn would grow up to expect their own children to know no other. In just this lay an excellent opportunity for an alert and reconstructed Conservatism.

Tories had agreed to the principle of a National Health Service when Labour first mooted it in the Commons in 1946, pointing out that it dated from a White Paper published by the coalition government two years previously. They were able to say, with truth, the same thing about Labour's nostrums for coal, gas, railways and insurance, since they could claim parentage of a series of commissions of investigation into all these subjects. (Only the nationalization of the steel industry was a resolution peculiar to Labour, and as a result it was bitterly opposed by the Tories, and was the single action that they repealed after they came to power.) In 1947 Butler insisted that Tories were not 'frightened at the use of the State', and that a good Tory had 'never in history been afraid of the State',[2] a

---

[1] C. L. Mowat, 'The Approach to the Welfare State in Great Britain', *American Historical Review*, lviii, 1952-3, 55 ff.
[2] A. Havighurst, *Twentieth Century Britain* (1962), p. 381.

remark that Disraeli—but not Balfour or Bonar Law—would have approved. They did not approve Labour's use of the weapon of taxation to bring about a redistribution of the country's wealth, but they could not undo what was being done, nor plan to renovate society on the old bases. A great amount of social 'levelling' had taken place: in 1949 only eighty-nine persons enjoyed, from earned income after taxes, more than £6,000 per year, compared with 6,560 in 1939. Yet the Conservative party while in opposition took care not to attack the paternalist principle of welfare, but to stress the dangers that were likely to prove an obstacle to its successful application in a country that, owing to governmental mismanagement, appeared to be living in a perpetual economic crisis, standing on the brink of a widening dollar gap, and weakening under a burden of chronic under-productivity. They made the point—one that the electorate came to approve—that Toryism was by its nature and tradition a state of mind that was trained to deal with things as they were; and, since the Conservative party was the home of this sane attitude, that party would clearly make better managers of a State machine than would doctrinaires without good business training, men who were accustomed and determined to see only one side of a question and only one half of the community.

Tories thus returned to the precepts of Peel in his Tamworth manifesto. They retired into that condition of 'political infidelity' which Disraeli in his political youth, and Newman all his life, had so condemned. They would do what the latter-day 'Friends of the People' were doing—but, by not doing it to excess, would do it better, and would do better by it. Yet they did not have the freedom of movement of Disraeli's era, and even the extent of their 'infidelity', or pragmatism, was circumscribed. Early Victorian Toryism, like early Victorian Whiggism, had inherited a paternalist role of long standing and acceptance. Early Elizabethan Toryism had not this good fortune. The democracy had now accustomed itself to the issue of a 'mandate' at a general election—a term that Labour politicians had perhaps overworked. The electors of Bristol had finally turned the tables on Edmund Burke. The people by their votes were prepared to delegate their will, to license a political party to administer a paternalist State on their behalf. Authority lay with them, and they granted a lease of it to persons whose administrative capacity they trusted, or at least for whose incapacity they had as yet no evidence. They did not look to these administrators for ideas, or for anything in the nature of radicalism. They had even a suspicion of planning for the future. Obvious needs must certainly be met: but needs that were not obvious were by definition not needs at all, and it was no business of a civil service to spend its time inventing them. If Burke had been defeated, it appeared to be Rousseau, with his concept of a general will, who had taken his place. Churchill was the last leader who was allowed a range of ideas. Attlee concealed what ideas he had even from his closest colleagues. Eden's career in diplomacy had debarred him from any detailed knowledge of the British community. Macmillan's mind was always enquiring, and he could perceive a wind of change when he heard one blowing: but he had no touch of the prophet, and was content to take Tory pragmatism to as developed a state as it could well reach.

Now as ever, this acceptance of things as they had become aroused strong support in the community. Conservatism had its particular place in a society which now had more than it had ever had to conserve. That security, wellbeing, and standards of living all had their price was something instinctively known, and a party whose members were apt to remind the electorate of this truth was not made unpopular by doing so. Conservatives did not set themselves, as their Victorian forebears had done, against the concept of social justice. The year 1946 had seen the passage through the Commons of eighty-four Bills: no other year was ever again to be so legislatively crowded. Tories contented themselves with pointing out, as Bentham and Arnold had done, that social justice was so tendentious and subjective a concept as to be impossible of a just fulfilment. The cry for social equality that mounted crescendo during the 1950s they reckoned a natural, and equally tendentious, corollary to this concept. In the field of public ideas, it was surely 'equality' that had the most colourful history of egotism, injustice, and tyranny, since no one could ever sincerely believe that he was just as good, but no better than, anyone else. The Tories therefore accepted the facts and consequences of six years of Labour government without accepting their implications. They did not seriously alter the structure of the State machine they took over in 1951. They fell out with Labour on the way to run the steel industry because they saw in this a symbol of the programme of efficiency which they were out to promote. The symbol served them well. It helped further impress upon the middle classes, many of them now escaped from their wartime flirtation with social idealism and divorced from any practical sympathy with Labour, that everything had its price and that everything also had its time; and that a time for cost accountancy had come. The world, owing no one a living, certainly owed no one a welfare state who was not prepared to work to keep it. The Conservative argument that sound Tory management would ensure the security both of the country and of its system of welfare took them far, winning for the party three elections in a row (1951, 1955 and 1959), an unheard-of-achievement—and this in an era wherein the British people, at long last, seemed to see a way open to them to that 'pursuit of happiness': that old democratic, republican, American, French ideal which members of the English Ascendancy for close on two centuries had denied was a worthwhile human endeavour in the first place.

But in a secular age which acknowledged no seer no one was prepared to deny the worth of human happiness, or to assert that here was a sphere that lay beyond the range of political processes. Yet—a man may be happy, but hardly a society. (It is arguable that the last time the British society was 'happy', in any meaningful sense of that term, was during the war.) Happiness was accordingly an odd principle on which to base the administration of a State. As both Tocqueville and Bentham had insisted, a democracy that built solely on a foundation of individualism had little to congratulate itself upon, and possibly as little to look forward to. Newman had attacked the utilitarian creed just on this ground, that it propagated its 'heathen nostrum' of looking out for Number One—but this was the accepted code of all those who were typified by the Saxon proletarian hero, Arthur Seaton, of *Saturday Night and Sunday Morning* (1950): 'All the rest is propaganda!'[1] This kind of cynicism signally stamped the 1950s under the presidency of the

[1] By Alan Sillitoe.

Conservative party. It could not be said that there was a Tory authority in the old sense, and it was because this could not be said that so many other things were said deliberately intended to wound. The Ascendancy had petrified into an Establishment, and it was this latter solid institution that bore the brunt of the attacks made by young intellectuals, instinctive Tories without a base from which to make forays, Radicals looking for a party to belong to, a new 'Young England' movement which could not find even a maypole for its emblem. They did not object to the exercise of moral authority. They objected to its absence, and they could not find enough certainty within to be confident of exercising it themselves. They asserted that the power and influence of the Establishment, whose doors were always open to men from the public schools, was entirely fraudulent, for its inmates, although they paid lip-service to the old creed of paternalist care for the country at large, were in reality looking out as sharply as any Arthur Seaton for Number One. Tories who were not fraudulent had to cope with this total non-alignment, and were baffled by it. Lord Chandos (Churchill's Colonial Secretary, Oliver Lyttelton, 1951–4) comments in his *Memoirs* how he liked to debate his colonial policy with undergraduates at Oxford; but he could find little to debate when one 'brilliant' young man opened a discussion by remarking it was a pity his colonial policy had so obviously failed.[1] Yet the youth represented his own generation better than a Lyttelton did his.

This absence of a genuinely Tory standard, of a Tory tone, together with the absence of the former popular acceptance and respect for a governing group—people who knew better and would do their best—affected social as well as political manners and conventions. In some parts of society a growing raffishness was observable, not unlike that often adopted by a white middle class in the tropics, where the habits of authority have always been conditioned by the heat. In this as in other things the 'fifties held some echoes of the 'twenties: but the 'Young Things' of the former period, intent only on a good time, had no true parallel. Young people who wanted a good time also wanted something else—and it was because they did not know exactly what, and no one was going to tell them what, that they

[1] *loc. cit.* (1962), pp. 389–90.

so sedulously honed and stropped their only weapons of anger and contempt. They envied the sense of commitment they found in their elders, the exiles from the 'thirties. They often found these people tedious, but still they envied them their Spanish War and their Communist dreams, their anti-fascism and most of all their great good fortune in having had in their world so enormously and patently wicked a villain as Adolf Hitler to gird their loins against.

The barometer of the social tone was now under the care of a new class, the ablest products of the Education Act of 1944 and the grants-in-aid scholarships to the universities. They preferred Redbrick to Oxbridge because they believed that the aspirations of those there, even when murky and low, were at least honestly held. They had no ingrained assumptions about the society they were clambering into, and were constantly shocked as they came in contact with people who regulated their whole lives and conduct on assumptions, and who were totally unable to distinguish between these and principles. Kingsley Amis's Lucky Jim, John Osborne's Jimmy Porter, the well-intentioned heroes of John Wain, are all moral men with a passionate distaste for 'phonies' —and they seldom encounter anyone else. (But their women, honest people with the life-principle to guard, are never phonies.) These romantic authors in their earlier novels and plays tried to break the stultifying old tradition that 'le highlife' was the only fit subject for drama; not because they disliked a civilized background with French windows, but because they could find nothing truly dramatic, nothing of value at all, to set in front of it. But as with women and Redbrick, their romanticism coloured their dealings with the proletariat, and they fell back on that sturdy middle-class standby of entertainment, the problem of sex relations—and thus the proletarian life they presented seemed as individualistic and irrelevant as that of the flannelled fools of the musical comedies of old. *I'm Talking About Jerusalem!* was the title of one of Arnold Wesker's proletarian plays (1960)—but few wanted to join such a conversation. Wesker himself sardonically underlined this, when he called a later and more successful piece *Chips with Everything* (1962).

For the welfare state was plainly not producing inhabitants for any new Jerusalem. A better standard of living did not give birth to a higher standard of thinking. 'The uses of literacy', as one critic discovered,[1] were many and various, but in no sense intellectual: mass literacy entailed merely a mass readership for mass-produced rubbish. The lower classes, brought by education to the wellsprings, did not prove themselves disciples of Tom Paine. The dramatists who investigated them thus became disillusioned as they discovered that neither destructiveness nor apathy had any dramatic core. With disillusionment came mannerism. In literature and cinematography the 'new school' developed a tendency to admire the crass and brutal simply because it was crass and brutal; and one realist film about life in the North, with all the emphasis on refuse-tip and smokestack, would turn out to be indistinguishable from another. Others meanwhile fell back 'beyond the fringe' of polite society in order to continue their satirical campaign, a campaign that had in it more of contempt than of satire proper, since the base from which it operated was never clearly established. They 'debunked' those in authority—accusing them not, as in pre-war days, of stupidity and wickedness, but of futility, since authority itself was obviously so futile a thing.

In fact, the real enemy of these committed critics was less authority than the materialism that authority appeared to be unable or unwilling to keep in control. This was not Tocqueville's state of virtuous materialism, either, but one of a distinctively amoral kind, as represented in the world of the take-over bid and the padded expense-account. Amid this absence of matter for poetry, the only frontier of imaginative adventure apparently left to many a city-dweller, who saw few works of nature, was to be found in a club where he could watch a woman strip while he lunched. In John Osborne's *The Entertainer* (1957), Britannia herself appeared as a 'non-stop nude'—thus effectively emphasizing two social perversions at once. T. S. Eliot warned *The Times* in 1955, when the government was on the point of licensing an 'independent' television network, commercially sponsored on the American pattern, of the disagreeable social consequences that would surely follow. For here was another realm for vicarious adventure. Was a nation whose millions sat nightly to 'watch the telly', who lived mentally with gunmen or in 'Z Cars'

[1] Richard Hoggart (1957).

or in 'Emergency Ward Ten', ever likely to be stirred by a cause? Or even to pay attention to reality? And were not these millions the same 'barbarian nomads of the future' whom Eliot had earlier discerned as the enemy in his *Idea of a Christian Society* (1939)? 'A mob,' in his diagnosis, 'will be no less a mob if it is well fed, well clothed, well housed, and well disciplined.' These were opinions of remarkable austerity. Eliot was reckoned humourless, and was certainly old—and age itself was easy enough to assess as another form of fraudulence. His criticisms, and others of the kind, were accordingly not criticized, but dismissed as irrelevant. Another elder, Somerset Maugham, unsurprisingly took his opportunity to reprimand the absence of integrity and craftsmanship in these new standards of literary criticism, and gave much offence when he identified the existence of a proliferating intellectual slum. Yet here he may have spoken for the audience his own works had long attracted, a middle-class audience which now laughed dutifully at satire levelled against itself, but which also felt a need for something with some better heart to it. The great popularity of the spectacular, theatrical 'period piece', depicting another time than this—whether *The King and I*, *My Fair Lady*, a cinemascope 'western' or a Biblical 'blockbuster'—seems to illustrate the wish of many to be emancipated for at least one evening from so bitter a world of diagnosed disenchantment.

Thus one reaction to the 'new society' was a display of emotional haste to get out of it and stay clear of it. Another, was a resolve to inject some purpose into it. Dissenters therefore abounded, ranging in kind from self-absorbed juveniles to those who obstructed traffic as a mark of their detestation of a society whose policies and purposes were physically controlled by stockpiles of nuclear weapons. Society as at present constituted appeared to present the image of a geometric absurdity: a series of tangents that lacked a central circle from which to project. Where the centre should traditionally have been, the hard work of the monarchy was rewarded less with respect for the principle of authority it was designed to embody than with gratitude for the glamour and colour of its physical appearance. Positions of influence were still a perquisite of those who had been brought up to become influential, since educational privilege was among the social assets included within the higher income brackets. The right accent was still a passport to acceptance. Success, a different thing, could be got without it; but success is never a perquisite of the majority, which puts a higher value accordingly on acceptance. Sometimes the right accent was a 'wrong' accent—as on the stage, or in parliament, where a proletarian pronunciation had its place—but this again was taken as a good illustration of the hypocrisy of the standard of values that prevailed. And plainly, more was always going to be heard of social levelling than was ever going to be done about it: for no one genuinely believed in it who found he was expected to expose his children to it, as a tally of the sons of left-wingers at public schools could easily show.

So buttressed, members of the Establishment were not discommoded either by that definition of their incorporation or by the anger, more often verging on petulance, of their attackers. Their predecessors in power had parried the assaults of Wells and Shaw. They themselves could dispose of this new crop of gad-flies by writing them off as so many envious youths who would, when they had made their way a little farther up a ladder of recognition, join the ranks of the established, and develop a habit of mind and behaviour accordingly—as many a radical generation before them had done. But they had to make their own way: no 'right of passage' was issued to anyone. Why should there be? the Tory asked, and felt it a question with point.

Harold Laski's name for this Establishment had been 'government by connection', and there were other names.[1] But it was a long-standing Tory opinion, that the tradition of authority was naturally a Tory tradition,[2] and, since this was so, that there would always be a great many people who disliked it. This was not something to dismay. There could, after all, be no intelligent radicalism in a country where there was no intelligible conservative tradition. Tom Paine had been an intelligent radical—and, among other things, he had in the second part of his *Rights of Man* proposed the abolition of the Poor Law, the imposition of estate-duties, the abolition of sinecure posts (including king and courtiers), the institution of old-age pensions and maternity

[1] The Service name for it was 'the old boy net'.
[2] Cecil, *Conservatism*, p. 247.

371

benefits, and a public works programme. Intelligent Tories who now found themselves living in Paine's world still thought themselves the right people to preside over it. Cobden too had been an intelligent radical, insisting—although he never produced anything in the nature of a concrete programme, since he was hampered by his adherence to *laisser-faire*—that there was no country where so much was required to be done 'before the mass of the people became what it is pretended they are, what they ought to be, and what I think they will yet be, as in England.'[1] He added that the people who were so anxious to civilize and Christianize Africa 'had a great deal to do at home within a stone's throw of where they were'.[2] Intelligent Tories who had inherited a programme that went far to meet Cobden's point saw themselves as the best paternalists available. Bryce had sonorously pronounced on the nature of the task before them. 'Though the people,' he wrote,

> cannot choose and guide the Means administration employs, they can prescribe the Ends: and so although government may not be By the People, it may be For the People. . . . A nation is tested and judged by the quality of those it chooses and supports as its leaders; and by their capacity it stands or falls.[3]

Intelligent Tories had no doubt that it was their own capacity which was best able to stand this test.

In this Tory armour of assurance there was now, however, an Achilles' heel. The accusation that, while they might indeed be as efficient as they claimed at doing what they had been given to do, they still had no genuine sense of purpose, was brushed aside rather than refuted. They had arrived at a position whose location Disraeli had divined in advance. A century before, while rejecting the principle of household suffrage, the Tory leader had warned his hearers that they would, in due season, with a democracy find that their property was less valuable and that their freedom was less complete. The greater the good qualities of the working classes, the greater the danger.[4] At the same time,

---

[1] Cobden, *Writings*, II, 375.
[2] 3H 113, July 19, 1850, 37–42.
[3] Bryce, *Modern Democracies*, II, 550–1.
[4] March 31, 1859: Monypenny and Buckle, *Disraeli* IV, 209.

AGENTS AND PATIENTS

Mill in his *On Liberty* was noting how there was now 'scarcely any outlet for energy in this country except business'. This wheel too seemed to have come full circle—Great Britain now wore the guise of a commercial republic. Mill's immediate posterity, the late Victorians, had found release from these narrow straits in the fascinations of building and then contemplating an Empire: but the century that had passed had also put an end to that.

For those who felt domestically frustrated did not feel their spirits rise as they looked out at the world beyond. Nor did those who felt domestically secure. The superiority of the European rate of productivity was possibly based on an even deeper devotion to the principle of happiness, since the countries of Europe, unlike Britain, had been psychologically as well as physically damaged by the war. But to the majority in Britain Europe was an unknown continent, another place of which they had only a tourist's view. Their people were known to be wayward and their ways incomprehensible. Across the Atlantic the United States of America was more readily recognizable—but American motivation had always been mysterious, and Americans were now combining their traditional pursuit of their own happiness with something new, a pursuit of it on others' behalf. They had experienced a moral commitment to uphold a particular kind of international order. The very intensity of this commitment, epitomized by the driving energies of the Secretary of State, John Foster Dulles (1952-8), tended to alienate the understanding of those whose own moral drives had diminished. Americans *cared* that there were Communists in, say, Cambodia, in a way that the British did not. Communists had been exposed, to everyone's embarrassment, within British governing circles. Doubtless, despite all precaution, this same thing might happen again. But public life in Britain did not produce, and public opinion in Britain would not have supported, so essentially mediaeval a figure as Senator Joseph McCarthy, who made a career of heresy-hunting, capitalizing on the American fear that Communists, 'working from within', would contaminate the principle of the American republic. The British saw Communism as a physical threat, not as a moral one: the ideology was now too plainly moth-eaten, and the ideologues, for all their talk of

N 373

THE HABIT OF AUTHORITY

Marxism and Leninism and determinism, were too obviously fascist careerists of a familiar brand. In the 'thirties Communist members had sat in the House of Commons: on the workshop floor Communist shop-stewards had long been a commonplace both to employers and to Transport House. These had not managed to overturn society when it was precariously balanced, and it was not thought likely that they were going to overthrow a far more comfortable community now.

The American insistence that there was a devil abroad in the world, one who by definition was an authoritarian anti-democrat, thus did not translate well across the Atlantic. Churchill had done business with this same devil as from June 1941—and if he, who could claim the status of a professional anti-Bolshevik of long standing, could swallow his ideological antipathies for the sake of protecting an overriding national interest, others felt they needed no excuse for doing the same. On a similar pragmatic principle Labour had recognized the government of Communist China in 1949, and the Conservatives that of General Franco in Spain in 1952. Neither in Britain nor in Europe was any such figure as Chiang Kai-shek allowed to exist, a *revenant* from the past come to cloud present policy. They could not afford to pay homage to a moral Formosa, reminding them of old hopes. What European countries, Great Britain with them, admired in the American democracy was not its morality, which they had never comprehended, but its success: in two centuries it had—somehow—become the greatest power in the world. American efficiency and technical skill constituted a passport to respect; American moral judgment did not. Americans indeed, as *parvenus* in the field of international diplomacy, in many ways paralleled the experience of the *parvenus* from the council school and Redbrick University amid the intricacies of the southern English class-structure. They had constantly to meet with, and bruise themselves against, assumptions which during their two centuries of isolated growth they had had no part in forming; and these they naturally suspected and disliked. But even here their tradition of adaptability worked in their favour, and they quickly developed an acceptable and on occasion a highly professional diplomatic sophistication. The Russians did no such thing, if they were to be fairly judged by the utterances of spokesmen who, while not displaying Stalin's pathological fears of foreign contamination, never seemed to grow any less ignorant of the ways of the world.

The British thus found themselves in a place and time governed by the physical power of Washington and Moscow: the Cuban crisis of October 1962 underlined the degree of their vulnerability. But they could see in neither a Mecca, radiating spiritual guidance to sustain them. Americans shared authority in the world with the Russians because both the United States and the Soviet Union were great powers. Over their own subjects both governments exercised a moral authority also, but this an outsider, while he might respect it, could hardly understand. From the time he first strode on to the world stage in 1940, Charles de Gaulle objected to the whole notion that a self-respecting nation could retain its self-respect, which was its soul, while under the leadership of something nebulously called 'the West' but more accurately called the United States; and he worked tirelessly to present the French nation with a new image for its especial use, one fashioned according to his own idiosyncrasies. Who could do the same for the British?

Britain, too, was a part of 'the West', devoted to the principle of a free democracy. But in her record, democracy had not arrived with a thunder-clap, to a sound of trumpets, amid Founding Fathers and heaven-sent legislators, as it had done (or at least as it was popularly reckoned to have done) in the American and French republics. Equality and levelling had been kept under control—and, as the educated invaders were now so loudly complaining, an entrenched Establishment was still determined so to keep them. Britain's distinctive contribution to democracy had been the theory, backed since 1832 by the practice, that it could be paternally guided and ultimately educated to a sense of responsibility—a sense of course much the same as that of the class which was guiding and educating. That the British Empire in its latest stages had been fashioned according to this theory all the books proclaimed: but that Great Britain also had taken that shape had not been so widely publicized. With this distinction in mind, British statesmen whether of Left or Right objected as did de Gaulle to the role of patient—patient in a world whose agencies were controlled by

375

people who not only did not share the British view but who had in their different days rejected it: Americans in 1776, Russians in 1917. They insisted that they had something distinctive to contribute to the Western alliance; and that in particular Great Britain enjoyed a 'special relationship' with the United States— a term which, as memories of war-time comradeship receded and President Kennedy succeeded President Eisenhower (1961), increasingly avoided accurate and positive definition.

Their sense of interior grievance was increased by the fact that Britain had not, like France, been defeated in war. She had been diminished by it. The publicized 'war-effort', as it turned out, squandered her assets and drained her resources, so that 'when in 1945 Britain voted into power a Labour government intent on improving the ordinary person's lot the country was financially insolvent for the first time in its modern history'. In such a situation, as Ernest Bevin discovered, it was a matter of extreme difficulty both to preserve a political influence at all and the will to assert it. It is in the last days of the British Empire, that old enclave of power and the paternalist assumption, that this process of strain, both of moral and material resources, can be most clearly seen.

In the post-war era Britain could not afford to defend her Empire against the rising tide of colonial nationalism. To do so would have required the mobilization of a standing army in India, and the marshalling of flying squadrons of military police, ready to hold down restive colonies the world over, for an unforeseeable length of time. She would have involved herself with a bitter and probably irreconcilable quarrel with the United States, for whom she was physically no match; and she would have been forced to retire from any participation in the United Nations' Organization, a body whose hostility to the continued existence of empires was made plain from the outset. She would also have had to spend untold sums of money, money which she did not have and which certainly no one would have lent her; and she would have drained the country of the manpower it needed to set the battered domestic economy back on its feet. Moreover, she would probably have had to cope with mutiny in a conscript Army which had been promised peace, or at any rate demobilization, when victory over the Japanese was attained. Not one of these things could be afforded—and the British learned in Malaya the lesson that the French Army refused to learn in Indo-China, and then in Algeria: that politics was still the art of the possible, and that this no longer included any possibility of preserving an empire by force, in an age when its prestige had gone.

Since, then, it was not a practicable proposition to preserve the British Empire, it was not preserved. The old Tory view of 'British interests' here obtained. Nothing was sensibly to be defined as a British interest which Britain in an emergency did not have the power to assert as such. To be able to declare an 'interest' at all, and to have it respected at large, is itself symbolic of power. To declare as such what cannot be upheld is to be exposed to contempt, and thus to find whatever influence remains weakened further still. It was in accordance with this reasoning that the business of decolonization, begun by Labour in India in 1947, was continued by the Tories at an accelerating pace throughout the 1950s. Persons were found who were declared fit to take over the imperial responsibilities, and given authority to do so. Princes in India, settlers in Africa, were to complain of desertion, and they had a point. But in a hard age it was not one that British politicians could afford to meet.

Yet however necessary it was to cut the imperial ties decolonization was not carried out without damage to the Tory concept of authority itself, with all its duty and habit. The British Empire was a famous organization, in which famous things had been done. Gathered together as an administrative whole after the American defection in 1783, its governance had been based on the principle that 'law and order' was itself a good, and its governors were people with assumptions to match. In the seventeenth century, when all concepts had to be examined afresh by men to whom problems of sovereignty had suddenly become concrete, Thomas Hobbes had examined the principle, and laid down the assumption for his posterity. 'The law is a command,' says he in his *Leviathan*, 'and a command consisteth in declaration or manifestation of him that commandeth.' This refreshing simplicity had much to commend it: and the Crown Colony system—with its governor, its executive council and, if there was one at all, its legislative council or assembly in the firm hands of a majority of nominated or 'official' members—was in the nineteenth century perfected to symbolize the harmonious relationship of tutor and taught, trustee and ward. The Colonial Governor had 'reserved powers' which he was expected to exercise if an emergency arose. In the British Cabinet he had the Colonial Secretary to back him, and consequently, units of the British Army or fleet to support him if needed. Public opinion, as in the case of Eyre in Jamaica in 1865, might later force his recall and repudiation: but that was an aftermath of the exercise of power, which did not diminish its efficacy. The essence of empire was control; the confidence to wield it; the capacity to enforce it if necessary. These were the three indivisibles of British authority overseas—and at home.

But a process of division had begun after 1919. Their exertions in the twentieth century's first world war had very seriously diminished the physical ability of the European powers to control and defend their empires. The confidence had also dwindled. They were no longer able to believe that a 'Golden Age' was just around the corner: journey's end for that hope had been reached somewhere in the mud of the Somme. The German Chancellor, Prince Bülow, had declared in 1900 that in the coming century the German Empire would prove either hammer or anvil; but, in the débris that littered Europe in 1919 neither hammer nor anvil could be confidently identified. In such circumstances the old imperialist assurance—its main attraction to subject-races, since men if they envy also admire authority—could not be maintained. Such words as had been used by Britain's Alfred Milner in South Africa at the time of the Boer War—

British influence is not exercised to impose an uncongenial foreign system upon a reluctant people. It is a force making for the triumph of the simplest ideas of honesty, humanity, and justice[1]

—were no longer relevant to or even meaningful in a world that wearily allowed the Treaty of Versailles to crown four years of struggle. The years that followed were those of the paper tigers.

[1] Quoted in Edward Crankshaw, *The Forsaken Idea* (1957), p. 29.

378

If the European empires did not display their weakness, that was because no one exposed it. In the seventeenth century the reputation of the imperial Spanish monarchy had far outstripped its capacity to assert its power, even although Francis Drake a century earlier had seen it as 'a colossus stuffed with clouts'. History now repeated itself. Once the Washington treaty had been signed in 1922, the Far Eastern empires of the United States, Britain, France and the Netherlands existed under sufferance of the Japanese Navy, although twenty years were to pass before the latter produced its own Francis Drake who made the position painfully clear.

In that interim, empire remained an accepted fact. Still under the shelter of the British Navy, the 'white' dominions asserted their freedom to define a status of independence without having to support it with any particular function; and although 'unrest' in India (always called by that name) was an embarrassment to Britain, it could be and was treated as a domestic, not as an international problem. The rebellious Congress party of the 1930s, unlike their more fortunate predecessors in the American colonies of the 1770s, could enlist no outside assistance, and had not themselves either the physical power or the moral assurance to unseat the British from the imperial saddle. Towards other colonies, adjudged less strategically significant, British statesmen pursued a liberal policy, increasing the degree of local representation and laying the foundations of an educational system that was expected to produce good civil servants for the extant régime. These in their turn were intended to act as the educators of others, the whole constituting a conservative white-collar middle-class, animated by Western values, whose function would be to interpret the wishes and ideas of the rulers to the illiterate mass. This policy derived from Macaulay's experience in India in the early 1830s, and it governed a colonial world of salaried, and sometimes of created, 'paramount chiefs'. (And had it been backed with zeal and money and statesmanship—had universities, for example, been established in the West Indies and in Malaya in the early 1920s instead of in the late 1940s—it might well have fulfilled its intentions.) But beyond these limits, British officialdom did not devote much thought to the future, say, of Africa. Africa was an undeveloped *area*. To develop it would make it no less an area. To the official mind it was never primarily the place where Africans lived, breathed and had ideas: Joyce Carey's *Mister Johnson* (1939) was read as an entertainment, not as a text-book. The idea that Sierra Leone was a 'nation'—as it now is (1961), and a member of the Commonwealth to boot—was one that would have caused merry laughter in the Colonial Office had anyone aired it there.

If the confidence of imperialism had been shaken by the century's first war, it was shattered by the second. It even had to endure a change of name. Seen from below, it was dubbed 'colonialism', American and Russian definitions of which were not far apart. The American *Webster's* defines 'colonialism' as 'the system in which a country maintains foreign colonies for their economic exploitation'. (In parenthesis, it is significant that the *Oxford English Dictionary* does not contain the word at all, and that the expression 'a foreign colony' strikes many English minds as a contradiction in terms.) The Russian definition expresses a similar sentiment, more robustly. The Russian language has no separate word for 'colonialism': one word serves for it and for 'colonization', and even that is carefully identified as a foreign importation. *The Soviet Dictionary of Foreign Words* defines *Kolonizatsiya* as 'the seizure of a country or region by imperialists, accompanied by the subjection, brutal exploitation, and sometimes annihilation of the local population'. Loaded with these objurgations, the imperialist of Milner's kind who had seen himself as a man with a mission, a trustee of civilization whose authority for the sake of civilization should remain unquestioned, felt himself the more inclined to leave the white man's burden by the roadside. Yet many a Tory conscience winced at this plain dereliction of duty. 'The Englishman,' so goes one embittered comment on the process of decolonization,

> deplores his grandfather's sins and tries to atone for them cheaply by betraying his grandfather's friends.[1]

A policy of pragmatism is not one that lifts anyone's heart. But what else could be followed? Six years of effort were this time crowned not by any peace treaty, however bad (no one was

[1] Crankshaw, op. cit., p. 37.

capable even of making a bad treaty) but by two international revolutions. In the East the forcible imposition of a Japanese Empire, although short-lived, made resuscitation of the former European Empires there impossible. In Europe, as Churchill had foreseen, the old balance-of-power ideal disappeared when Germany, the European centre, was destroyed and partitioned. In one sense Europe itself disappeared, for it soon became a zone of strategic manoeuvre between the power of the United States and power of the Soviet Union. These were no circumstances for the crusader.

So, too, the Labour party, never lacking in crusaders, discovered. The party had a long history of anti-imperialism, and, since it had first allied with the Liberals in 1906, had successfully instructed the electorate that paternalism, like charity, properly began at home. But Labour's leaders, mindful of the brotherhood of man, took as moral a view of the overseas world as of that at home. Economic freedom was everyone's birthright, and from 1921 'Dominion Status' for India was a plank of the party's platform. With this outlook, Labour could not but see the process of decolonization as something of positive virtue and value. It was slower to calculate the kind of deduction that others were to draw from it. Empire in India, as nineteenth-century Tories such as Palmerston and Curzon had always pointed out, could not be given up without cracking the walls of the entire imperial structure. Even in its own time, Attlee's 'timetable' plan of winding up the British *Raj* proved an odd bedfellow for Bevin's programme for finding some solution to the problems of another area of British responsibility, Palestine —and one wonders how far, if at all, these policies were concerted before their contradictions struck everyone as obvious. The security of the *Raj* in India had always depended more upon the will of an authoritative class than on manpower and money, although it needed all three: once the men and the money had been withdrawn, it was naturally assumed that the British will to protect the country's interests had evaporated also. This appeared to remove any *raison d'être* for a British presence in the Middle East: and the story which begins in Palestine in 1947, despite the Tory traditional views of Ernest Bevin concerning the nature of British interests, and which ends in Egypt in 1956 and in Cyprus in 1959, illustrates the grinding process by which the British themselves were forced to recognize that they had no means, no convincing argument, with which to combat this alien assessment.

Tories who fell heir to Labour's policy of granting self-government to the dependencies thus applied it without any great conviction that these areas were likely to put their independence to any great use. If they sought to promote methods of 'gradualism', they were handicapped, as Oliver Lyttelton found out, by the widespread popularity of the 'timetable' theory. Colonial nationalists wanted the nationalism, and the seats of power with it, to be given to them, not to their posterity. The Tories made one last moral stand at Suez in 1956, an invasion of Egypt carried out in the interests of Britain—but it was not so that the world regarded it, and the Tories themselves found they had not the assurance to carry the business through. It was this self-realization, rather than any deep respect for world opinion (never a British attribute), which caused official Toryism thereafter to lose all interest in imperialism, and consequently in the fate of those parts of the empire that still existed. A Central African Federation was the last imperial structure to be built (1953); but when mined from within by black nationalism, white nationalism found no support in London, and the structure was allowed to collapse after a ten years' existence. In the West Indies another federation (1958) fell apart after four.

Imperial ideas, and the authority that accompanied them, had long presented a target for attack to the educated in Great Britain. Tory heads had once been shaken at a Whig East India Company; Whig heads at the grandiosities of Chatham. Humanitarians had inveighed against the existence of slave-plantations; economist utilitarians against the cost of imperial garrisons. Liberals had complained about the fiscal burden of ostensibly self-governing colonies; against Anglo-Indian dreams of a 'scientific frontier', Disraeli's 'spirited foreign policy', and the kind of jingoism on which the sun never set. Labour objected to the diversion of policies of missionary paternalism from the domestic arena, wherein they were clearly most needed. Irishmen objected to English tyranny, throughout. Democrats attacked the essentially non-democratic nature of imperial

governance, and had long disliked the type of imperialist who
saw all political education for subject-races as a form of subversion. But the death of British imperialism left a curious void.
It was not only a target that was removed, but an influence that
everyone in the country had felt the force of, and a way of life
that had conditioned the Englishman's world to the limits of
national memory. The mass of the people, who shared few of the
attitudes listed above since their main interest was not concerned at all with policy, imperial or other, but with making a
living, had none the less known that there *was* an empire. They
knew nothing about its organization, and could not have
identified with any confidence its component parts; but their
feelings of patriotism were stirred by the sight of the map
painted red. For the British Empire, whatever else it was, was a
monument to British exuberance, British abilities, British
institutions and above all to British power and influence in the
world. They had certainly not been accustomed to consider
Great Britain as Europe's offshore islands, nor to suppose that
the British attitude and outlook was as significant as, but not
more so than, that of any of the unknown states of 'the Continent'.

But, as the 1960s drew on, Great Britain appeared to be
gravitating towards the position of what had been her own 'white
Dominions'. These had the status of independence, accorded to
them by Britain at the imperial conference of 1926 and sealed by
the Statute of Westminster of 1931. But they had not found any
peculiar function or sphere of operation. Australia's physical
security, like Canada's, depended on the goodwill of the United
States. The Commonwealth of Nations had no institutional
basis, and it signified just as much as, but no more than, an
individual enthusiast thought it to signify. It was democratic in
spirit, and could not accommodate any spirit that diverged, such
as South Africa's in 1961; although, as South Africans pointed
out, it did not appear to object to the forms of authoritarianism
that were in vogue in Ghana and Pakistan. But it had too little
that was concrete, and lacked authority accordingly. The 'new'
countries with a shared colonial past adhered to it and continued
to do so as long as they considered that their own interests,
strategic and economic, were served by the maintenance of the
connection: but they dealt always not with 'the Commonwealth',

as such, but with the Commonwealth Relations Office in White-hall if there was anything they particularly wanted to discuss. Great Britain was thus left a degree of administrative responsibility which she did not especially want, but which none of her Commonwealth partners, who had troubles of their own, especially wanted to share. British official opinion towards the Commonwealth was mixed, and in some cases coloured with an emotional attachment to the old imperial tradition of responsibility: but this was a wasting asset, and the determined campaign of the Macmillan government to enter the European Common Market (1961-2), had it succeeded, would clearly have damaged the commercial ties of the Commonwealth; and with these, much else would also have parted.

In these circumstances the democracy in Great Britain was left to look for some *raison d'être*, and it did not warm to commentators who pointed out that, say, the countries of Scandinavia had no particular *raison d'être* either. The world the British people lived in now had no ascertainable map, red or otherwise. The future had no ascertainable shape, since the conditions that had shaped the future of every generation since the time of Napoleon were no longer to obtain: an authoritative world-position, recognized as such. The call was out for leadership, the leadership of a group not readily identifiable on the present political scene—wherein Left and Right were channelled in the same grooves, and competed with each other to achieve the same things—which would act as chart-makers and seers, and whose cartography and prophecy would prove correct. It was a formidable summons, almost as difficult to issue as it was to receive. Arrived at this watershed of the national life, the democracy was faced with the decision whether it would give its 'mandate' once more to the concept once again of a paternalist authority, finding for the country its best course to pursue; or whether it would settle for a continuance of things as they were, in the hope that happenstance would do the work of foresight and somehow, in some way, engineer this continuance.

For want of an alternative, the Labour party once more, as it had done towards the close of the war, fell heir to its own public reputation as a repository for zeal and commitment. Circumstance helped it use this legacy, as it was clear there was no other asset to invest. At this late date its members could scarcely claim that they were better pragmatists than the Tories, who had now had thirteen years' practice. Already the success of Liberal candidates in the by-elections of the early 1960s pointed to the rising middle-class dissatisfaction with the Tory policy of pragmatism. Labour had a chance to exploit this, and it was apparently in a position to do so because, under Hugh Gaitskell's manful leadership throughout the 1950s, the party had at long last been able to bury its sad history of internecine quarrelling and turn a coherent front towards the electorate. It remained to be seen, however, whether the latter could be persuaded to give it their trust.

In the American democracy there was some parallel to this British predicament. Eight years with Eisenhower's prosperous republic, which included three years with Senator McCarthy, were considered by a majority of Democrats as several years too many. Thus the presidential campaign mounted by John F. Kennedy in 1960 underlined the need for the United States to march towards a 'new frontier'. Its nature was not clearly defined, and in fact as Kennedy's presidential term passed not many Americans went to look for it; but the image itself caught the imagination because of its optimism that there was, some-where, such a thing as a new frontier, which men of goodwill, sagacity, fortitude, and intelligence could reach. It argued that what was already in people's experience could be expanded; and it did not take the normal critical line of the social reformer by arguing that the present experience was anyway fraudulent. There was nothing wrong in better food, better housing, and better standards of living. There was nothing wrong even in television as a diversion. The people who warned against affluence did not object to money; they did not contradict the popular view that wealth, even if it could not actually buy happi-ness, at any rate paved a way towards it. What they objected to was the state of anarchy into which, as Arnold had predicted, too affluent a society might fall, beset with laziness, lack of enter-prise, and both public and private selfishness. In fact they were speaking of decadence—a term they did not however use, since its only acceptable application in the popular estimation was either to ancient Rome—or to Mauve, or Yellow, decades.

In Britain's case this warning had some point. The self-absorption of *fin de siècle*, at the turn of the twentieth century, had helped produce an unthinking jingoism in foreign and imperial affairs, while the 'condition-of-England' remained uncared for. Now, as the mid-century passed, Britain had clearly reached a genuine end of an era, and such a period held specific dangers. Here the parallel with the problems of contemporaries came also to its end. What the British course should now be, was a question that could not be solved by looking at other people's difficulties and actions. The British State, the British community, was still *sui generis*, 'inlaid with a peerage and topped with a Crown'. The British democracy was neither of the American nor the French type. These were both of long standing: Britain's was a creation of the twentieth century itself, and much less forward-looking than either. Unlike them, it did not distrust the presence of a strong central government, since the entire evolution of the country—its laws, its liberties, and its assumptions about both—was dependent on that government's efficiency at any given time. It was still habituated to authority, and still—despite the satire from the flanks of the middle-class —inclined to that deference to it that Bagehot had commented on a century before, although now more perceptive as to its nature. It still felt that 'government *for* the people' was the truly essential component of the democratic trinity as laid down in Lincoln's famous definition. The British people still lived within distinctive social strata, and were likely to remain in these until some major 'nationalization' of the educational system was carried out. They were still slow to recognize facts of life: only twenty years after the fall of Singapore (March 1942) did a majority come to understand something of the nature of the revolution in status which had been triggered by that event—and even then it was dangerous for a politician to refer openly to the diminution of power, or to point out that the 'independent deterrent' in Britain's armoury was neither independent nor likely to deter. They were as insular as they had ever been in their ideas. Even the intellectual rebels, railing at hypocrisy and incompetence, seldom urged that what they so complained of was ordered better in France.

In consequence, the British people were disinclined to follow precepts that they, or someone on their behalf, had not tested. They would not trust their future to any political party that did not own a respectable pedigree, nor to any person whom they could not, in the social context, vouch for. 'Democratic politics,' one analyst has remarked, 'is the art of reaching decisions that are generally acceptable.'[1] There was still, therefore, a place for Bentham's legislator—but he had first to be recognized as such. He could not claim such a status, it had to be accorded him. The people did not want analysis, but they expected insight. They continued to ask of their legislators what they had always asked for, and what they had usually been lucky enough, in periods of national crisis, to get. They asked for those same indivisible qualities that had given the now-liquidated British Empire its reputation in the world. They asked of their governors authority, assurance and capacity. In England social privilege had been the charter of political power, from the time of the Normans onwards. Its last charter was ability. The last Ascendancy must be composed of able men. 'A great part of all power,' as yet another analyst had observed a century before, 'consists in will.'[2]

It remained to be seen, as 1964 closed, whether this traditional habit still accompanied those who sought from the people the authority to govern. The election in October had returned the Labour Party, under Harold Wilson's chairmanship, to a position it had once known only too well: that of office, not power. The people had voted men out of power—not other men into it. Time therefore had still to show whether the people could be persuaded, by the will and capacity of their new leaders, to accord to them their own traditional habit of acceptance.

[1] John Plamenatz, *On Alien Rule and Self-Government* (1961), p. 104.
[2] J. S. Mill, *Responsible Government* (1861).

INDEX

Acton, Lord, on American spoils system, 122; on Tocqueville, 190; on liberty, 198

Adams, John, on government, 100; on parliamentary authority, 124; on property and judgment, 132

Adams, John Quincy, on burning of Washington, 84; sees no parallel in American and French Revolutions, 131

Adrian IV, Pope, and Ireland, 36

Alger, Horatio, philosophy of, 307

Algiers, Newman in, 204

Alison, Archibald, on 1793, 86; a victim of a prank, 98; on Scottish society, 98

Alphege, Saint, disparaged, 30

Alsatia, never a State of the Union, 27

American Civil War, English attitudes to, 215 ff.

American colonists, respect of, for Locke and Blackstone, 13

American Constitution, function of, 135; all sail and no anchor, 160; no English counterpart, 229

American 'experiment', nature of, 136

American Federation of Labor, not socialist, 327

American Loyalists, English historians and, 15

American republicans, want of loyalty diagnosed in, 14, 157

American Revolution, Adam Smith on, 100; an unpleasantness, 104

American Studies, British Association for, a latecomer, 15

Andrews, C. M., on naval corruption, 264

Anglicans, cultivate garden, 202

Anne, Tsarina, boyars force Charter on, 38

Annual Register, 1831, hostile to 'speaking-trumpets', 186

Anstey, F., *Vice Versa*, 284

Anti-Corn Law-League, antipathy of, to Chartists, 187; vulgarity of, 213

Argyll, Duke of, on Scottish aristocracy, 162; on Whig origins, 270; on sheep, 273

Aristotle, *Politics*, a tory text-book, 96

Army Bureau of Current Affairs, out of favour, 356

Arnold, Matthew, on Methodists, 212; *Culture and Anarchy*, on middle classes, 241; catholic distastes of, 260

Arthur, King, normanized, 30; not in Scotland, 33

Ashley, Lord, disputes with Bright on factory legislation, 189; puts through Mines Bill, 213

Asquith, H. H., dubbed a Whig, 294; displacement of, 329

Atlantic Charter, implications of, 353

Attlee, Clement, a social reformer, 326; on mess of centuries, 356

Attwood, Thomas, founds political unions, 187

Austen, Jane, ignores Napoleon, 168

Australia, toryism in, 144; colonies of, social condition discussed, 296 ff.

Australian Colonies Government Act, passage of, 163

Austrian Empire, need for, 214

Bagehot, Walter, hostile to employers and traders, 184; stresses need for leadership, 230; on Palmerston, 237; on sensible men, 293

balance of power, a Whig doctrine, 168, 237

Balcarres, Lord, on loaves and fishes, 121

Baldwin, Stanley, born 1867, 229; an unknown, 332; political skills of, 344; popularity of, runs out, 348

Balfour, A. J., unCobdenite, 223; on House of Lords, 305; loses election three times, 314

Ball, John, on lure of freehold, 40

Bancroft, George, *History of the United States*, impact of, 125, 262; quoted, 129

Barbados, royalism in, 113

Barebones Parliament, views of, 55

Barrie, J. M., *What Every Woman Knows*, 251; fey insight of, 276

Beaverbrook, Lord, and Socialism, 325

Becket, Thomas, reputation of, 35

Beit, Alfred, and Oxford bequest, 313

Bell, Clive, *Civilisation*, quoted, 21

Bengal, Clive and his sepoys in, 30; North's Regulating Act for, purpose of, 115; Permanent Settlement in, effect of, 153

Bentham, Jeremy, on House of Lords, 85; on equality, 134; and commonsense, 178 ff.; opinions of, 180; dislikes history, 200; and mean sensual man, 200; no reputation in Edinburgh, 270

Bevan, Aneurin, on need for socialism, 325; keeper of the flame, 359

Beveridge, Sir William, *Report* of, 356

Bevin, Ernest, image of, 325

Bible, King James', appeal of, 253

Bill of Rights (1689), Tom Paine's view of, 61

Bismarck, Prince, political skills of, 236

Blackstone, William, American devotion to, 13; *Commentaries*, impact of, 73, 180; Bentham disparages, 180

Blatchford, Robert, *Britain for the British*, 303, 317

Bolingbroke, Lord, *Patriot King*, on establishment, 64

Bolshevism, reputation of, 82

Boomerang, William Lane's, on Chinese menace, 298

border, Scottish, a no man's land, 32

boroughmongering, 71

Boston Tea Party, Lord Mayor of London and, 105

Botany Bay, Muir escapes from, 91

boyars, Russian, force Charter on Tsarina Anne, 38

Brailsford, H. N., on music and beauty, 304

Braxfield, Lord, views of, on Constitution, 91

Bray, village of, squire and parson in, 57

Bright, John, notes differences between England and Scotland, 33; on Australian Colonies Government Bill, 163; combats aristocratic viewpoint, 168; self-confidence of, 184; urges need for middle-class action, 189; disputes with Ashley, 189; on cottage squalor, 189; Russell asks to dinner, 209; on Disraeli, 210; on

Corn Laws, 218; denies love of numbers, 219; wants Constitution restored to people, 220; for household suffrage and ballot, 222; admiration of, for American constitution, 219

British Association for American Studies, recent incorporation of, 15–16

British Broadcasting Corporation, a public oracle, 356

British Commonwealth, name of, 353

British Constitution, not written down, 135; a chance-medley, 179; Russell on, 182

British Empire, existence of impossible without habit of authority, 16; an irrelevance, 315; talent drained into, 338; zenith of influence of, 351; a monument, 383

British interests, definition of, 237

Brooks' club, headquarters of 'Friends of the People', 90; shrine of Fox, 194

Brougham, Lord, defines middle class, 183; and royal marital troubles, 191; Woolsacked, 194

Brummell, Beau, will not serve in Manchester, 250

Brunswick, Duke of, manifesto of, 83

Bryan, W. J., views of, on England, 158; ideas of, 310–11

Bryce, James, on Reform Act (1832), 159; on Disraeli, 211; on the Confederate cause, 217; on American politics, 236; on boroughs, 277; on ends and means, 372

Buccleuch, Duke of, rent-roll of, 276

Bull Run, English reaction to Northern rout at, 216

Burdett, Sir Francis, on the people, 173; on participation in law-making, 184

Burke, Edmund, appeals to custom not law, 19, 169; on innovation, 59; on 1688, 124; on East Indians in parliament, 67–8; on chains of influence, 73; *Thoughts on Present Discontents*, on necessity of control, 75; on old and new Whigs, 77; on American disturbances, 79; on Fox and his following, 79; on mutiny in the navy, 84; *Reflections on the French Revolution*, influence of, discussed, 78, 95;

agent for New York, 102; on reasons for the American rebellion, 124; on trusteeship, 151–2; on conditions in Bengal, 152; on the British Government, 170; on magistracy, 282; Marx gibes at, 320

Burns, Robert, possible fate of, 169; 'Tree of Liberty' poems of, 95; and right of passage, 270

Butler, R. A., on role of the State, 363

Butler, Samuel, *Way of All Flesh*, on education, 249

Butterfield, Herbert, and nature of English history and governance, 15, 17

Cade, Jack, grievances of, 42–3; suspected presence of, in Barbados, 46; nickname for Joseph Chamberlain, 291

Calais, loss of a symbol, 108

Calton Hill, Edinburgh, memorial to 'Martyrs' on, 93

Calvinism, an aristocratic religion, 98, 269

Cambridge University, enfranchised by James I, 43; bishops not supposed to be produced by, 267

Canada, Americans attack (1812), 130; Loyalists in, 140, 142; toryism in, 144; Strachan and Gourlay's activities in, 144–5; Lord Durham and, 148; Constitutional Act (1791), effect of, 142; Trade Act (1825), purpose of, 143; bilingualism in, 144; rebellion in (1837), 150; absence of socialism from, 296

Canning, George, on flame of liberty, 85; and liberal toryism, 159; on nonsense, 179; on British Constitution, 185; and the Six Acts, 185

Carey, Joyce, *Mister Johnson*, 380

Caribs, exterminated, 111

Carlyle, Thomas, dislikes Saxons and Scots, 29; on French Revolution, 167; on egotism, 200; on cash-nexus, 260

Carnegie, Andrew, practices of, 309

Carton, Sydney, adventures of, 168

Cartwright, Major John, retains property qualification, 170; view of, on universal suffrage, 207

Castlereagh, Lord, public reaction to

death of, 191; and European statesmen, 214

Cecil, Lord Hugh, *Conservatism*, quoted, 315

Cecil, Lord Robert (see also Marquess of Salisbury), analyses Reform Act (1832), 222 ff.; on pay and journeymoney, 223; on pervading falseness, 226; on acceptance of political defeat, 238–9

Chalmers, Dr Thomas, and Scottish Disruption, 161; and Arnold, 212 n.

Chamberlain, Neville, establishes protection, 314; lacks political skills, 344

Chamberlain, Joseph, and unlocking the land, 166; never given elbow-room, 226, 288; Radical programme of, 248, 289–90; appeals to Scotland, 273; 'Jack Cade', vanishes, 291

Chandos, Lord, *Memoirs*, quoted on Churchill's Caretaker government, 367

Charles Edward, Prince, inflation of numbers who followed, 94

Charles I, offers Cromwell knighthood, 21; political tactics of, 45; a paternalist, 48; and Quebec, 112; and Colchester brewers, 256

Charles II, long parliament of, 45; on Dissent, 57, 250; Bombay and Dunkirk, 112; like Disraeli, a comedian, 210; and Massachusetts, 45

Chartists, make Cade their hero, 42; unpatronized, 86; their monument to Martyrs in Edinburgh, 93; antipathy of, to Anti-Corn Law League, 187; aims of, 188; absorbed, 217; cause exasperation, 248; translated to Australia, 297

Chatham, Lord (see also William Pitt the elder), on House of Commons, 62; a political liability, 63; rhetoric of, on America, 102

Chatterley, Sir Clifford and Lady (D. H. Lawrence), as symbols, 251, 341

Chesterton, G. K., on the people, 316

Chiang Kai-shek, a *revenant*, 374

Chinese labour, in Australia, 298; in South Africa, 302

Christian Socialists, ideas of, 318–19

Church, in Norman England, a form of

L'Esprit des Lois, assumptions of, 180

Montague, C. E., on American capital, 293

Montfort, Simon de, a Victorian hero, 46

Moody and Sankey, debarred from Eton, 243

More, Hannah, style of Evangelicalism of, 203

Morgan, J. P., Cobden magnified, 309

Morley, John, on Church of England, 255

Morris, Gouverneur, views of, on democracy, 130

Morris, William, ideas of, 321, 323

Mosley, Sir Oswald, looked on as coming man, 216

Motley, J. L., and democracy in England, 216

Muir, Thomas, trial of, 91

Municipal Corporation Act (1834), blow to toryism of, 195

Munster, Ireland, colonization in, 110

Namier, Sir Lewis, on role of George III, 65; on the role of the Crown, 112

Napoleon I, English reputation of, 168

Napoleon III, distrusted, 214

National Debt, a Whig job, 67

National Health Insurance Act (1911), principle of, 295

National Health Service, 361

Navigation Acts, repealed, 218

Nazi-Soviet Pact (1939), a tombstone to its age, 346

Nesbit, E., stories of, 262

New Amsterdam, taken 1664, 112

New Brunswick, Loyalists in, 142

New England, economic uselessness of, 101; illicit trade in, 123

New France, conquest of, 115

Newgate, Wakefield writes *Letter from Sydney* in, 22

Newman, John Francis, criticizes Tamworth, 197; lapses to Rome, 202

New Model Army, commonalty in, 19

New South Wales, life in, 22; governed like man-of-war, 141; 'tartars' wander out of, 149

'New Whigs', plans of, 182; keep Fox's flame, 178

New Zealand, colonization in, 149; Grey and responsible government in, 151; social conditions in, 300

nonconformists, relieved of statutory disqualifications, 201

Nore, mutiny at the, 84

Norfolk, Duke of, toasts the sovereign people, 87

Norman Conquest, nature of, discussed, 25 ff.

Normans, a litigious race, 25; embed themselves in English social system, 25–6; seen as heroes, 34; and as stage-managers, 22

Norman yoke, defined, 19; condemned by Bentham, 180

North, Lord, on petitioners, 74; coalition of, with Fox, 104; on colonial government, 140

Nottingham, activities of mob in, 192

O'Connell, Daniel, none in Scotland, 97

Odo, ravages Northumbria, 27

Offa King of Mercia, a charter attributed to, 41

Ohio country, speculation in the, 111

Old Age Pension Act (1908), principle of, 295

Old Contemptibles, 329

Oldfield, William, *Representative History*, on county Down, 71

Orderic Vitalis, on Norman behaviour, 26–7

Orwell, George, few imitators of, 346

Osborne, John, *The Entertainer*, 369

Osborne judgment (1909), 305; reversed 1913, 325

Ottoman Empire, need for, 214

Owen, Robert, ideas of, 317

Oxford Movement, nature of, 201; attitude of, to poor, 204; influence of, on 'Young England', 211

Oxford University, James I enfranchises, 43; imperial history endowed at, 313; Cyril Connolly on, 335

Page, W. H., pictures future, 330

Paine, Tom, *Rights of Man*, argument of, 23; on Normans, 23ff.; on Bill of Rights, 61; works proscribed, 87; analysis of social justice, 169

Palermo, Norman bridgehead at, 26

Raj, British, in India, not designed to represent Indians, 156

Raleigh, Sir Walter, Irish enterprises of, 110

Rebellion, English, disrepute of, 60

Redesdale, Earl of, as publicized by daughters, 346

'Red Flag', the, 324

Redmond, John, on repossession of Irish soil, 36

Reform Act (1832), effects of, 221 ff.; Lord R. Cecil on, 222 ff.

republicanism, no English status, 54

Revolution, English, glorious reputation of, 60

Rhodes, Cecil, *rhodomontade* of, 252

Ricardo, David, on landlords' interest, 173; on political economy, 179

Richard I, an unlikely English hero, 29

Richard II, and Peasants' Revolt, 41; nominates knights of the shire, 43

Richards, Frank, significance of stories of, 284

Richmond, Duke of, a maverick, 76; ideas of, 207

right of passage, in Scotland, 234

Ritchie, R. L. G., *The Normans in Scotland*, quoted, 31, 32

Roberts, Lord, on German socialists, 328

Robespierre, ideas of, 81

Rockefeller, J. D., and God, 308

Rodney, Admiral Lord, on slave nutrition, 212 n.

Romilly, Sir Samuel, on barbarian laws, 179; dubbed a Whig by Bentham, 179

Roosevelt, President Franklin, at Yalta, 355

Roosevelt, President Theodore, and strikes, 310

Rosebery, Lord, his policy of continuity, 238; popularity of, 268; an instinctive tory, 301; on socialism, 285

Rothschild, Lionel, peerage for, 255

Rothschild, Nathaniel, no peerage for, 255

Round, J. H., on social standards, 251; on middle class, 183

Rousseau, Jean-Jacques, on the English, 75

Royal Air Force, a Cinderella, 350

Royal Commission on Physical Deterioration (1903), findings of, 316

Royal Commissions, tory attitude to, 213

Runnymede, baronial monument at, 25

Russell, Lord John, and responsible government, 150; and unreformed Commons, 182; respect of, for British Constitution, 182; bewildered by Chartists, 188; hands back poisoned chalice, 192; asks John Bright to dinner, 209

Russell, W. H., Crimean dispatches of, 220

Russian Revolution, and Labour party, 336

Saint-Just, Antoine, ideas of, 81

Saints, Clapham, ideas of, 170

Saints, in parliament, disappearance of, 56

Saintsbury, George, on French Revolution, 167; on literary realism, 255

Salisbury, Earl of (1381), on Peasants' Revolt, 41

Salisbury, Marquess of (see also Cecil, Lord Robert), on Irishmen as governing agencies, 165; on street legislation, 233; pessimism of, 267; on Liberalism, 290; puts out boathooks, 293

Saxons, part of, in English story, 15, 23; despised by Carlyle, 29; in *Ivanhoe*, 23

Scotland, not colonized, 31; a place of refuge, 32; David I feudalizes, 32; no villeinage in, 33; Council of State and, 51; union with England, abolished, 58; Friends of the People in, 90; trials of 'martyrs' in, 91; constitution of, 98; no O'Connell in, 97; Reform Bill (1832) in, 98; Kersaint on, 98; not a colony, 99; Quebec compared with, 115; habits of mind in, 97, 269; voting record in, in nineteenth century, 270

Scott, Sir Walter, and Richard Coeur-de-Lion, 29; picture of Saxons, in *Ivanhoe*, 23; on India, 93; *Rob Roy*, quoted, 273

Seeley, Sir John, on aristocracy, 17; on role of George III, 65; aphorism of, on absence of mind, 108

GEORGE ALLEN & UNWIN LTD

London: 40 Museum Street, W.C.1

Auckland: Box 36013, Northcote Central, N4
Bombay: 15 Graham Road, Ballard Estate, Bombay 1
Bridgetown: P.O. Box 222
Buenos Aires: Escritorio 454–459, Florida 165
Calcutta: 17 Chittaranjan Avenue, Calcutta 13
Cape Town: 68 Shortmarket Street
Hong Kong: 44 Mody Road, Kowloon
Ibadan: P.O. Box 62
Karachi: Karachi Chambers, McLeod Road
Madras: Mohan Mansions, 38c Mount Road, Madras 6
Mexico: Villalongin 32–10, Piso, Mexico 5, D.F.
Nairobi: P.O. Box 4536
New Delhi: 13–14 Asaf Ali Road, New Delhi 1
Ontario: 81 Curlew Drive, Don Mills
São Paulo: Caixa Postal 8675
Singapore: 36c Prinsep Street, Singapore 7
Sydney, N.S.W.: Bradbury House, 55 York Street
Tokyo: 10 Kanda-Ogawamachi, 3-Chome, Chiyoda-Ku

W. L. BURN

THE AGE OF EQUIPOISE

Small Royal 8vo   *45s net*

This book is neither an 'exposure' of the mid-Victorian generation nor an attempt to recover a vanished enchantment. What the author has sought to do is 'to examine and describe certain aspects of English life and thought between 1852-1867, certain ways of looking at things, certain men and woman whose actions and opinions formed or at least illustrate those ways'. He is aware of the difficulty of his task—'the gap between the mid-Victorian age and ours widens and narrows and widens again': at one moment it seems that our great-great-grandfathers were very much as we are; at another their thoughts and actions appear so bizarre, so little credible, that they could have been the inhabitants, not just of another century but of another world.

As the author sees them they were people living in a society which (despite all the talk about *laissez-faire*) was in many ways rigidly disciplined. The disciplines made for national stability though not necessarily for individual comfort or security. They were also people much less sophisticated than they liked to think themselves, contented with 'broad, simple truths' and rough-hewn, often crude, distinctions. This was part of their strength although the consequences were not invariably pleasant. The author's prejudice against what he calls 'selective Victorianism' is evident. 'What is not permissible,' he says, 'is to select from the past those things which we happen to like and to keep them apart from their contemporary context.' With this in mind he has sought to throw light on what is still in some respects a curiously 'dark' period of nineteenth-century history.

As Professor Asa Briggs has written, this is 'A work of great scholarship, based on wide reading in the rich field of mid-nineteenth century literature, social investigation and political pamphleteering'. It is also exceedingly readable. Only an author who has lived with his material can re-create, as does Professor Burn, a world in which the reader in turn will live and will find himself immersed.

GEORGE ALLEN AND UNWIN LTD